THE LIFE
SHE WISHED
TO LIVE

ALSO BY ANN McCUTCHAN

*Where's the Moon: A Memoir of the Space Coast
and the Florida Dream*

River Music: An Atchafalaya Story

Circular Breathing: Meditations from a Musical Life

*The Muse That Sings: Composers Speak About
the Creative Process*

Marcel Moyse: Voice of the Flute

The Yearling [handwritten]

THE FLUTTER-MILL [struck through]

Thin and straight [handwritten]

A column of smoke rose from the cabin chimney,~~xx thin and straight as a cat-tail.~~ The smoke was blue where it left the red of the clay. Then it ~~xxxxgxxxxxxxxxxxx~~ trailed into the blue of the April sky and, ~~strangely,~~ was no longer blue but gray.

The boy Jody watched it, speculating. The fire on the kitchen hearth was dying away. His mother was ~~finishing~~ hanging up ~~the~~ pots and pans after the noon dinner. The day was Friday. She would sweep the floor with a broom of ti-ti and then, if he were lucky, she would scrub it with the corn-shucks scrub and never miss him until he had reached the creek. He stood a minute, balancing the hoe on his shoulder. ~~Txxxxkxxxxxxxxxxxxx~~

unweeded

The clearing itself was pleasant if the/rows of young shafts of corn were not before him. The wild bees had found the chinaberry tree by the front gate. They burrowed into the ~~xx~~ fragile lavender blooms as greedily as though there were no other flowers in the scrub; as though they had forgotten the yellow jessamine of March; the sweet bay and the magnolias ahead of them in May. It occurred to him that he could follow the swift line of flight of the black and gold bodies, and so find a bee-tree

full of amber honey.

tree. The winter's cane syrup was gone, ~~the honey~~ and the jellies. ~~Hix fxxxxxxxxxxxxxx~~ Finding a bee-tree was nobler work than hoeing, and the corn could wait another ~~whole~~ day. An afternoon ~~...~~ with such a balmy stirring were not to ~~...~~

THE LIFE
SHE WISHED
TO LIVE

A Biography of

Marjorie Kinnan Rawlings,

Author of *The Yearling*

ANN McCUTCHAN

W. W. NORTON & COMPANY
Independent Publishers Since 1923

For information about permission to reproduce selections from this book, write to
Permissions, W. W. Norton & Company, Inc., 500 Fifth Avenue, New York, NY 10110

For information about special discounts for bulk purchases, please contact
W. W. Norton Special Sales at specialsales@wwnorton.com or 800-233-4830

Manufacturing by BVG Fairfield
Production manager: Julia Druskin

Library of Congress Cataloging-in-Publication Data

Names: McCutchan, Ann, author.
Title: The life she wished to live : a biography of Marjorie Kinnan Rawlings,
    author of The yearling / Ann McCutchan.
Description: First edition. | New York, N.Y. : W.W. Norton & Company, [2021] |
    Includes bibliographical references and index.
Identifiers: LCCN 2020056028 | ISBN 9780393353495 (hardcover) |
    ISBN 9780393353501 (epub)
Subjects: LCSH: Rawlings, Marjorie Kinnan, 1896–1953. | Women authors,
    American—Biography.
Classification: LCC PS3535.A845 Z834 2021 | DDC 813/.52 [B]—dc23
LC record available at https://lccn.loc.gov/2020056028

W. W. Norton & Company, Inc., 500 Fifth Avenue, New York, N.Y. 10110
www.wwnorton.com

W. W. Norton & Company Ltd., 15 Carlisle Street, London W1D 3BS

1 2 3 4 5 6 7 8 9 0

Dedicated to the memory of Joanne K. and Richard C. Bartlett

CONTENTS

INTRODUCTION

I first heard about Marjorie Kinnan Rawlings from my fourth-grade teacher at McNab Elementary in Pompano Beach, Florida. It was early spring, and Mrs. Chapman, a Florida native, decided it was a good time to share Rawlings's best-known novel, *The Yearling*, with twenty nine-year-olds. Every day after lunch, for weeks, she read aloud a few pages, inviting the class to listen for the author's beautiful sentences and the backwoods Florida world they brought to life. All of us, northern transplants whose families had been lured to the state by the postwar boom, were entranced by the story, delivered during that delicious drowsiness following milk and sandwiches by an old-timer whose voice was as soft and suggestive as distant radio waves. *The Yearling* was our first impression of Old Florida, the peoples' speech and traditions, and Mrs. Chapman's reading seemed a private thing, a gift from her to us. We didn't know that the book, a coming-of-age story about a boy, his pet deer, and his parents, who farmed the north-central Florida scrub, had been the best-selling novel of 1938. Nor did we know the book had won the Pulitzer Prize and been translated into twenty-nine languages, or that Metro-Goldwyn-Mayer had made a popular film of it, starring Gregory Peck and Jane Wyman—all before we were born. By the time Mrs. Chapman read it to us, *The Yearling* had come to be thought of as a children's book, because it centered on a young boy. It was a staple of the elementary school story hour.

I loved *The Yearling* as one loves a fairy tale or a dream, and Mrs. Chapman's reading became one of my fondest memories. Much later, I read the novel by myself, silently, admiring it as magnificent storytelling, as literature. The novel's lyricism, its fine rendering of country life, its use of local dialect, its structure and emotional range revealed Rawlings the artist, and I wanted to know how she, born in 1896, had become one. For clues, I took up her 1942 memoir *Cross Creek*, also a best seller in its day, and reveled in stories of the tiny Florida settlement where she'd established her writing career in the 1930s. Cross Creek was the place out of which she wrote, no doubt a magical spot, and finally, I traveled to the area, which had changed very little since she'd lived there. The hamlet was still a rural community on a stream between two lakes, Orange and Lochloosa, altered only by the soft conversion of Marjorie Rawlings's farmhouse, outbuildings, and orange grove into a state park with a paved road and guided walking tours. It was easy to imagine writing here. Still, I wondered, who was the artist whose life and work had made a shrine of this outpost? Where, beyond her two best-known books and Floridians' sentimental tributes to her memory, was evidence of the complex woman Rawlings must have been?

In 2014, it seemed the only answer would be to pursue a biography of Rawlings—just one existed, and it was more than twenty-five years old. When I contacted Florence Turcotte, the archivist for the Marjorie Kinnan Rawlings Papers at the University of Florida, I asked if there would be enough material to work with. "No problem—it's one-stop shopping here," Flo said, and I quickly learned that the Rawlings archive is *many*-stops shopping, because the collection, including letters, manuscripts, news clippings, and photographs, is vast—which I found both reassuring and intimidating. Even so, I suspected there were more resources to be discovered, and in time, that suspicion proved correct.

While I relied on every possible source to create Marjorie's portrait, two large bodies of work were critical. First, the more than four thousand letters to and from Marjorie and her many friends, lovers, family members, and professional associates offer an extraordinary look into the writer's public, private, and interior lives. Her writings contain descriptions of experiences in New York City, Rochester, Cross Creek, and other locations; reactions to books, articles, and political developments; encounters with other writers; reports on her uneven health; armchair analyses of pals, acquaintances, and employees; and gossip. Letter writing in her lifetime was a standard form of extended, long-distance communication. Depending on where one lived, telephone use was to various degrees limited and expensive, and at Cross Creek, even when phones were finally available, the service was spotty and complicated by party lines.

Marjorie wrote many letters longhand—and her hand *was* long: a bold, backhanded scrawl broken by extended dashes, as if she were speaking aloud, off the cuff. Possibly, she dashed off her boldest communiqués while drinking—a problem illuminated by her correspondence. Other letters were carefully composed and typed. Some read like set pieces worthy of a literary memoirist or a raconteuse, both of which she was. (Occasionally, some of these pieces or anecdotes appeared nearly word for word in letters to more than one person.) But whether set down by hand or type, Marjorie's letters are full-voiced, often performative. I might note here that quotations from the letters between Marjorie and Maxwell Perkins, her editor, and those from Marjorie to Norton Baskin, her second husband, reflect the punctuation decisions of Rodger L. Tarr, editor of *Max and Marjorie: The Correspondence between Maxwell E. Perkins and Marjorie Kinnan Rawlings*, and *The Private Marjorie: The Love Letters of Marjorie Kinnan Rawlings and Norton S. Baskin*. Punctuation decisions for quotations from other letters are mine.

I have frequently treated her correspondence as I might handle interview material for a documentary. That is, I have listened for the most telling or significant lines, paragraphs, or whole letters to reveal various aspects of the author and the ways she expressed herself in conversation with others, as well as to establish facts. In 1998, when the George A. Smathers Libraries at the University of Florida acquired a rich cache of letters between Marjorie and her second husband, Norton Baskin, curator of manuscripts Frank Orser wrote: "As factual, detailed resources, they are the principal source for her biography, almost constituting an autobiography. As literature, they are often gems." Marjorie herself would have agreed. Toward the end of her life, in a speech given for the dedication of a new addition to the University of Florida library system, which would contain her papers, she remarked that "letters, particularly those of more than casual interest, I think, should be a very important part of the collection. Because anyone who has done research of any sort knows the treasure trove in coming across letters that picture the period and the personalities in a period far beyond the publications of the day."

Two years later, as Marjorie researched a biography of novelist Ellen

Glasgow and learned that Glasgow's letters had been destroyed, she expressed deep disappointment: "This saddens me, as the very essence of a personality is often evinced in personal letters as in no other way." Certainly she was thinking of her copious correspondence with Scribner's editor Maxwell Perkins; her husbands, Charles Rawlings and Norton Baskin; and close friends like Julia Scribner Bigham, Macmillan editor Norman Berg, and writers including Zora Neale Hurston, Ernest Hemingway, and Sigrid Undset. With all, she shared her creative struggles. Without those letters, it would be impossible to tell how Marjorie got any writing done while running a productive orange grove and leading an increasingly public life—for she was, as soon as she left public relations and journalism work in the North for the Florida wilderness, a businesswoman and, after *The Yearling*'s success, a celebrity as well.

The second significant body of work, Marjorie's two autobiographical manuscripts, nearly bookend her Florida writing years (her final novel, *The Sojourner*, was set in Michigan and largely accomplished in rural New York). The first manuscript, *Blood of My Blood*, is an account of her childhood, youth, and young adulthood; it stops at her mother's death in 1923. She completed it after moving to Florida in 1928 and entered it unsuccessfully in a novel-writing contest. However, *Blood of My Blood* is more memoir than fiction, featuring her parents, brother, teachers, and others true to her life (all properly named) and focuses primarily on Marjorie's difficult relationship with her mother, Ida Kinnan, whose ghost she needed to confront.

Though Marjorie excoriated her mother, barely redeeming her at the end, she admitted her own imperfections as a spoiled, manipulative child, understanding that she, too, was a flawed character. She wrote in the first and the third person, alternating intimacy and distance, and dramatized scenes like the saucy Hearst feature writer she had been, detailing physical surroundings with an observant journalist's eye. Settings were geographically and historically grounded, individuals convincingly rendered. Peeling away the passion, the need, of this document, one can discern facts useful to a biographer. I have incorporated such information as confirmed by research, which included Marjorie's later correspondence with her brother and other intimates. However, passion itself is helpful: it divulges an author's driving obsessions. (When she gave her papers to the University of Florida, Marjorie destroyed an earlier memoir, "Diary of a Schoolgirl." "In my first year of college," she wrote Clifford and Gladys Lyons—he was a professor at the University of Florida English Department and, later, at the University of North Carolina—"I had set out to *re-write* a perfectly honest diary of adolescent days, with literary intent. I remember having destroyed the original diary, quite certain that I had achieved a masterpiece of memoir in the re-writing. The early one would probably have been fun, but I hope the edited version never even caught the eye of God.")

The second manuscript, *Cross Creek*, published in 1942 and as much a classic as *The Yearling*, is a creative nonfiction chronicle of Marjorie's life at the Creek, a succession of graceful, sometimes humorous narratives describing encounters with friends, neighbors, farmhands, wildlife, weather, and flora and fauna. It is a treasury of true people, places, and events, meticulously, imaginatively, and urgently drawn. (It is not to be confused with the 1983 movie *Cross Creek*, an account of Marjorie's early struggles to write in Florida.)

Besides Marjorie's letters and memoiristic manuscripts, the various drafts and published versions of her work, from juvenilia to *The Sojourner*, offer a close look at her development as a writer, including themes and character types (such as the desire for home and the preadolescent boy) that persisted throughout her career. However, this biography is not intended as a work of literary criticism. I very much concur with Jeanette Winterson's warning against "tying in the writer's life with the writer's work so that the work becomes a diary; small, private, explainable, and explained away, much as Freud tried to explain art away." I seek to illuminate instead Marjorie's humanity: her heart and mind.

One more word about sources: certainly, I have consulted many others, but in doing so I have most valued Marjorie's contemporary accounts of events and people, as well as contemporary accounts by others, over memories or memoirs produced long after her death—for remembrances are often inaccurate, self-serving, or tidied and raised up as myth. Part of my challenge has been to determine the veracity of well-loved tales about Marjorie Rawlings and, if found useful, couch them in terms that make their origins and reasons for perpetuation clear.

To some extent, writers reflect who they read. Although Rawlings's personal library was scattered after her death, one can trace her vora-

cious reading habits in her letters. She was interested in so much: literature, politics, history, science, philosophy, biography, the art of writing.
She loved Proust and detested Faulkner. She read and reread the Bible,
although she was not religious in any conventional sense. She often
consulted William Bartram's eighteenth-century *Travels*, particularly
the naturalist's observations of Florida. She took on massive histories,
dwelled on single poems. She once said she read "about a book a day." I
have included her reactions to certain books when they seemed directly
connected to writing projects.

Also critical to understanding Rawlings are the times in which she
lived. Although she aspired to write literary stories and novels, she was
a woman of limited means, and directly after college, she needed to find
a job—any job. Hoping to use her writing skills, she started out as a
YWCA publicist. This led to a spotty journalism career in the 1920s,
when women reporters were rare, mostly freelance, and assigned light-
weight features for the new "women's pages," which multiplied after
women gained the vote. In this, she was rewarded for facile storytelling,
a natural ability her University of Wisconsin professor William Ellery
Leonard warned her against, and with which she would struggle when
writing serious fiction.

In the years containing most of her Florida output, 1930 through
1945, she was profoundly a writer of her time. During the Great Depression and leading up to World War II, a significant number of American
authors chronicled, in fiction and nonfiction, culturally isolated corners
of the country that hadn't been changed by modern life. Some writers felt
an anthropological impulse, the field burgeoning in response to studies
such as Margaret Mead's ground-breaking *Coming of Age in Samoa* and
personal narratives like Luther Standing Bear's *My People the Sioux*,
both published in 1928. This urge teamed naturally with investigative
reporting, a practice just a few decades old, which would lead to what is
now referred to as immersion or participatory journalism—the reporter
fully involving herself with a situation, sometimes incognito. Other writers were moved by America's long-standing rural ideal, increasingly worshipped, feared for, or nostalgically mourned in the wake of the Industrial
Revolution and the First World War. Some southern authors, notably
Erskine Caldwell, worked to reveal the "waste land" and the "unknown
people" of the rural South, characterizing them (white or black) as piti-

fully backward and judging their lack of connection to contemporary civilization. Such writers considered themselves agents of social change.

It is no accident that in Margaret Mead's and Luther Standing Bear's signal year—1928—the Library of Congress established the Archive of American Folk-Song, sending pioneering folklorist John Lomax and his son Alan on expeditions to gather authentic folk songs before traditional tunes could be overridden by radio's new *Billboard* hits. Following that, the Works Progress Administration's Federal Writers' Project, established in 1935, deployed hundreds of writers from coast to coast to document regional American life. On the popular front, *Fortune* magazine sent writer James Agee and photographer Walker Evans to Alabama for six weeks to live with the families of three tenant farmers, their material finally appearing in book form as *Let Us Now Praise Famous Men* in 1941. And the southern literary renaissance was in full swing. Thomas Wolfe (*Look Homeward, Angel,* 1929) and William Faulkner (*The Sound and the Fury,* 1929) were among those who pulled away from romances about the antebellum South and responded to southern culture after the Civil War. Among the renaissance landmarks was Julia Peterkin's Pulitzer Prize for her 1928 novel, *Scarlet Sister Mary,* which portrays black folklife in South Carolina's Lowcountry. Peterkin was the first southern woman writer to win the prize.

It so happened that in 1928—the year of Peterkin's win, Mead's debut, and the folk song archive's founding—Marjorie Rawlings decided to leave city newspaper work in Rochester, New York, to try writing fiction in Cross Creek, Florida. With a small inheritance, she bought, sight unseen, a seventy-two-acre orange grove and farmhouse, determined, along with her first husband, Charles Rawlings, to write in deep, undocumented country full-time, living on citrus profits. As it turned out, the grove required far more labor than she had imagined—a saga in itself—yet Marjorie also saw in backwoods Florida a striking opportunity to immerse herself in a little-known culture and transform reporting into literary fiction. Within a few years of her arrival in north-central Florida, she had put the region, and herself, on the national literary map.

Over the course of her years at the Creek, Marjorie made friends with the handful of Cracker families scattered about the surrounding scrub and swamp and forest. ("Cracker" meaning descendants of white Scots-Irish and English settlers.) She stayed in local households at various points, observing and experiencing firsthand her neighbors' ways of living, taking copious notes on everything they did and what they said in their local dialect. She had an uncanny ear for speech and idioms. She was accepted in the tiny community, albeit as an outsider and, at times, an eccentric, but like everyone else, she lent a hand, bartered, spun yarns. She learned to catch crabs from a johnboat at night, to hunt fowl with her shotgun, accompanied by dogs—a long line of them—and to make moonshine in a swampland still. She enjoyed these activities, especially hunting with friends: local folks and, as she gained notoriety beyond the Creek, an increasing number from Ocala and Gainesville, home of the University of Florida. From neighbor women and her various housekeepers, she learned to cook with ingredients she and her farm employees raised: poultry; fruits and vegetables such as mangos, pecans, and collard greens; and milk, cream, and butter from Dora, her dairy cow. She took pride in throwing dinner parties for friends and associates passing through Florida, from snowbird relatives to luminaries like Robert Frost and Wallace Stevens.

Everything Marjorie Rawlings experienced at Cross Creek contributed to her books and stories, and their successes, in time, expanded her circle, and her life, well beyond that secluded spot. For although she stated more than once that she hated cities, she was also drawn to them, and she left the Creek often for metropolitan areas such as Atlanta, Washington, D.C., and New York. Here, she conducted the social business of her writing life, savoring contact with the writers, artists, and thinkers who were her peers. She attended concerts, plays, and museum openings. She gave readings. She was a guest at the White House.

Admittedly peripatetic, she was full of contradictions.

ONE MIGHT VIEW Rawlings's work solely as the result of her particular sociopolitical time or a literary movement, but my aim here has been to discover and show how she created the life she wished to live as a writer with a poetic, philosophical impulse toward art-making, and a strong urge to manifest it on her own terms. It is the strongest story running through the personal materials she left for us to consider. Since her college years as an aspiring poet and dramatist at the University of Wisconsin, she had been obsessed with natural beauty and the notion of cosmic consciousness, the purview of Whitman and other poets she studied and with whom she felt a kinship. At Cross Creek, she found the perfect unspoiled environment out of which to attempt stories and novels reflecting the ideal. It is true that this section of Florida had yet to be significantly explored in imaginative literature, offering Rawlings a first-come opportunity, but just as importantly, its isolation harbored living examples of the radical interconnections between all living people and things—a concept fundamental to cosmic consciousness. She loved it when an occasional critic caught on to that wider inspiration. Even after she moved her writing headquarters to an upstate New York farm village in the late 1940s, she continued to explore the theme, made most explicit in *The Sojourner*, her last novel, set in rural Michigan, where her mother had grown up.

NOVELIST JOHN GARDNER could have been describing Marjorie when he wrote, "True artists, whatever smiling faces they may show you, are obsessive, driven people." Often, her pleasant face dissolved into frustration, her mouth pressing into a thin line. In letters to close friends and her editor Maxwell Perkins, Marjorie repeatedly confirmed her drive, and the struggle to balance the desire for solitary work with the demands of social needs, obligations, and outward events, as most writers do. "I have an acute need for solitude," she scrawled one morning, after her first husband and her brother-in-law left the Creek to run errands. "Too constant contact with other personalities has often weighed on me, and I am glad to be free for a day." She would have agreed with the poet William Stafford, who described his life as two rivers that blend. "One part is easy to tell; the times, the places, events, people," Stafford wrote. "The other part is mysterious; it is my thoughts, the flow of my inner life, the reveries and impulses that never get known—perhaps even to me." This second part, he continued, has its own story, which sometimes touches the outer one. But it is not the same.

For Marjorie, the outward story included relationships with her warm, nature-loving father, whom she adored, and her cool, ambitious mother, whom she did not; her brother, an affectionate lost soul; two husbands, one demanding and intense, the other supportive and easygoing; and various friends, suitors, and professional contacts, including fellow Scribner's authors Scott Fitzgerald and Ernest Hemingway, as well as Zora Neale Hurston, whose friendship forced her to come to terms with the racism she had grown up with and which she subsequently argued against. Her early places and periods include a childhood in Washington, D.C., at the close of the Gilded Age, before World War I; the University of Wisconsin in wartime; and then hack writing and editing in postwar Manhattan and publicity and journalism jobs in Louisville and Rochester in the 1920s.

After 1928, and her acquisition of the Cross Creek grove, Marjorie eventually enjoyed and adjusted to literary success, even as it sealed the dissolution of her first marriage. She continued to guard her privacy, refusing some invitations or expressing relief when an event was canceled, but took part in enough public occasions to expand her circle. With her second husband, Norton Baskin, a sociable hotelier who grew up in Alabama, she was able to maintain a separate writing life, which he respected. Their copious correspondence, much of it between Cross Creek, where she wrote, and St. Augustine, where he worked, seventy miles to the east, offers rich details about daily life in both places and describes a relationship—call it a weekend marriage—that supported Marjorie's calling.

Still, she experienced significant interruptions. One, the U.S. involvement in World War II, she accepted willingly. During those years, she corresponded with the many soldiers who had read her work in military-issue paperbacks and been moved to write to her. And when her husband left Florida to serve for a year as an ambulance driver in India, she wrote to him regularly, worrying constantly about his well-being and whereabouts. From the beach near St. Augustine, she volunteered as a plane spotter. These and related activities constituted her contribution to the war effort, and often consumed her.

But another interruption, unbidden, had lasting consequences: a painful, sustained lawsuit filed in 1943 by a neighbor angered by Marjorie's brief description of her in *Cross Creek*. Although the suit was resolved after five years (in a fashion neither woman could call satisfying), it spelled the end of Marjorie's Florida writing. Coincidentally, Marjorie's beloved editor Maxwell Perkins died suddenly just as the lawsuit approached resolution. It was the greatest loss of her literary life; if not for the editorial advice of her friend Norman Berg, she might not have completed *The Sojourner*. And finally, but not incidentally, through all of her years at the Creek and afterward, Marjorie coped with recurrent, long-standing physical and emotional problems exacerbated by a penchant for rich food and strong drink. Together, they obstructed her thoughts. They tested her friendships and marriages. They contributed to her death in 1953.

Marjorie's inward story did not run along a clear-cut timeline. If not for her notes and letters, especially the prodigious and often personal correspondence with Maxwell Perkins and, after Perkins's death, Norman Berg, understanding her creative development would depend on an even larger dose of speculation and interpretation than a biographer would be comfortable with when creating a coherent narrative. Other inward themes or obsessions, often evolving from outward situations, include: Marjorie's intimate relationships with men; her struggles as an ambitious, independent woman; her friendships with women as independent as herself; her lifelong concern for her troubled brother; the ongoing specter of her mother and fond memory of her father; her struggle with racism and her curiosity about African-American art (particularly literature and dance performance); and, finally, her love and defense of Florida's natural environment.

IN 1945, MARJORIE WROTE: "If human wantonness and human greed have here and there destroyed Arcadia, with the careless cutting and burning of forests, the useless and destructive draining of lands that were refuges for all the wild things; with the erection of billboards and transient camps; if avid purveyors of Florida's great cash crop, the tourist, have a little spoiled the beauty and overcharged the seeker of loveliness, lay the blame fairly where it belongs, as all such things as greed and war and man's general inhumanity to man, must be laid, on the frailty of human nature, and not on Florida, great and gracious tropical queen."

No one agreed with her more than the late Richard C. and Joanne K. Bartlett, the dedicatees of this book. Dick Bartlett spent part of his youth along one of the wildest stretches of Florida's Atlantic coast in the 1950s and '60s and attended the University of Florida, where his lifelong love of Rawlings's work began. After his business career took him to Texas, Dick became active in conservation work, serving as chairman of the Nature Conservancy in Texas and authoring two books, one with Joanne, on Texas conservation and outdoor sport. Together, the Bartletts founded the Thinking Like a Mountain Foundation, a residency for artists and thinkers working on environmentally themed projects. This biography, conceived by Joanne after Dick's death and generously funded by the foundation, is part of the Bartletts' enormous legacy and a direct product of Rawlings's inspiration. Although Joanne Bartlett did not live to see *The Life She Wished to Live* published, her interest and energy animated the work to its completion.

THE LIFE
SHE WISHED
TO LIVE

Chapter One

Origins

WHEN MARJORIE KINNAN WAS nine years old, her mother, convinced she'd birthed a nightingale, took the child to a voice teacher near their home in Washington, D.C., for an audition. The man listened to Marjorie sing a ditty and offered a quick assessment. "Do not waste one cent, Madam," he said. "I do not always dare to be so positive, for adolescence, maturity, often change the whole texture of a voice. But here—no. Never."

Ida Kinnan was disappointed. She believed that her little girl was musically talented. She needed to believe it, for she'd spent her entire pregnancy attending concerts, trusting in theories of prenatal influence to give her a songbird, one who would sing, "and the world would be at her feet." According to the daughter years later, the child was to be an extension of the mother, fulfilling dreams of a notable, sophisticated life—and in 1905, what better vehicle than the musical show? For the past two years, Victor Herbert's operetta *Babes in Toyland* had been the rage in New York and even toured. It offered plenty of roles for children, to the delight of stage mothers everywhere. But since the voice teacher had so quickly dismissed Marjorie's musical potential, Ida switched gears and began watching for signs of other talents in her girl. Finally, to her relief, a more promising gift surfaced when Marjorie entered a children's writing contest in the *Washington Post* and won two dollars.

Ida's daughter had an ear for language and, after all, signs of a voice—on the page.

Newly energized, Ida encouraged her daughter to continue writing and entering more contests, rewarding her by matching her earnings and excusing her from chores when "inspiration" struck. Marjorie delivered the goods and eventually placed second in *McCall's* 1912 Child Authorship Contest with a sentimental story, "The Reincarnation of Miss Hetty," which appeared in the August issue. It was her first national publication, a sign that she might be more than a local talent. Ida's dreams took definite shape. Marjorie would become a famous writer, marry well, grow rich.

MARJORIE WAS BORN ON August 8, 1896, in the turreted second-floor bedroom of the Kinnans' American Queen Anne–style house, whose address is now 1221 Newton Street in Brookland, a Washington, D.C., neighborhood just undergoing development then. She was Ida and Arthur Kinnan's first child after nine years of marriage. Dramatizing the event in *Blood of My Blood*, an autobiographical manuscript about her youth and early adulthood, Marjorie described her own existence as Ida's consolation prize for an inability to crack Washington society—the pregnancy itself a gesture against Arthur, who, as the eldest of a large brood, hadn't wanted children and who, Ida had been disappointed to learn, did not possess the temperament of a social climber. According to Marjorie, Ida's condition had been a shock to him. It would seem the couple had scrupulously avoided conception for nearly a decade. Now Ida made motherhood her mission.

"Before this child she would unroll the rosy carpet her own feet could never tread," Marjorie proclaimed. "In this child she would attain the distant places, sweet with sophisticated music and florists' flowers. She would control the girl's associates, her school; she could contrive fine clothes for her. In this radiant city she could see that in the girl's youth she was thrown with the children of the great, who would become her friends.

"We see the phenomenon of a deliberate extension of her own life for a deliberate purpose," Marjorie concluded. "A peculiarly ruthless mother love is at work."

Marjorie, who by turns described her child-self as victimized, culpable, or ridiculous, wryly described her own appearance as a baby: the round Dutch face, the straight black hair. "It is almost impossible for any female infant, if not deformed, to be totally unattractive when immaculately clean and 'cunningly' dressed," she commented. "It is doubtless one of Nature's devices for getting them raised to maturity. . . . The baby wore real lace and a soft blue broadcloth coat, bordered with otter fur. Pinned inside the edge of the otter-trimmed blue bonnet was a row of artificial curls."

Following fashion trends, Ida tried lightening Marjorie's freckles with expensive lotions, dressed her in organdy, and once, when she sat down in a mud puddle—of which Brookland, with its unpaved streets, had many after a rain—punished her severely. Marjorie "reached full maturity before she was able to shake off a tense stiffness when in fresh clothes." Occasionally, Arthur made fun of his wife's fastidiousness, which must have relieved his daughter.

Ida threw lavish birthday parties, enrolled Marjorie in dancing school, and sought the hopeless voice lessons. More than once, she had the little girl photographed in a studio. A shot taken when Marjorie was a toddler shows a child posed stiffly against throw pillows and ball-fringed draperies and engulfed in a voluminous dress tucked under her chin like a dinner napkin. The straight black hair appears to have been bent and singed by an electrical appliance, a desperate effort at styling. The expression on Marjorie's face is not one of the easily cajoled. Anyone urging her to sit still and "watch the birdie" had been met with a look of perplexity, boredom, or suspicion: the horizontal eyebrows, the flat stare, the closed lips turned down. Her mouth bore "the compressed thinness of the egoist." How much of a person's expression can be attributed to facial construction is hard to say, but if the eyes are most telling, Marjorie's carry a clear message: "Let me out of here." Plenty of little girls would have acquiesced, even enjoyed being fussed over, but not this one.

MARJORIE CONSISTENTLY PORTRAYED her mother as a manipulator who would make of her girl a performing monkey. But her father,

Arthur, who preferred a pastoral existence, she worshipped as an ally. Of the two parents, both raised on midwestern farms, he was the one who best understood Marjorie. Though he had studied law and secured a government job in the nation's capital, he grew disenchanted with city life when his daughter was young and retreated to land he bought beyond the suburbs, raising crops and dairy cows part-time, enjoying his work outdoors more with each year, to his socially ambitious wife's dismay, until his untimely death. In *Blood of My Blood*, Marjorie recalled a moment in her childhood that expressed her parents' differences. It happened one evening when Ida discovered their little girl outdoors, dancing around a chestnut tree in her nightgown. Arthur dismissed his wife's horror, remarking that Marjorie, who had slipped out by climbing from her bedroom window into a cherry tree, was doing "the only sensible thing on a moonlit night like this."

In later years, Marjorie would criticize *Blood of My Blood*'s sentimental, ironic style, comparing it to Jane Austen's, stating that she'd intended an objective study of Ida Kinnan and regretted the preponderance of "unhappy details." Defined for a writing contest as a novel, *Blood of My Blood* contains much reliable information and fine detail about its primary settings—Washington, D.C., and Madison, Wisconsin, where Marjorie attended college. Missing from the account is an admission of how much Marjorie enjoyed storytelling and writing at a young age and how ambitious she was for herself. Her creative output would bear that out. That Ida hovered as Marjorie discovered her own natural love of language and narrative was unfortunate. The entanglement chafed at the writer long after her mother died, in 1923; only *after* Ida's death did Marjorie, at twenty-six, begin moving toward an unconventional writing life that made sense to her and would have horrified—but eventually thrilled—her earliest backer.

YET ALL ALONG, Marjorie kept her father's affirmation close to her heart. She would always credit him for her love of nature, her sensitivity to weather and seasons, plants, animals, and people, and the dignity and satisfaction found in tending the soil. Her success came not from arias aimed at box seats but from poetic, pastoral writings about rural landscapes and scrappy settlements around Cross Creek, the Florida hamlet where she and her first husband settled down to write. With her mother's bequest, she bought, sight unseen, a run-down farmhouse and a scruffy orange grove. Here, she turned her back on a patchwork career as a journalist and publicist and began writing fiction, drawing on her experiences in the Florida scrub, where mosquitoes and feral hogs whined and grunted in coarse counterpoint to the mourning doves and mockingbirds. Her white neighbors, native Floridians, or southern Crackers, and her black neighbors, descendants of slaves, were the antitheses of the high society her mother had imagined for her. They sewed their own clothes; caught, shot, or grew their food; and worked on the land, tending citrus trees, harvesting logs, and distilling moonshine. Living among them, Marjorie said, she felt she had come home.

A few years after the move south, *Scribner's Magazine* published Marjorie's poem marking the dramatic change, the defining one of her life. In "Having Left Cities Behind Me," she reflected,

> . . . I find those various
> Great towns I knew fused into one, burned
> Together in the fire of my despising.
> And I recall of them only those things
> Irrelevant to cities: murmurings
> Of rain and wind; moons setting and moons rising.

But that vehement rejection, like *Blood of My Blood*, contained conflict, a possible disingenuousness, for after her third novel, *The Yearling*, won the Pulitzer Prize, Marjorie Kinnan Rawlings enjoyed visiting cities, where she took in cultural events not available in Florida, and where many of her closest friends, writers and artists, lived. Practically speaking, her life was divided between city and country, mirroring her parents' duality. She drew sustenance from both.

As her writing career blossomed and her personal life extended well beyond Florida's interior, Marjorie continued to plant gardens, keep chickens and cows, and run her farm and grove business at Cross Creek, with its many responsibilities: soil maintenance, harvesting, packing and shipping, hiring and firing workers. She was, in a very real sense, mistress of a small plantation, which she ran by herself. Her tumultuous marriage to Charles Rawlings ended at the Creek. Her second husband, Norton Baskin, was a gregarious Alabamian and city man who spent time there but never took up sustained residence, preferring their penthouse in his St. Augustine hotel or their oceanfront cottage on Crescent Beach. The Rawlings-Baskin alliance could be described as a long-distance marriage, measured by the two-hour drive between St. Augustine and Cross Creek or the train travel between Florida and New York, as dictated by Marjorie's needs as a writer.

Although she insisted that Cross Creek was home, it seemed she was born not to the farm or the city but to the provisional territory between. The period aphorism "A ship in harbor is safe, but that is not what ships are built for" might apply to Marjorie or most any creative individual, "harbor" referring to any enduring measure of security. In her early thirties, Marjorie identified for a friend "the cauliflower aspect of my nature—I have found that my growing habits are similar to that vegetable—I need to be transplanted frequently. Five years in one place is all I can stand. I get desperate, caged-in." Something was always pressing her to move, to be in motion, even if it meant no more than a week in New York City, a summer touring the English countryside, or three months in a North Carolina mountain cabin. It was the same force that first drove her to the Creek: an ongoing quest for the life she wished to live.

MARJORIE KINNAN DESCENDED from generations of farm families on both sides. As a child, she knew her maternal grandparents, Abram Traphagen (1839–1925), of mixed German and Dutch blood, and Fanny Osmun (1847–1925), of Norwegian heritage. Abram and Fanny had grown up in Michigan, and after their marriage, Abram established a farm in Linden, a tiny settlement about sixty miles northwest of Detroit. Their daughter Ida May, Marjorie's mother, was born in nearby Holly in 1868.

Abram raised potatoes, corn, wheat, and rye, and by the time Ida was close to adulthood, he was making a comfortable living. "His barns were good and sheltered a herd of a dozen milch cows and his own bull; several work horses, two of them of sufficient beauty to serve, when not overworked, as carriage horses," Marjorie recounted. According to family stories, Abram enjoyed farming. Fanny, who had no doubt journeyed to Detroit—in 1880 a bustling city of more than 116,000—frequently complained about her husband's focus on his land and animals, his leisurely gift of gab. "Your pa's yarns won't buy you any silk dresses," she'd say to Ida, reinforcing the idea that silk, obtained in a sophisticated environment, was to be desired over hogs and sheep. While her husband was content with a traditional life, Fanny had caught the postbellum fever of improvement and renewal, manifested in small towns as aspirations for big-city ways.

Marjorie's mother attended school in Fenton, a town of about two thousand. In 1887, when Ida was nineteen, Fenton welcomed its first piano, purchased by Mrs. Benjamin Rockwall, a sister of Mrs. W. M. Fenton, the town's founder. Mrs. Rockwall and Mrs. Fenton knew how to play the instrument, and they had it installed in a large room of the local hotel so all could admire and enjoy it. News of this marvelous object fascinated the chief of a Native American tribe that frequented the area, and one day he appeared at the hotel specifically to hear the piano. Known as King Fisher, the chief would appear on his visits "dressed in a frock coat of navy blue, a tall hat of furs, ornamented with silver bands and medals, rings pendent from his ears, gaiters and leggings of deerskin and strings of wampum and beads appended." At the hotel, he was offered a chair and sat quietly, awaiting the sound. A local observer remembered King Fisher's dignified bearing and how, after "the piece [was] played, the song sung," the enchanted chief asked Mrs. Fenton to dance. She declined—it would have been unseemly. Finally, "arising with the dignity peculiar to his race, Fisher exclaimed, as he gazed at the piano, 'Man could not make it; Manitou [life force, Great Spirit] made it!' "

Ida Traphagen might have attended this memorable event. Surely she knew about the striking juxtaposition of town ladies plinking the ivories and a lavishly appointed chief attributing the instrument to a creator from his spirit world. Under Fanny's influence, Ida would have admired most the ladies' musical talents and their stylish dresses from Detroit. Even small-town Michigan offered lessons in performance, physical glamour, and social status—possible seeds of ambition.

On her father's side, Marjorie's line in America stemmed from Norwegian and Dutch roots. Her paternal grandparents were Asahel Simeon Kinnan (1832–1880) and Ethelinda Gabriella Pearce (1832–1928), both born in Ohio. Arthur Frank Kinnan, Marjorie's father, was born in 1859, in Anderson or Noblesville, Indiana, small towns northeast of Indianapolis. His early childhood encompassed the Civil War; more than fifteen hundred men from the area served in the Union army. Farming ran in everyone's blood, especially, according to family lore, on the Pearce side.

Arthur's father, Asahel, head of a "savagely religious" Methodist farm household, died when Arthur was twenty-one, leaving him to support his mother and eight younger children—seven of them girls—by working in a brick kiln. He studied at night, and in his late teens or early twenties he entered Michigan State University, a prototype for land-grant institutions under the Morrill Act of 1862. It was the first school of higher learning to teach "scientific agriculture." When Arthur attended, the enrollment was less than two hundred. He had so few resources, he lived in a shack he built on the edge of East Lansing and made his own bread.

Arthur graduated with a B.S., cum laude, in 1883 and moved to Fenton to teach, shortly rising to Fenton High School principal, then school superintendent. Ida, nine years younger, was a student at Fenton High. After she graduated, Arthur courted her for two years in the traditional manner: Sunday evening visits, with parents nearby. "The psychology of mis-mating awaits an analyst," Marjorie would later write. Arthur, a tall, good-looking fellow, was known to be charming, disciplined, sanguine, and possessed of a good sense of humor. Having provided for his mother, his siblings, and himself with hard work and spartan living, he had matured early. Ida, the plainer of the two, and sheltered, aspired to social and material improvement, and though her suitor lacked the worldliness she imagined she wanted, she saw that he offered stability and a life beyond farming. Besides, she hadn't many choices. Her chief pleasure outside her parents' home was playing the tuba in the Fenton Ladies Band. The pair married in 1887, the year the first piano had come to town, and moved to Big Spring, Texas, a community of about one thousand frontier settlers, where both took teaching positions. For the first two years of their marriage, Ida referred to her husband as "Mr. Kinnan," which Marjorie interpreted as cold and "an enslavement to convention . . . a glimpse of the motivating force of her life: her ambition, the fierce urge of the mediocre to rise above the commonplace."

Ida, yearning for a life beyond the farm, was typical of her time, place, and background.

COMPARED TO VERDANT FENTON, Big Spring in the 1880s was a dusty encampment. Only a decade before, it had functioned as a stopover for buffalo hunters pushing west. Aided by powerful firearms, they destroyed the plentiful animals, about 4.5 million between 1871 and 1874, depriving Native Americans of their meat source, forcing them onto reservation lands, and profiting from the sale of meat, hide, and bones. Ranchers came, too. Big Spring's first permanent structure was a butcher's shop. In 1880, the Texas Rangers were sent to the region ahead of the impending Texas and Pacific Railway to pacify ranchers and cowboys, and to protect citizens from the remaining Comanche. When the railroad was completed, Big Spring became a railroad town, bursting with noisy saloons and hastily nailed up gambling halls. In 1883, a real English earl, the Earl of Aylesford, fled the fallout from his high-society divorce by exiling himself to Big Spring and purchasing a twenty-five-hundred-acre ranch north of town. To the middle of nowhere, he brought servants, horses, and fine household goods. He built an eight-room house north of town known as the "Texas Castle" and stocked it with guns. As if the earl's presence signified the establishment of civilized life, the county's first commissioners created a school district and authorized the building of a schoolhouse in Big Spring. For this, the Michigan newlyweds journeyed south and west.

On the face of it, Arthur had taken a step down professionally. Big Spring, named for a dependable water source, was a high plains crossroads of sandy loam, cactus, and mesquite—an oasis that drew travelers but not permanent residents. The closest settlements were Knott and Elbow, the nearest towns of any size Fort Worth, 268 miles east, and El Paso 350 miles west. In thirty years, oil would be struck in Big Spring, and the town would boom. But Arthur couldn't foresee that, and he didn't plan to stick around. The reason he spirited Ida southwest, to a dry, homely place where one could hardly grow a household garden, was strictly financial: the Texans had offered him a much higher salary than Fenton, Michigan's, as well as one for her—an extremely attractive prospect, given their circumstances. At the time, Arthur's paycheck was not

entirely his own. He still contributed to his mother's support and probably assisted his brother and sisters as they attended the University of
Michigan. He was also ambitious for himself, studying law on the side.
If he and Ida could bank some Texas money, he could attend law school
somewhere and start a practice.

Arthur and Ida stayed in Big Spring for about two years. On arrival,
they were feted with a prairie-style housewarming, to which townspeople
brought gifts of food, utensils, and even a wildcat hide. When the town
fiddler struck up a lively tune, Arthur Kinnan broke into a Highland
fling, delighting everyone, while Ida, who might otherwise be embarrassed by her husband's lack of dignity, basked in the attention of the
frontier women, who admired her more sophisticated clothing.

According to county records, Arthur, Ida, and a Miss Beal constituted the Big Spring school faculty in the fall of 1887, teaching in a "two-
story box building which was occupied so rapidly that there was not time
to paint it." Arthur drew $30 in September, $70 in October, and $100
a month thereafter ($2,717 a month in 2020 dollars, or an annual sal-
ary of $32,608). The women received $50 a month. In September 1888,
Arthur was paid an additional $50 as "principal," the first reference to
an administrative position. By November he was back to $100 a month.
Ida's salary remained unchanged.

At first, Ida was able to make an adventure of the whole enterprise. She
enjoyed respect as a teacher and the wife of the educator in charge. After
a chapter of the Order of the Eastern Star was chartered, she was named
the first "Worthy Matron," or presiding officer, a mark of distinction
in the little community. But the slapped-up houses, the dry wilderness
crawling with spiders, snakes, and prairie dogs, and the unpredictable
extremes of Texas weather disturbed her. Ida's objections surfaced when
she and Arthur were invited to spend a week at "Moody's ranch," presumably the panhandle holdings of another Englishman, Robert Moody,
who had recently taken possession of the PO Ranch from his partners
after the "Big Die-Up," a series of winter blizzards and summer droughts
that killed off thousands of cattle. Now Moody was taking advantage
of his position, buying more acreage, drilling for water, installing wind-
mills, fencing open land. Arthur and Ida looked forward to the trip,
though it would require two days of travel in a covered wagon.

After a night in the ranch house, Moody treated Ida and Arthur to a tour—a ride through open plains not unlike the terrain around Big Spring, where the land stretches out and away so far and so flat that one can follow more than one weather system in the distance. As Moody described ranching work, Arthur suddenly "exploded with enthusiasm," proclaiming Moody's life far superior to that of a professional's, such as his own. "It was her first inkling of the madness that was to possess him. She sensed his frenzy, for the very soil itself," Marjorie wrote of her mother. Matters got worse when an oncoming storm blackened the sky. They'd never make it back to the ranch by dark. Moody led them to a bunker he called "the ground-hog's hole," a dugout containing a bed, stove, and chair, and rode on alone to the ranch. By morning, the storm had hammered the bunker door. Water stood everywhere. Arthur took it in stride, but for Ida, this might have been the last straw.

FROM THEIR BRIEF STINT in the Wild West, the Kinnans appear to have moved straight to Washington, D.C., in 1889 or 1890, where Arthur sought a government job. His younger brother, William, led the way; in the 1888 and 1889 city directories, William is listed as a War Department clerk. The following year, Arthur appears as a U.S. Patent Office clerk, having passed the civil service exam. In 1890, the brothers are listed at the same address: 1916 Larch Street NW, which no longer exists but was probably near Howard University. Marjorie described her parents' first Washington home as a suite of two rooms in a P Street boardinghouse. She was likely mistaken about the address, though the period furnishings, possibly drawn from her mother's recollections, or even a magazine, are quite precise. According to Marjorie, her parents' landlady, a Miss Renée, had appointed the rooms with a green Brussels carpet, black walnut furniture, and starched white curtains, "looped back to show neat ferns on window-sills." There was a white porcelain washstand, a dresser of bird's-eye maple, and "calendars of sunset scenes, with a wooden receptacle like a bird bath, for matches, and a precise square of paper on which to strike them." Only one room in the house had ever "suffered the social catastrophe of having matches struck on the wallpaper. The room had been repapered and the occupant dismissed."

Almost as soon as he and Ida had unpacked at Miss Renée's, Arthur bought land in the Brookland neighborhood, at the time a new development northeast of the city, securing a building permit for the Queen

Anne house. The following year, 1891, the city directory lists him as a Brookland resident. Now Arthur and Ida had their first true home, its asymmetrical façade suggesting an irregular interior floor plan. There were fish-scale shingles, dentils, great eaves overhanging a generous wraparound porch with painted spindle balusters, a dormer window, and a three-sided tower—the second-floor bedroom—with relief panels mounted over each of its three windows. The house was pretty and fashionable but not, for the times, ostentatious.

Arthur couldn't have afforded the city center, and, with the farm and prairie in his blood, he gravitated toward open space, anyway. His preference for Brookland, while an expression of his heritage, also went right along with the period's rise of the rural ideal, straight from Jefferson's vision of an agrarian democracy. In the industrial age, it was often conveyed through the popular notion that life was healthier in the country than the city. The air was cleaner and breezier, an abundance of scenic open spaces invited outdoor play, and large lots could accommodate gardens. One might still keep a cow or chickens.

Like many suburban communities, Brookland had been transformed over the decades from woodland to farmland to a large family spread and, finally, to a patchwork of new subdivisions. The Kinnans were among the first to set up house where the estate of gentleman farmer Jehiel Brooks and the adjoining farms had been carved into streets and building sites. Arthur bought not one but three oak-filled lots on Providence Street (later changed to Newton), walking distance to the train station and the new elementary school, built the same year as the Kinnans' home.

Marjorie's parents made frequent rail trips across town to watch the house go up. When the couple moved in, Ida was pleased. "The furniture was decent enough," Marjorie recounted. "Her linens were impeccable. There were lace curtains, a Polar bear rug, a silk scarf draped over the black marble mantel in the double parlor, a settee upholstered in mulberry silk, a reed chair, two gilt chairs for the hall; the Stag at Bay; the portrait of the lion whose eyes followed you; all the up-to-date paraphernalia of the era; and over all the shine and polish of Ida's blood-sweating housekeeping."

Arthur's new post as an examiner in the United States Patent Office's electrical division paid well enough, and now that he had planted himself and his wife in Brookland, he could study law more diligently, with his goal of a comfortable career in sight. Ida, fresh from easy celebrity on the Texas prairie and expecting a perch, imagined herself as a Washington hostess, sipping tea with diplomats' wives. She and Arthur would find a way into high society, Ida thought.

But dreamy ambition can cloud a newcomer's sight, and a woman who'd known only farming and ranching towns topping out at two thousand residents couldn't know what awaited her in the nation's capital, a city of a quarter million, including Georgetown, and growing fast. Several social circles spun about in postbellum Washington, among them old southern families who had ruled society before the Civil War; congressmen and their families, who increased as states and representatives were added; the diplomatic community, also growing; and high military officers and their families. Add to that a regular turnover, depending on elections and other political changes, and tracking who was who and where one might find an entry point could be difficult, if not impossible.

To guide newcomers, and each other, a number of notable Washington hostesses wrote etiquette books, a booming genre. But not everyone behaved accordingly. New millionaires from the West not schooled in, or giving a damn about, polite society shocked the city, among them mining magnate and short-term Colorado senator Horace "Silver King" Tabor, who left his wife of nearly thirty years for the divorcée "Baby" Doe and in 1883 staged a costly sham wedding at the Willard Hotel, normally frequented by presidents and ambassadors. As well, the Panic of 1893, the financial depression that began shortly after Ida and Arthur moved to Washington, had drawn a gloomy curtain on the Gilded Age. In 1894, Washington was besieged by Coxey's Army: more than five hundred unemployed workers participating in the nation's first notable protest march. Outside the city, several thousand more had set up camp. The Kinnans had arrived in a time of flux, when many middle- and upper-class citizens lost their bearings—grasping at life, rather than experiencing it.

And still, rich newcomers continued to flood the city. At that moment, the scene was not just rule-bound *and* changeable but run by well-heeled women whose spouses were busily engaged in political or military or business matters. Although the women's suffrage movement was underway, traditional roles prevailed. Here, a female had little power aside from those she could exercise in the parlor, representing her husband (or father) as hostess and tastemaker.

WHEN THE KINNANS LEFT TEXAS, Ida might have imagined that her husband's Washington career would confer social standing well beyond the Order of the Eastern Star. Instead, it only assured them of a path to the city's middle class. Arthur was but one in a sea of government workers, moving with the crowds in and out of large official buildings. The Patent Office building, a massive Greek Revival structure, its porticoes said to be exact reproductions of the Parthenon's, dwarfed its entrants. (A previous employee in the building, Walt Whitman, was fired from the Bureau of Indian Affairs in 1865, when James Harlan, the secretary of the interior and a former Methodist minister, discovered in the poet's desk a copy of *Leaves of Grass*.)

Thus, with a busy husband and no position, Ida was left to determine a role for herself. At first, she was called on by wives of other Patent Office examiners, as well as an acquaintance from Michigan, plus "an elderly eccentric . . . who called on everyone within a radius of six blocks," this last woman possibly an invention or an exaggeration, but certainly believable—many neighborhoods harbor such a person. Ida explored Washington's shops and museums, strolled the National Mall to gaze at the formidable red sandstone Smithsonian Institution castle and a newly completed white obelisk, the Washington Monument. She toured the Capitol and attended congressional sessions. She read the society pages. She did her best to entertain in Brookland. One "delightful evening at home" she and Arthur hosted was cited in a modest report of Brookland activities in the Washington *Evening Star*.

Soon enough, Ida discovered that she was unlikely to stand out in Washington; neither was Arthur, who responded to the city differently. Quickly discerning the soul-robbing character of government work, he aimed for professional independence, not a perch in the middle of things. He focused on his studies at Columbian University (later renamed George Washington University), receiving a B.A. in 1895 and a master of patent law in 1899. He sank his neighborly impulses into the Brookland community. A founder of the King David Lodge, he helped build the Masonic temple. He joined the Brookland Baptist Church, along with many of the neighborhood's prominent residents (the church, a white wooden edifice, was right across the street from the Kinnan house), and served as president of the Brookland Citizens Association. He lobbied hard, though without success, for a Carnegie library and campaigned to extend streetcar service between Brookland and the heart of the city. But "as time went on, it was apparent that he had chosen the cheaper part of town, and that the development in its direction was low-class. As a matter of fact, he had bought his site in the raw suburb because he could get three times as much ground for the same price," Marjorie observed.

In the early 1890s, Brookland was not a low-class neighborhood, but neither was it Dupont Circle. Its population and character were only beginning to show. The area was still wild and free enough to invite an archaeological dig in 1892, yielding Paleolithic spearheads and other implements. One of its most distinguished citizens was the ornithologist Robert Ridgway, curator of birds at the Smithsonian and future author of the eight-volume *The Birds of North and Middle America*. Brookland sat on a north-south migratory flyway, offering birds the food and shelter missing in more developed areas. Here, Ridgeway could sit on his lawn with a pair of field glasses and monitor passing species. Another Smithsonian curator, Danish botanist Theodor Holm, built a house two blocks from the Kinnans and tended a garden complex enough to use for his botanical collection. "For Sale" signs marked weedy home sites. The packed-dirt streets slickened when it rained, and the wooden sidewalks would warp. There were few streetlamps.

A feature Ida might have questioned was the proximity of the new Catholic University campus, just east of Brookland. Its first building, massive Divinity Hall, had been completed in 1889, welcoming the initial class of students. More buildings went up, and other Catholic institutions affiliated with the school, adding to the large campus, which, despite new construction, preserved its bucolic feel—there was that much land. The lack of ambient light in the area invited the installation of an observatory in 1890; here, important comet sightings were recorded. Even if Brookland were to transform into a grid of elegant townhouses, Catholic University's presence would always ensure spacious quietude nearby. The neighborhood became known as "Little Rome."

And not unlike Washington, which had long supported a substantial population of African-Americans, drawn to the city during Reconstruction for jobs or education (Howard University was founded in

1867), Brookland was racially mixed. Some of its black citizens were descended from freed slaves who had worked adjacent farms as share-croppers. Others had bought tracts of land and, in turn, sold lots to other African-Americans. The community was segregated; racially restrictive covenants were established. In the 1890s, Brookland counted seventy-six African-Americans, about one-tenth of the population, and the segment continued to grow.

There is little evidence that the Kinnans disliked the racial mix, although, as a representative of the Brookland Citizen's Association, Arthur opposed building a "colored school" in the heart of the community, arguing for a location farther out. One assumes Ida would have considered anything that looked like integration to be a barrier to a wider, whiter circle—even though, as her daughter would later claim, the Traphagens and Kinnans weren't particularly racist. Whatever her motives, Ida began casting about for ways to improve their situation. What could she do? There had to be a way to change her life.

Chapter Two

The Perfect Daughter

1900-1913

IDA KINNAN'S PLANS FOR a daughter worthy of the upper classes were complicated by a second, and unbidden, pregnancy. In April 1900, when Marjorie was not yet four, her brother Arthur was born. Although Marjorie hadn't been given a middle name, ostensibly to leave room for her future husband's, Arthur's full name would be in limbo for years, presaging the character of his adult life. In the 1900 census, he is listed as Liston A.; in his father's will, he is named as Arthur Liston. But by college age, the boy called himself Arthur Houston, which he used for the rest of his life. (Both Liston and Houston are family names on Arthur Sr.'s side.)

According to Marjorie, Arthur's birth dismayed Ida. It seemed her mother might have welcomed a miscarriage rather than carry this child to term. Whatever the reason, Ida failed to give her son the attention she'd heaped on her daughter. Young Arthur frequently threw tantrums for no reason Ida could discern, and when she publicly compared the children, she complained that one was good, one bad. As the older, preferred child, Marjorie took advantage of her superior position, teasing her brother, knowing she wouldn't be punished for it. But she also began to rebel against her mother. One financially lean spring, when Ida, in an effort to refashion one of her daughter's old hats, turned down the brim of the perky tricorn for a new look, Marjorie found that "by walking in apparent demureness and giving her ears a strong twitch, she could make the done-over hat suddenly shoot up its sides to their original position." Already in the habit of entertaining the neighborhood children, she strolled up and down the street in the hat, flipping the brim, rewarded with screams of laughter.

Arthur Sr. surprised Ida, and probably himself, with his deep fondness for Marjorie. He adored her. When he left the house before she awoke, he might leave her a little message or a verse. ("I love my little daughter / from her head clear to her toes / I even love the little bit / of turkey-egg nose.") His values were at odds with his wife's: social position, fine clothing, and wealth were unimportant. Fame was fine, if "noble and deserved." Marjorie took his values for her own.

For several years, Arthur Kinnan's salary covered elegant wardrobes for everyone, including Ida, who, Marjorie discovered, wore a pair of false breasts. As both Brookland and Arthur's fortunes grew, the elder Kinnans continued to participate in community life. Arthur's sister-in-law, Jenny, brought Ida into a small society of higher-class women who would admire a tasteful new ensemble, and promoted her membership in a ladies' embroidery club, whose purpose was to make "utterly useless and indefinable knick-knacks meant for Christmas presents," as Marjorie put it.

But the club's secondary aim, a tasty luncheon, often highlighted Ida's cooking skills, learned from her mother, Fanny Traphagen. Although Ida discouraged Marjorie's attempts at domestic activities "through the mistaken idea that they were ignoble" and allowed her to make only Parker House rolls, "because it seemed like an amusing accomplishment for a child," Marjorie eventually grew to love cooking, and in her forties, she published her mother's recipes for egg croquettes, jellied chicken, almond cake, and other delicacies in *Cross Creek Cookery*. The Kinnan table was well laden. At supper, Arthur blessed his wife's efforts: "Receive our thanks our Heavenly Father, for these mercies. Bless them to our bodies' good, for Thy name's sake. Amen."

As a public servant, Arthur occasionally spoke at a school or community event, in a frock coat and silk hat. In his years as president of the Brookland Citizens Association (1903–04 and 1906), he must have led many a town meeting. The family could afford summer visits to the Traphagen farm in Michigan, as well as vacations in West Virginia and Maine. They employed a maid or a housekeeper—this would most likely have been a young black woman or an Irish girl from the larger Catholic population—though the only household help Marjorie ever cited was her Aunt Jenny and Uncle Will's "old brown Emma," who made excellent custard ice cream.

JUST AS THIS ACTIVITY BEGAN to resemble, a little, Ida's dreams, Arthur announced his plan to buy a farm, proof that his excitement over the Texas ranch had been not an anomaly but an expression of his genetic code or a baseline passion. He'd found an attractive piece of land in Garrett Park, Maryland, ten miles outside Washington, and while continuing to work at his office job, he intended to build a dairy to sustain the family, enabling them to leave the city and return to rural life. Washington was growing in that direction, Arthur said—the land would support them one way or another. To raise funds for the farm purchase, he sold the lovely Queen Anne home on Newton Street and the lot abutting its east side and built a plainer house on the west lot, mortgaging the property. Ida objected. The financial undertaking was too much, the whole idea a dream and a regression. Yet she had no choice but to go along with it. Arthur bought the farm in 1905, the year of the singing audition, when Marjorie turned nine.

Writing of this time, Marjorie remembered the farmland as "scenically beautiful and all but sterile. One length of its two hundred and forty acres lay along Rock Creek. The other boundaries were gracious woods. It sloped up and down, up and down, in curves as lovely as Venus's body." There was an old white farmhouse, a cold spring, a "wild park" of various trees, a brook lined with lilies and ferns. She noted her father's trips to the land on weekends by train or trolley, his efforts to improve the soil by studying agriculture manuals; buying fertilizer, feed, and equipment; rotating crops; and overseeing tenant farmers. He bought a few cows and by the end of eight years had nearly a hundred head of Holsteins and Guernseys, "richly black and white and spotted against the Maryland meadows." He built barns, drove mules, laid pipe, created a modern dairy, and eventually sold his milk and cream to a Washington

lunch chain—all while working his office job. "He was architect, engineer, carpenter, and Hunky."

Marjorie loved the farm. How could she—a girl who had climbed
from a second-floor window into a tree, whose mother, fearing a mess
in the house, often sent her outside to play, whose neighborhood offered
open spaces reminiscent of farmland—not be drawn to it? As her father
labored to grow corn, oats, and rye, Marjorie and her brother sometimes
joined him, playing on the land, in the creek, picking wild berries. That
first summer, Arthur brought the whole family to camp on the property
and set up a large tent near Rock Creek. Marjorie recalled the first night
and morning: "the whippoorwills in the valley below sobbed all night
in the moonlight. The wind shivered the thin locust leaves. The frogs
shrilled on their silver pipes, and the deep cow bells sounded, and then
were still, and tinkled again, as Peg and Laura and Bess and the gray
heifer grazed and moved." In the evening, she heard Kensington's church
bells. "The air was spiced with pennyroyal, with clover, with locust blossoms, wild roses and the grassy smell of the cows."

IDA COULDN'T ARGUE WITH her husband's farm purchase; neither
could she fight Marjorie's affinity for the land. But she figured that her
daughter, still young, might yet reveal a special talent worthy of a city's
attention, and two years after the failed voice lesson, Marjorie did. One
Sunday when she was visiting her Uncle Will and Aunt Jenny, Marjorie
was given a magazine containing a simple story. After reading it, she saw
a children's writing contest announced in the Washington Post, rewrote
the story in her own way (later, she would call it plagiarism), and sent
it in, winning two dollars. "The Best Spell" is a fairy tale ending in a
perfect love. An ingratiating reference Marjorie planted in the story for
its intended reader probably didn't hurt its chances. The enchanter "had
two little nieces to provide for, and sometimes it was hard to make ends
meet, for he had ogres to fight, called editors (although not all editors are
ogres)." Grateful for her prize, perhaps even coached by Ida, Marjorie
wrote to the children's editor, "Aunt Anna" (Cecilia Reynolds Robert-
son) to say that the two dollars was the first money she had earned. "So
this morning I went downtown with father and started a bank account,"
she announced, self-satisfied, adding that she would earn 2 percent, with
compound interest.

Her mother "pounced on this morsel, a mouse for a long-hungry cat" and a siege began. Ida became consumed with her daughter's future writing career, seeking more contests, freeing Marjorie from chores to follow her "inspiration," holding her up to others as a budding genius. Marjorie recalled the puffery and slick sentences her mother encouraged: "Self-confidence is a great loosener of tongues and of words," Marjorie wrote, looking back. "With this Rock of Gibraltar behind her, the girl did not falter with phrases. The result was a certain precocity, a meaningless smoothness, that took prizes away from normal, groping children. By a wiser mother, pseudo-adult writing would have been recognized for sounding brass—the most dangerous development possible." Yet Marjorie might have been projecting part of an internal conflict onto her ambitious mother.

Having published on the *Post*'s children's page in the Sunday supplement, Marjorie was named to the Cousins' Club, a group of young contributors who submitted letters about writing and literature. Members used pen names; Marjorie's was Fidelity. She continued to enter the *Post*'s contests, often placing first or second with stories or poems. At the Brookland School, she spun yarns for her classmates. She was a natural raconteur and preferred an audience of boys. Already, she was developing a bawdy streak.

By the time Marjorie was fourteen and ready to enter high school, Ida had decided that Brookland was not good enough for her daughter's social development and education, and she pressured Arthur for a change. At first, the couple considered a generous offer from a friend who owned a college prep school for girls, but neither wanted to see their daughter a charity student among the rich. In Ida's mind, the alternative was a wholesale move out of Brookland, close to a prestigious public school, and when she nearly broke down over the quandary, Arthur agreed to sell their second Brookland house and let his wife make whatever new living arrangements she wanted.

Ida quickly moved the family into the passably attractive Hammond Court apartments on Thirtieth Street NW in Georgetown; there Marjorie would have access to Western High School, an imposing Classical Revival edifice in Columbia Heights, where many wealthy and influential people lived. At Western High, Marjorie would attend classes with the children of government officials and diplomats, and in this neighborhood, the family would be much closer to the capital city's heart, and the events that drew people to it.

During Marjorie's high school years, for example, Washington saw its first suffragist parade (the Woman Suffrage Procession, March 3, 1913), routed along Pennsylvania Avenue, one end of which was six blocks from Hammond Court. With eight thousand marchers, including nine bands, four mounted brigades, and twenty floats, the parade, held the day before President Woodrow Wilson's inauguration, attracted tens of thousands of spectators, some eager to ridicule the cause. Dozens of marchers were blocked, tripped, or assaulted; one hundred wound up in the hospital. Clearly, the Kinnans were now close to the middle of things. To afford it, Ida determined that they would spend summers on the Maryland farm and sublet the apartment.

To WESTERN HIGH SCHOOL, Marjorie carried the linked expectations she had learned to bear: high social status and notable accomplishment. Her mother looked forward to daily reports: who had spoken to her daughter or invited her to a party, who had noticed her talent or praised her writing assignments. Under such pressure, Marjorie remembered, she tried too hard to make the "right" friends and, failing, concentrated on writing for the school magazine, the *Western*. Despite this obvious vehicle for her daughter's talent, such focus made Ida nervous. Was the girl turning into an intellectual, unattractive to young men? No doubt Ida, whose single wooer had offered his hand after two years of Sundays on a country porch, was anxiously reading everything she could on "modern" courtship, which had grown markedly different in just one generation. Women and girls, especially in cities, increasingly often participated in public life, giving rise to the ritual of the "date" outside the home. Combined with her outsized hopes for Marjorie, such freedom of movement and choice must have given Ida many sleepless nights.

But in time, a balance was struck. Nice boys called on the girl who lived in the Italianate building with the courtyard and fountain. The girl who wrote joined a sorority. "Over her left breast," Marjorie wrote of herself, "she wore a display of high school jewelry, class and fraternity pins, worthy of a wounded war hero." To pay for dancing lessons and party dresses beyond their means, the family extended its rent-free summers on the farm.

Marjorie recalled two romances from the Western High years. The first was an anonymous admirer who for weeks ordered a fresh floral corsage delivered to her door every Tuesday. The admirer turned out to be a girl indulging a "morbid crush." The second was more promising: a boy from a well-to-do family who invited Marjorie to the dancing school's spring cotillion. She liked the boy well enough, but it was his mother who drew her in. Warm and confident, without pretension, the woman invited her into the family's elegant home and treated her son and Marjorie to dinners, concerts, the theater, and a New Year's Eve celebration with champagne. For a special occasion, she lent Marjorie pieces of her own fine jewelry. Besides these luxuries, Marjorie found her beau's mother easy to talk to. Although Ida approved of the social connection, she eventually grew jealous of the other mother, who seemed to have won more of Marjorie's heart than she had. When the beau's mother invited Ida to a party, the woman from Holly, Michigan, attended warily, nervous and tongue-tied.

Many years later, Marjorie recalled another situation revealing her mother's naïveté, this time with regard to a Hammond Court neighbor, Mrs. Nolan, "a spectacular blonde with an ermine coat." Marjorie related that this neighbor

fancied herself as a high soprano and her voice, above the haphazard piano notes of her own striking, was as shrill as a hawk's. When she let loose, one of her parrots screamed with her, then, outclassed, shrieked, "What the hell! What the hell!" Mrs. Nolan kept large numbers of birds and we had a strong suspicion that large numbers of men kept Mrs. Nolan. There seemed no other way to account for men's voices late at night, through our bedroom wall which adjoined Mrs. Nolan's bedroom wall. There was a Mr. Nolan, very fat and inclined to drunkenness, who came home only occasionally. One day Mrs. Nolan, wrapped in the ermine coat, her hair freshly blondined and topped with a black velvet hat with an egret plume, was sweeping out to go downtown on her mysterious errand. She stopped to pass the time of day with Mother, to whom, for some strange reason, she was devoted, for there could not have been two more dissimilar women. Years later, I found among Mother's things one of those old-fashioned photographs of postcard size, of Mrs. Nolan in the ermine coat and black velvet hat and egret plume. Across it was scrawled, "To my nearest and dearest neighbor." Studying the portrait with the eye of maturity, I knew for a fact that Mrs. Nolan had been our nearest and dearest whore.

Marjorie continued to write for the *Western*, holding the associate and literary editorships (1911–12 and 1913–14, respectively) and continued entering the *Post*'s contests. In her first year at Western, she won a first prize for a poem titled "The Traveler." It begins:

> *I guess I have the wanderlust*
> *For I am always on the go;*
> *Behind the plow's too tame for me,*
> *As also is the hoe.*

From here, the speaker travels to Africa, Venice, Switzerland, Scotland, France, Russia, and China but is ultimately glad to see the Statue of Liberty and New York's skyscrapers, signing off with "Be it ever so humble / There's no place like home!"

Marjorie's high school poems and stories continue in this vein. They are romantic, sentimental, and unoriginal. That is, one can detect the young woman imitating, parroting, as one might in the early stages of artistic development. But she was also writing for a particular audience delighted by the superficial, the patriotic, or the familiar: her mother, "Aunt Anna," and her teachers and classmates.

At fifteen, she won another *Post* contest with what the children's editor described as "a thrilling tale of the sea." "A Battle for Life" opens with an extended Gothic flourish: "Ah, gentle reader, 'tis a fearful tale I shall unfold—a story that will make cold shivers run up and down your spine, a narrative calculated to make your nerves tingle, to make you shudder and grip the steady arms of your cozy chair and peer fearfully and apprehensively into the darkness of the hallway—the story of the weighing in the balance of seven human lives in the scales that ever tipped toward death."

Yet farther on, the overwriting subsides and the author's voice changes, eases, as if now that Marjorie has pleased her audience, she can write less dramatically, yet with no lack of description: "The water was thick, thick as oil, dark and cruel. As the oars dipped into the strange substance no gentle splash followed—only a dull gurgle. . . . The skies overhead were dull and leaden. The gentle rose-pink rays of the setting sun seemed to shun the place. Half-terrified, the men pushed the boat against the only semblance to a beach offered."

The story concludes with a positive, if not happy, ending. Always, in Marjorie's juvenilia, someone is conventionally saved, rewarded, taught a lesson—and sometimes, a dear little animal dies.

IN 1912, AT SIXTEEN, Marjorie submitted a story to *McCall's Magazine*'s Child Authorship Contest and won second prize. "The Reincarnation of Miss Hetty" tells of a prim spinster who has been emotionally stunted since the accidental drowning of her baby brother, under her care, long ago. On a trip to town one day, Miss Hetty encounters an orphan boy who wants to sell her his dog in order to eat, and, envisioning her baby brother, she suddenly breaks down. In the brief final scene, the golden-haired child is fast asleep in Miss Hetty's house, in a "little white bed by the window." Miss Hetty's heart is "at rest."

In *Blood of My Blood*, Marjorie depicted her brother, Arthur, as a nuisance to her mother. He is not afforded the intense focus Marjorie was and seems underfoot, wanting for attention. Reading details of an artist's personal life in their imaginative output can be no more than an academic exercise—many years later, Marjorie would put forth the idea that the private life and personality of an author had little to do with their work. However, her dismissal seems self-protective, as writers do draw from experience, consciously or unconsciously. It's worth noting that "Miss Hetty" is the first of several stories (including *The Yearling*) with a vulnerable young boy at its center. Not only did Marjorie prefer an audience of boys; she tended to feature them in her work and look after a few in her adult life.

Also in 1912, Marjorie published the first of several poems featuring dialect, revealing another aspect of an absorbent, discerning ear and an awareness—conscious or not—of trends. One of her childhood heroes was James Whitcomb Riley, a friend and admirer of Mark Twain, whose *Adventures of Huckleberry Finn*, one of the earliest American novels written in vernacular English, had been published in 1885, fewer than thirty years before. Riley's children's poetry and dialect works were popular; in 1912, the *Post* awarded Marjorie a first prize for her tribute poem "To James Whitcomb Riley." Following Riley's lead, she could both mimic and transcribe. For example, in her poem "The Freshman's Side of It," a red-headed Freshie speaks like a toddler:

> *We Fweshman do to all de games,*
> *An' join de 'ssociation,*
> *An' pay our dues, join de debate*
> *An' den our consolation.*

In "H'it's a Bear, H'it's a Bear, H'it's a Bear, There!" an upper-class Englishman holds forth, applying the *h* sound before a vowel, distinguishing himself from lower-class Britons, who drop their *h*'s. And in the 1913 story "A Surprise," which took first place in another *Washington Post* contest, Marjorie channeled Mandy, a working-class American girl who is advised by a pair of snobbish friends to stop socializing with her own kind. Mandy responds in the vernacular: "I don't reckon you ought to talk about the girls I go with. Mebbe they ain't what you call ladies, but I think they've got a good bit more manners and refinement than some of those you think are the finest in the school. They don't keer 'bout what I've got on, it's the heart that's under my old-fashion dress."

Riley and Twain weren't the only popular authors employing the vernacular. Nine years before Huckleberry Finn appeared, Joel Chandler Harris, a native Georgian and a columnist for the *Atlanta Constitution*, created the Uncle Remus character and, starting in 1879, published Uncle Remus's African-American folktales, not just in the *Constitution* and other southern newspapers but in nearly every state from New York to California. Harris based the tales on his close associations with slaves during the Civil War. As a very young man, he had worked on a newspaper published by a plantation owner, and being shy, and self-conscious about his Irish ancestry, he felt more comfortable spending his off-hours in the slave quarters than the plantation house. He absorbed the slaves' language and stories, even as he availed himself of his employer's library, reading the likes of Chaucer, Shakespeare, and Poe. In an interview published the year Marjorie was born, he told a reporter that Uncle Remus was a composite of "three or four old negroes who I knew as a boy. I have combined them and perhaps have added something to them." He could hear Uncle Remus talk; "his voice rings in my ears as I write." The stories, he said, were "the folk-lore of the negro," some with African or even Indian origins. Brer Rabbit, for instance, was a trickster figure.

The Uncle Remus stories had appeared in the Washington, D.C., *Evening Star*, and by the time Marjorie could read, they had been collected in a best-selling book. Four collections of Uncle Remus stories were published during Marjorie's childhood and adolescence, and Harris's books were invariably included—along with *Huckleberry Finn* and *The Adventures of Tom Sawyer*—on Christmas book lists for children. It's reasonable to assume that Marjorie was familiar with some, if not all, of them. Ida and Arthur might have placed copies under the tree. "Uncle Remus is one of the saints of the holiday season," wrote Frank Carpenter in the Washington *Evening Star* when Marjorie was four months old. "He is almost as much a part of our children's lives as Santa Claus." The southern Negro dialect Marjorie would employ later had come first to her not just from Brookland neighbors, but very likely through her reading.

IN MARJORIE'S SENIOR YEAR at Western (1913–14), the Kinnan family underwent several major changes. Arthur Jr.'s temperament softened after two minor operations and his tantrums abated, relieving some tension in the household. Ida threw herself into planning Marjorie's college career, ideally at prestigious Bryn Mawr, encouraging an egoism in her daughter that finally caught the attention of her husband—one day, Arthur heard Marjorie fling an insult at her mother and boxed her ears for it. Around the same time, Ida finally realized that she had indulged her daughter too much and restricted some of Marjorie's social activities, chastening the girl and retrieving some of her own self-respect.

But the most significant event, one apparently no one saw coming, was Arthur Sr.'s death. He had suffered blinding headaches for some time, but the sedative prescribed by the society doctor Ida preferred did little but put him to sleep or make him talk "wildly of his plans." One day when Arthur slept until noon, Ida phoned the doctor, who told her to let him continue napping. By evening, when Marjorie's most promising date yet, a young banker, called at the apartment, Arthur was, unbeknownst to them all, breathing his final hour. The family doctor was called again, but he was attending to someone else and sent his assistant, who immedi-

ately diagnosed an acute uremic coma and fled, leaving the family awaiting his superior. By now the tragedy unfolding behind the bedroom door
could not be hidden from the visiting banker, who Marjorie sent out
for another doctor. This one witnessed Arthur's last moments, and laid
out the body. Finally, the family physician arrived, shocked, protesting
he had detected no symptoms of uremia. When Ida asked him if Arthur
could have been saved, the doctor told her no.

Arthur's large family and Ida's parents traveled to Washington for
the funeral, which also drew some surprise mourners: young men Arthur
had, unbeknownst to Ida, helped through school, as he had helped his
brother and sisters, and her brothers. He had kept the extent of his gener-
osity to himself. His remains were taken to Oakwood Cemetery in Fenton. Much later, when Marjorie was an established author and crediting
her father for early grounding, she often said he had lived the true life of
his mind and heart on the Maryland farm.

Chapter Three

Wisconsin

1914-18

AFTER HER FATHER'S DEATH in the fall of 1913, Marjorie continued her senior year at Western, writing for the school magazine and submitting more work to the *Washington Post*. In May, she won a first prize for "Alonzo Perceval Van Clyne," the story of Snubby (Alonzo), a pug-nosed boy who tells ghost stories of "stellar magnitude," draws clusters of less daring boys, and can't stop skipping school to frolic and explore outdoors. When Miss Casterlin, his pretty, sympathetic teacher, warns him that she will lose her job if he doesn't stay in his seat, the youngster, whose family situation is unclear, explains that he can't help himself. "Somethin' pulls me, an' I—I jes' go. It's mostly him, I guess. I can always feel when he is lonesome, or sick, or tired. It's 'cause he loves me so, I 'pose, an' I love him, 'cause I always know when he wants me, or has somethin' in the woods to show me, or a new story."

Miss Casterlin imagines that Snubby's "him" is the call of the wild, which she understands, but she tells Snubby that if she loses her job she will starve, because she has no parents. Her mother died when she was small, and her father was lost in a shipwreck. "He loved the woods and the fields, too," she says, producing a picture of her father. Snubby smiles at the picture and promises not to run away again. But one glorious May day, he slips out of the schoolhouse, races into the woods, and returns with a white-haired man he calls Daddy Joe. The man is both Snubby's "him" and Miss Casterlin's father. A tearful reunion ensues. The father's survival and retreat to the woods is never explained—the point is that Snubby has found him and everyone is happy.

As Marjorie finished her classes and penned the class song (sung to the tune of "Believe Me, If All Those Endearing Young Charms"), Ida worked out a plan for her daughter's college education. She couldn't afford the Ivy League schools many of Marjorie's classmates at Western would attend; nor could she remain close to the high end of Washington. Arthur's sisters offered to send both Marjorie and Arthur to the University of Michigan, but Ida refused their help. The way Marjorie saw it, her mother feared assistance from "the enemy's camp," women "dedicated to high doctrines of mind and soul—women unfashionable and unworldly." Instead, Ida studied the situation surrounding her inheritance—the Maryland farm—and discovered that a syndicate planned to build a major highway that would run through the property. Her husband had been correct on one point: the land would be valuable when the Washington suburbs stretched in that direction. The timing was good, for the countryside was still farmland and the highway had yet to be built. She felt she could make an agreeable sale to the right investors, and did. The proceeds provided sufficient interest income for herself and the children—not riches, but enough to get by. Once the deal was struck, she held an auction to liquidate the farm equipment and registered stock. She planned the whole thing herself, hiring the best auctioneer and riding around Rockville in a horse and buggy, posting advertisements. The morning of the auction, Marjorie refused to be part of it.

By now, Ida had determined that her children would attend the University of Wisconsin. The school was said to be first-rate since the 1903 appointment of President Charles Van Hise, who, with the backing of Governor Robert La Follette, had undertaken an agenda of promoting scholarly research and established a graduate program. The English Department had an excellent reputation. (In 1927, Eudora Welty would transfer to Wisconsin from the Mississippi State College for Women.) Marjorie knew Robert La Follette Jr., who was a year ahead of her at Western High School, and his brother, Philip, a year behind her. Their father had resigned the Wisconsin governorship in 1906 to serve in the U.S. Senate and had moved his family to Washington. Robert was currently attending the University of Wisconsin, as Philip would later.

Marjorie was no shoo-in for the school, though, despite her overall fine grades (math and science were not her strong suits). On the confidential application form, under "Give a general estimate of the work and character of the student," Western High's principal wrote, "Miss Kinnan has great natural ability, particularly in the line of literary work and languages. She is capable of doing rather extraordinary work—tho' she is easily distracted by social interests!" Beneath this, a UW official typed, "Candidate to be admitted on probation if grades are <u>Good</u>." She was required to maintain a minimum 75 percent average for a full load in her freshman year.

In August 1914, the three Kinnans and their furniture were en route to Madison. By September 1, Ida had rented a large apartment beyond her means in a nice section of town, on Lake Mendota; to cover the cost, she took in two student boarders. Two weeks later, from 625 Mendota Court, she wrote to the university that she had come to Wisconsin to establish a permanent residence. Marjorie was granted resident status. When classes began, the freshman co-ed had a closetful of new clothes to go with her lakeside address. As one college friend later put it, "I remember seeing her on registration day. She was so lovely. She always wore high heels and gloves, as they did in those days, and I remember thinking, 'She looks the way a girl ought to look.'"

Ida's dreams for her daughter continued to hold sway: Marjorie was going to distinguish herself on campus, both scholastically and socially, and eventually land a notable husband—but not too early. Ida envisioned her daughter making her literary mark first, then marrying, say, a governor in her late twenties. Marjorie recalled that Ida scrimped on everything for her daughter's benefit, wearing cotton stockings so Marjorie could have silk, letting her shoes fall apart so Marjorie could have kidskin slippers. Ida continued to live for Marjorie's daily reports.

Very soon, Marjorie was placed in the advanced composition class taught by William Ellery Leonard, the first teacher to soundly criticize her, "flicking down adjectives and destroying adverbs by the dozen." She reveled in his intelligence and irreverence—she might have known that

Professor Leonard was, or would become, a legendary teacher. Leonard had come to Wisconsin in 1906 and would remain until his death in 1944. Literary critic Leslie Fiedler, who earned his graduate degrees at Wisconsin, dedicated his *Love and Death in the American Novel* to Leonard, for "the rich, tragic quality of his own being as well as by the excitement he engendered in the classroom." In a biography of the professor, University of Wisconsin graduate Neale Reinitz praised Leonard for demonstrating that "literature can be a fulfillment of life." By the time Reinitz encountered him in the early 1940s, Leonard "had white hair and wore a flowing purple tie. . . . He had written a popular volume of sonnets and had been married four times. He taught a strange combination of courses that included *Beowulf* and the poetry of Robert Burns, and had published more than a dozen books." Reinitz recalled Leonard's unusual phobia that confined him to a few blocks near campus. It involved a pathological fear of railroad trains, which Leonard wrote about in his book *The Locomotive-God.*

Leonard is the only professor Marjorie described at any length in *Blood of My Blood.* When she entered his classroom in 1914, he was just three years past the suicide of his first wife and was deep into revisions for *Two Lives,* a collection of sonnets in response to his marriage and its tragedy. Despite the emergence of his lifelong agoraphobia, Leonard had begun courting a twenty-three-year-old summer school student, and in October 1914, he married her. He participated in amateur theatrics and wrote "farce-comedies" for the Faculty Club. He digressed during lectures, dressed as an eccentric: "high laced boots, a cane, and a green Harvard book bag."

According to Leonard's biographer, Marjorie was one of his shining lights. She must have been thrilled by his searching, unconventional mind. Yet Ida, who'd heard tales of the professor's behavior, refused to hear Marjorie defend his brilliance. When Leonard commanded her to write a story without adjectives and adverbs and Marjorie protested it couldn't be done, the professor bellowed, "And I say it can! I guess I ought to know more about adjectives and adverbs than a chit of a school girl!" She pulled it off, learning the value of strong nouns and verbs, but Ida thought the exercise insulting. "I don't call that encouragement," she said. She preferred her daughter's old flowery style. Marjorie replied, "Sometimes I think that what I need is not encouragement, but killing."

Later, she wrote of her mother, "Pity that she could not see that a succession of Leonards would have been the only thing to save the girl. The later professors were 'darling'—but they were too lenient."

In her remembrance, Marjorie briefly mentioned two other professors: O. J. Campbell and R. E. Neil Dodge. With Dodge she took courses in the Romantic and Victorian movements. With Campbell, it's not clear. His topical offerings don't include the other English courses Marjorie signed up for: American Literature, Chaucer, two surveys of English literature, two semesters of Shakespeare, six semesters of Composition, two of Narration, one course in journalism, and one that may be (if I am reading the registrar's shorthand correctly) Dramatic Writing. She also continued her studies in French and German, having come from Western High with two years of German, three of French, and four of Latin. The rest of her transcript shows two semesters of botany, four of history, three of philosophy, one of public speaking, and one of "political economy."

SOCIALLY, Marjorie gradually made her way. At first, she tried too hard to impress the four sororities that rushed her, exaggerating her Washington connections and scattering her bodices with her high school pins. When she failed to receive a bid from the sorority she was most interested in, she turned to other pursuits, liberated from the ordeal of trying to fit in. A few months later, the group she'd wanted, Kappa Alpha Theta, whose impressive house was furnished in the fashionable American Craftsman style, offered her a bid.

At the same time, she was active in the Dixie Club, which she described as "a shoddy little affair of queer Southerners," and which apparently hurt her standing with some campus men. The club, part of a young national organization with chapters as far-flung as the University of California and Cornell, was part of a trend toward campus groups celebrating various regions, no doubt a comfort to out-of-state students. Some of them even had their own houses, like fraternities and sororities. (The trend, and most of the clubs, died out before World War II.)

The Dixie Club welcomed members from below the Mason-Dixon Line. Marjorie, born just beneath that line, and the child of Yankees, barely qualified. As well, she was running with an "intellectual bunch" and "talking crazy, philosophical talk," which wouldn't have attracted the sorts of beaus her mother preferred. Anxious about her daughter's prospects, Ida monitored Marjorie's dating strategies, which included: keeping an eye on the campus events schedule weeks out, putting off the average fellow or stalling for time in case a more desirable one called, breaking one date for another, keeping her machinations vague or secret so that no man knew he was being manipulated, and feigning confusion when caught playing. The Dixie Club hadn't driven everyone away. Marjorie named admirers: Little Southern Woody, Good old Dick, Fritz the Milwaukee aristocrat, "Speed" the track man, Marty and Fred, Alvin and Hod and Gil and Kim. Ted. Gyp. The more social traction Marjorie gained, the more she took advantage of her mother's sacrificial position, expecting new clothes and other privileges, even as she lost respect for her.

Marjorie enjoyed considerable campus successes beyond the Thetas and the Dixie Club, starting with the theater, a natural fit. Gertrude Johnson, her speech and drama coach, encouraged the young actress and served as a role model; she was one of Wisconsin's few women faculty members, recently hired to establish a theater program. In January 1916, as a sophomore, Marjorie played the role of "Tweeny," a common servant girl who is enthralled by the lead character, a butler, in J. M. Barrie's *The Admirable Crichton*, which had had a long run in London and been produced on Broadway in 1903. Marjorie the raconteur, the vernacularist, must have savored lines like this one: "I'm full o' vulgar words and ways; and though I may keep them in their holes when you are by, as soon as I'm by myself out they comes in a rush like beetles when the house is dark."

The play was a co-production of the Red Domino Dramatic Club (women) and the Edwin Booth Dramatic Club (men). At the time, the sexes were segregated, as the university frowned on men and women traveling together for performances outside Madison. In Red Domino, Marjorie began a lifelong friendship with Beatrice "Bee" Humiston (later McNeil), who also played a servant in the Barrie play and would become a high school English and drama teacher and a published playwright for works intended for secondary schools.

By the fall of her junior year, Marjorie had composed a play of her own, *Into the Nowhere*. Described as "a fantasy," and in the December 1916 program as "An Original Pantomime in Black and White," the play had a large cast, including a pianist. It won first place in the annual contest sponsored by Union Vodvil, an organization raising funds for the student union building. *Into the Nowhere* was a huge success, copyrighted by the Dramatics Club and reportedly performed by school and college groups across the United States. To date, no copy of the manuscript has turned up, fueling the notion that the play depended entirely on pantomime to carry the action. However, the program's 230-word synopsis offers enough detail for envisioning a performance, and perhaps it is the extent of the script. It begins:

> The two maids prepare the stage by carefully dusting the hedge trees. The clown kisses them in rapture. Coquette dances into the garden. The clown disapproves of her little hat, and offers his own. Having kissed the maids, he wishes to kiss her also. She slaps him and runs away. Pierrette and Pierrot find the garden and dance. The Fliffy-Fluffs dance about the happy couple. The Villain and Witch hypnotize Pierrot and Pierrette. The anxious Parson is shocked.

And so on, toward a wedding, until the maids return to dust the trees again and prepare for the next performance. Here, Marjorie combined and parodied commedia dell'arte characters, music, and dance—a modernist gesture. Her "pantomime in black and white" came just two years after Charlie Chaplin's first American film was released; by the time Marjorie graduated from Wisconsin, he was a worldwide celebrity. Pantomime, with its reliance on physical expression, fascinated many artists at the time, driving all the movies until sound technology arrived, in 1927. If Marjorie directed *Into the Nowhere*, she must have selected the musical accompaniment and demonstrated or described the physical movements she wanted.

In January 1917, a month after *Into the Nowhere*'s premiere, Marjorie played Madam Jeanne Marie Napoleon de Gallifet Didier in the Domino-Booth production of another British play, *'Op-o'-Me-Thumb*, a 1904 one-act by Frederick Fenn and Richard Pryce. Bee Humiston landed the lead role of Amanda Afflick. In March, Marjorie was Celia Faraday ("an unaffected woman of twenty-nine, with a sense of humor") in the junior play, *Green Stockings*. This, too, was a fairly new work—the New York production had opened in 1911. It was also Marjorie's third performance in four months. It appears she exhausted herself that academic year, presaging a lifelong pattern of overwork and collapse. In the fall, she had been allowed to take just twelve credits in view of her work on *The Badger*, the university's yearbook, and she withdrew from all classes in February, even as she kept her role in *Green Stockings*. Her transcript cites her withdrawal as due to "health." Presumably this coincided with her tonsillectomy, as she published a humorous poem alluding to it in the November 1917 issue of the *Wisconsin Literary Magazine*. She was permitted to make up one course: Chaucer.

In January 1918, Marjorie, Bee, and another student, J. Bloom, took third prize in a Union Vodvil contest for their performance of Alfred Kreymborg's play *Lima Beans*, an expressionist verse drama. This experimental play had premiered at the Provincetown Playhouse during the 1914–15 season, with William Carlos Williams and Mina Loy playing the married couple, "He" and "She." (At Wisconsin, Marjorie was "She" and Bee, "He.") Apparently, Marjorie contacted the playwright herself, and naïvely, for in a letter to her, Kreymborg refused her permission to perform the play without paying royalties.

The *Lima Beans* plot is simple: every night, the couple has lima beans for dinner. But one night, the wife tries something different and buys string beans from the Huckster. When the husband gets home and discovers that there are no limas, he throws a fit. The Huckster returns, the wife buys lima beans, and the couple reconciles. It is easy to picture Marjorie—veteran of dancing lessons, impromptu storytelling, and numerous flirtations—as the clever wife who surprises her husband, tussles with him, and finally gives in to his staid preference, accepting his kisses and winking at the audience as the curtain lowers, as if to say, "Boys will be boys." The campus newspaper, the *Daily Cardinal*, commented that both Marjorie and Bee "had drawn freely upon their imaginations," "evidence enough of their ability, versatility, mobility of expression and real enjoyment ipso facto."

Beyond the theater, Marjorie gathered academic and social honors. In 1917, she was elected to Phi Beta Kappa and Mortar Board. She was on the 1917 *Badger* yearbook's board (listed under "Satire"), was "woman's editor" of the 1918 edition, and was one of two "special features" editors for 1919. She was vice president of Red Domino. She was on the staff of the *Wisconsin Literary Magazine* (hereafter *WLM*), rising to associate editor, and contributed to the *Daily Cardinal*. In these publications, one can track some of her progress as a writer.

Her short stories still listed toward the sentimental. In "The Brute," published in WLM her sophomore year, she explored masculinity and femininity, both inner qualities and social roles undergoing dramatic shifts in the early twentieth century. She would question these themes, and struggle with them, for most of her life. "The Brute" features a man "every inch of six feet eight virility" whose appearance frightens everyone but his wife, who understands his goodness and tenderness. "Your heart, I think, must be that of a woman," she tells him. "Your heart is one of love, love that cannot restrain itself, that craves a return, in sympathy, and more love. I give you that return, I let you pour out all the love within your soul—here."

Yet, she confirms, the outside world expects brutality of a man his size, and so he meets the world's expectations by accidentally killing a clerk who raises his hand to an innocent street urchin. Dazed by his action, the Brute faints and falls from his office window to the city pavement. When he awakes in the hospital, the doctor delivers bad news and good news. The bad: he is a quadriplegic. The good: his wife has given birth to a son with "the beauty of his mother." When the doctor wheels the Brute outdoors, a little girl nearby regards him as a "nice man," because his ugly face has been "softened by pain, and the network of lines, under the hair streaked with the white of suffering, seemed the map of a heart, all gentleness, kindliness and love."

The entertainer in Marjorie swung toward farce. For example, in the December 1916 issue of *WLM*, she published "The Captivating Odors of the Kitchen," a humorous yarn about Jedediah Hoskins, a single man whose life is changed when he dines at his boss's home and enjoys cooking far exceeding his mother's. After this, he refuses his mother's cooking and eats out. As a result, it would seem, he receives a promotion and is sent to a new town. By now he has decided that he must be married, and to a woman who can really cook. One day the delicious fragrance of fried chicken wafts from a window, and he wonders if the woman he hears singing inside is "the one." He catches sight of her. She is desperately homely: "Her tiny black eyes had a tendency to cross at the most alarming moments, her mouth had a listless, pouty droop that betokened a nature of mixed sulks and slatternliness, and her form bore no relation to any previous feminine model." Yet he pursues and marries her. But the joke's on him when his new wife reveals that the cooking odors were the work of a previous boarder. Like Jedediah, she is only looking out for herself, and now that she can depend on his salary, she'll hire a maid and economize on food. "I don't believe in wastin' a lot o' time on fancy dishes for a man," she says, chomping on a large slice of bread.

Marjorie published book and drama reviews in *WLM*, too. And poems. One, "The Mouse Speaks," was listed under "other poems of distinction" in *Poets of the Future: A College Anthology for 1916–1917*. The speaker is a man addressing a woman practiced in manipulating beaus. It opens:

> *I scarce can see your eyes beneath your lashes—*
> *You drop them, coy, and shy, and most demure;*
> *I only get a bit of blue, in flashes—*
> *You do it all on purpose, I am sure.*

Other poems are less clever, more mysterious. Appearing in the following issue of *WLM*, "Creation of Soul" seems inspired by Edna Millay's early masterpiece "Renascence." Two stanzas:

> *The cross-roads Calvary shone ruddy gold,*
> *Warmed in the soft glow of the evening sun,*
> *When he, my vagabond, sweet alien,*
> *Came framed against it, tall, and dark, and bold.*
>
> *And I was his from Time's first happy day,*
> *And god-like, did he ask, and take, my all;*
> *And god-like, too, gave radiance to the thrall.*
> *And I shall follow where he leads, for aye.*

And in April 1917 came "The Stuff of Dreams," describing a "low-roofed, sprawling house" and "a garden, filled with roses, larkspur and columbines." It ends:

> *Out of the noise, the push, the whirl,*
> *Out of the aches that will not cease,*
> *Out of the satisfaction, pain—*
> *I dream of this—of this—and peace.*

Beyond campus publications, Marjorie submitted poems to national magazines like the *Century* and the *Atlantic Monthly.* No acceptances came, though Ida read encouragement in the perfunctory rejections. Still, Marjorie wanted most to be a poet. In the April 1918 issue of *WLM,* her essay "On Poetry and Vachel Lindsay" appeared; it was an argument, or a preaching, for poetry as an ideal food for the soul. The essay opens with a long preamble about the existence of souls and the presence of a "soul-nucleus" in those who seek an education. "I believe that every one of us here has undreamt-of spiritual possibilities; put the baby on the right diet, and he'll grow," she wrote. From here, she suggested contemporary poetry for a first course, recommending Lindsay, a dramatic, entertaining declaimer known as the Prairie Troubadour. Then: "Try other moderns. *Read them aloud.* Read them in different moods. Fit them to your moods. And see if it doesn't satisfy something that beer or canoeing won't touch."

In her senior year, Marjorie won the English Department's William C. Vilas Prize for an essay on the Belgian Symbolist poet Émile Verhaeren and submitted her thesis, "Paganism in English Poetry." She was named one of Wisconsin's "Representative Women," the criteria being "Spirit, Competency, and Womanliness." In a special portrait for *The Badger,* typical of the period, she is wearing a gauzy gown with rosettes applied to the shoulders and fluffy marabou encircling the three-quarter-length sleeves and overskirt. Marjorie's hands lie folded in her lap. Her head is bowed demurely, eyes cast down, like a Maxfield Parrish virgin gazing into a pool of water.

That Marjorie omitted this last sort of honor from *Blood of My Blood* speaks volumes. The notoriety must have pleased Ida, but it's fair to say that her daughter quickly dismissed it. As her college career progressed, Marjorie had become increasingly independent; while still a member of Kappa Alpha Theta, she joined a movement to ban sororities. In May of her senior year, in the *Daily Cardinal,* she described sororities as "unwholesome, pernicious, and undemocratic." They "perpetuate a caste system that is unfair to other university alumnae who are not from sororities," she wrote.

The mother-daughter connection finally ruptured. Marjorie was, as she later described herself, "filled with the usual juvenile despair at life's futility," probably fueled by the "intellectual bunch," she ran with, which would have included fellow staffers on *WLM*. Her mother "did not know that at this time youth chooses its subsequent philosophy; permanent despair, courage; retreat into the herd, into the utmost possible mediocrity; or finds a renewed appetite for the adventure of living." "Convictions," a theme Marjorie wrote for an unidentified professor, opens, "I am as acutely conscious of the futility of man's destiny as Wordsworth was of his immortality." She discusses the universe, faith, and God, criticizes people who say they know God, and describes a powerful personal experience, the symbolic birth of "cosmic consciousness" in her.

"I trust my instinct," she wrote, "because it is cosmic. I experienced the universe—once. I was wide awake, and was thinking of some trivial thing in a text-book I was reading. And it came on me suddenly, my feeling, my consciousness, embraced without warning—infinity and eternity, I comprehended them. They were <u>in me</u>, and my thought encompassed them like a veil. It was the one moment of exaltation in my life. I was so powerful, so omniscient, that I felt 'If there were a God, He would feel like this.' And on the heels of that came a consciousness, 'I am as much God as anyone. For this moment, I am God. Because my thought includes infinity and eternity.' "

One day Marjorie baited Ida, saying she'd considered suicide, and instead of registering shock or offering reassurance, Ida called her ungrateful. "I owe you nothing," Marjorie replied, citing the selfishness driving her mother's attention. "You fuss at me to write, to write. Then when I do, you criticize it if it isn't sweet and pretty. You're wrapped up in what people think, and I despise it." Later, she regretted the outburst. Yet she would foil Ida's ideal of late-twenties, post-fame marriage. Marjorie described the start of it: "In the early spring of 1918, the senior year, the catastrophe occurred. Out of the safe void, appeared a young man on crutches, to whom the girl addressed herself with the matter-of-fact tone she used around the house. None of the sprightliness, the gay affections, the coyness, of her past relations with her beaus. . . . The girl spoke to the young man with the broken leg as though she had known him all her life. As Ida soon understood, there was indeed the fatal recognition."

How did Marjorie meet Charles "Chuck" Rawlings? He wasn't a member of her class and rarely appears in *The Badger*. But in her senior

year, Marjorie had one course with Chuck each semester: The Romantic
Movement in the fall, Advanced Composition in the spring. Chuck was
a member of the student theater community, including the Haresfoot
Club, an all-male dramatic society that toured light productions around
the state. In the spring of 1918, he contributed to *WLM*, where Marjorie enjoyed a prominent position. In their last semester, both appeared
in *WLM*'s pages several times. Bee Humiston McNeil said Charles had
wanted to meet Marjorie after reading a draft of her senior thesis—she
had given a copy to someone in his fraternity house. "He was adorable,"
she recalled. "The girls would fall all over him to impress him. I remember not being able to take my eyes off of him in the library. He was apple-
cheeked and kind of blonde." Both were attractive, high-spirited, and
ambitious for their writing. It seemed only a matter of time before their
paths would cross.

WITH CHUCK, an aspiring writer and the dapper son of a Rochester,
New York, shoe company foreman, Marjorie had dropped her preten-
sions. "He summed up for her all she asked of life," Bee related. "He was
the core of her puzzle, and the other jagged pieces would just have to fit
around him." The couple announced their engagement at his fraternity
house without telling her mother. Ida was furious, and insisted on a private meeting with Chuck, laying out her plans for Marjorie. Instead of
being helpful, Ida believed, he would be a hindrance. Chuck accused
Ida of spoiling Marjorie. "You've got her wanting the things you want.
Money and clothes and society columns. . . . You've tried to tell me how
high a valuation you put on your daughter. And I tell you, you hold her
cheap. You'd sell her to the first dog with a million dollars."

At Marjorie's graduation, Chuck and Ida sat together in a temporary
truce. When Marjorie recited the class poem, Ida urged Chuck to admit
that her daughter was talented—that the poem was beautiful. But, Marjorie remembered, he refused. "Terrible rot," he sneered. "Sentimental
and cheap. She tossed it off yesterday afternoon."

IF THE SECRET TO marriage is to want the same thing in life, Chuck and
Marjorie had it. They wanted to be writers. It didn't matter whether he
took her to the prom at the new state capitol and twirled her beneath the

golden rotunda on marble floors. It didn't matter if he had given her his fraternity pin, and it certainly didn't matter if either of them had any money. They had bigger plans.

Chuck did not finish a B.A. in 1918, as Marjorie did, and given his uneven high school and college careers, he might not have expected to. Born in Rochester in 1894, two years before Marjorie, he was the eldest of Anne Tarrant Rawlings and Charles A. Rawlings's three sons. Of his early life, little is known, except that he was interested in boating and that his family spent summers in "White City," a seasonal community outside Rochester overlooking Lake Ontario. Here, more than a hundred families pitched white canvas tents on wooden frames and fished, swam, played tennis and baseball, and held special events, including the annual torching of the outhouses. Fathers rode the trolley to and from their day jobs in the city. Young boys ran wild.

Whether or not Chuck's freewheeling summers held him back, his education was somehow delayed. He entered Rochester's West High School in September 1910, at age sixteen, and completed his coursework five years later, passing a delinquent exam in Modern European History shortly before his twenty-first birthday, cementing a solid C average. Urged by a friend who had left Rochester for the University of Wisconsin, he applied as an "adult special student." Special students could choose only from freshman courses; for advanced studies, they had to demonstrate "special preparation or special necessity."

Chuck arrived in Madison for the fall 1915 semester, and by February 1916 he had been advised to withdraw, mainly because of his poor performance in Spanish, or to continue on probation if he could pull up his grade. A year later, he was still on probation over the Spanish problem, and in the fall of 1917 he was allowed a reduced course load of five hours, to accommodate a broken leg from an accident in a friend's Ford Runabout. When he finally met Marjorie at a school dance, he was limping around on crutches. She asked to write on his cast, and he refused: "As famous a writer as you are, no." He wanted to keep the cast clean. He liked her immediately: "I should have been in awe of her," he recalled much later. "Her brilliance, scholastically and dramatically. She was a damn fine actress and captivated the campus. I remember her conversation. Her conversation was music to my ears." By then, he had pledged

Chi Psi fraternity; had been tapped, inexplicably, for Skull and Crescent, a Greek men's leadership honorary; and was loading up on English courses.

AT MARJORIE'S GRADUATION, the couple's plans were set. She would move to New York to start a writing career, and Chuck would, like many American college men at the time, enlist in the army. The First World War had begun the summer before Marjorie entered Wisconsin and was, in the great historian Paul Fussell's words, "perhaps the last [war] to be conceived as taking place within a seamless, purposeful 'history' involving a coherent stream of time running from past to present to future. . . . Compared with ours, [it was] a static world, where the values appeared stable and where the meanings of abstractions seemed permanent and reliable." Though the United States didn't enter the war until April 1917, when massive casualties in Europe were all over the news, enthusiastic, patriotic American men stepped up to serve with what Fussell describes as "the universal commitment to the sporting spirit," referring to the male madness for physical fitness (leading, among other things, to the growth of college athletics) and its upright twin, character building—both expressions of perpetual rebirth, so dear to American Protestantism. These passions, a late nineteenth-century reaction to industrial and commercial life, but long bred in the culture, morphed easily into militarism. Historian Jackson Lears put it this way: "For those eager to harmonize manliness and morality, there was no melody so pleasing as the threnody of military heroism."

Proof of that tune may be found in Marjorie's last *Badger* yearbook, featuring photographs of UW men in uniform, the captions celebrating feats and heroic survival, not service or gravity. For example: "Lieutenant E. L. Hahn, '18, is seen with his airplane just before he undertook a cross-country flight from Kelly Field, San Antonio, which nearly cost him his life. A thirty-five mile gale dashed his machine to earth, and as a result of his injuries he was confined to the hospital for two months." In the January 1918 issue of *Kappa Alpha Theta Magazine*, Marjorie, sentimental, callow, reported on male alums seen at the previous fall's homecoming: "Hundreds of 'dear departeds' walked once more around the campus; many of them in uniform, very self-conscious in their new role, and very stern under the weight of great determination. Have you noticed how they have aged—these youngsters? The boys we have played with have become men over night, and although it hurts to see it, there is consolation in the fact that they seem infinitely finer and deeper than before. And it does seem so much harder, doesn't it, to stay home and just think! Handling a machine gun must be such a satisfactory way of expressing oneself."

Chapter Four

New York

1918-19

"*OVERTURE. LIGHTS!*" That is what Marjorie titled the post-Wisconsin chapter of *Blood of My Blood*—the pages chronicling her move to New York City, her mother's involvement, the weeks spent seeking work, the start of her marriage to Chuck. "This then was the beginning of life," she wrote. "Here was the audience. The programs were rustling. The curtain quivered on stage. There was a flutter in the proscenium. The orchestra struck up the overture. Lights!"

Marjorie continued: "It was the fall of 1918, and the overgrown village was vital with the thrill of war. The girl was tip-toe with ecstasy. She longed to try her strength against those massive doors, to carve her initials on the substantiality of their insolent oak. Ida trailed her like a moth, trembling before the careless young flame of her."

Ida stayed in New York long enough to help her daughter find temporary lodgings. Marjorie had saved enough literary prize money—as always, matched by her mother—to get by while she looked for employment. The war had removed many young men from the workforce, and opportunities for women, who anticipated the right to vote, were rising. Professor Dodge had given her letters of introduction for Philip Littell, a founding editor of the budding progressive publication the *New Repub-*

lic, and Honoré Willsie, a novelist, a University of Wisconsin graduate, and an editor at the *Delineator*, a popular women's magazine touting fashion and homemaking, yet retaining a progressive tone from Theodore Dreiser's editorship (1907–10). Willsie, a tall woman born Nora Bryant McCue, was, like Professor Leonard, something of an iconoclast. She had drawn attention on the UW campus by striding about with Cedric, her Great Dane, and had abandoned "Nora" for her pen name. She would divorce her first husband in 1922 and marry William Morrow, who would establish the publishing house of that name.

In a letter to her mother, Marjorie reported Willsie's advice. "She said, 'Well, you've got the gift of gab all right. Only God Almighty can tell you whether you'll do anything with it. I suppose you are too young to know that you have to have something to say. You have to have some private gospel that you want terribly to preach. I don't mean moralizing. I mean that there has to be something close to your heart that you want to talk about." Willsie advised Marjorie to "get any kind of job in the world except a literary job. 'Go ahead and live and work, and if you've got the spark in you, it'll burn you up until you let it out. You'll be wild to get at your writing. You'll sit up nights to do it. If you do hack stuff in a magazine office, you'll go stale.'"

Ida deemed it poor advice. Connections were everything, she insisted, singing her same old song. "They tell me contact is most important in selling stories," she wrote, enlisting, not for the first time, the mysterious "they." Ida's anxiety and implied disappointment in Marjorie's father surfaced in other remarks, such as "Do you know, my dear, that it takes *conceit*, lots of it, gall, nerve, self-esteem, self-satisfaction, aggressiveness, optimism, with a *little* ability, to get through the world?" Honoré Willsie did offer Marjorie a job, but she turned it down, unhappy with the woman (a Miss Blaine) she would be working under.

Marjorie next checked in with Philip Littell, who referred her to another of the *New Republic*'s co-founders, Irish author and critic Francis Hackett and his wife, Danish writer Signe Toksvig, who also worked at the magazine. "They have just been married but she is going right on with her work," Marjorie observed. Littell and Toksvig passed Marjorie on to James Oppenheim, who had founded the short-lived literary magazine the *Seven Arts*, publishing the likes of Dreiser, Frost, D. H. Lawrence, Amy Lowell, and Kahlil Gibran. Oppenheim was a lay analyst and early follower of Carl Jung, whose *Psychology of the Unconscious*, published just a few years before (1912), had caused his break with Freud. Marjorie reported, "He said, 'You have the writer's gift. I can't tell you any more than that.' He advised me to go in for psycho-analysis. Said it was the greatest thing in the world for a writer, to help him probe into human motives and emotions." In fact, psychoanalysis was in its infancy—Freud's initial opus, *Studies on Hysteria*, was not twenty-five years old—and Marjorie might have gained as much from tarot cards.

She kept pounding the pavement. Someone sent her to Eugene Saxton, who was associated with the *Bookman*, a staid journal offering book reviews and publishing industry news. It also published short fiction. Apparently, the *Bookman* planned to give her an editing test, as she wrote desperately to Chuck, asking for "everything about proofreading signs." Her fiancé, who had enlisted in the army at Fort Slocum, a large recruiting facility at New Rochelle, was now stationed at Camp Upton, Long Island. He hoped to go into aeronautics. Chuck responded by return mail with detailed drawings and instructions—an editing handbook. It must have arrived too late. Marjorie wasn't hired.

Later, while trying on a "darling" hat she'd admired in a shop window, she discovered that her purse had been snatched, trooped down to the *New Republic*, and confessed her bad luck to Signe Toksvig, who gave her ten dollars and told her to, in effect, pay it forward. When Chuck heard about it, he wired Marjorie his two months' salary—another confirmation of their bond. He would continue all fall to supplement her income when she ran short, scolding her when she sent him an accounting of what she owed him. It gave him pleasure, he wrote, to "go around broke, knowing it was because you had what you needed and I could help you." Ida, still in town, was furious—why hadn't her daughter asked *her* for money?

Neither was Ida happy that, after a chance meeting on Fifth Avenue—near the imposing Charles Scribner's Sons Building, where a young editor named Maxwell Perkins was cultivating his first discovery, an army officer named F. Scott Fitzgerald—Marjorie ran into one of her sorority sisters. That young woman, having arrived in New York earlier, was able to get Marjorie a publicity job on the YWCA's War Work Council. Marjorie wrote to Chuck, "They give you the material, letters, and facts from overseas and we write them up and sneak in a mention of the Y.W.

as often but as quietly as we can, and the publicity director places them with all the magazines. It's a cinch."

None of Marjorie's literary connections or Ida's "they" had mattered a whit, and though the aspiring writer was cranking out formula, she could now pay her own way. Refusing to live downtown, "near things," with two friends who were "bad managers, and unambitious," she rented a room from a Miss Matthews, who sublet space in her Carolyn Court apartment on West 121st Street, half a block from Morningside Park. "I'd rather take a little longer to get to and from work, and have a better, healthier, quieter residence district to go home to," Marjorie wrote to Chuck. "Mother asked where the girls received men callers, and she [Miss Matthews] said, 'Oh, right in their rooms. It's considered perfectly proper. All of us are going back and forth along the hall constantly, and if anything seems wrong I would know about it. . . . The girls usually leave their doors part-way open when they have callers, though not necessarily. And of course, 'tho I try to look out for my girls, I expect them to take care of themselves.' "

Ida appeared to be satisfied with the situation—but, still, not with Chuck. In another letter to her beau, Marjorie wrote, "Chuck sweetheart—you've got to make most whopping good, if only to give me a little peace and comfort, from her. She acts worse every day. She makes some horrid comments now, *every time* I mention your name. . . . She said tonight, 'If you could explain to me just what you love about him, perhaps I could understand the situation a little better.' . . . She keeps me sick at heart all the time, although she worships me—or rather the part of me that does *creditable* things."

At this point, Marjorie had met and charmed her future in-laws in Rochester, gaining a sympathetic set of parents. Both wrote her encouraging letters. "Daddy" Rawlings provided a publication contact. Chuck and Marjorie wrote back and forth several times a week, sharing their experiences, pining for each other, imagining their future together, wisecracking. When Marjorie landed the YWCA job, Chuck wrote gleefully: "My sweet Christian cherub: Oh! I knew that someday you would see the true light. You little sacrilegious crook, you! Oh, this is almost too good. . . . You! You of the Indie posterity cynicisms; you of the scorn of the true light—Oh ye! ye!, hypocrites and Pharisees. You're going to hell when you die sure as God made little green apples. We'll go together, tho'. I absolutely refuse to have you walking off to hell alone. I'll have to do something; break up some happy home or steal money out of milk bottles to catch up."

When the Y hired her, Marjorie was asked for proof of church affiliation, and she didn't have any. The minister of the Congregational church in Madison, where she "did my praying," had died, and she didn't expect Brookland Baptist to have records past the cradle roll. If she couldn't dig up evidence, she would have to undergo a baptism. "I don't see any way out of it," she wrote Chuck, "except to have the holy water sprinkled inside my shirt. No Baptist trip to God for me! The River Jordan is all right—good river—but the immersion idea in November is all wrong!"

Somewhere along the line, Marjorie was referred (probably by Oppenheim) to Beatrice Hinkle, a psychoanalyst in Gramercy Park who had studied with Freud in Vienna, rejected his notion of the female psyche, and aligned herself with Jung's theories. Hinkle, an avowed feminist, had recently translated Jung's 1912 *Psychology of the Unconscious* and needed a literary secretary to answer mail and help her write her own book, no doubt *The Re-creating of the Individual: A Study of Psychological Types and Their Relation to Psychoanalysis* (1923). At first Marjorie thought it a good opportunity, but then she noticed that the therapist's nails "were bitten to the quick, and her hands trembled, and she pointed to her cabinets and whispered, 'If you work for me you've got to know AWFUL things about people,' and it gave me the creeps." Marjorie turned down the position, though the prospect confused her mightily. She wrote, in part, to Chuck: "I'm unconsciously mixed-up tonight. In fact, dear, I feel so confused I don't believe I can write much. I don't believe I could follow out a logical sequence of thought. . . . I'm at such an obvious crossroads . . . and the fog on either side is so thick. . . . I think I'm tangled up in that Hinkle woman's psychic radiations or something. I felt her concentrating on me last night about 11 o'clock."

Apparently, Marjorie consulted a Miss Avery, who probably had experience with psychoanalysis, about taking the job. Marjorie described the phone call to Chuck:

> She felt as I do, that it might be the making of me as a writer—I
> feel that I might do something really big as a result of it, Chuck, if
> I took it—but she put into words my secret fear that it might spoil

my happiness as a wholesome, normal human being. She said that since I was really so young, after all, it might have a morbid effect on me to get into that line of thought and know the most intimate cores of people's lives and thoughts—things they couldn't even tell to themselves, except under this sort of hypnotic psycho-analysis— under it they deliver up their very souls. It involves sex a great deal, you know—it might be fearfully unhealthy. Meanwhile, I go ahead taking Y.W. notes from the religious weeklies. Religion is an awfully morbid thing, isn't it? . . . Much more unnatural than sex problems!

She closed the letter with misgivings about their future together—a theme that ran operatically on both sides during their separation. Here, she wanted him to answer big questions, guide her, be her superior: "Can I go ahead with that psycho-analysis job, get my big material out of it, and keep rational and normal and happy? Can I be a bigger writer than I ever before thought I had a chance of being, and yet make the right go of our two lives together? Can you gather all of me, my work, my thoughts, my queer female inconsistencies—into one coordinated whole under your guidance? Do you have the big, quiet strength to do it? Can I be as big as I want to be and yet know you're bigger?"

Chuck replied, thoughtfully reiterating the position's pros and cons, and encouraging her to take the job if she wanted it. But he wouldn't tell her what to do. "Remember, inspiration or materials be hanged, you stay Marge Kinnan. . . . You will have to decide it yourself. It's your life— becoming more so every day, just the way I can feel my life becoming my own little fight! We've started off apart, damn it, and I guess we will have to solve it that way and then write our answers. It's your life, Skinny. All I can do is love you from the sidelines."

Chuck had his own concerns. Several times, he confessed to Marjorie that he felt inferior or inadequate. He would never be, he told her, as "big as you are." He sensed that he had not grown up, though Camp Upton helped. "How damnably weak I used to be; almost effeminate in some things," he wrote. "How you ever did it I will never be able to under- stand." In one letter, he explained that his "will and control and half my confidence" had not been in him but had been ceded to Marjorie. "You were the stronger of the two and I was leaning on you," he wrote. "And

I have been getting them back, little by little. . . . I've got to be strong all the time. . . . I am the <u>man</u> and things <u>have</u> to be that way to be right."

As well, he yearned for a chance to write, and he described some characters and situations that excited him, closing: "I can write; I have always <u>felt</u> it, even when I should have proved to myself by my efforts that I couldn't, and I've got to get all I can out of this game to help me when I get out. I am seriously . . . going to write. I presume the notion makes you smile, but maybe I'll show you."

Meanwhile, Marjorie was growing fond of city life, and in breezier letters, she described some of her outings. One night, she and her friend Imogene went to a YWCA event in Brooklyn, via "miles and miles of subways and surface cars full of Jew shop-girls who jostled us furiously when they saw the Y.W. insignia." When they arrived at the appointed address, "a huge Jewish men's club," they discovered they'd come on the wrong night. So they took themselves out to dinner, starting with Clover Club cocktails. "There was slick music," she wrote, "and an interesting crowd—and you can't imagine how wonderful New York looks at night from the Brooklyn Bridge—the tall buildings are nothing but high piles of tiny gold squares of light, from the windows—they surely do work late, down in the Wall St. district. We only hope the Y.W. doesn't ask us to itemize our expense account for the trip, as the Clover Clubs were charged to 'Bar'!!! Oh, we felt so deliciously wicked—but <u>safely</u> so, since we were with each other. I wouldn't take a cocktail of any sort with a man, except you."

Marjorie did, however, blithely accept dates with other men, to enjoy nights on the town she needed an escort for or couldn't afford. In September, for example, an unnamed fellow took her to *Daddies*, John Hobble's new comedy at the Belasco Theatre, and supper. "Don't worry," she wrote Chuck beforehand, "I hate the poor devil, but I figure his money is as good, or better, than mine, for seeing a good show." Afterward, she reported, conspiratorially, possibly overdoing displeasure to assuage Chuck's jealousy: "Wonderful chicken salad at Murray's! But ye Gods, who can enjoy food opposite a runt? Then he insisted on dancing and he climbed all over my ankles. I could have killed him with good grace. I pray to God he sails soon."

The couple's letters were equally full of affection, longing, and dreaming. They waxed poetically, as young lovers do, imagining by turns exotic travels all over the world and a cozy country bungalow with a warm fireplace, where they would nestle side by side, forever and ever. One note from Chuck mirrors similar sentiments from Marjorie: "There's a little place, like a shrine, in the very core of me, that is lit perpetually with candles and filled with incense; and it is you and yours. It's the center of all things. It was <u>always</u> you. I realize now, that the thrill that comes over me before anything beautiful, that the pain of twilight and of sunset, are <u>you</u>, and the longing for you."

The two occasionally touched on ideas. In one letter, Marjorie referred to a past conversation and the contents of her "cosmic" college essay: "You know, I'm coming around to your belief of the outside consciousness. . . . Bought an interesting little book today—'Twenty Minutes of Reality'—somebody else had that same experience I had—experiencing—oh, eternity—whatever you want to call it. It will interest you, I know." (*Twenty Minutes of Reality: An Experience, with Some Illuminating Letters Concerning It*, by Margaret Prescott Montague, originated in the *Atlantic Monthly* as column material about enlightenment.) Following a long thread, Chuck responded: "To me we are like a cup holding the 'soul' (cussed word) and, our brain, the 'ultimate cause' (jolly old chap, old 'ulti;' he's helped me over some tough ones) is the force that makes it possible for us, the cup, to hold and pour thoughts and dreams greater than our dirty, hairy body can ever be, for the glory. Something must come from outside, and that something—is my God. I don't like it because I can't see him. I hate to strain in the dark, but he's there."

Marjorie was giddy with delight. "We, old moody-and-depressed-and-cynical us, we can have such a gloriously jolly existence that nothing can phase [*sic*] us!" She added, "My silly nerves and tendency to cry are gone. I have a hunch that the two operations I had this summer were just what I needed. And I haven't been having a tiny bit of trouble with that abdominal difficulty I spoke of to you. My regular life is good for me." Marjorie was probably referring to her tonsillectomy in Madison and, possibly, a mastoid operation. Chuck had noticed the scar behind her ear. Mastoiditis is commonly caused by a middle-ear infection; its symptoms include irritability and pain, and if not treated soon enough, it can affect the brain. Surgery to remove infected bone must have been the best treatment, as antibiotics were years away. Marjorie's abdominal problems, though, were just beginning.

Marjorie offered news of freelance work outside her day job at the Y, like the $15 fee from *Young's Magazine* for "a trashy story I dashed off one night here in N.Y. It's so punk I almost used a nom-de-plume. . . . It was Littell himself, on *The New Republic*, who said, "Sell anything you aren't actually ashamed to sign your name to." She reported on former suitors who tracked her down. It's easy to imagine that Ida offered them her new address. Dick Knott, for instance, sent a long, slightly mournful letter, conveying his confidence in her selection of Chuck. Knott made it clear she'd had plenty of choices at Wisconsin. "If he felt badly," she wrote to Chuck, "it certainly never showed. . . . I know he's perfectly sincere in his good wishes. He's a real friend, and I can guarantee that you'll like him." She ended her letter with a description of a fancy restaurant luncheon she'd attended: "We had chicken patties (the patties were very thin, sweet, crispy ones) with huge chunks of the white meat and fat oysters, etc. . . . And heart-melting ice cream in fancy shapes, —and fancy cakes—and coffee and hot chocolate with thick whipped cream." She couldn't wait for the two of them to be together and cook all the dishes they loved.

Chuck addressed the God question again, suggesting a continued struggle with being equal to, and man enough, for Marjorie: "Sweetheart. There is a God. I'm not weak there. There is no stage in my development that has to overcome that fact. I've got the one thing I need now to be sure I'm bigger than you. I won't say anything else about it, but I'm glad, glad, glad it's just the way it is. Watch how it plays out."

Two days later, Marjorie stayed home from work to write Chuck a nine-page letter. She was glad he felt "bigger" but was enraged over his decision to wait two weeks for a visit, even though a quarantine—likely related to the 1918 flu pandemic—had been lifted and he was free to travel. What was he waiting for, she demanded to know. If it was money for a more luxurious hotel room and fine food, she could return some of what he'd sent her; plus, he knew she was about to be paid again. ("Do you mean it, that you're happier broke—away from me?") If his delay meant he was asserting his new "strength," she considered it a weakness, cynical. "The process going on in you has gotten past my comprehension. If getting 'straight' is going to make a typical, selfish, self-sufficient man out of you—I'll wish you weak again. I don't want you so self-sufficient, God knows, that you don't need me at all. . . . Maybe all this damnable mess is just a phase of your finding yourself." The letter concluded warmly, but nine more pages, written that evening, alluded to a new letter that had just arrived. "I could kill you for that letter waiting for me when I got home tonight. I could kill you for it." She had also received a nasty letter from Ida, complaining of Chuck's unfitness for Marjorie. "She said I reminded her of a fond mother, 'rushing to the defense of your baby, as it were.' She disparaged completely my telling of your making good at camp, and being put in Development work. Called it 'more dignified than peeling potatoes.' She said that whenever 'the name of your little God is involved, at once, biff, bang, you seem to be bereft of the power to reason or be fair.' I have to swallow that."

Marjorie added, "I fight back the tears—and turn to your letter, saying to myself, 'Bless his heart, what a contrast this will be. How he'll prove to me how fine he is.' And what do I get? A flippant request to keep the home fires from smoking and think of things to eat."

The emotional pages continued. Marjorie blamed Chuck for caving in to friends advising him to string her along. "Sometimes I think you're <u>very</u> susceptible to other people's opinions," she wrote. "Don't you have any philosophy of your own?" Just because she loved him didn't mean she'd come crawling back to him. She might have given him "what I could never give any other man," she explained, but "[I] could love you desperately and still tell you to go to the devil."

Two days later, the pair made up in letters that probably crossed in the mail. By November, their letters were equally weighted with romantic love offerings, light confidences, and talk of practical matters like jobs and money. He reminded her that neither of them was "regular army." "You are a wonderful example of a shell game with your soul as the pea," he wrote. "God knows which walnut shell you will find it under next. If anyone asks you what you are, tell them that." Marjorie responded with a line she might have emblazoned on her forehead for all who would know her: "You musn't interpret a mood as a permanent state of mind." She was, and always would be, susceptible to swift, deep changes in temperament.

On November 11, 1918, Germany and the Allies signed an armistice and the Great War ended. Marjorie and Chuck turned only slightly toward the near future, as he still had work to do at Camp Upton and wouldn't be able to visit her at Thanksgiving. She was being considered for a promotion at the Y, a possible assignment in Russia. She had run into other Wisconsin friends, including a very happy married couple, and had heard of a former professor and his wife who had gone to Italy with the Red Cross. Maybe, she suggested, she and Chuck could be sent overseas—Russia or France or Italy—and get "a couple of books and lots of articles" out of it, and when they returned, the papers and magazines would "gobble us up." "And think of how fond of each other we'd be among foreigners," she added. "We'd never fuss at all." On she wrote, imagining drinking goat's milk, riding in oxcarts, and wearing fur coats in Russia. They ought to do it now, she said, because if Chuck went into the newspaper business, they certainly wouldn't be able to afford it later. Let's put off the bungalow and newspapers and magazines and babies and comfort and quiet, she pleaded, her fantasy marked with underscores and exclamation points.

In his next letter, Charles eliminated one of her nicknames. She responded, "Why is it 'getting wrong' to call me 'dear old chap?' I love to be called that. Don't you think I'm a good scout any more, or a good pal,—or what? I like to think I can be anything to you, according to your needs—chum—lover—mother—baby—Harlequin—" Aside from that, she was feeling upbeat, and having some luck with her poetry. "The Monastery," which had appeared the previous spring in the *Wisconsin Literary Magazine*, was chosen for Henry T. Schnittkind's annual college anthology, *The Poets of the Future*, for 1918.

By now, Chuck's parents had made it clear that they wanted the couple to settle in Rochester. In a long letter to Charles on December 15, Marjorie issued one of her many manifestos. Going to Rochester ran contrary to them, individually and as a couple. "We're so intensely individualistic, both of us—it just happens that our individualities cuddle down in the same box together, like the two halves of a pecan (*very* good simile, don't you think?); and we can't stand it to be unduly interfered with. What's right for us is perfectly wild to the average, normal human being. . . . We've got to be out, where things are moving, and we can catch some of the enchantment and swing of life—and feel free to tear off and do perfectly absurd, glorious, romantic things." In Rochester, they'd be Mr. and Mrs. C. A. Rawlings Jr., not Marjorie Kinnan and

Chuck Rawlings. "And what would I do there? However good the opportunities for you, there certainly wouldn't be as good ones for me." She urged Chuck to explain that he needed to make good in New York first, then return to his hometown, a big success.

In February 1919 Chuck left the army and took a job in New York with the Federal Export Company for $25 a week, matching Marjorie's salary. They rented an apartment at 42 East Seventy-Eighth Street. Cohabitating without the benefit of marriage was unusual for the times. In April, Marjorie wrote to Ida, announcing a May wedding in New York. In Marjorie's theatrical re-creation of her mother's reply, Ida responded as if from a fainting couch: "Oh my daughter— If you do this thing, this mad thing, this wasting of yourself on the sullen stripling, never reproach me with not having warned you of the consequences. If you do it, you are doomed." She went on:

> I awoke last night in a cold sweat. I had dreamt that I saw you falling down a steep flight of stairs, down and down. I could not stop you, I could not save you. I could only watch that fatal plunge. When I reached you at the foot you were white and limp—I can see it now— with your slim neck broken. This morning—your letter. I am not a superstitious woman, but surely the omen must frighten you, as it does me.

According to Marjorie, she and Chuck laughed themselves silly over "the flight of stairs and the slim broken neck."

The wedding was on.

Chuck wrote to Ida, apologizing for his inability to visit her in Madison and stating his intention to marry Marjorie the first week in May. "You were quite right," he acknowledged, "last spring; there was a pretty much no-account chap sitting on your front divan most of the time. And now you see difficulty. I am no longer sitting on your front divan and I am no longer worthless. Right at present, I am assistant to the over-seas advertising manager of perhaps the best futured export house in New York." His success depended only on "the degree to which American export trade flourishes"—an outcome that seemed unquestioned. He added, "Marjorie insists upon hanging on to this Y.W.C.A. outfit. I don't know whether it is the thing she should do or not. It is her own work and her own life. I have no desire or right to put anything—an Englishman's pride least of all—in its way. All I know is that she can stop and depend upon me if she so desires and any insistence either way would be unjust—and fatal, as you know Marjorie."

He assured Ida about Marjorie's affections: "She loves you very deeply—more deeply than I think either of you realize or you would not hurt each other so.—I adore her and she loves you and you are her mother; therefore because you are her mother, something she loves, I must, too. I am not going to break your heart!"

No reply from Ida exists, but she traveled to New York for the wedding. The night before the ceremony, Ida brought up the subject of birth control, and Marjorie snapped, slapping her. As the curtain came down on New York, Marjorie imagined Ida's reaction: "This strange female creature was blood of her blood, bone of her bone, flesh of her flesh, but the spirit around which blood, bone, and flesh were built, was a fragment broken off from the cosmic consciousness and was not hers at all."

Chapter Five

Louisville

1919-22

CHUCK AND MARJORIE weren't in New York long. The postwar economy was unstable. A recession was brewing. Chuck's company went out of business, and Marjorie's job at the YWCA ended, presumably without a church baptism. Marjorie kept trying, and failing, to sell poems. A typical rejection note, from Hazel Deyo Batchelor, fiction editor of the *Pictorial Review* read: "My dear Miss Kinnan: This little poem is very sweet but just at present we are so well supplied with verse that we are not buying anything new." Mrs. Batchelor, still in her twenties, was an aspiring poet herself and a popular author of serials about love and marriage, with titles like "And So They Were Married" and "The Testing of Julia Grant." The following year, the *Pictorial Review* serialized Edith Wharton's *The Age of Innocence* prior to its hardcover publication and subsequent Pulitzer Prize—the first awarded to a woman.

Marjorie succeeded in selling a coquettish tale, "His Little Cabbage Head," to *Young's Magazine*, a publication touting "realistic stories" (not to be confused with realism). Other titles in the issue—"Blush Pink and Silver," "The Engaged Mr. Lamb," "The Wine of Life"—indicate the level of affectation. Marjorie was clearly conforming to the market, setting aside William Ellery Leonard's warning against overwriting. (In a wince-inducing moment, one of Marjorie's characters says café au lait is "to the tongue as Italian silk underwear is to the body.") Most of her paid work during the spring of 1919 was freelance nonfiction for magazines and publicity copy for the George H. Doran Publishing Company, where Sinclair Lewis had worked briefly five years before. She was savvy enough to build on her assignments for the Y, placing articles on women's contributions to the war effort, although some of these pieces might have been written before she left her job, a component of her staff work. In "The Blue Triangle Follows the Switchboard," which appeared in *Telephone Topics*, an employee periodical for New England Telephone, Marjorie celebrated "the first time in history a great war has been carried to a successful conclusion with women recognized officially as part of the army." These women, telephone operators of the Signal Corps, were often stationed just a few miles behind the firing lines, and after the Armistice, they joined the army of occupation in Germany. Their housing, before and after the war, was procured by the YWCA, described in the sort of detail only a Y staffer would have had at her fingertips.

A longer piece, "Women as Constructionists," published in the *New France*, acknowledged the impact of the war on women, as well as that of women on the war and on the immediate future. "An enforced independence has awakened their sense of responsibility as citizens, as constructionists," Marjorie wrote. "They can never go back to unadulterated domesticity." The YWCA's Foyers des Alliées, hostels for the battle-weary in France, had proved the value of teamwork, cooperation, and a welcoming atmosphere created by women. "All women," Marjorie wrote, "whatever their race or creed, are sisters—daughters of the modern order—servers of humanity."

Marjorie also placed more domestic articles, such as a compendium of YWCA church supper recipes and an upbeat guide to planning a girls' club modeled on the Girl Scouts, founded seven years before. Overall, her job at the Y, at that particular point in history, had positioned her to continue writing about women's accomplishments. Their skills and patriotism had been essential to the war effort, and suffrage naysayers were forced to change their minds. In June 1919, the struggle for women's voting rights ended when the Senate approved the Nineteenth Amendment. The required thirty-six states ratified it the following year.

Now women were increasingly in the news, not always as social append-ages to men but as citizens willing and able to take significant roles in public life.

THAT MARJORIE LATCHED ONTO Chuck at exactly this point might help explain both her attraction to him and some of the forces that eventually ended their marriage. When he had written to her, "You are a wonder-ful example of a shell game," he might have been referring to Marjorie's moodiness or, just as easily, projecting his own ambivalence. Chuck also might have seen tripartite conflict in his future wife: a necessity to extri-cate herself from Ida's complicated influence; a fundamental need, apart from Ida's projections, to develop and flourish as a writer; and a desire for loving companionship. That these three concerns were spectacu-larly alight within a lively, intelligent, ambitious, and physically delicate twenty-two-year-old during a year containing college graduation, a solo move to New York City, the end of World War I, and a key moment in the women's rights movement, lays to rest any notion that Marjorie was, at the root, inconsistent. She had identified an artistic life she wished to live, but her outward and inward situations, both now and in the years to come, were often opposed.

ONCE, EARLY IN HER MARRIAGE, Marjorie visited her mother in Madi-son, where, again, Ida made it clear that she disapproved of her daughter's husband and the footloose life they led. Not for the first time, Marjorie accused her mother of trying to live her dreams through her daughter. In a composed scene, she explained to Ida that she was not a prodigy. Her creative work would take time. "I only mean that there is something vital in me that must find ultimate expression," she told Ida. "I'm not ready to write. I'm full of theories about people that I've got to prove or disprove by living and studying a little longer. I want to write books about things I don't know enough about yet."

During that visit, Marjorie called on Professor Dodge. "I've stopped being in such an awful hurry to write and get 'on the market,'" she remem-bered telling him. "There isn't the rush I thought there was. You know, I think a great deal of the present successful writing by young authors is only the exuberance of youth. They simply bubble over into print."

To this he answered, "Of course in such cases, their writing wouldn't be what we call 'the real thing.' It wouldn't last."

Exactly how or when Marjorie came to this realization isn't clear. Her slick remark about "the exuberance of youth" sounds imitative or even, because the scene was written several years later, self-serving. But her leap from shallow to deep water was likely the result of trying to write and sell facile work that paid little, bored her, or both, in contrast to her literary education and the voracious reading habit fueling her aim to make art, not magazine copy. Spending nearly a year in New York had offered necessary perspective—a crash course on the wider literary world. And she did have something to say, a "private gospel" she wanted to preach, as Honoré Willsie, the editor at the *Delineator*, had insisted she should. "There has to be something close to your heart that you want to talk about," Willsie had told her. For Marjorie, that something was coalescing around the idea of cosmic connection.

MARJORIE AND CHUCK REMAINED in New York through the summer of 1919. In July, Marjorie's brother, Arthur, or "Artie," a tall, handsome young man still in Wisconsin under his mother's wing, wrote a long, anguished letter to his sister (addressed to "Peaches") lamenting his college experience and wishing she had given him more advice. "I have often wondered why you never told me some of the things that are of common occurrence in the university that were very uncommon to me while in high school. . . . All my ideals have flown," he confided, "and it certainly is hard for me to find—without success—new ideals. In the first place, I learned what a booze-fighting lot the students are." He no longer respected his Chi Psi fraternity brothers, who were as bad as the rest. "I have gotten of late so that I don't give a damn what happens," he said. "Mother has been very worried about me for fear I'll start drinking— God no, after seeing those bums rock around like animals." Many of the girls he met were "nothing but a bunch of insincere skirts trying to be the whole damn show on a barrel of hot air." He admitted that his grades were uneven and blamed himself for allowing the spring weather, good-looking girls, and fraternity sports to distract him. He was desperate for guidance, "especially without a kind, great-hearted father, like the one I lost." He wanted to know about his sister's married life, as well as her ideals and thoughts about the future, and he begged for a "real honest-to-goodness letter—one that comes from the heart. . . . I want to know everything from you and not indirect from mother, for you know how she is, poor woman."

In early August, writing from a summer job in Ashland, Wisconsin, Arthur wished Marjorie a happy birthday and apologized for failing to send a gift. He was "very low" on funds. "I'm so low that I owe quite a few dollars at present," he confessed.

WHEN THEIR MONEY RAN OUT at the end of the summer, Marjorie and Chuck gave up their New York apartment and briefly decamped to Rochester, which pleased his parents. The young couple considered spending the winter in the North Carolina mountains and "writing hard," but they chose the commercial route again when Chuck took a job as advertising manager for Stewart's Dry Goods, a grand, seven-floor department store in Louisville, Kentucky. Marjorie found work as publicity secretary for the Louisville YWCA, housed in the landmark mansion built by cotton planter J. C. Ford in the 1850s. Their new home was a tiny apartment on Third Street, near their jobs downtown, where trolleys and automobiles conveyed shoppers and business folk to and fro and policemen directed traffic by hand with "stop" and "go" signs. The city, along the Ohio River, took pride in its railroad and shipping activity, its factories and warehouses, its stockyard, its airfield. And though it called itself "The Gateway to the South," it had long been on the fence, depending on the situation. During the Civil War, Kentucky had sided with the Union, yet it failed to abolish slavery until the war was over—and then it established Jim Crow laws. But its business aspirations were decidedly northern. It stood as a gateway, in either direction.

Marjorie's work situation was a good fit, building on her New York credentials. She wrote copy for the YWCA, and the Louisville *Courier-Journal*'s October 24, 1920, Sunday magazine published her long piece about the local Y's health center for women and girls. (It is the first known article with Marjorie's married byline.) That article probably led to her short-term Sunday magazine series titled "Live Women in Live Louisville," which offered five profiles of women excelling in male-dominated professions—the sort of series women's suffrage inspired. The first installment appeared on February 6, 1921, the last on April 10.

"Live Women" could be described as a column, since it opened with a personal flourish—the storyteller warming up on her own entertaining terms before getting down to business. The February 6 piece on Dr. Lillian South, the only woman state biologist in the United States, begins: "About the time I was lisping prayers at my mother's knee, and earnestly invoking heaven to send measles to me in light but school-preventing form, I was taught that for pure, breath-taking speed you couldn't beat the minute man of early Colonial days. But wisdom came to me, perhaps with the measles, and now I know why the minute man is represented by a statue: he was a motionless piece of bric-a-brac compared with the modern phenomenon, the mile-a-minute woman."

There follow more than twice as many words describing "women on wheels everywhere at once" before Marjorie introduces Dr. South, whose work and influence is chronicled more professionally. That is, Marjorie drops the long, first-person lead so reminiscent of her college writing and switches to an efficient, journalistic voice. The strategy—or indulgence—must have pleased her editors and readers, because she kept it up. Insurance underwriter Theresa Moellman received this flippant introduction: "O for the virile pen of Horatio Alger. What does it matter that the hero is a woman? She has trod the path to success in the very manner which that leader of ambitious youth has sponsored, and I feel the need of his solemn style. I would like to picture my lady hero, surrounded in early youth by a bevy of girls indifferent to their employer's welfare, but with her own eyes fixed firmly on the goal ahead, working whole-heartedly for 'the firm.'"

Nearly a century later, it's easy see how, by introducing her women subjects superficially, Marjorie diminished their achievements, patronizing both them and herself by backing into an otherwise serious profile, tap-dancing and waving a fan. It wasn't as if she didn't have better models. Though women journalists were a distinct minority, the pioneer Nellie Bly (born in 1864) had already made her mark as an investigative reporter for the New York *World*. Her first-person articles were marked by straightforward storytelling via lean, declarative sentences.

However, Marjorie was writing not for the *World* but for the deeply southern *Courier-Journal*, and she was not the upstart Nellie Bly (nor a man) but a self-conscious young woman with creative ambitions, in need of an outlet, if not a job. Her newspaper work mirrored the period. In the 1936 tome *Ladies of the Press: The Story of Women in Journalism by an Insider*, onetime *New-York Tribune* reporter Ishbel Ross (1897–1975), a contemporary of Rawlings's, assigned labels to the previous four decades of women's work in the press, covering Marjorie's contributions to newspapers, from the *Washington Post* juvenilia to her later work for the *Rochester Evening Journal* and the *Rochester American*, the Sunday paper. The divisions are artificially crisp, but useful to understanding the times. They included 1890–1900, "The Stunt Era"; 1900–1910, "The Sob Era"; 1910–20, "The Suffrage Era"; and 1920–30, "The Tabloid Era."

Nellie Bly came to journalism in the 1880s, one of the few full-time women reporters, but it was her "stunts," her self-dramatization, culminating in a trip around the world, that inspired "a wild outcropping of girls who freely risked their lives and reputations in order to crash the papers." For women lucky enough to find newspaper work at the end of the 1890s, Ross says, "it was either clothes and the cookery book, or the stunt girl." By the turn of the century, the stunt fad was over, although Bly's work contributed to the development of the undercover story. Now, as women's magazines proliferated, newspapers saw a market in women readers, and by 1903, the year the *Ladies' Home Journal* reached one million subscribers, more than three hundred women across the country were employed as reporters. In this decade, the Sob Era, women were sent to write about whatever they happened to find, such as society events, women's clubs, and the ubiquitous teas. Gossip and other girl-talk features proliferated. ("Reflections of a Bachelor Girl," columns by Helen Rowland, which appeared in the New York *World*, were gathered into popular books.) Any news covered by a woman was secondary to her sympathetic, even tearful, reaction to it. Assignments were often random. "A girl might be asked on her first day to interview a ward politician, on her second to interview a monkey, on her third to tell how to trim an Easter bonnet," Ross notes. Women's pages coalesced around this material, often with children's pages, such as the *Washington Post*'s, appended.

During the Suffrage Era, 1910–20, more women were hired to cover hearth, home, and accomplishments outside the home. They "invaded the front pages of the most conservative papers with their stories of feminist's doings," Ross wrote. "The general tone, however, was jocular." Marjorie's "Live Women in Live Louisville" series fits nicely here. But

Marjorie would also work during the Tabloid Era, 1920–30, launched a year after the New York *Daily News*, the first American tabloid, was founded. The *Daily News* and its followers offered opportunities to women writers who would "astonish, bemuse, dazzle and horrify the reader." This was the heyday of Hearst, at the time the world's largest media conglomerate. The 1920s also saw the rise of advice columnist Dorothy Dix (1861–1951), "America's Mother Confessor," the highest-paid newspaperwoman in the world. These developments explain the sensationalism in Marjorie's work, in her breathless leads for the *Courier-Journal* and her later coverage for the *Rochester Evening Journal* and the *Rochester American*. In an interview long afterward, Marjorie referred to her duties as a "Hearst sob-sister," and commented, "It was a rough school, but I wouldn't have missed it. So long as you can avoid the stereotyped pattern you learn a lot when you must put down what people said and how they acted in great crises in their lives. And it teaches you objectivity."

IN LOUISVILLE, Chuck and Marjorie socialized with Lois Clark Hardy, a friend from Wisconsin, and her husband, James E. "Ed" Hardy, also a Wisconsin graduate. A war veteran, Ed had joined his father's farm equipment firm in Louisville. With the Hardys, Chuck and Marjorie joined the wild throng at the 1921 Kentucky Derby, where thousands of spectators, inside and outside the park—including a few boys who shinnied up the center field flagpole—strained toward the track, the women's eyes shielded by large, flowery hats, the men's by fedoras and straw boaters. The winner, American thoroughbred Behave Yourself (followed by Black Servant and Prudery), was immediately rushed by the noisy crowd. Behave Yourself must have occasioned many a joke and a julep before and after the race, as the Hardys, Rawlingses, and others in their company drank and smoked heavily, defying Prohibition, which had taken effect in 1920. Indeed, Charles Rawlings Sr.—"Daddy" Rawlings—tended his home brews in Rochester, writing to the kids about his luck with peach brandy.

As a woman publicist and a freelance journalist in this climate, Marjorie functioned well. She wrote assuredly and, sharp-eared, could imitate almost any style—or styles—required of a publication. But where was her own voice—the one that might carry a long, sustaining line?

Evidence lies in the first page—the only page that survives—of a pastoral story titled "Jenny," which Marjorie wrote in Louisville and might have submitted to magazines, as the header contains her name, Louisville street address, and a word count of 4,800. It opens plainly, realistically, and instead of leaping or twirling into sensational business, the story moves steadily, at leisure, setting a rural scene with delicate, declarative care.

In the late summer of 1868 Jeff Maddis took Jenny for his bride. The ceremony over, he led her from her mother's house, helped her into the high seat of his rough board lumber wagon, and drove silently down the Michigan roads toward the newly acquired farm. The forests edged the way deeply, hickory, oak and maple. Here and there a clearing showed a group of wooden buildings, a ploughed stretch dotted with stumps; children, chickens, dogs. The open spaces, hot beneath the sun, died into the woods again, where the air was chill, and velvet green and dark like the trees. The wagon wheels creaked; a loose board rattled; chipmunks darted across the deep-rutted road; the infinite wood voices shrilled and hummed within the stillness.

The shadows lay long when the thin church spire of Baxter became visible. Two miles beyond waited the farm. This region was more populous, with plentiful streams and meadows; the smell of new hay was strong in the evening. The last half-mile ran over the hills—

The story, set in Michigan farmland, shows Marjorie practicing a voice shaped and clarified outside the popular market, married to an interest in depicting rural life. It's possible that "Jenny" was inspired by the 1920 English translation of Knut Hamsun's 1917 pastoral novel *Growth of the Soil*, which had brought Hamsun the Nobel Prize for Literature—Marjorie later cited the novel as an influence on her work. But "Jenny" might also have been prompted by her February 1921 trip to see her mother in Madison. The visit was her first since the wedding, and not altogether pleasant. In letters leading up to the trip, Ida had regaled Marjorie with extensive news—gossip, really—of former classmates who had married for money and position; they dressed expensively, traveled widely, and consorted with notable people. For these reports, Marjorie had given Ida the silent treatment, but she finally showed up in Madison for "the sole secret reason that she had a new gray squirrel coat." She made it clear that she would have nothing to do with her mother's dreams and would take her time developing her work. "Perhaps I'll only live in my books," Marjorie told Ida, standing her ground. "Life seems to me an exploration, an expedition into the unknown. One's enjoyment and profit of it depend on one's like or dislike of mental travel."

The visit ended when Chuck, missing his wife, called long-distance, and Marjorie "packed and left with an unseemly eagerness."

MARJORIE AND CHUCK spent just under two years in Louisville, arriving sometime in 1920 and returning to Rochester before the close of 1922. Both are listed in the 1921 Louisville city directory, but in 1922, only Chuck is listed, suggesting that Marjorie was left out of the directory, as women sometimes were, or had resigned her job at the Y. Back in his hometown, Chuck took a traveling sales position with the Leach Shoe Company, where his father worked. The couple moved in with his parents at 213 Kenwood Avenue, in a pleasant, treed residential area not far from the city center. It was financially wise, convenient, and, with Chuck gone so often, a proper choice for Marjorie, the explorer turned road widow.

In January 1922, Marjorie visited her aunt Ethel Riggs on the Linden, Michigan, farm established by Ida's father, Abram Traphagen. In a letter to Chuck, Marjorie wrote of her maternal grandfather's farmhouse. The description seems connected to the "Jenny" fragment from Louisville. "It's on a knoll, and overlooks little hills and valleys, woods and a tiny lake. The whole front of her house, almost, is one big living room—with an alcove that widens it still further at one end. It has six big cheery windows, facing East and South, and the bright winter sun has been streaming in all morning through the snowy white dotted Swiss curtains."

Marjorie continued, describing the pleasure of turning a cream separator, with the reward of "a whole pail of golden, thick cream. I was also given the privilege—at my request—of washing the separator—which has some 50 different be-creamed parts to be laundered!"

And there was the amateur production of *Emily's Mistake* at the local opera house. Marjorie, the raconteur, delighted in its earnestly achieved flaws: "The orchestry sounded like a deliberate take-off and attempt to be funny—the worst collection of discords you can imagine. No two instruments hit the same note or the same key at the same time. There was a 'fairy'—a country lass with a voice like Ontario's fog horn. 'I am a fairy,' she announced in train caller's tones." Eight little boys portrayed Scottish chiefs: "About two of the eight were doing the singing, and in so feeble a voice, so fragmentary a manner, that 'fierce battle song' would never have alarmed a rabbit. It was delicious."

The letter ended with news of her accidental fall through a trap door in the farmhouse: "There I was in space, with the heavy cellar steps banging past me. Aunt Ethel saw me go, and said I turned a complete somersault in the air, landed on my behind, and fell with my head crashing against the stone wall at the bottom. By every right I should have broken, first, my neck, and then every other bone in my body." Yet she suffered only minor bumps and bruises. "Poor Chuck," she wrote, "they cannot kill me! You are doomed to have me on your hearth for many moons."

BUT AFTER A PROMISING beginning, 1922 offered several major changes in Marjorie's life and the lives of those she loved. On May 1, Charles Rawlings Sr. died, leaving Anne Rawlings head of the Kenwood house. A few weeks later, Arthur Kinnan graduated from the University of Wisconsin, and Ida took him to New York to seek his fortune, then returned to Madison, for the last, short chapter of her life, working as chaperone at the Kappa Alpha Theta house. At first, in letters to Marjorie, she described how much closer she had come to her ideal existence. "Everything possible is done for my happiness and comfort. I have three new gowns, really very handsome. You would not know me." But after a while, she admitted a growing sense of desolation, and Marjorie wrote to her more frequently, out of pity. Later, Marjorie summed up her mother's condition: "She had lived too long in other lives, and the penalty was loneliness."

In the months that followed, Ida grew unexplainably weak, and her letters sounded sadder. Her children wouldn't come home for Thanksgiving; neither would they be there at Christmas. "I did not know that so little could matter to me, that mattered before," she wrote.

Her daughter had little time to sympathize. She had just landed her first real newspaper job.

Chapter Six

Rochester

1922-28

I N September 1922, Marjorie was hired by the *Rochester Evening Journal*, a new Hearst paper managed by Harry Gray, a veteran of Hearst papers in San Francisco, Chicago, Detroit, and New York. The chain, which peddled sensational copy, was not expected to succeed in conservative Rochester, and in time, that prediction was borne out. But at the beginning, Gray was given free rein, and when the paper made a big splash, Marjorie was part of it. From its first issue, September 12, to November 17, under Gray, Marjorie published forty photograph-illustrated hard-news or human-interest features in the *Rochester Evening Journal* and the *Rochester American*, the accompanying Sunday paper, nearly all of them prominently placed on page 3 or high in the women's pages. One piece landed on the front page—a rarity for a woman reporter, and especially for the sort of story Marjorie was assigned, usually four times a week. Many were tabloid-worthy. Some sample headlines:

"Come Back," Cries Bride, 50, Forsaken
Husband, 61, Leaves Her After Month of Wedded Bliss
Was Rapid-Fire Romance

Couple Married Few Days After Meeting in Denver—
Past of Husband Is Clouded

Lonely Spinster Had Premonition of Tragic End
Neighbor Tells of Warning in Dream
Victim Pleaded with Friend to Hunt Down Slayer
If She Was Ever Found Killed

"Easiest Thing in World to Get Dope," Cries Woman Addict
Victim of Rochester Ring Descends from Respected Life
to Penitentiary Cell

Softer pieces addressed fashion, health, and behavior:

The Cookie Jar Keeps Husbands at Home, Says Food Expert
Old-Time Molasses Cakes Look Better to a Man Than Blonde Curls,
Is Claim

Path to Slimness Is Mountainous, Declares Prima Donna
Lovely Singer Who Longed to "Do" Salome Gives Reducing Secret

Girl's Charm Goes Farthest in Business, Says Woman Banker
No Need for Her to Emulate the Mummy—
Should Develop Her Own Personality

But though her subject matter was, by turns, lurid or mundane, Marjorie's style was more consistent than it had been in Louisville. Gone were the extended, overcooked leads. The deserted fifty-year-old bride, for example, received sympathy in an opening that was dramatic but cut right to the story's heart with a controlled scene, a function of the real reporting Marjorie had been assigned. Daily, she crisscrossed the growing manufacturing city of three hundred thousand, reporter's tablet in hand, observing, interviewing, listening, scratching notes. Back at a typewriter in the newsroom, she pounded out copy on short deadlines, in tandem with her driven colleagues, mostly men.

BECAUSE CHUCK WAS on the road so often that fall, mainly in Kentucky and Ohio, the couple again began to write letters back and forth, revealing the pattern of grand passion, misunderstanding, pent-up anger, and tearful apologies begun in their wartime correspondence. Chuck's ongoing fear that Marjorie was the stronger of the pair emerged again. Suspecting that she and Harry Gray were having an affair, he asked her to resign from her job. She defended herself—she had been only a friend to Gray—though like other newsroom women of the day, she probably felt obliged to lend a sympathetic, womanly ear to her male boss. Sympathy often led to flirtation. Marjorie, who'd dated other men while engaged to Chuck, might have described her exchanges with Gray once too often. To keep her marriage on track, she complied with Chuck's request.

A week after her last feature ran, Chuck wrote from the Hotel Gibson in Cincinnati to explain his anxiety, referring to a past situation in Louisville, probably with C. E. Brett, his boss at Stewart's Dry Goods. (What "three months" refers to is unclear. Marjorie probably wrote ad copy for Stewart's. As well, Chuck traveled for his advertising job.) Had Chuck pulled Marjorie from Louisville out of jealousy? He elaborated on his misgivings:

> Now about this Gray business. Skinny, until this last time, have I ever mistrusted you? Look at it honestly. There was Brett. For three months I could have killed him. I hated his sugary, sickening smirking at you. I knew that given the opportunity for evil, he would move in only one way. That through all that time we were apart, I knew for a sure bet that nothing could change your being what you were or what you would do, drunk or sober. I have an enormous capability for trusting you.
>
> Did I even scowl at you when you were running all over for those tough stories? Did I even bother to care what this damn fool Gray was like until things began, even tho' you were down there alone with him time and again. Do you think that even now, tho' you were ever so fond of this bounder, that I would let you stay at this job if he hadn't gone over the Keep Off the Grass sign?

Chuck continued, imagining what had happened between his wife and her editor, complaining of a stomachache, of going "a bit mad," then offering lavish apologies, explanations for his weaknesses, and declarations of love. Yet he returned to Harry Gray, sounding the same themes: Gray was an ogre; Marjorie had invited trouble or had used bad judgment. He would write to Gray himself and explain why he'd insisted that Marjorie quit.

Marjorie responded to one of Chuck's phone calls, recounting fondly the sound of his voice and how she enjoyed pressing his clothes, caressing his baby blue pajamas "with a warm and tender iron." Then she switched gears, moving toward one of her manifestos:

> But now, Chuck Rawlings, you just see here! You stop this monkey business about thinking I'm out with Gray, etc., or you won't have a wife. I told you once and for all I wouldn't see him or go out with him, and that goes.
>
> After tearing me up by the roots from a perfectly harmless job, the least you can do is stop your damn fool imaginings. I won't stand for it. Why in God's name did I leave the job, if not to show you that I was looking out for your selfish, boggish happiness? And then you call up from Youngstown and ask, "Were you out with Gray today?" I may sound as if I were kidding, but I'm in earnest. You give me the same square deal that I'm giving you, old lover!"

And in a letter written a week after her last feature ran, Marjorie, having quaffed three glasses of "Uncle Fred's hard cider" ("and no three highballs ever made me feel any better") pulled out all the stops:

> You say you aren't trying to make me "confess" or "probe my very depths," but that's just what you want. You get the jimmies— and bingo!—you expect me to come across with a nice juicy little acknowledgement of having longed for some other man or some such fool idea to justify your crazy notions and imaginings. Well, you're all off. I have missed my job, naturally, just as any active mind misses accustomed activity. But I have NOT longed for "Gray's companionship"—or anything of Gray's except his $45 a week.
>
> There are times when I long to be a ragamuffin, fighting the world for a living. I love the scramble. I love to be the tattered scrambler, buffeting other writers for my bread and butter. There are times

when I want to be alone, all alone, in New York, working, fighting, making my name, owing no one, with no one owing me. It's exactly the same sort of thing you have, I imagine, when you've wanted to go to sea alone—except I have been more in love with the fight.

It's the conflict between the adventurous, worldly mind in me, sexless, aggressive, wanting to lick life on its own terms—Heavens, I love it!—and on the other side, my entirely female desire for my own fireside and you coming home to me and my babies. . . .

There are times when I resent—almost to madness—being a woman. I want to fare forth alone. . . . I want to be a solitary fighter, loving no one, with no one loving me. Then—I come out of that—and all of Heaven or earth I want is my home, with you and children.

That is my one problem. . . . I think there is an answer, however. When I am freed of financial press, I think I can turn my literary energy to work at home—which I am unable to do now because of financial uncertainty. I have always written for money—and since leaving college I have written for a living. As long as money is scarce, I cannot give myself the leisure to write at home, when I know I can make anywhere from $25 to $60 a week by purely commercial writing.

The next day, she wrote breezily about the weather, her domestic chores, and how she would now read A. S. M. Hutchinson's new novel *This Freedom*, whose central question was, Could a woman have a career and a family, too? The answer, in so many words, was no. Ida had sent the book to Marjorie.

"Someday, I shall write a great feminist novel," Marjorie declared, "urging women to gird on their armor and kill all the men. That would give them a few years of peace before they (the women) died off. Then the monkeys could begin evolving again—perhaps with better results than they have obtained so far."

WITH THE END OF HER short-lived reporting career, Marjorie turned toward Mother Rawlings's company. In good weather she walked the downtown routes she'd followed as a journalist, no doubt climbing to the top of the grand Powers Building for a bird's-eye view of the Kodak Tower and other skyscrapers, the Genesee River, and Lake Ontario, or perhaps loitering in the sumptuous Hotel Rochester's lobby, strolling the Reynolds Arcade, circling the marble columns of the Monroe County courthouse, and appraising the new Eastman Theatre, built by photography entrepreneur George Eastman for the city orchestra he'd founded. Where once she had been an insider, Marjorie now haunted Rochester from the outside, with little else to do but wait for Chuck to get off the road.

FOR THE 1922 CHRISTMAS HOLIDAY, Marjorie's mother traveled from Wisconsin to the Linden farm to visit her elderly parents. There, Ida Kinnan was acknowledged to be seriously ill, hovering close to death. Marjorie and Arthur, summoned by telegram, rushed to Michigan. Their mother died in January 1923, probably of a throat infection. Like Arthur Sr.'s decline as a result of uremia, her demise might have been due to inattention. In Marjorie's composed scene, Ida struggles in agony to her last breath, while Abram "goes out into the woodshed and beats his gaunt bony fists on the cordwood he has split" and "Fanny wails up and down like an old peasant hag. 'Oh Idy! She came home to her mother's arms to die!'" But there is no record of Marjorie's own reaction to her mother's final hours.

By the time Marjorie returned to Rochester, the dailies had seen editorial changes. Gone were the regular local sob stories—most tearjerkers came from news services reporting from afar. This held for softer women's stories, too. Marjorie might have contributed unsigned work, such as bridal announcements, but it's more likely that a staffer covered these. Overall, neither Hearst nor its direct competitors, the Rochester Times-Union and the Rochester Democrat and Chronicle, were counting on sensationalism to sell papers, and neither ran her byline. What Marjorie wrote in 1923 or published without a credit is not documented, and it's likely she wasn't employed at all, except for keeping house, keeping Mother Rawlings company, and strolling solo to keep Chuck sane.

However, it is reasonable to speculate that, with time on her hands and her mother gone, Marjorie made notes for, or at least pondered, material for Blood of My Blood, the self-narrative of her family heritage, her youth and young adulthood, with a lens trained sharply on her mother, and ending with her mother's death. (More than once, she described how her work underwent a long gestation period prior to a white-hot first draft.) In the manuscript, she employed re-created or representative scenes—techniques common to memoirists and fiction writers. The style of *Blood of My Blood* also bears some resemblance to the sob stories Marjorie churned out for Hearst. Though it is written primarily in third-person omniscient voice, the author occasionally interrupts with personal commentary—wise or wry—or a passionate outburst.

SOMETIME IN 1923 OR 1924, Marjorie wrote and probably sent out an essay on the child artist turned writer, disguised as a short story ("Boil, Little Pot, Boil!"), giving her address as 192 Mill Street, Charles's business address. The couple, together with Anne Rawlings, who worked as a saleswoman downtown, had moved from the Kenwood house to one on Ericsson Street.

In April 1924 Marjorie landed a short-lived job as social critic with the Rochester magazine *Five O'Clock*, which was devoted to "verses, jokes, and other material with local color." Writing under the nom de plume Lady Alicia Thwaite ("not only a third cousin of the Earl of Bentleigh, but one of London's most scintillating cognoscenti"), she satirically critiqued cultural events. But she contributed just four times, covering a purported burlesque at the Corinthian Theater, a fictional wrestler at the center of Rochester culture, a wrestling event at the city's Convention Hall, and a bogus May coming-out of Rochester's waitresses. She was introduced with the April 29 issue, and in the May 20 number, the editors bade her farewell: "This is the last of a series of articles by Lady Thwaite. Her life has been so repeatedly threatened that she has been forced to retire, for the time being, from print."

Why Marjorie suddenly ceased writing for *Five O'Clock* is a mystery, and one wonders if Chuck had anything to do with it. Her writing is lively, witty, and razor-sharp—clearly, she was having fun, at the top of her lighter powers. At the Corinthian Theater, she noted, for example, that with Rochester audiences, "the scantier the costume, the louder their cheers. Indeed, when Miss Pauline Russell bites her lips, lifts her chin and steps bravely before the footlights in three pitiful little squares of silk, the pit, galleries and stalls unite in their applause and call her back again and again and again to show their appreciation of a true artist's indomitable pluck." Henry Clune, the *Democrat and Chronicle*'s longtime columnist, who served as *Five O'Clock*'s editor (the magazine folded after eleven months), later remembered that Marjorie had suggested a weekly piece, and that he'd put her to work. "She picked out her own assignments and they were hardly congruous with her fancy title . . . the girl had the touch. Even my limited editorial judgment told me that," he wrote. But he didn't indicate why Marjorie abruptly stopped writing for him.

Early the following year, in January 1925, Marjorie, Chuck, and Mother Rawlings moved to a new three-bedroom home at 8 Kent Road in Brighton, a suburb. In a letter inviting a college friend, the writer Ethel Fairmont Beebe, and her husband, Murray, to visit, Marjorie described the house as "a very small affair, with no 'show' points" but added that "it is most comfortable, and we think, attractive. We couldn't offer you the wild intellectual debauchery of New York, but might rake up a newspaperman or so with whom you could argue."

It appeared that Anne Rawlings was not a burden, traveled frequently, and was good company at home. "She is a theosophist, is studying astrology, etc., and needs only concentrated training to be a real student of philosophy," Marjorie explained to Ethel. Marjorie and her mother-in-law must have had a lot to talk about, theosophy covering a wide spectrum of mystical beliefs and suppositions; its concerns with myth, creative imagination, and awakening to the divine might have fed Marjorie's interest in cosmic consciousness. Indeed, Helena Petrovna Blavatsky of the modern theosophical movement taught that of the seven planes of existence, the lower four are planes of cosmic consciousness, or the intelligent soul. But for Marjorie, whose notion of cosmic consciousness was felt, not intellectualized, this sort of mental organization ultimately must have been irritating.

Marjorie added that Chuck was now writing for the *Rochester Herald*. Having grown up on Lake Ontario, he loved boating, and he was now covering yachting and other water activities. "A telegram would reach us best at home, here, as we have a phone and I am here most of the time," Marjorie wrote. Apparently, she was not employed beyond Kent Road, although she sold a piece to the sensational magazine the *World:* a dramatic account of a highly publicized Rochester love quartet—clueless husband, scheming wife, scheming lover, duped ex-lover—that ended in the husband's murder and the sentencing of the other three.

From the short years in that house, two completed fiction manuscripts exist, one an unpublished children's story, "Under the Lily Pond," signed Mrs. Charles Rawlings. It opens conventionally: "Jean and Jenny never in the world expected to go under the lily pond, but this is how it happened." Another story, "The Heaven of Arlette," is a fantastic morality tale whose heroine, Arlette, a creature with cloven hands and a long, silky tail, plays bridge in Heaven, where the Holy Ghost, a magnificent gentleman who is "faintly furry," catches her in a lie about apple blossoms and inspires her to find God. Neither story reaches much farther than those Marjorie wrote in her college years.

IN 1926, the *Herald* was subsumed by the *Rochester Democrat and Chronicle*, and Chuck moved over to its building on Exchange Boulevard. In May, after at least two years at home, Marjorie began a column-in-verse for the *Times-Union*, Gannett's evening paper. "This series is an entirely new thought in the feature line, that of making a romance of housework," the introducing editor wrote. "Songs of a Housewife" appeared six times a week until February 1928 and celebrated everything domestic: cleaning, cooking, gardening, children, and animals. (By now, Chuck and Marjorie had two household pets— a cat and a dog.) Readers suggested subjects. The series was quickly syndicated, running in dozens of papers from New York to Oregon. More than four hundred poems appeared. Intended for the working-class woman, each contained three or four light, rhymed stanzas, and they were often rough, as Marjorie turned out nearly one a day. Of the many, here is a sample:

The Symphony of Supper-time

I like the sound of silver,
* When the table's being set,*
In the early Winter twilight,
* With the lamps unlighted yet.*

I like to hear the kitchen door
* Swing slowly out, and then,*
When Mary passes, laden, through,
* Swing slowly back again.*

I like to hear the kettle sing;
The hissing of the roast;
The children coming in from play,
A hungry, noisy host.

I like to hear the murmurings
When my dessert appears.
The symphony of supper-time
Is music to my ears!

Chuck was still working for the *Democrat* in 1927, but the couple had moved yet again, to 5 Lincoln Avenue in Irondequoit, northeast of Rochester. In 1928, Marjorie's "Songs" ceased, coinciding with Gannett's purchase of the *Democrat*, which became the company's flagship paper. The young writers kept moving.

In March, immediately after the "Songs" vanished, they took a Clyde Line steamship from New York City to the port of Jacksonville, Florida, to visit Chuck's brothers, Jimmy and Wray, who, drawn south by the Florida land boom, were running a service station in tiny Island Grove, a village southwest of Jacksonville. Jacksonville then was the gateway to the state, with access to the great Atlantic coast beaches, via Henry Flagler's railroad. Newcomers like Chuck and Marjorie shivered with anticipation, imagining adventures in a state long promoted as a land of pleasure, exoticism, and opportunity. They were met at the dock by Zelma Cason, a woman in her late thirties, a native of Island Grove who knew Jimmy and Wray. She installed the couple in a hotel, and Chuck's brothers came up to collect them. For several days the four roamed around Florida's raw interior, trekking through the wilderness, floating on the Ocklawaha and Withlacoochee Rivers, crossing over to the west coast for excellent fishing in the Gulf of Mexico. Marjorie and Chuck were captivated by rural Florida's beauty, its rustic farms, and its earthy inhabitants living frontier lives on what they found, grew, or created from their wild surroundings. A romantic notion struck the romantics: Might they make an easy living with an orange grove in the middle of nowhere, giving them ample time to write?

After Chuck and Marjorie sailed back north, Jimmy and Wray promised to watch for a good deal. The wait was short. Florida's land boom (and attendant growth) had recently gone bust, largely due to disasters: a 1925 railroad strike that cut off building supplies, the September 1926 hurricane, which devastated south Florida, and the banking crisis that followed. Real estate and tourism had yet to revive, although the Orange Blossom Special, Seaboard Air Line's luxury train carrying winter tourists from New York to Florida, continued to run. Plenty of people were hard up, especially in rural areas, and to complete the bleak picture, another destructive hurricane in September 1928 (the "Okeechobee hurricane") made landfall near West Palm Beach, damaging more property and killing at least two thousand people. Florida was in a momentary slump. With the small inheritance from Ida—the residual of the Maryland farm sale—Marjorie bought, sight unseen, a farm and orange grove in the tiny hamlet of Cross Creek, about four miles northwest of Island Grove in southern Alachua County

In November 1928, she and Chuck loaded Dinghy, their Scottish terrier, and Jib, the tiger cat, into their car and drove about fifteen hundred miles south. To Ethel Beebe, Marjorie explained the move: "We both got in a panic as to where the salaried life in a city like Rochester, in a profession like the newspaper profession, was leading us. Chuck was happy in his yachting writing, but aside from that he could see fat paunches and boredom overtaking his friends." If he remained a freelancer, he wouldn't advance, and embracing executive work, "which he loathes," would merely lead to "higher priced cars, a bigger house—and the same old routine."

She acknowledged "the cauliflower aspect of my nature," how she needed to be "transplanted frequently," and added, "I know one thing tho, from this migration. Further moves will always be south. The tropics offer the most for your time and money."

She regretted having spent so much time in Rochester, which, after New York, had been a painful letdown, telling Ethel, "Most of the interesting people there are the musical cliché [crowd], which lets us literary lights right out of the picture." They'd made a few friends, but "the town is smug and awfully small-town, the 'upper class' is fearfully affected, and Blah, and you go around wanting to slap people's faces, which is not the community spirit at all." She might have added that she'd had little to do there until "Songs of a Housewife," no doubt approved by her husband, caught on. Finally, she'd had a job she wasn't forced to quit. Instead, it had quit her.

Sometime that year, Marjorie completed *Blood of My Blood*, underway or finished before the move to Florida. To a friend, she referred to the manuscript as a biography, and when she entered it, unsuccessfully, in a 1929 fiction contest sponsored by the Atlantic Monthly Press, she called it a novel. No doubt the judges recognized its personal mission. After the failed contest effort, Marjorie scrawled three lines across the final typescript: "Written 1928 / And Jane Austen / to a turn!" To a correspondent, she noted that the work had been written quickly, under pressure, and "whatever merit it may have had, potentially, was lost in the scramble."

Although the Atlantic Monthly Press rejected the manuscript, Marjorie had succeeded in examining and dramatizing her family story, detaching from Ida, and taking her leave in the name of art. And, with Ida's last gift, she had purchased a home she wanted: a random farm that would have horrified the giver.

Chapter Seven

The Creek

1928-31

"WHEN I CAME TO THE CREEK, and knew the old grove and farmhouse at once as home, there was some terror, such as one feels in the first recognition of a human love," Marjorie wrote after the move. "For the joining of person to place, as of person to person, is a commitment to shared sorrow, even as to shared joy."

When her aunt Madelaine, one of her father's sisters, heard about Cross Creek, she commented, "You have in you that fatal drop of Pearce blood, clamoring for change and adventure, and above all, for a farm. I never knew a Pearce who didn't secretly long for a farm." Marjorie replied, "It is more important to live the life one wishes to live, and to go down with it if necessary, quite contentedly, than to live more profitably but less happily."

CROSS CREEK WAS barely a dot on the map, eighty-five miles southwest of Jacksonville, the largest city in Florida at the time, and seventy miles west of the old coastal community of St. Augustine. Cross Creek was named for the slight waterway joining Orange and Lochloosa Lakes. The lakes connect to the Ocklawaha River, a major tributary of the great north-flowing St. Johns. In 1928, the hamlet lay in a remote, forbidding area, a mixture of hardwood forest, scrub, swamp, and water whose original occupants—snakes, alligators, deer, boars, bears, bobcats—lurked in great numbers. Human residents, mostly descendants of white settlers and black slaves whose forebears had come from neighboring states, lived off the land and the fugitive waters, farming, fishing, hunting, ranching, logging, and moonshining.

The closest sizable town to where Marjorie and Chuck had now settled was Gainesville, population ten thousand, the seat of Alachua County and the home of the University of Florida. It had recently paved some streets for motor traffic and built its first modern hospital. Gainesville was situated along the Atlantic Coast Line Railroad line, and as a rail hub, it offered hotels for tourists close to the station and the town square, plus proximity to Ocala (population seven thousand), the seat of Marion County and the gateway to Silver Springs, one of Florida's oldest tourist attractions, featuring rides in glass-bottomed boats. Visitors from the North were good for commerce in Gainesville and Ocala, although, like other Florida towns, these two had been highly resistant to change after the Civil War. Both Alachua and Marion Counties formed part of the state's "lynching belt."

One wonders how Cross Creek could have captured Marjorie so completely. She would say it was the legacy of her father, with whom, as a young girl, she'd practiced rudimentary farm tasks and walked the Maryland woods, dreaming the same dream of living in the Maryland countryside. In tandem, a nostalgic pastoralism—so thoroughly American, before, then, and now—held sway among many writers in the late 1920s and early 1930s, as economic instability and another world war loomed.

Until this move, Marjorie had said she liked to be transplanted regularly, and skipping from Wisconsin to New York to Louisville to Rochester in eight years had borne that out—at least for a young, ambitious woman in her twenties. But after she turned thirty-two, an early, fleeting fantasy of a cozy country bungalow seemed to catch up with her, alongside the deepening desire to create serious literature, not hackwork for city newspapers or the popular fiction market she'd never cracked. The idea that a woman might claim her own artistic space was in the air, and in the news. In October 1928, Virginia Woolf delivered the two lectures leading to *A Room of One's Own*, just one month before Marjorie and

Chuck arrived in Florida. And Marjorie the journalist must have realized that the area offered bounteous, unrefined material, ripe for exploration in stories—an irresistible invitation.

Still, opportunity and cultural context do not fully explain Marjorie's attraction to Florida's wilderness and the striking transformation in her writing that followed. One must circle back to the first seed planted. Marjorie once maintained that had Ida Kinnan been the parent to die early, she would have lived on the Maryland farm with her father, and her writings would have been set there. The "Jenny" story fragment from her Louisville days shows her attempt to depict life on a Michigan farm—the farm she then had access to—in a voice that suited it. Now, moved by a cluster of circumstances and desires, she would transfer the dream shared with her father to a Florida orange grove. The leisurely, poetic turn her writing took at Cross Creek was linked to her childhood wanderings near Rock Creek. She could imagine writing from the beating heart of this new world because she felt it so clearly. She might have explained that feeling as a cosmic connection.

AFTER A GREAT REVELATION comes work. The Cross Creek farm had been bought cheaply, but it had fallen on hard times, and those hard times would continue with the 1929 stock market crash. Marjorie and Chuck, arriving at the start of the 1928 citrus harvest, found structures and machinery that needed mending, repairing, or rebuilding. The farmhouse itself was barely habitable, with no bathroom, only an outdoor tin stall shower and a screen-doored outhouse. (When Marjorie first entertained guests in the dining room, she always took the seat facing the window that looked out to the privy.) The kitchen, at least, had cold running water. The fruit trees, in fair shape, required immediate and ongoing nurturing. Grove workers, mostly blacks on the lowest rung of the southern caste ladder, victims of the Jim Crow laws, had to be hired and trained. (Florida had been among the first states to pass the more restrictive precursor to Jim Crow laws—the infamous Black Codes—in 1865.) Chuck's brothers signed on to help, and dove in. The closest neighbors, Tom and Pearlee Glisson, offered welcome advice. Besides the Glissons, three white families lived nearby: "Old Boss" Brice, the MacKays, and the Basses. So did two black families: Henry Woodward (who lived in the Brice tenant house) and the Mickenses.

Marjorie focused on freshening the farmhouse, cooking meals, planting a garden, and adding farm animals, including chickens and a cow. Jib, the Rochester cat, took to Florida right away, catching, she reported, "everything from barn and field rats, through rabbit and partridge to lizards and snakes." But Dinghy, the terrier, failed to thrive and was sent back north to friends, to be replaced with a series of hunting dogs. To the end of her life, Marjorie kept an assortment of beloved pets. "If you didn't like cats and dogs, you didn't like her," a former housekeeper remembered. "Just imagine riding in the car. Wherever you sat, you got dog hairs."

To a college friend, Marjorie expressed girlish excitement about Cross Creek: "The life here is one adventure after another. The people and the conditions are a constant delight, while to the 'eye-minded' the beauty of the place is a perpetual treat." In the same breath, however, she admitted, "We are hovering on the brink of financial disaster." Since April, Florida citrus groves had been infested by the Mediterranean fruit fly, cutting or delaying fruit shipment across the state. The problem wouldn't abate for another year. Yet the Cross Creek area, at the northernmost part of the citrus region, still grew fine oranges, and the state had begun using fruit as a tourist draw—a symbol of the good life. The Rawlingses' trees were, Marjorie said, beautiful. "If we can ship," she wrote optimistically, "the year's income ought to be high enough almost to pay back our investment at once. . . . Depending of course on freezes and on the market price for oranges—you can live the life of country gentlefolk, with plenty of cheap labor under you, in beautiful surroundings, and close to two oceans, a wealth of rivers and lakes for small boat traveling, which we both crave, and a fascinating, pioneer playground in any direction. To say nothing of the climate, which is all its fondest boosters ever claimed for it." Hers was the voice of the innocent newcomer who responds at once to lush growth, warm waters, and soft air and has not yet experienced the peninsula's extreme weather, creeping wildlife, and puzzling culture. But Marjorie's—and Chuck's—reactions to their new home soon acquired texture.

MARJORIE WANTED TO TRY writing about Cross Creek and its people, but between house and grove work and entertaining the first of many visitors eager for a Florida winter vacation, she found it nearly impossible. All the same, she was listening carefully. "The Crackers, the natives here, are a strange breed, speaking a quaint Elizabethan English," she observed in a letter. She pulled out her reporter's notebook, copied out phrases.

Besides help from Jimmy, Wray, the Glissons, and paid grove workers, Marjorie and Chuck hired household assistance. A local widow, Mrs. Slater, and her six children, did odd jobs for a while. The eldest son, Snow, tended the grove after his mother moved away. Martha Mickens, the matriarch of the Mickens family, and the first person to greet Marjorie and Chuck at Cross Creek, helped over the years, as would her husband, Old Will, several of their offspring, and other relatives. In time, Marjorie came to wish for a maid who would function not only as a servant but as a co-cook in the kitchen and a sort of amanuensis, protecting the author's privacy, shielding her from unwanted visitors, and both respecting and tidying the papers tossed about on the writing table or thrown to the floor. To various degrees, she was able to train a succession of young black women who would withstand her moods and her treatment of them, alternately as friend and hired help.

Black household employees lived behind the main farmhouse in an unpainted tenant shack consisting of a front room, two bedrooms separated by a sheet, and a kitchen—cramped quarters. Additional workers came from both white and black populations. The grove pickers, mainly black, were trucked in from other points during harvest months and occasionally had to be replaced, as some fled the area for better opportunities in cities like St. Petersburg, where construction jobs were available, or northern climes, as part of the Great Migration. The ratio of whites to blacks in Florida was about two to one, with a larger percentage of blacks in rural areas. Many depended on whites for employment and, when it was offered, other forms of support, such as medical care, the use of a car, or intervention on their behalf when they were threatened or mistreated—Florida's Ku Klux Klan was in full flower. Chuck and Marjorie adopted a paternalistic, benevolent white position toward their black employees. And although Marjorie plunged into farm and kitchen work, often alongside her hired help, she also expected to be served well: the eggs had to be prepared just right. She set herself apart from people, according to a neighbor, "by displaying an air of intellectual and social superiority." She was the mistress of her house.

As EXPENSES MOUNTED and Florida's fickle weather and natural predators threatened crops, Chuck's brothers returned to the North, leaving Chuck and Marjorie to their Florida dream. Nearby, the Glissons faced a mountain of work with their grove, so Tom Glisson and Chuck helped each other, pruning and setting new trees. Together, they cleared brush, shoveled muck, and improved production on both properties. The Glisson's son, J.T., said his mother gave Chuck and Marjorie her highest compliment: "We are lucky to have honest neighbors." He remembered, "Mrs. Rawlings, a pretty woman who examined everything with an unquenchable thirst for the smallest details, came to the grove with lemonade or water. My dad told Momma she was high-strung and likeable." Glisson summarized the impression Marjorie made at the Creek, over time:

> She exuded an aura of energy and controversy. She was charismatic and antisocial and unyielding, a force that could not be ignored. She smoked in public at a time when most women smoked in secret and publicized her taste for good liquor when most of the country buried their empty bottles. Her fast driving, reckless accusations, and occasional profanity all created an image not always admired but never ignored.
>
> Mrs. Rawlings was looked upon as a temperamental character who vacillated from warm and friendly to snobbish. She clearly valued her independence and privacy. But to be fair to her, that same description fit most everybody at the Creek.

As CROSS CREEK ADJUSTED to Marjorie, she adjusted to the Creek. At first, she read her new neighbors' friendly overtures as bids for charity, and because some of the locals' livelihood was "quasi-illegal," they tended to keep their daily business from her. After settling in, Chuck and Marjorie met people outside the Creek. Among their first friends were sportswoman Dessie Smith Vinson and her husband, urologist Dr. Clifford Vinson, Tampa residents who owned a hunting and fishing camp: a log home Dessie had built herself in Sparr, another hamlet, south of Cross Creek. The Rawlings-Vinson meeting came by way of the grapevine, when someone suggested that the Vinsons visit the Rawlings couple, who were in bad financial shape. The price of fruit had fallen to thirty cents a box, when it cost fifteen cents a box to pack and ship. Dessie, a petite woman in her twenties, drove to the farmhouse, and though Chuck wasn't home, Marjorie was, and the two women hit it off.

ALONG WITH ZELMA CASON, the Island Grove resident Marjorie met on her first visit to Florida, Dessie would stand among a handful of Marjorie's Florida women friends who did not conform to conventional American womanhood. Like Zelma, Dessie was a native of Island Grove. She had supported herself with a variety of jobs since her early teens; her father had died when she was two years old, and her mother had succumbed to flu in the 1918 epidemic. It's fair to say that she was not simply assertive but fearless. Soon, she and Marjorie went hunting together, and when Dessie saw how badly the writer's big shotgun "kicked like a Jersey mule," she insisted that Marjorie take her smaller one, easier to handle.

Later, Marjorie admitted to a fellow writer—Ernest Hemingway—that she had never shot a gun until she came to Florida, "and then I was turned loose with a 12-gauge shotgun that later kicked a six-foot game warden in the canal. . . . It was a year before anyone noticed that I was holding the damn gun stock against my chest like a perfume atomizer. It was two years more before anyone noticed that the stock was about four inches too long for me. I've had to learn, alone, to correct flinching. Had to get over sheer paralysis. Made myself get over that, and now shoot too quickly."

Dessie introduced Marjorie to foxhunting on horseback, and they went several times, starting at eight or nine o'clock in the evening with their dogs, heading to the prairie west of the hammock—an elevated hardwood forest in the midst of wetlands—staying out until dawn. According to Dessie, they rarely killed a fox. "We usually just got the dogs off after they had treed or holed one and let the fox go for another good race," she reflected later. The women never went to town. "We did not go to night clubs or anything like that," Dessie said. "We made our own fun." Dessie also taught Marjorie to shoot the squirrels that raided the pecan tree by the Cross Creek farmhouse. At one moment in the

Rawlings marriage, Chuck mistook his wife's aim at a squirrel for her intention to fire at him, and disappeared for hours.

Marjorie's friendship with Zelma Cason deepened when Zelma was hired to take the 1930 census in rural Alachua County and invited Marjorie to join her, riding about on horseback, meeting people. "She was the logical census taker for our district," Marjorie remembered. "She knew all the inhabitants, black and white, and every road and trail leading to their houses. None of the places could be reached by a main road, and traveling by automobile would leave most of the noses uncounted." Such a person also knew everyone's business, and what everyone knew of Zelma, besides a basic neighborliness, was her judgmental streak, stubbornness, and love of profanity. J. T. Glisson said his father characterized Zelma as "an 'old maid politician' who liked everybody except the damn fools who didn't agree with her."

In two posed photographs, Zelma appears stern, sharp-nosed, her mouth set, not given to smiling. Yet for some time, the two women got along, and it seemed their friendship promoted the newcomer's acceptance in the region. Marjorie was grateful for a no-nonsense companion with an insider's history, a person who would, by her support, legitimize her. Zelma assumed a proprietorship, having befriended and oriented the newcomer. Holding a prominent place in the community was important to her.

CHUCK, THE BOATING ENTHUSIAST, began wandering the Gulf Coast for material and periodically returned north to cover yacht races, while Marjorie remained at the Creek, took copious notes, and began writing. Her best time was in the morning—in bed, after a breakfast ritual that would evolve over the years. At seven o'clock, her maid would prepare coffee, fresh-squeezed orange juice, an egg, and toast, arranging the dishes, coffeepot, creamer, and sugar bowl on a silver tray, with linen and a fresh garden flower in a silver vase. In one corner, the maid placed a can of food and a bowl of milk for Marjorie's cat, which ate straight from the tray. When Marjorie and her kitty were satisfied, the dishes were removed and Marjorie wrote, using the tray as a sort of desk. After lunch, she typically moved to her typewriter table—handmade by Chuck—on the screened porch.

Marjorie was aware of her status as a new writer in Florida, though she was not the first one to journey down from the North, nor the first woman writer to run an orange grove. In 1866, Harriett Beecher Stowe had rented an old plantation on the St. Johns River for a thousand-acre "cotton experiment" offering work to freed slaves, and put her troubled son Frederick in charge of it. The following year, Stowe became enamored of Mandarin, a settlement across the river, and envisioned a "line of churches" along the St. Johns. She purchased a house in Mandarin as a winter home. The property included an orange grove, and, assured by locals that her crop would earn $2,000 a year, she hired a cousin to move down and manage it. Her northbound crates were marked "Oranges from Harriet Beecher Stowe, Mandarin, Fla."

But Stowe's chief interest in the village was religious education for black and white children, and she took up writing again, to fund it. Among her projects was the 1873 volume of Florida sketches titled *Palmetto Leaves*, which likely boosted Florida's tourist trade. The sketches, originally written for the *Christian Union*, were confined to her own patch of paradise, including St. Augustine, Palatka, and Ocklawaha, and portrayed life there as idyllic, bountiful, happy-go-lucky. Her colorful descriptions of nature, particularly plants, led northern readers to inquire about land prices. She replied that the best land in the state had probably been taken up already, but there were thousands of acres of good land near the St. Johns. She mentioned a horticulturist who planned to plant a massive rose garden nearby but, anticipating the ruin of Florida's natural environment, warned the reader: "These places in Florida must not in any wise be compared with the finished ones of the Northern states. They are spots torn out of the very heart of the forest, and where Nature is rebelling daily, and rushing with all her might back again into the wild freedom from which she had been a moment held captive."

Whether Marjorie had read *Palmetto Leaves* is unknown. Stowe died the year Marjorie was born. But she sought out living writers who had arrived in Florida before her. In 1930 or 1931 she introduced herself by letter to Minneapolis-born, Wellesley-educated Marjory Stoneman Douglas, a former staff editor and columnist for the *Miami Herald*, now a notable freelance writer for the *Saturday Evening Post* and other publications. Douglas, like Dessie Smith and Zelma Cason, was an unusually independent woman, the kind of friend Marjorie gravitated to. Much of Douglas's fiction and nonfiction was set in south Florida, particularly the Everglades. Her work and reputation as an environmentalist was just beginning to build. In Douglas's writer-to-writer reply, she invited Marjorie to visit her "little thatched roof workshop in Coconut Grove, where I spend my days and some nights." It had no telephone or radio, only the sounds of insects, animals, and a ticking clock. She wished to speak of books and Marjorie's writing plans, and answered a question Marjorie had obviously posed. "There was never any doubt in my mind that there was room for both of us in Florida," Douglas wrote. "There is so much in it, of variety and stimulation that a dozen writers who care for it couldn't exhaust it."

EARLY IN 1930, Marjorie sent eight fictional sketches based on her white neighbors to a *Scribner's Magazine* editor who had once encouraged her. In March, Alfred Dashiell offered her $150 for the group, "Cracker Chidlings." "You ask how I happened to become interested in this material and how I gathered my facts," she wrote to him.

> This wild, beautiful country, tucked off the tourists' highways by no large number of actual miles, is in itself a challenge to the imagination. I had met only two or three of the neighboring Crackers when I realized that isolation had done something to these people. Rather, perhaps civilization had remained too remote, physically and spiritually, to take something from them, something vital. They have a primal quality against their background of jungle hammock, moss-hung, against the tremendous silence of the scrub country. The only ingredients of their lives are the elemental things. They are a people of dignity, speaking often in Chaucerian phrases, aloof but friendly and neighborly once even a Yankee has proved himself not too hopelessly alien. I have gathered my facts first-hand. Most of the material is to my personal knowledge. The rest has been told me here and there in the locality, and is equally authentic.

"CRACKER CHIDLINGS," Marjorie's first literary publication, is presented as a collection of local tales, most of them in the voice of a jocular, regional storyteller. (Chidlings, pieces of fried pork intestines, also known as "chitterlings" or "chitlins," denote the pieces' brevity and spirit.) They depend on Marjorie's knack as a mimic and raconteur more than her straightforward voice in the Michigan fragment "Jenny." A sketch titled "Georgia Money" opens with: "Sam Whitman, whose daddy's daddy killed a bear and panther on the Ocklawaha, hates a Georgian worse than most Florida Crackers, because he married one."

Sam "lived a happy, drunken life" until he married a "lean spinster" from Georgia who caught him at 'shinin'' (moonshining). To make a living, the couple set up a café, which Sam ran into the ground. His wife "departed wailing to her Georgia home" and returned with a deal from "her daddy," who has offered to start the business again, "if'n I'll leave the till alone." But "dogged if I'll let him do it," Sam declares, because it would mean bringing Georgia money into Florida.

When *Scribner's* included "Cracker Chidlings" in its February 1931 issue, some Floridians took note of it, including the editor of the *Ocala Evening Star*, who complained that Marjorie had "painted her portrait of backwoods life with the hand of a crude artist." She had "interwoven into her stories some sort of dialect which sounds as if it must be spoken somewhere." He accused her of using speech from the Blue Ridge and Cumberland Mountains and handling her subjects unsympathetically to meet market demands. "For after all it is not realism so much as what the editors *demand* as realism that sells fiction. The literary field of America has reached the lowest dregs in history with editors demanding bootleggers, gunmen and criminals." The editor defended the rural populace ("The average native is fairly well educated") and soft-pedaled the Florida-Georgia rivalry, claiming that it barely existed, while plenty of tension boiled up between Georgians and arrivals from other states, he said—effectively blaming Georgians for any conflicts. In a huff, he concluded that by presenting "Cracker Chidlings," *Scribner's Magazine* was guilty of libel "against the citizenship of Florida."

Even as a newcomer, Marjorie was not about to roll over dead, and although she had just undergone an appendectomy in Jacksonville, she responded immediately, and at length. She denied any familiarity with the Cumberlands, suggesting that the editor was guilty of bathing fact in "comforting illusions." She declared that her sketches were "so true, that I have softened, not colored them, for fear that if they came to the chance attention of one of the subjects—all within a forty-mile radius of my home—offense would be taken at my frankness, where none was intended."

She defended her use of dialect, at which she worked hard, in successive revisions. "Perhaps my newness in this country gives a pristine quality to the oddities of speech that come to my ears," she suggested. "Perhaps my interest as a student of etymology has made me alert to quaintness and to archaisms deep-rooted in the English language. One of my Cracker acquaintances . . . said to me of 'coon-meat, of which he is exceedingly fond, 'It has a kind of foolish taste.' Do you know that one must go far back into Anglo-Saxon speech to find the word 'foolish' used currently in the sense in which he used it. And have you noticed that the Georgia 'hit' for 'it,' which persists hereabouts, is likely to be used at the beginning of a sentence, but not necessarily afterward?"

She returned the editor's insults with some of her own. Of course, not all Florida natives speak in dialect, she shot back, only those in places "uncontaminated by the tourist or the Rotary Club." She wrote,

> Sir, you would eliminate individuality. You would annihilate personality. . . . The lack of sympathy is yours, not mine. These people are to me all that is delightful. Yet they offend you. I am so sorry. . . . I have only begun my recreation of this section and these people. I am going leisurely, for I wish only to write of what I know. Added to past days and nights in the scrub, there must be weeks; there must be longer and further prowlings through the piney-woods and the shadowy hammocks—where, alas, my dear sir, I am never likely to meet you.

SOON AFTER "Cracker Chidlings" appeared, Marjorie enlisted a fourteen-year-old Island Grove boy, Buren Clayton, to take her on her first alligator hunt. She and Chuck had stayed with his family for a short time before the Cross Creek farmhouse was habitable. Later, the boy worked for Marjorie, packing Brussels sprouts. One night, in Clayton's boat, the pair eased out into Orange Prairie, a shallow part of the lake sizzling with saw grass and water moccasins. Clayton told Marjorie how to use her headlamp: flash the light in a waking gator's eyes, hold them with the beam, shoot. One false move of the lamp, and the gator would sink to safety. Marjorie's first try was a bust—"she couldn't hold the beam on the gator," Clayton remembered. "Her disappointment was almost a tangible thing." They poled along, finally encountering "the granddaddy of all gators."

"Suddenly, out of the blackness, he seemed to spring into the circle of light." Marjorie took aim, shot. She was sure she had hit him, but Clayton saw the alligator slip away. "I'm not the gator hunter you thought I was," Marjorie told her companion. He replied, "For a one night gator hunter, you are pretty good."

"More than ever," he said later, "I liked and respected this amazing woman, who in such a short time fitted into the pattern of Florida backwoods living." He'd hoped Marjorie would write about their outing, but she told him, "No gator, no story."

THE TUSSLE BETWEEN the Ocala editor and the Cross Creek author continued, and it didn't go unnoticed elsewhere. In late March 1931, the tiny *High Springs Telegram* (located forty miles northwest of Cross Creek) reported that Marjorie had paid a personal visit to the *Ocala Evening Star* to convince "the powers that be that, in choosing seven characters bordering more or less on the 'derelict' that she did not mean them to represent typical Florida rural characters." Everything would be all right, the *Telegram* said, if Marjorie could convince *Scribner's* readers of the same thing.

The *Evening Star*'s response to the *High Springs Telegram*'s story about the Ocala paper's ongoing argument with Marjorie ran as long as its original editorial. "Kipling was right," it declared, "when he said 'the female of the species is more deadly than the male'—and that goes for the newspaper arguments, too. . . . We should like to sound a warning to all our brother editors to stick to their Southern Gentleman ethics and never get embroiled in debate with a lady writer." The editor admitted that he had read Marjorie's first long Florida story, "Jacob's Ladder," in *Scribner's* April issue. While he felt that Marjorie had "injected too many gnats, mosquitoes, reptiles, hurricanes and hardships into the local color," he found Marjorie in person to be "a charming little woman, so enamored of her adopted state and not really disagreeing with our point of view, that instead of criticising her 'Jacob's Ladder,' we recommend that all Floridians read it for the pleasure they will obtain, with reservations"—because, of course, "Jacob's Ladder" was not real but fiction.

Marjorie may not have liked being called "a charming little woman," or being forgiven her trespasses because of a love of Florida, but at least the editor had pointed local readers to her second Florida-based publication. "Jacob's Ladder" is a fully developed work, establishing Marjorie's Florida-inspired voice, her cosmic lens. It depicts a pair of poor young Crackers, based on the couple living in Marjorie's tenant house. On first meeting, Mart and Florry know, without speaking, that they are inevitably connected, as if part of a greater pattern. Soon afterward, in the midst of a hurricane, from out of nowhere, Mart appears to rescue Florry from her abusive father, "like a bird-dog guided by the scent." "I kin feel them things a-comin', a long ways," Florry says of the storm. "I could kind o' feel you comin'."

The couple leaves, stands before a parson, sets up house in the swamp, and as their fortunes wax and mostly wane, they endure a medley of hard livings common to poor whites in rural Florida. Mart labors at trapping, fishing, working an orange grove, moonshining. The pair moves from place to place, Florry setting up house in various borrowed shacks, a tenant home, the woods; Mart toiling for thoughtless or dishonest men who always cheat or betray him, forcing him to move on. Their plight is made all the more tenuous by extreme weather and the dangers of living in the wilds. Florry barely survives malaria, and their ill-nourished infant dies in its first year. A garden she manages to raise up is flooded by a storm. After the unnamed infant dies, she adopts pets she must leave behind with each move. In one scene, on a beautiful afternoon, she and Mart are rowing a tidal river to the gulf. It seems their luck is turning. As she sings "Jacob's Ladder," the couple relaxes, their burdens laid down—for a while.

"Jacob's Ladder" offers a closely observed catalog of Cracker domestic ways and speech. Early on, Mart prepares a turtle for cooking: "He drew out the long, leathery neck with a hooked wire and cut off the sharp-beaked head with his knife. He separated the neck and four thick legs deftly from the shell, trimmed off sections of the translucent border, flexible like thin gristle. The female was full of yellow fat and still yellower eggs, some of them encased in paper-white shells, ready for depositing in a hole in the sand."

"Coons and skunks is wild fer cooter eggs," Mart tells Florry. "You kin allus tell when it's fixin' to come a rain, for a cooter's got sense enough to lay jest aforehand, so's the rain'll wash out her tracks and fool the varmints."

Mart cooks the turtle, too. "He boned the pieces of pink and white meat, dipped them in meal and salt, and fried them in the black iron Dutch oven that was their only cooking utensil. The lid vibrated alarmingly and in a few moments he lifted it to show her the heart still beating in the bubbling grease and the muscles of the legs twitching spasmodically."

Florry, who has never cooked a turtle, says, "Dogged iffen I wants to eat anything you has to stand on the lid to keep it from poppin' out o' the pan."

The story—a novella, really—holds abundant, poetic depictions of natural phenomena, as essential to Marjorie's full voice as her ear for speech, eye for customs, and growing sensitivity to individual lives. Natural surroundings, the seasons they sustain, the cosmic web they represent, are rich, essential context for her characters. In "Jacob's Ladder," a single tree receives its due:

A magnolia sixty feet tall shaded the tenant house. It was covered from top to bottom with tall white candles that burst wide into dazzling glories, opening from the top down, like a Christmas tree slowly being lighted. The blossoming was leisurely. The great white blooms were above her head for weeks. Then the white petals began to drop down and turn russet on the ground. The yellow stamens fell. The huge green leaves, brown-faced, drifted down with a soft rattling on the roof. In summer, the white candles shone red. Tall red cones were thick with glistening seeds and the birds rustled in and out among the branches.

WHEN MARJORIE SUBMITTED "Jacob's Ladder" to *Scribner's Magazine* in 1930, both Dashiell and Maxwell Perkins read it. Perkins wrote to Marjorie, praising and tentatively accepting it, with three suggestions:

that she change the original title ("High Winds"), make the inventory of subsistence struggles subservient to her characters' development, and create a stronger ending in which Mart and Florry find a resting place rather than continued misery. Perkins also observed that Marjorie, as narrator, intruded too often, telling readers about characters where action and speech would suffice and, in fact, be stronger. In his soft, elegant manner, Perkins advised her to show, not tell. "If, after reading this letter, you feel inclined to reconsider the manuscript in light of these suggestions, we shall return it," he wrote. "It will be considered for the prize we offer, by the judges, but apart from that matter, we should like to arrange to publish it, but should greatly hope that you might think well of revising it for that purpose."

Marjorie accepted his advice and returned a revision. "The ending I have worked out does, I believe, make a rounder unit," she wrote. "You see, I began with my mind full of the power of this environment—and after all, from the human if not the cosmic point of view, the courage of these people is more important."

YET THE NORTH FLORIDA PRESS again failed to appreciate her. The Gainesville *News* wrote that "Jacob's Ladder" "purports to be a 'human document' based on the lives of two Florida Crackers." "We found it interesting enough to read to the end," the sour critic wrote, "but would be reluctant to admit that it is true to Cracker life, the Cracker dialect, or to Florida geography or climatic conditions. It is supposed to be 'typical.' But any story of Florida running along a period of two or three years and encountering two hurricanes and a snow within that period of time cannot be dignified as such, much as we would like to hand laurels to the lady." In fact, it is quite possible that north Florida could experience such extreme weather within a few years.

In south Florida, though, the urbane *Miami Herald* praised Marjorie's work and scolded its neighbors to the north. "Ocala, Marion county Fla. people are torn and almost bleeding. Floridians in counties adjoining are sympathetic and almost equally exercised. All of their affliction emanates from a few simple strokes of a writer's pen though some of the Floridians regard the strokes as stabs."

The *Herald* praised "Jacob's Ladder" as "splendid from a literary angle." The editorial's writer noted, "The characters are certainly not typical of all Floridians. Neither are Palm Beach winter residents." Rawlings understood her characters "with all the compassion of a woman's great heart."

"If we Florida 'crackers' do not like ourselves as reflected by the mirror of literature," the critic chided, "we must do something about it and produce more and better 'crackers.'"

LOCAL KERFUFFLES MATTERED LITTLE to Marjorie's prospects. For one thing, the $700 she had received for "Jacob's Ladder" enabled her to install a real bathroom in the Cross Creek farmhouse. More significantly, *Scribner's* announced that her story had brought a new writer to the literary scene. She was the "real find" of its recent novel competition. The finder, Maxwell Perkins, added Marjorie to a stable already occupied by protégés F. Scott Fitzgerald, Thomas Wolfe, and Ernest Hemingway. Thus began an extraordinary relationship between a writer and her editor, a professional alliance and a friendship, carried out mostly in seventeen years of correspondence: 698 letters, notes, and telegrams and a pile of well-marked manuscripts. Marjorie might have secluded herself in a dank pocket of the South, but by shining light on it, she had stepped onto a national stage.

Chapter Eight

South Moon Under

1931-33

IN FEBRUARY 1931, after accepting "Jacob's Ladder," Maxwell Perkins sent Marjorie an appreciation, closing with "Is there any chance that you will write a novel? If you do, you can depend upon a very eager and prompt consideration of it from us." Nearly two months later she replied, "I am vibrating with material like a hive of bees in swarm. It would take pages of necessarily vague ramblings to discuss it. At present I see four books very definitely. Two of them need several more years of note-taking." She described a plot that would come to drive her second novel, *Golden Apples*, set largely in and around orange groves during the Great Freeze of 1894–95. But the first novel would take place in the present-day Big Scrub, an area roughly equivalent to what is now the Ocala National Forest, bordered by the Ocklawaha and St. Johns Rivers—a sandy plateau supporting dense stands of tall, pencil-thin southern pines, surrounded by riverine swamp and hammock. "So far I have not come on the necessary thread of continuity," she wrote. "When it occurs to me, I think it will force me to drop whatever else I may be doing. Once I know where I am going, the book will almost write itself."

Max offered respect and support: "You would be by far the best judge, of course, and apparently you intend to be the judge, and to write when you come to that point where you feel the necessary confidence, and that compulsion which is the best indication that the book should be done." Receiving no answer, after a couple of months he posted a gentlemanly nudge: "I really ought not to trouble you with this enquiry because you would inform me when you are ready, but I'm very anxious to know if your plans for a novel, or other writing, have advanced since you last wrote. Could you send us a line?"

She did: a report on three stories in progress and "a dozen or so" sketches, plus preparations for her Big Scrub novel. She had befriended three families and had arranged to live in the Leonard Fiddia house-hold, which included "a boy as indigenous to the scrub as the deer, and his ninety-pound wisp of a white-haired mother, who ploughs, and last week with an axe cut a sapling and killed a rattlesnake in her field." Leonard, not a boy, but a young man of twenty-nine, ran moonshine, and insisted that Marjorie help him. "The federal agents have been very active lately," she told Max, "so don't be too surprised if your correspondent has the misfortune to be run in! If it should happen, please don't bail me out, because the jail-house would be a splendid place for quiet work!" Her novel had no story line yet, but she felt it would come once she was immersed in the Fiddias' world. When she returned to the Creek, it would be well-formed, and she would name a completion date. She recalled a writer friend who read for Houghton Mifflin and, realizing how many others wrote well, had decided that she could best contribute to literature by getting out of it. "I am not so high-minded," Marjorie told Max. "You have given me a fatal encouragement. I am like the old Cracker . . . who fiddled in ecstasy as long as a single soul would listen to him."

Meanwhile, she finished one of the stories, and when *Scribner's Magazine* turned it down, she offered it to the *Atlantic Monthly*. "Lord Bill of the Suwannee River" was based on research up the storied stream, where she had gathered tales about Bill Bell, a larger-than-life building foreman for the Atlantic Coast Line Railroad who became the town leader of Trenton, Florida. Marjorie had spent some time in the small town (population 706), west of Gainesville. Bell's widow had referred her to her husband's friends. "He was a man's man," she told Marjorie. "You will have to go to the men who knew him." In her cover letter to the *Atlantic*'s Ellery Sedgwick, Marjorie cited her recent Florida writings in *Scribner's* and described her submission: "The legendary quality of this character gives a fiction cast to the material—yet except for the changing of names, the story is true from beginning to end." She named her informants, both Crackers and high-ranking citizens. But Sedgwick responded with a terse rejection. "Dear Mrs. Rawlings: This is pleasant reading, but we think it is rather a pity that you haven't told a genuine story instead of piecing together these scraps of legend." Lord Bill went into a drawer.

IN AUGUST 1931, Marjorie moved in with the Fiddias for two and a half months. In early November, she wrote at length to Max from Cross Creek. "I have voluminous notes of the intimate type, for which the most prolific imagination is no substitute," she reported. She knew that the scrub people were "gentle, honest," and their living precarious. "But just how hand-to-mouth it is, surprised me. I was also astonished by the utter lack of bleakness or despair, in a group momentarily on the very edge of starvation and danger. Whatever else my story turns out to be, it will not be a gloomy, morose, 'novel of the soil.' I found a zestfulness in living, a humor, an alertness to beauty, quite unexpected, and of definite value to record, if I can 'get' it."

The scrub residents bothered no one, she said, living as well as they could on wasted land cleared of timber and animal habitat. They tended to settle along the occasional small lake with its attendant marsh or "prairie," or "along the river edges, where the natural hammock growth has been bitten into by settlers' clearings. It is a fringe of life, following the waterways," she explained. The deeply forested scrub was "a vast wall, keeping out the timid and the alien."

Moonshine was their only sure product, sold illegally to townspeople. 'Shining, Marjorie said, would be a part of her novel's background— "a part of the whole resistance of the scrub country to the civilizing process," as she saw it.

During her time with the Fiddias, Marjorie took part in illegal activities: stalked deer out of season at night, helped dynamite mullet from a boat, "kept the family in squirrels," shot a limpkin (a large, heron-like bird) and waded waist-deep through the swamp to retrieve it. Had a federal agent caught her, she might have gone to jail. When roasted, the bird was delicious. "With food scarce, these people kill, quite correctly,

I think, what they need," she wrote Max. "Incidentally, *only* what they need for food." Licensed hunters, she observed, killed much more than they would use.

Marjorie helped the Fiddias with household chores—washed quilts, minded the sweet potato patch. She hunted bear with family members and neighbors and sat around the campfire, listening. All the while, she took notes on the Fiddias' speech, offering Max examples. "Many expressions are very beautiful. The fish and deer, in fact most of the game, feed 'on the moon'—at moon-rise, moon-down, south-moon-over and south-moon-under. The people are conscious at all times of the position of the sun and moon and stars and wind. They *feel* the moon under the earth—south-moon-under."

By now Marjorie had secured a literary agent, Brandt & Brandt, to place work and negotiate contracts, and in December 1931, *Scribner's Magazine* published another Cracker story, "A Plumb Clare Conscience," about a moonshiner named Tim who outfoxes a federal agent. Tim's saga is told mostly in Cracker dialogue and, like all of Marjorie's Cracker tales, is sympathetic to the underdogs, who live by codes often opposed to the law and the privileged. To understand the distinctions, Marjorie had extended her research beyond Cross Creek and the Fiddias' property. She had studied the law, for one thing—fishing regulations, bag limits—and observed how it was carried out, or not, both in the backwoods and the courtroom.

In May, Max wrote again, gently inquiring about Marjorie's progress. "Circumstances" had taken a toll over the winter, she told him, but she would send a draft of her novel by the end of July. What had held her up, she didn't say. It could have been grove business—the Florida orange harvest might start as early as October and run through April, depending on the variety grown, and the industry was in a slump. But in an April letter to Ethel Beebe, Marjorie suggested ongoing problems with Chuck, who, with the help of Clifford Vinson, had gained access to the Greek sponge-fishing community at Tarpon Springs, on the Gulf Coast. Vinson had treated their families and knew Louis Pappas, owner of the popular Riverside Café, a restaurant and bar. Vinson took Chuck to the café, introduced him around, and with Pappas serving up plenty of lamb, Greek salad, and spiked orange pop for all, a party ensued. The next day, Chuck was on a sponge-fishing boat, gone with the fleet for six weeks. Afterward, he wrote an article with photographs and sent it to the *Atlantic Monthly*, which rejected it. When Marjorie discovered that Chuck hadn't attached a cover letter to introduce himself and his subject, she offered to write one for him. "I knew the manuscript had never gotten past the first reader," she told Ethel Beebe. The article was accepted for the April 1932 issue. In a diary of Cracker notes, Marjorie uncharacteristically jotted a personal remark: "Chuck sold a sponge story to the 'Boston Bastards.' Celebrated by letting loose a whole barnful of guineas and game chickens." But when the piece appeared with a biographical note Chuck didn't like, he blew up at Marjorie, as if it were her fault.

"Chuck's disposition is still rotten, but he has lots of room to bellow in, and he looks, blissfully, like a beachcomber most of the time," Marjorie explained to Ethel. Chuck and a veterinarian, she said, were giving their female pointer aphrodisiac pills, to hurry a litter along. "I live in constant terror that Chuck will slip one in my coffee—or worse still, in his own!

"However, the ribald Chuck has gone high-brow on me, and will have to take in his horns," she wrote, referring to the *Atlantic* story. "He will have to stop beating me now. You don't mind it from a journalist or an orange grower, but damned if a woman feels like taking it from a contributor to The Atlantic!"

AT LEAST BOTH WRITERS were making progress. The *Saturday Evening Post* contacted Chuck for more sponge fishing coverage. In May 1932, *Scribner's Magazine* published Marjorie's "A Crop of Beans," a story based on an experience at Cross Creek. Marjorie, Chuck, and a hired black family "covered five acres of young bean plants with dirt and brought them through a freeze, and for $9 a hamper for the first picking," she wrote Ethel. "Everything in the bean story is true. The young woman in the story died this winter; flu, poverty, miscarriage."

Also that spring, Marjorie's agent sold "Gal Young Un," a fifteen-thousand-word story *Scribner's* had turned down, to *Harpers Magazine*. It ran in two parts, June and July. Its protagonist is Matt, a lonely, middle-aged widow living by herself deep in the woods, still grieving her husband, fifteen years gone. She is conned into marriage by Trax, a slick young opportunist who's heard she is rich. With Matt's resources in property and cash, he builds a moonshine still and starts a business, even turning Matt's great room into a roadhouse. For some time, Matt remains in a fog of infatuation, doing his bidding, overlooking Trax's patronizing demands and lack of affection. But when her husband disappears for days and weeks at a time, finally bringing a giggling young conquest named Elly into the house and expecting Matt to accept her, her fog lifts, and she achieves revenge, first depriving Elly of food, then, in a satisfying sweep, destroying Trax's still, setting fire to his shiny new automobile, threatening him with a shotgun, and ordering Trax and Elly to leave. Trax takes to the road, but Elly, homeless, remains huddled at the edge of the property, not knowing where to go. Hearing the girl's whimpers, and reflecting on the situation—Trax's cruelty to the naïve girl, and her own—Matt takes her in.

Scribner's had turned down the story as "too stridently feminist," an odd call, even for the times. Its setting, the Florida backwoods, and its chief dramatic drive, Matt's emotional trajectory, are set down unhurriedly, and together support a gripping narrative. The story also recalls Marjorie's less literary pursuits: two features for Hearst, plus a wire story that ran in the *Rochester Evening Journal* the week after she resigned her position. In the first of her features, a widow secluded in a weather-beaten house surrounded by trees, grieving her fiancé ten or fifteen years dead, is inexplicably murdered. In the second, a sixteen-year-old girl from a small town runs away to the big city of Rochester, takes up with a married man, and keeps house for him, believing he will seek a divorce and marry her, even as he goes out with other women. Eventually the pair lands in jail and the man is convicted of stealing a car. In the wire story, a woman whose estranged husband has impregnated his lover takes in the woman and the resulting child, saying it is "nothing more than any woman acquaintance would do. I sympathized with her."

In fact, Marjorie considered "Gal Young Un" a bit of a potboiler.

IN JULY, Max prompted Marjorie again about the novel. She replied that she had crossed the finish line, but the manuscript required more editing. The process on this book would foretell a pattern for those that followed it. Form was her biggest challenge here. She had written a series of episodes covering forty-five years and wasn't sure if the whole thing hung together. Two other publishers (Bobbs-Merrill and Harper & Brothers) had shown interest in it, but she preferred to "bring it up to meet your high critical standards than to have it brought out at once in an imperfect form."

Two weeks later, having sent the manuscript, she sailed to New York to meet Chuck, who had been covering yachting events on Lake Ontario, and offered to visit Perkins in New York. He had read the novel, and the two discussed it. Afterward, he wrote a remarkably long, thoughtful follow-up letter detailing their talk. "My suggestions come only from the fact that the material is presented rather from the point of view of a social chronicle than from that of a novel," he wrote. "To form a novel these episodes should be woven together by fictional devices, which arouse expectation in the reader as to the outcome of certain complications which have arisen between the principal characters and enforce a continuity of interest." There followed suggestions, chapter by chapter, most having to do with structure and pacing. He recommended some substantial cuts, as well as subtle changes in viewpoint. Marjorie still tended to impede narrative flow by interpolating her own comments or otherwise taking the reader out of the story—habits carried over from journalistic reporting and the habits of popular fiction. But, Max assured her, "The very ending of the book is splendid."

"Your diagnosis and prescription are so specific," Marjorie replied, "that I think between us we can have the patient on his feet in no great while. You have a truly amazing genius for taking the product of another's imagination in the hollow of your hand. It is the height, I suppose, of critical sympathy and understanding."

She admitted, "The direct narrative form throughout is so patently required—and through so much of the book I seem perversely to have avoided it. Looking back to my earliest conception of the book, I do not believe that I ever planned it as a true novel, but, as you express it, 'a social chronicle.'" She had been afraid of two things: writing too long a narrative and not being detached enough. She would finish revisions, she promised, by the end of October. "I probably work better under pressure," she said. "The bad part of the book is the part I dawdled over."

In early October, she thanked Max for a copy of Hemingway's *Death in the Afternoon*: "One of those books on which you can see the mark of an inner compulsion in the writer," she commented. Chuck had read it, too, and the couple fought over it. He thought the book a depraved work, and in a dialogue Marjorie composed for Max, Chuck called Marjorie, for defending Hemingway's artistry, "a vulgar woman with an obscene tongue, without fineness of taste or perception." To Chuck, who she described as "the most offensive sort of Anglophile," she replied, "I am not decadent. I am only detached. Life is not to me the intensely personal matter that it is to such people as you, with your fixed ideas. I accept all of life as an abstract phenomenon, and nothing in it shocks me nor too greatly concerns me. I am interested in ideas as ideas, in facts as facts, in emotions as emotions. I really have the advantage of you. I too had conceived of bull-fighting as cruel and vicious, but Hemingway passes on to me a terrific emotion that he had felt; reveals a beauty he has seen." She recalled her years as a journalist, when she was enamored of wrestling matches. "If architecture is frozen music, then good wrestling and good bull-fighting are rhythmic sculpture," she wrote. "Add to the beauty of line . . . a certain abstraction of death, as Hemingway writes of it—and I can share with him an overpowering cosmic excitement."

Their argument "shook the walls of the Rawlings shack," Marjorie confided. "Blows were dealt that will be perhaps be too long remembered."

In early November, she announced that the manuscript would be ready in about two weeks. "If you like the book, I shall drink a quart of Bacardi in celebration," she wrote Max. "If you don't like it, I shall drink a quart of Bacardi." She was doing her own copying. Good typists were scarce.

Finally, she mailed the pages. "By the way, this is my only copy of the new form," she told Max. If he decided to put out the book, "I must have three or four weeks before the manuscript goes to the printer's hands." Max wired to say that he would return all but the first chapter. He was saving it for dummies (a mock-up of the book). He would market the book in January, with publication soon after. Marjorie was both surprised and nervous, proposing that she send her final revision "day by day as I get it done."

Still, she invited feedback. "I am anxious to know just how the revision strikes you. Now that it is done, I realize that it is not the book I wanted to write—not the picture I wanted to give. Very possibly it is a better book—probably more readable—but somehow or other the emotion I intended to convey has escaped me. Probably it is always so with any writer except a true genius. The thing that sweeps across you, clamoring for expression, is probably always more powerful than the flabby words and phrases you begin to trot out about it."

In the heat of revising, she wrote again, no doubt after a drink or two. "The more I think about it, the more put-out I am at you. . . . I don't give a damn about Scribner's wanting to hurry to get the book published—I wanted it as good as possible—and you didn't even read it."

"You have one swell guarantee of my hurrying with my editing—hunting season opens November 20th."

Max assured her that she could still make changes when the book was in galleys and mentioned that they had never discussed contractual terms, offering 10 percent on the first five thousand copies, 15 percent on the rest. She accepted them, then lobbed a new wrench into the mix. Chuck had read some of her chapters, thrown down the manuscript, and insisted that she remove all of the profanity. If she would do this, her husband said, the book could be marketed to boys. She blew up at him, was "soothed with copious draughts of native rye," and came to see what he meant. Maybe Chuck's idea was a good one. Maybe *South Moon Under*—as the novel was titled, suggesting the feel of the moon beneath the earth—could be Florida's *Huckleberry Finn* or *Treasure Island*.

She continued to muse: "It sounds like an affectation to say that I don't particularly care whether or not the book sells. I just happen to mean it. I should rather have it considered good by people of discernment, than popular." But she was open to changes that might broaden the appeal if the book's integrity stood.

She asked Max what he thought about certain coarse words and phrases, and begged him to figure out the whole thing. But she wanted honesty. "Don't let me emasculate either character or story or a very problematical end," she implored. "Don't let me turn a rough woodsman into a Boy Scout!"

More rapid exchanges followed. A slightly better contract was offered. The profanity question was addressed. Max felt that nothing needed to be changed but said they'd consider these issues again when they had the proofs. On November 23, Chuck wrote to Perkins that Marjorie had fallen ill; he enclosed the rest of her manuscript, four of the chapters being "in a crude state." On December 1, Max began sending galleys of chapters, in batches. The same day, Chuck wrote Perkins to say that Marjorie had double malaria but was beginning to recover. Perkins replied:

I don't want to tell Mrs. Rawlings too much about the book because publication is always a speculation, and in these times everything is against success. But if it can be between you and me, I should like to say that I find it a very remarkable piece of work. It is most uncommon to find a book which is good through and through. You find people who can do excellent dialogue, or excellent description, or have a sense of character, or any one or two, or three, of the half dozen requirements of a truly fine thing. But this book is good in all those respects."

That same day, Marjorie wrote to Perkins from bed, her portable typewriter on a tray. On profanity, she said, "I think we shall end by making substitutions for the many 'sons of bitches,' otherwise not doing much." The rest of the month saw another flurry of last-minute revisions—details he caught, second thoughts of hers. Marjorie was still not well. "I seem to do everything I do, with a perfectly pointless intensity," she wrote, "and the malaria is a case in point." She cited side effects of "absurd quantities of quinine," including dizziness, nervousness, and confusion. "It does outlandish things to one's nerves and balance—both physical and mental."

With Christmas 1932 came a pause, while Max hunted in Arkansas with Hemingway, and Marjorie and Chuck vacationed at the Vinsons' hunting lodge. In a note to her brother, Arthur, now based in Seattle, Marjorie described the liquid courses of what was probably a New Year's feast: "Southern egg-nog all morning. Martinis before dinner. Sparkling Burgundy with the turkey. Yellow Chartreuse for a liqueur. Then, later, champagne, Chauvet 1920—and Dr. Vinson apologized for the vintage! That's all right I says, anybody used to getting rosy on corn liquor can manage very nicely on 1920 Chauvet." Arthur, familiar with his sister's increasing love of liquor, scolded her for mistreating herself. "Can it be that [so much] success has gone to your head that you feel entitled to cavort about the swamps down there lapping up in dog-like fashion all of the rotten likker you see stagnating in every pool? . . . Get on the wagon and stay on."

By mid-January 1933, *South Moon Under* had been named the Book-of-the-Month Club's March selection—a $4,000 windfall for Marjorie, who saw in it a new cypress shingle roof. Even the editor of the *Ocala*

Banner had requested an advance copy. It seemed there was nothing left for Marjorie to do but hold her first book in her hands. But on January 26, Max sent her a telegram:

LENGTH OF ALLIGATOR ON PAGE 184 QUESTIONED
AS TOO GREAT STOP IS THIRTY AN ERROR FOR THIRTEEN
QUESTION CAN CORRECT

Two days later, she replied:

THIRTY INTENTIONAL BUT MAKE IT TWENTY
TO AVOID QUESTIONING

At the end of February, *South Moon Under* was released to glowing reviews. Faber and Faber bought the English rights to the book and asked to option Marjorie's next three novels. The critics were "more generous than I had expected," Marjorie wrote to Max, "but they sadden me. I feel quite cheap, quite the Judas, at having apparently delivered the Cracker into the hands of the Philistines."

SOUTH MOON UNDER emerged directly from Marjorie's experiences with the Fiddias and revolves around several generations of a family and its precarious life in the Big Scrub, dwelling first on old man Lantry, who dotes on his youngest daughter, Piety. (Incidentally, Piety is the only "real" name Marjorie used in the novel. Piety Fiddia was Leonard's mother.) The girl, something of a tomboy, enjoys assisting her father with the crops and other outdoor chores while her sister, Martha, helps their mother keep house. Lantry is haunted by a secret, which, at the end of his life, he finally reveals to Piety: he had come to the Big Scrub from another southern state because he'd killed a man—a "revenooer"—and feared being caught. Though indifferent to marriage, Piety takes a local husband and bears a son, Lant, who inherits some of his grandfather's looks and all of a nameless fear. Piety loses her husband to a logging accident, and as the story of her backwoods life, and Lant's, progresses, she grows into widowhood and wise old age, reflecting an acceptance that marked many of Marjorie's Cracker characters: "But if the road had been hard, it was also pleasant. If a living was uncertain, and the sustaining of breath precarious, why, existence took on an added value and a greater sweetness. The tissues of life were food and danger. These were the warp and woof, and all else was an incidental pattern, picked out with vari-coloured wools. Love and lust, hate and friendship, grief and frolicking, even birthing and dying, were thin grey and scarlet threads across the sun-browned, thick and sturdy stuff that was life itself."

Lant, who has a natural affinity for the scrub's land and water, can't stand more than two years of school and makes a living in a variety of Cracker ways, living on the edge, with dignity. He falls for a privileged family's delicate daughter, learning a hard lesson about the region's caste system, and loses a much better match he grew up with to his untrustworthy cousin Cleve. He deals with Arkansas and Alabama outsiders, who try to change the local customs. Finally, he manifests his nameless fear. Like his grandfather, Lant, too, is compelled to kill a man—Cleve, who has betrayed him—and, pondering a flock of ducks in flight, owls hooting in the dark night, the position of the moon, he experiences a mysterious revelation: "Perhaps all men were moved against their will. A man ordered his life, and then an obscurity of circumstance sent him down a road that was not of his own desire or choosing. Something beyond a man's immediate choice and will reached through the earth and stirred him. He did not see how any man might escape it."

Mississippi-born critic Herschel Brickell offered a lavish appreciation of the novel in the *New York Herald Tribune*, criticizing only the above passage as "thoughts that are the author's," not Lant's. "It seems a little surprising that an editorial pencil did not remove this small bit of evidence that Miss Rawlings is not already a novelist of experience and reputation," he complained faintly, as if obligated to insert a mite of discord, and implying that a Cracker couldn't think deeply. Nevertheless, he concluded that "the book is rich in the humor of the natural man, seasoned with the salt of earthy speech, and touched many times with beauty, the beauty of a strange country which the author evidently knows with the utmost intimacy.... Those who know what it is to love the earth and the people who live near it will find in it a profound satisfaction."

The *New York Times* book critic Percy Hutchison sounded the same chords, praising *South Moon Under* for introducing "a people and a setting new to literary fiction," without forcing dramatic notes. Yet the novel held the reader and was, "in every true sense of the word, dramatic. The answer is in the cunning weave of the chronicle to the pattern of life set by the scrub."

South Moon Under, Hutchison wrote, was "both a living document and a book of which one must say that it is distinguished art."

Chapter Nine

Coming Apart

1933-34

W ITH *SOUTH MOON UNDER* COMPLETED, Marjorie relaxed into a comfortable domestic routine. She replanted her vegetable garden, and in early spring, she harvested lettuce, Chinese cabbage, broccoli, parsley, beets, and collard greens. She caught up on letter writing—she would always be a prolific correspondent—including notes to old Wisconsin friends like Bee Humiston McNeil, who now lived in southern California, writing and producing children's plays. *South Moon Under* was selling well at the Hollywood Bookstore, Bee reported, adding, "What a man's man you have become, running around shooting off guns!"

Regional reaction to the novel was enthusiastic. Jacksonville librarian and promoter of literary culture Carl Bohnenberger proclaimed in the *Florida Times-Union*, "Mrs. Rawlings has reproduced the voice of the scrub lands. The sense of living is at every turn and the appeal of common humanity is in every line. . . . Her reproduction of their [the Crackers'] language is uncannily accurate. All of their rites and rituals have passed before our eyes. Their unsuspected beliefs and codes are known to her." He was glad the book had been written before the Cracker culture had disappeared.

A letter arrived from Edith Pope, a twenty-eight-year-old novelist from a prominent St. Augustine family whose husband, Verle, a real estate agent and rising politician, had called on Marjorie. Edith praised *South Moon Under* and invited Marjorie to lunch. Edith had hoped someone would write a good book about the Crackers but thought "a Cracker couldn't do it, nor any Floridian." Only a person "to whom the expressions and ways were new and arresting" might manage it. In time, Marjorie and Edith became close friends. This new connection with the Popes and others in Florida's "Oldest City," just south of Jacksonville and notable for its seventeenth-century fort, Spanish Renaissance Revival architecture, and lavishly appointed hotels, marked the start of a social and professional life beyond the Creek—indeed, beyond Florida. In five years, Marjorie had disappeared into an unknown southern backwater, written about it, and emerged a celebrated author.

Still, sales in north-central Florida were dismal. All of Ocala, Marjorie reported, was "standing in line" to read the public library's two copies. "Everyone tells me with great pride, 'I've got my name on the list to read your book. I can hardly wait,'" Marjorie wrote Max. She accepted such tributes, although privately she wanted to exclaim, "Do you think I'm a damn orchid, that I can live on air?"

Sales were steady in large cities, but overall, the book business was not healthy. Neither was the season's orange harvest. Marjorie worried about overdue bills and her rickety car, and asked Max for an advance on her slow-moving Book-of-the-Month Club check. She wondered if *South Moon Under*'s release could have been timed more advantageously, and fretted about readers' tendency to buy the book of the moment, ignoring better books they'd missed a year or more before. The U.S. economy was still on the skids. On March 3, shortly after her novel's debut and on the eve of President Franklin Roosevelt's inauguration, Marjorie received a tip that twenty-six Florida banks would fold on Monday, March 5. It might have been a rumor, but she drove to her Ocala bank and pulled out a chunk of cash, just in case. As it turned out, the new president announced a bank holiday, lasting through March 9, when Congress passed the Emergency Banking Act, restoring some confidence. The Depression continued, and it's fair to say Marjorie's writing, in tandem with the grove, ultimately kept her afloat.

Chuck continued his trips away from the Creek, investigating and writing about water events. He had not taken his wife's success well. There was a "show-down" in March, after *South Moon Under* was released. As the possibility of divorce hung heavy in the air, Marjorie grew deeply depressed and agreed to a getaway trip with Dessie Smith Vinson down the St. Johns River.

With an eighteen-foot rowboat outfitted with two outboard motors and camping supplies, the women put in beyond the headwaters, near Fort Christmas, where the river was "a blue smear through the marsh," Marjorie recalled in her account. "It sprawled to the four points of the compass; flat; interminable; meaningless." Marjorie navigated with a compass, a river chart, and a book of pilot rules, while Dessie manned the boat. Over the several days it took to reach the Ocklawaha and the Creek, they got confused or completely lost several times, as the changeable St. Johns leaned, curved, spread, and contracted, as it will, seasonally or not—plus, the women's map was thirty years old. At one point, Marjorie noted, "We were in a labyrinth. The stretch of open water was merely the fluid heart of a maze." The women finally came to rely on free-floating beds of water hyacinths. When disoriented, they shut off the boat's motor and studied the hyacinths "until we caught, in one direction, a swifter pulsing, as though we put our hands closer and closer to the river's heart." Dessie recalled that the hyacinths were blown by the wind; she, instead, would kick a little dirt or trash out of the boat, watch it go under, and follow the current carrying it away. Hers was a less poetic, but more accurate, compass.

In the evenings, the women made camp on banks and sandbars, enduring bloodthirsty mosquitoes and the threat of snakes. Dessie, who wore a leather belt with a bowie knife and revolver, caught or shot dinner. One morning, she bagged a duck for breakfast with her .22. Marjorie took the domestic role, having packed ham, bacon, canned goods, and ingredients for bread and biscuits. She cooked meals in a Dutch oven over a fire, a method perfected at the Creek—the year before, she had published an article about Dutch oven cookery in *Sunrise*, a Florida promotional magazine. One night, she discovered that she'd even brought ingredients for tartar sauce—a luxury. When their boat took on water, the women dragged it to shore and caulked two seams with fabric strips torn from a shirt.

Marjorie and Dessie had the river mostly to themselves, though it seemed every time they shucked their clothes to skinny-dip, a fisherman's skiff hove into view. They ran into various characters, from a surly hut squatter to a yacht captain. Along the river, word had spread that two women were making their way north. A group of fishermen admitted they'd been watching for them.

According to Dessie, Marjorie made no notes on the trip—she was too busy. But she chronicled it in "Hyacinth Drift," published in the September 1933 issue of *Scribner's Magazine*. The piece opens, "Once I lost touch with the Creek. I had had hardships that seemed to me more than one could bear alone. I loved the Creek, I loved the grove, I loved the shabby farmhouse. Suddenly they were nothing." At the end of the trip, when she and Dessie finally turned up the Ocklawaha, she panicked: "I was afraid once more of all the circumstances of living.

"But," she continued, "when the dry ground was under us, the world no longer fluid, I found a forgotten loveliness in all the things that have nothing to do with men. Beauty is pervasive, and fills, like perfume, more than the object that contains it. Because I had known intimately a river, the earth pulsed under me. The Creek was home.

"I knew, for a moment, that the only nightmare is the masochistic human mind."

Dessie believed that on that trip, Marjorie decided that she would divorce Chuck.

Just not yet.

MARJORIE ENJOYED HER CELEBRITY, though mostly at a distance, which suited her. She had turned down Max's invitation to a Friends of the Princeton Library dinner in New York, even though writers like Willa Cather would attend. ("I can't say I'm sorry," she replied. "I can well imagine that, as you say, the dinner will be better than most such, but even so, can you imagine anything more revolting than a large room crawling with authors!") The *New York Herald Tribune* published a list of six books she'd read in the past year and would recommend. "I've been well marooned away from new books for five years," she wrote for the column. "In the past year I have happened to read and enjoy these." They were Hemingway's *Death in the Afternoon;* Willa Cather's *Shadows on the Rock;* James Gould Cozzens's novel *The Last Adam,* about a New England country doctor and his town's typhoid epidemic; the

T. E. Shaw translation of Homer's *Odyssey*; William Bartram's *Travels Through North and South Carolina, Georgia, East and West Florida*; and *Flight into Darkness*, a novella by Arthur Schnitzler that depicts the gradual onset of madness. But Marjorie could no longer claim to be isolated from the publishing world. As soon as Max Perkins had taken her under his wing, and to the end of his life, he regularly sent new books to Marjorie, whether or not Scribner's published them.

The same month, Chuck was back at Tarpon Springs, having rented a dilapidated place to work by himself; he had hired a local woman to cook and clean. Brandt & Brandt, also his agent, had sent encouraging suggestions for a story he'd submitted. Chuck was happy and loved his surroundings. He, too, had navigated intricate waters. "My most fun has been coming home at night down the very complicated Anclote Channel," he wrote. "There has been no moon but I have seen islands as big as Australia loom up over my bow—appear right under the cutwater and the next day discover them to be about as big as my boat house. Getting out of the main bayou is a thrill. It curves and then splits into three channels. You take the middle one and watch for red lights on a bridge."

Chuck indicated that the Tarpon Springs rental had been conceived as a solution to their problems. "If you are all right then it is going to be a good idea. I can feel myself growing into a near normal damn fool again and I can see no reason why we have to tear our lives all to pieces. I certainly realize now that it would not be the brave thing I thought it was a week ago. I also realize we must not be all tied up in an irritated knot again. We could not help being satiated with each other. I am getting unsatiated and the thought of seeing you is good. Can you come down next week, C."

FROM HIS NEW HOME IN ALASKA, Arthur Kinnan had sensed his sister's marriage faltering and sent her a long letter of support and advice. There are only two sorts of men, he said, and it can't be helped—it's in their blood. Both sorts want to be king of their castle. "The first is a 'kindly' king, the second is a 'weakling' king, but all kings nevertheless," he wrote. The kindly sort were "strong, tolerant, brave, courageous, decent and kind," like their father. The weaklings were cowards, bullies, and cheats, only appearing to be powerful. A weakling "wouldn't dare abuse a kindly king and he seldom does. In their presence he masquerades as one of them—and usually is never found out." Arthur thought Chuck fell into the latter group.

In marrying Marjorie, a woman who didn't need her husband's provision or protection, Chuck's domain was encroached upon, Arthur explained. "Women, I don't believe, question their positions as attendants to their kings. As you yourself stated, your desire was first to be the wife, next the writer. In your case, Marjorie, you have done nothing to interfere with Chuck. Your success, which he purported before your marriage to extol, has no more bearing on your matrimonial relationship than were you an expert horsewoman, swimmer, or golfer. He's just like millions of other men—kings—and can't stand this subject casting a shadow against his brilliance. It is perfectly understandable and natural for him to resent your supplying the sustenance of life for both of you."

And yet, Arthur felt, even if Marjorie had stopped writing to tend house full-time, Chuck would criticize her for not living up to her potential. Arthur hoped she'd jump clear, not worry about what anyone thought, and "don't be a softy in the payoff. Take and keep everything—everything that is yours, everything to which you hold the merest semblance of title. You've carried the load, paid the freight, now dump it and salvage every bag of oats." Engage competent counsel, he added. Lean on true friends. And "for heavens sake, Marjorie, pour out your worries to your old good for nothing brother . . . I'll worry my head off unless you keep me posted."

BY THE SUMMER OF 1933, Chuck and Marjorie had agreed to divorce. He would strike out on his own, while she remained at the Creek. J. T. Glisson, the neighbor boy Marjorie had befriended, remembered how Chuck publicly handled his departure from the community. The couple visited the Glisson house—"I'd never seen them walking together"—and Chuck shook hands with J.T.'s father, saying he had come to say good-bye. "Marjorie and I are too high-strung to live together," he told Tom and Pearlee Glisson. "I also wanted to ask you, please don't let my leaving affect the wonderful relationship you and your family have with Marjorie." The Island Grove depot agent reported that the couple came to the station, shared a last kiss, and parted.

"All we knew was he caught the southbound train," Glisson said. "Most people leaving here are going back north."

DESPITE HER TUMULTUOUS PERSONAL LIFE, Marjorie had begun planning her second novel while *South Moon Under* was in galleys. She had dismissed much of the public praise for her first book. "Any good journalist, able to get the material, could have made a readable book out of the scrub stuff," she told Max. The next book would have to meet higher standards, and the main character would not be a Cracker; instead, she wanted to write about a cultured outsider who attempts rural life. Marjorie had thought about this on the St. Johns trip, and she was concerned that part of the new book might become too "raw and disgusting." "I am so weary of the Faulkner school of filth," she confided. Yet her main character, an Englishman sent to Florida to run an orange grove, would have to behave badly among his guileless neighbors before attempting to redeem himself. Marjorie planned to spend August and much of September in England, researching a location for her Englishman's original home. She didn't want an aristocrat. Upper middle class, rather scholarly, would do. The novel's time period would cover the peak of Florida's orange industry before the Great Freeze of 1894–95. Marjorie had tracked down a few elderly Englishmen and Englishwomen in Florida to interview; one of them had sent to England for diaries of the period. Carl Bohnenberger, who had favorably reviewed *South Moon Under* and worked as an assistant librarian at the Jacksonville Public Library, offered to help.

In late July 1933, Marjorie set sail for England from New York, but not before meeting with Max, who had suggested she write a book about a child in the Big Scrub. "It would be designed for what we have to call younger readers," he said. He recalled Chuck's comment from the previous November, that parts of *South Moon Under* would be especially attractive to boys, like *Huckleberry Finn*. He didn't want to interfere with her new novel; he was just planting a seed. "When one plans a thing of that kind, the mind works on it, even if unconsciously," he noted.

Marjorie spent about six weeks in England, touring about in a rented automobile, staying in country inns. To an old Wisconsin beau who had sent a note congratulating her on *South Moon Under*, she wrote that the

English people were agreeable enough: "If you sit quietly at table and don't speak and don't spill things, all of a sudden someone passes you the toast and accepts you."

But there was more on her mind than observing the English. As she sailed back home, she was moved to write a long letter to her friend and neighbor Zelma Cason, the census-taker who had introduced her around Alachua County three years earlier and was known for a "special brand of profanity." Apparently, the two women had quarreled, or come to grudges, before the trip. The rift might have begun as early as 1931, when, according to Zelma, Marjorie had said to Zelma's family, "some man should take me down across his knees and give me a good spanking for my little red flannel tongue." In Marjorie's account, Zelma had grown jealous of her friendships with Dessie Smith and Fred Tomkins, a fishing buddy, insisting she break off with both. At this moment Marjorie, possibly depressed by her divorce, wanted to patch things up, but not without demonstrating she might be right about the situation. She wrote: "My dear foolish Zelma, the thought of coming back to another long grind of hard work with you refusing to be a friend, is very painful to me. Doesn't it strike you as rather a useless state of affairs?

"Your 'vicious little tongue,' for which you 'need to be spanked' is your worst—your *only*—enemy. Those of us who have loved you and enjoyed you, have done so in spite of your habit of saying cruel and unkind things about people. The world is far too hard and unhappy a place for any of us to be unkind to one another, in speech or deed, and I only hope you will take this letter as an expression of my friendship and affection for you, an interest in your own good, instead of considering it an unwarranted attack."

How Zelma responded is unknown, but their story did not end with Marjorie's letter. Zelma's judgmental streak, as described by Tom Glisson, continued to rule, and as a community insider, he said, she had the power to manipulate a reputation, including one of an individual not "from here."

After her trip to England, Marjorie celebrated another publication in the *Saturday Evening Post*. "Alligators," written in first-person Cracker dialect, is an assembly of tales about the "pebble-hided knockers," courtesy of her neighbor Fred Tompkins. The piece is signed "Marjorie Kinnan Rawlings and Fred Tompkins," and when payment for the story arrived, Marjorie tried to share it with Fred, whose wife refused it—there was a difference between telling a tale and writing it, she said.

The British edition of *South Moon Under* appeared in October, and the London *Times Literary Supplement* pointed out the book's cosmic absorption, gratifying Marjorie. But she was still depressed and couldn't work. Her divorce would soon be final, and she struggled with the new novel's plot—both she and Max had feared it would be too melodramatic. Still, another story inspired by Tompkins found its home. In October, *Scribner's Magazine* published "Benny and the Bird Dogs," the first of several comic tales narrated by the fictitious Cracker woman Quincey Dover, whose speech is punctuated with expressions like "He gets excited the way fat men do, and he swelled up like a spreading adder" and "She has a disposition, by nature, as sweet as new cane syrup. When she settled down for a lifetime's quarreling with him, it was for the same reason syrup sours—the heat had just been put to her too long." The story's hero tricks an outsider by selling him dogs that have been trained to escape and run back home. Marjorie admitted that Dora was her alter ego, and once wrote to Max, "My friends call me 'Dora Rolley' a great deal of the time, especially for the half of my schizophrenic personality that doesn't behave as well as the other half."

Now she told Max she was considering putting the novel, tentatively titled "Hamaca" (Spanish for "hammock"), on hold and writing the boy's book instead. "I happen to be in a distressed mental condition, and while I don't think personal happiness or unhappiness makes a scrap of difference in writing, it might be just as well to have my thinking a bit clearer for so complicated a piece of work as my Englishman's psychology."

In mid-month, she went to stay with Cal Long and his wife. Cal, a hunter and moonshiner, was the area's longtime hooch supplier, known for a clean brew out of spring-fed water running into the Ocklawaha. He screened his containers to keep squirrels from falling in, and he delivered his 'shine in new ten-gallon white oak kegs that had been charred inside. His customers, Marjorie included, aged it for about six months, then siphoned it into smaller kegs or bottles. Now he was growing old, and Marjorie intended to stay as long as necessary to draw out his stories. Possibly, time in the scrub would help generate the boy's book. Cal's place was "in the very core of the scrub," she told Max, "where he has lived since 1872—falling into decay under the exquisite mantle of flowering vines. They are hard put to it to make a living, principally because the deer and foxes eat their crops almost faster than they can raise them." The Longs' home stood on Pat's Island, a spot of piney woods within the Ocala National Forest, which had been created in 1908, nearly thirty years after Cal's house went up. Killing game within its borders was against the law now.

Cal, another seasoned storyteller, offered Marjorie a lot of material, but his tales took time to unwind. After a week's stay, Marjorie reported to Max that she intended to return, asked how old the boy in the boy's book should be, and wondered if he could send five hundred dollars to her bank—she'd run out of money. For the next month, she was engrossed in the project, collecting more stories from Cal, including the tale of a pet deer he'd had as a boy. When the deer grew big enough to clear fences and disturb crops, Cal's father demanded that he shoot it. He did, and the sad memory of it had stuck.

Throughout the month, Max and Marjorie continued corresponding about the boy's book, as if it were already being written. They discussed a possible illustrator for it. Yet the story had yet to be conceived. How old should the boy be, Marjorie continued to ask. Was the book for a juvenile audience or an adult one? She couldn't write it as an adult novel, she asserted. It would have to be for juveniles, but not written down to a particular age. Maybe she would use a pseudonym, or at least sign it M. Kinnan Rawlings, so boys wouldn't be put off by a woman author. On it went, until late October, when Max quietly cut to the chase. The age of the boy didn't matter, he wrote: "The truth is the best part of a man is a boy. It is the subject matter that counts, and the fact that the hero is a boy." The sales department would want a novel, he cautioned. "They want to turn everything into a novel. They would have turned the New Testament into a novel if it had come to us for publication. . . . The thing for you to do is write it as you feel it and want it, without regard to anybody at all."

Just then, Marjorie learned that she—and "Gal Young Un"—had won the O. Henry Memorial Award for the best short story of 1932. (Years later, she told interviewers that the $500 arrived when she was down to a box of Uneeda biscuits and a can of tomato soup—surely an exaggeration, since *South Moon Under* was doing so well.) She confided to Max that it felt "like being handed a medal for committing murder" and feared she'd have to go to New York to collect the award. Marjory Stoneman Douglas had told her about winning second place one year and being obliged to go up to accept it and make a speech on the art of the short story. She wound up spending nearly all of the $250 prize money on travel expenses, she said, and had "never felt quite so imbecilic in her life." For herself, Marjorie felt that prizes had little to do with merit. "The moment arrives when material things go astonishingly right for awhile—then, as astonishingly and unreasonably, they go wrong." The trick was to avoid thinking anything would stay the same.

On November 10, 1933, five years after Marjorie and Chuck Rawlings moved to Florida, their union was legally over. He received $2,000, representing his interest in their Rochester house. That night, supportive friends from Ocala drove to Cross Creek, bringing along the new manager of the Marion Hotel, Norton Sanford Baskin, an agreeable, gregarious man five years Marjorie's junior. A native of Union Springs, Alabama, and one of six children, he had graduated from his county high school, and though he hadn't attended college, he enjoyed reading and knew many of the classics. As Norton later recalled, he had recently overseen a luncheon for the St. Agnes Guild of the Episcopal Church. The event had been reported in the paper.

Marjorie greeted him enthusiastically. "I've wanted to meet you," she said, and when Norton expressed surprise, she continued: "It said in the paper that you passed water at every table. I wanted to meet the man who could do that."

"It isn't easy," he replied. "You have to save up."

Afterward, one of Marjorie's friends asked what she thought of Baskin. "Oh, he's just one of those personality boys," she said. "Throw him back." When Baskin heard about this, he refused to accept the rejection—"Who was she not to accept my charm?"—and kept visiting her at the Creek. He would be one of several suitors Marjorie entertained. As well, he headed a friendly threesome Marjorie dubbed "the Three Musketeers," men like brothers to her, always on call to assist the lady writer living alone in the woods. Cecil Clark, the owner of an Ocala hardware store, and artist Bob (Robert C.) Camp, the director of a WPA art gallery in Ocala and a member of a prominent Ocala family, were the other two. But no matter who was stopping by Marjorie's place—pals or suitors—Norton Baskin was her steadiest guest.

The next day, Marjorie wrote to her former husband. "Dear Chuck: The divorce was granted yesterday—You're free as the wind, big boy, and I hope you'll make the most of it. Take the women as they come—we're a tough breed, and can stand considerable man-handling." Anne Rawlings had sent her a friendly letter; Marjorie related that she was "glad she and I can go our ways with mutual respect and affection." Then, news of the Creek. The new roof was on. Friends visited. In her absence one day, a handyman had lined a closet all too well. "Came home to find he had completely sealed up the 10 gals. of liquor I have up there!" Marjorie had him cut a hatch big enough to let her retrieve her treasure.

ALTHOUGH A NEW CHAPTER had begun for Marjorie, her former marriage shadowed the new year. Early on, Chuck wrote from Nova Scotia about their 1933 tax returns, which, since he was out of the country, Marjorie would have to handle. He should have thought about it before he left, he acknowledged, but "somehow incomes have never been much on my mind."

"My development, for some reason, had been arrested for years," he wrote by way of apology. "I was naked when I sauntered away. That is the best way to feel how cold the wind can blow. . . . You are kind to label the oppression mutual. It was, of course, nothing of the sort. I—for whatever reason—the chemistry of our union, my own destiny, in some unseen way, my own fault, I don't know, but whatever it was, it was the real culprit—was held suspended in life.

"I would not possibly have been happy or made anyone else happy that way, in that place. There is nothing the matter with us, you as you, I as I. We really are two very decent people and we should get our break. I certainly hope with all my heart that you get yours."

For Bee Humiston McNeil, Marjorie summarized the marriage from her point of view: "We were never happy for very long. Everything I did was wrong. Nothing suited Chuck. When we came to a show-down a year ago in March, he said that he realized he had always had an inferiority complex as far as I was concerned. You will remember that rather ingratiating shyness and self-deprecation. He never got over it."

She confided, "It almost broke me—the alternative to my divorce was, frankly, suicide. Life just wasn't worth living with the black cloud of his daily disagreeableness over me."

Marjorie had hoped the Florida move would make things right, but it did not. "The last winter we were together, he tried to convince me I was going crazy. A little old aunt [Ida Tarrant] was with us, and that old dame almost tore him down. She said if she ever caught him at such a vicious thing again, she'd make his life hell. You can imagine how he acted when my Florida stuff began to be accepted."

"Of course," Marjorie admitted, "I've given him a black sheet and myself a white one, and that can never be accurate. All I ask of him is to leave me in peace. I have begun to find a little of the joy in living I always had."

Marjorie's suicide remark to Bee was serious. Although no personal diary exists (or remains), a few brief, introspective forays lie tucked within her research notes. Among her *South Moon Under* papers, she had inserted this philosophical response to her difficulties:

> Mankind could go on a vast sit-down strike; could trouble itself, protesting, to the grave. But it would be the most thoughtful of us who would go, the most sensitive, the most eager for place and beauty. And our longing for loveliness would be buried with us. And most of all I fear the cosmic forces would be quite indifferent to our going. It is, perhaps, a privilege, to be tortured. Perhaps out of that torture will come the community of spirit that will allay the cosmic nostalgia—the sense of loneliness that destroys us. I rejected today, with what I hope is a permanent intention, the thought of suicide.

Chuck kept in touch with the Glissons, who bore him no malice. "We didn't hear a word from him for at least a year, and maybe more than that," J.T. recalled later. "But articles by Charles Rawlings began to crop up in *Collier's*, the *Saturday Evening Post*, that kind of thing." Glisson confirmed Chuck's continued independence: "Publishers wanted to tell him where to go and what to do, and of course he wasn't that kind of person." When World War II started, Glisson said, Chuck bought a two-masted schooner in Tampa, had it outfitted, and set out to the Pacific as a freelancer. "He sailed around the Cape and covered World War II when there were no other correspondents doing it. He disguised his whole boat. He was ahead of some invasions, in some places."

Chuck contracted malaria again and again, and by the end of the war, Glisson said, "His health was shot. They shipped him back to the States." A 1945 anthology, *The 100 Best True Stories of World War II*, contained three of his stories for the *Saturday Evening Post*, all from the Pacific Zone. Chuck eventually settled in Bunker Hill, a hamlet of about a dozen families near Alna, Maine, overlooking Damariscotta Lake. It was a New England version of Cross Creek, with a fourteen-party telephone line. Known there as a former war correspondent, he continued writing for the *Saturday Evening Post*, remarried several times, and outlived Marjorie by twenty-one years. In a 1970 letter, he wrote of her, "I think her ear was a great, great ear. Her ability to listen to a Cracker conversation—to go in and depict it, to suggest the nuances, the touches that were necessary to let it come into perfect light—was absolutely miraculous. It's a joy to read Marjorie. I admire her still."

Chapter Ten

Golden Apples

1934-35

FIVE YEARS INTO THE Florida experiment, her marriage over, Marjorie took stock of her earnings and property, hers alone to manage. By early 1934, she had earned about $6,000 ($116,000 in 2020 dollars) on *South Moon Under*, $4,000 of which had come from the Book-of-the-Month Club; actual sales of the book were disappointing. She learned that the citrus packing house Chuck had engaged had overcharged them; she corrected the arrangement. She paid off old bills—some several years old—bought a new car, and added small structures to the farm, including a new tenant house. Sales of oranges and short stories would have to cover her regular expenses, like taxes and mortgage payments. She brought in experts from the University of Florida to assess the grove and learned that her fruit was subpar because the trees had been underfertilized. The trees could be brought back with proper attention, they told her, and she invested in more trees and nutrients. Among snatches of Cracker dialogue in a pocket notebook, one finds reminders for fertilizer formula (8-4-8: nitrogen, phosphorus, potassium) and pest control (nicotine sulphate). "It is going to be nip and tuck," she wrote to Chuck's aunt Ida Tarrant, her defender, with whom she remained close. But "by staying put and living quietly, if nothing queer happens, I will be all right."

She had achieved some peace of mind, notwithstanding Anne Rawlings's short-lived attempt, through a local friend, to bring Chuck and Marjorie back together. "I am enjoying life more than since I was a girl in college. Everyone says I am like a different person and 10 years younger," she told Aunt Ida.

One of Marjorie's first adventures as a single woman was a four-day rattlesnake hunt on Big Prairie, a wild expanse west of Lake Okeechobee, with herpetologist Ross Allen, who had recently established the Reptile Institute at Silver Springs, the popular tourist attraction near Ocala known for tours in glass-bottomed boats. Like other commercial ventures in Florida, the institute straddled a line between education and entertainment: visitors could learn about Florida's cold-blooded creatures and thrill to spectacles like alligator wrestling, too. Allen wanted publicity for his project. Some years later, Marjorie transformed her notes into "The Ancient Enmity," a chapter in her 1942 non-fiction chronicle, *Cross Creek*. The chapter, a personal essay anchored by reportage, explores common fears of snakes, then launches into the trip, as she admires the magnificent wetlands and Allen demonstrates to his phobic guest the biological and behavioral habits of snakes. He hopes she will pick one up, and though she only manages to hook one with the customary L-shaped stick, then drop it, Marjorie returns to the Creek somewhat victorious, and meditates further on the snakes she encounters there. "It would be impossible for me ever to feel affection for a snake," she wrote from the safety of her screened porch. But now she could observe them with interest, "consider them as personalities."

THOUGH THE DIVORCE clouded her days, Marjorie cultivated a new social life and kept up with an increasing number of engagements in Florida. Soon after *South Moon Under* was published, Jacksonville critic and librarian Carl Bohnenberger approached her about speaking to the Menshiviki, a small private club (named for the Russian socialist faction) of men who met monthly in the city for lunch and a program. The new novel thrilled them all, but by rule, they couldn't invite a woman to lunch. Marjorie solved it by inviting them to Cross Creek, where she set up a bar, served them a fine meal, and told stories—an adult version of her childhood pleasure, spinning yarns for an audience of boys. She entertained the Menshiviki several times, until *The Yearling*'s fame claimed more of her schedule. From this group, she selected her doctor, Dr. T. Z. Cason (Zelma Cason's brother), and her attorney, Philip May Sr. Many members agreed that Marjorie's dinners were unforgettable.

In February, she read from *South Moon Under* at Rollins College as part of the Animated Magazine, an annual assembly of distinguished speakers who appeared outdoors, amplified for thousands of listeners. This year, the speakers included two members of President Roosevelt's cabinet—Attorney General Homer Cummings and Secretary of Commerce Daniel C. Roper—along with publisher and philanthropist George Arthur Plimpton and the popular novelist Fannie Hurst. Marjorie was well received, and would read for the Animated Magazine again in 1937, 1938, 1941, and 1945. At the gala dinner, Marjorie met novelist Robert Herrick, who, she reported to Max, "has something of your peculiarly understanding quality, and we disgraced ourselves by getting in a far corner and talking . . . ignoring the party all evening." Herrick admired *South Moon Under* and had urged his brother-in-law, a member of the Pulitzer committee, to give it the 1933 novel prize. He even volunteered to look at "Hamaca" and advise Marjorie, but Max cautioned against it. "He writes fine novels, but they belong to a time that we have entirely left behind," he ascertained. Marjorie read some of Herrick's work and concurred. As Max put it, "His personality is infinitely beyond his literary gifts."

FOR MOST OF 1934, Marjorie continued to struggle with "Hamaca." She wondered if she suffered from the same malaise Scott Fitzgerald and Thomas Wolfe had faced, best summed up as "second book syndrome," the anxiety a writer might experience after a highly successful debut. In February, she again thanked Max for his belief in her. "You do encourage me by indicating that difficulty in 'getting going' is not necessarily a sign of complete incompetence." She'd always thought that "to allow personal turbulence to interfere with one's work was a fatal weakness, and a sure sign that the artistic impulse was not valid." Physical problems never bothered her, she claimed, "but when I am emotionally torn up I find myself submerged in a miasma with clear thought seemingly impossible." If she forced herself to write in a foggy psychological state she produced "un-true rubbish."

By June, she had started the novel six times. She had thought that the story—of a British remittance man and two orphaned Crackers found squatting on his family's property—should start in the outsider's home territory, England. She finally realized the book had to open in the hammock—as much a character as the humans within it. She was eager to speak with Max about this new turn and invited him to stop by on his way to a vacation in Key West, but the editor refused, saying he'd postponed his trip to work with another novelist. "I am engaged in a kind of life and death struggle with Mr. Thomas Wolfe still, and it is likely to last through the summer," he explained. (The book in question was *Of Time and the River.*)

Max never would visit Marjorie in Florida, despite her urging. In a letter to Hemingway later that year, he confessed: "I never did feel comfortable alone with women (I suppose there is some complex involved in it) and the idea of visiting one with nobody else around (she is divorced) scares me to death."

Later that month, Marjorie sent him the first ten thousand words of "Hamaca." If he thought it was going well, she said, she could average one thousand words a day and submit the complete manuscript in November. Max responded: "I could have gone on reading a manuscript of that quality all day and called it a holiday." He advised her on balancing her main characters: Tordell the Englishman and the Cracker siblings Luke and Allie. Marjorie replied with relief, adding, "I hope you haven't thrown away the 35 pages I sent you—that was my first draft and only copy." Max had recalled the same situation with *South Moon Under,* so, fortunately, he had kept the pages and now sent them back. Marjorie reported again, considering several ways the story might develop, stating emphatically, "I despise working with an outline."

IN ITS AUGUST 1934 ISSUE, *Scribner's Magazine* published Marjorie's short story "The Pardon," the tale of a man who is unexpectedly released from prison after serving seven years of a twenty-year sentence for a crime he didn't commit. Back home, he discovers that his wife has birthed a son by another man. The story concludes with two of Marjorie's frequent character types—the stray boy and the wronged, sensitive man—in familial embrace.

The publication of "The Pardon" must have been a welcome diversion. At the time, Max was reading a new section of "Hamaca," and in early August, he suggested, carefully, that "it does not seem to be quite right in every respect" but "is certainly part of a very fine book." Marjorie trusted him to tell her what was wrong, and how to fix it. "I will bring up a live rattlesnake and drop it on your desk if you are ever polite about my stuff and I catch you at it," she warned. "The truth is the most difficult thing in the world to get at, and I always felt that the closest approach to truth is the greatest kindness." She also confessed, "I do a very peculiar thing sometimes in my writing . . . I get definitely off-key, into a queer plane that is without reality. I simply do not know how or why I do it. My only hope is that I have become reasonably able to at least recognize it once it has happened." She discussed Louis Bromfield's novel *The Farm*, based on his experiences on a self-sufficient family farm. Its form would drive Perkins crazy, she warned, but "as a study of a way of life, I found it magnificent."

THE HEAT WAS ON—it seemed the new novel was heading to completion. Max posted the marked manuscript with pages of notes. Most of his suggestions had to do with timing—an event happened too quickly, or its exposition and development might be slowed down. "The truth is you are a writer, and no one need have any anxiety about what you do," he assured the nervous author. "I never saw anybody so quick to understand what a book needed." Marjorie aimed to finish by the end of October and revise in November, but the work went more slowly than expected. Toggling between the hammock and the civilized scenes created problems with form, tone, and characterizations. She felt that in avoiding melodrama, she had sacrificed necessary details. Her Englishman's voice was problematic. "I ran out of anything to read last night," she told Max, "and picked up *Jane Eyre*, which I had happened never to read—and the worst of that sounds exactly like some of my stuff now, when I get stilted. At least I know what I'm trying to avoid!" She asked Max not to give a completion date to Scribner's business side.

In November, she was still struggling. "But even through my intense dissatisfaction with this manuscript a conviction comes to me that even if it is very bad indeed, someday I shall write a good book," she told him. Max replied with a copy of Henry James's *The Art of the Novel*, a collection of James's critical prefaces to his own novels. Scribner's had just published it. Marjorie found it helpful, even consoling—James had fretted over time schemes, too. She wrote to Max: "My great fear is that what should and could be authentic drama, becomes melodrama, without reality. I like to write in a series of dramatic scenes, building each chapter up to its own little climax. If it works, it gives the emotional intensity I want to achieve above everything else."

"Don't take Henry James too seriously," Max advised. "I think you have a right diagnosis of your own weaknesses . . . but I think you exaggerate them very much, and that knowing them, you will also know how to correct them."

Two days before Thanksgiving, the novel was finished, but Marjorie would have to type a clean copy herself, because only she could read her penciled notes. She mailed the whole thing before Christmas, with a letter saying she was disgusted with it and would submit a list of criticisms. But before she could do so, Max read it and sent her a detailed discussion on how it could be improved, mainly in the final third, when several themes converged. He still saw inconsistencies of tone and point of view. Motivations were not always clear or believable. One secondary but important character was not "a success." This last section was melodramatic—it moved too rapidly, too much happened. Max suggested fixes and praised the rich context: the world of oranges and orange growing. He thought the hammock region "magnificently given," better than in *South Moon Under*.

Marjorie replied with relief: "I am staying home from a deer-hunt to write you, because I am so much stirred by your letter. . . . Once again, you have clarified for me what I recognized as a muddle." She addressed each of his suggestions and welcomed further ideas. "That the thing is not utterly impossible is like firm ground under my feet after struggling in quicksand. So many times the effort to keep the grove going properly, the struggle to build some personal happiness, and so on, have seemed absurdly hopeless, and if the book had come out a total failure, things would have been difficult for me mentally. As it is, I feel great hope in all directions."

MARJORIE COULDN'T HAVE exaggerated her concerns over her grove. The first major freeze of the century (December 12–13, 1934) had just descended, destroying 40 percent of the state's orange crop. Florida governor David Sholtz toured the central Florida Citrus Belt soon afterward, surveying the scattered damage. Trees on one side of a road might be dead, while on the other side, all remained healthy. Such were the vagaries of Florida weather. The governor was convinced that "substantial citizens" who had never received federal relief would have to apply for it. In response to the freeze, the Federal-State Frost Warning Service was created the following year, and the state legislature passed the Florida Citrus Code, establishing the Florida Citrus Commission and the Florida Department of Citrus, which offered marketing, research, and regulatory support. There had been problems in the past with uneven quality, for example, and some growers shipped fruit too soon or sent out fruit that had frozen. (An orange frozen solid like a baseball is mealy and mushy when thawed.) Now, too, there was a question of heating groves when frost was imminent. Smudge pots, oil-burning devices developed after a freeze in southern California, would become part of every grower's equipment, set out between trees when cold temperatures were predicted.

For Marjorie, these developments meant additional protection—and expense.

On the last day of 1934, Max wrote to applaud Marjorie's proposed changes and confirmed that *Golden Apples* would be the new novel's title. She would receive the highest royalty Scribner's could offer: 15 percent from the start. In the current economy, he said, the publisher did not give advances, but in light of Cross Creek's recent losses, he offered her the choice. She shared some of this information with Carl Brandt, who up to now had handled her short work and foreign book rights. Brandt suggested a "nominal" $1,500 advance and asked Marjorie to allow him to deal with Scribner's on everything, from there on out. It would not interfere with her editorial relationship, and she would more than earn back Brandt's 10 percent commission.

ALONGSIDE THE HARD BIRTH of *Golden Apples*, *South Moon Under* continued garnering praise. There was a question of serializing it in the *Ocala Banner*, which Marjorie dismissed, feeling everyone had already read it; plus, bringing it out again would revive speculations begun when the book first appeared. Like any novel set in a small, specific place, with some characters based on real people or composites of several, *South Moon Under* had generated local gossip: Who was she really writing about? Marjorie refused to repeat the experience. Fan mail continued, and occasionally, an individual sought a copy signed by the author in person. Some even made a pilgrimage to Cross Creek. At first, Marjorie didn't mind when an admiring stranger interrupted her writing day. Later, she sternly guarded her privacy. "A car driving up to the gate in the middle of the day produces muffled curses," she wrote in 1942. "The same car arriving as the sun is dropping over Orange Lake is welcomed with unqualified joy."

At least one early pilgrim enjoyed a pleasant encounter. Neal Smith, a student living in the Florida panhandle, set out to meet Marjorie, stopping in smaller and smaller hamlets for directions just vague enough to confuse the outsider, and made it to the author's home, known to have the only working bathroom within a twenty-mile radius. In a letter to his mother recounting the visit, Smith, who would keep in touch with Marjorie and become a Hawthorne scholar, offered a quaint but immediate portrait of the writer and her domain: "There was the little cottage near the edge of the narrow road, set among the orange trees with perfect naturalness. A few plants struggled in the sand: Turk's cap, allamanda, plumbago, asparagus fern. Repairs were evidently going on: at the left was a half-finished port-cochère, on the roof was a lone man hammering on the last row of new shingles. 'Is anyone home?' I asked. He looked at me curiously: 'Well, cook's here, and Margie ought to be around somewhere.'"

Smith walked around to the back of the house, where, through a screened porch, he could see a woman in the kitchen. It was Marjorie, in a housedress, mixing cake batter in a bowl. She invited him in. Smith found her friendly, unpretentious. The maid, Beatrice (also known as 'Geechee), assisted her, barefoot. Then: "Mrs. Rawlings kicked at the draft of the woodstove, opened the oven door, and put three of the cakes inside. 'Beatrice, you watch these pans and turn them around,' she admonished. 'Come on out on the porch, Neal.'

"All this time I had been looking at her with incredulity. Her hair, evidently waved at home, hung in short wisps around her shining face, the strap of an undergarment had slipped down on her arm. I was at once at ease and happy to find her so <u>human</u>."

Marjorie left Smith on the front porch while she freshened up. "At one end was a chintz-covered couch. There was a small table or two, some comfortable chairs, potted sansevieria, a portable typewriter in a mix-up of correspondence on a big round table where Mrs. Rawlings works. Letters were everywhere, flying helter-skelter."

When Marjorie returned, "She wore a simple pink silk dress, and had combed her short hair to the back of her neck; her face was no longer shiny, and she was cheerful and composed. She is not very tall; she is slender, moves gracefully and quickly. Her voice is soft and Southern. She has brown hair and quiet eyes that are steady and sympathetic; she used no lip rouge and wore no ornament."

The pair talked of plants, including gardenias, which Marjorie loved. She confessed that she had "dug one up from a Negro's yard, paid fifty cents for it; it died, she says, to show her sin. She is interested in the welfare of the folk about but refuses to be a martyr."

The grove helped support Marjorie, but maintaining it was an immense job for one person, she admitted to Smith. " 'When I had a husband,' she said, 'he took care of this for me,' moving her hands in a wide sweep." There was more talk—of books, of travel. When the cakes were done, Marjorie made fresh coconut icing and served cake to her guest, with hot tea. She clearly took pride in her culinary skills. But "she nearly caused my strangulation when she told me a joke while I was drinking tea," Smith remembered. "She smiled at my compliments and made me eat two huge portions of cake. After a while we went into the yard and inspected her calendulas and Italian cypresses." When a line of ducks filed by, Marjorie asked Smith to inquire of a friend how to tell old ducks from young ones. "I want to kill the young ones," she told him, "and don't know which they are."

MARJORIE CONTINUED SENDING revisions to Max, fussing, discussing. Should a scene go or stay? Was a character promiscuous? Why or why not? Early in 1935, Marjorie had a physician friend (probably Clifford Vinson) read the manuscript and offer medical-psychological diagnoses of two characters, which helped her reshape them. But the ending of the book was still "badly blurred." "My God," she wrote Max, "it's so sickening at this stage of the game."

Almost predictably, she fell ill, narrowly avoiding bronchial pneumonia. In February, she began addressing her editor as "Max" instead of "Mr. Perkins," and he in turn addressed her as "Marjorie." In the midst of this, *Cosmopolitan* asked to serialize the new novel, requiring a version cut from 130,000 words to 80,000. Marjorie took this on even as she struggled to get the full version right—the magazine would pay her $7,200 (worth about $136,000 in 2020). "I wish the Cosmopolitan sale was at the bottom of the sea," she confided to Max, "but that's literally biting the hand that feeds me." The added income would make the next year or two "much simpler." Indeed, she would be able to make more improvements to the farmhouse, including adding a second bathroom. At the same time, Marjorie was thinking of the "boy's book," next in line. Who would illustrate it? Then, back to *Golden Apples*, and her struggle to revise one character ("still melodramatic traces"). Desperate, she wired Max about coming to New York to review the manuscript in person.

But before he could answer, Marjorie was thrown off a horse, fracturing her skull, and checked into a hospital. "Thought it was only muscular injury," she wrote, "but the pain kept getting more severe." She had traveled 120 miles to Tampa for X-rays, revealing the fracture and a chipped vertebra. "They put me in a brace at once, devilishly uncomfortable, but you get used to anything." She had mailed the third of four installments to *Cosmopolitan* just before going to Tampa—meaning she must have been in real pain as she completed it.

How or where the horse incident took place is lost to history, but immediate condolences came from Major Otto Lange, a West Point graduate and army commander, at the time an instructor for the University of Florida's ROTC program. Major Lange was an avid hunter, fisherman, and gardener. Marjorie had hunted ducks, doves, and quail with him that winter, and with their shared interests in outdoor sport and the preservation of wild Florida, it's likely that their friendship, ultimately a liaison, had begun earlier. In their correspondence, Lange addressed Marjorie as "Dearest Diana," presumably paying homage to her love of the hunt. Marjorie, now a fixture on the academic cocktail circuit, had mentioned to Max having been at Major Lange's home for drinks, prelude to a dinner party given by University of Florida president Dr. John J. Tigert. "Dr. Tigert is a prig and a fanatical dry," Marjorie wrote, "and the Major deliberately set in to get me high, saying that his ambition was to deposit me on the Tigert doorstep and say, 'Here's your guest.' He accomplished his purpose." When everyone was seated, Marjorie discovered that her dinner partner was a preacher, "and I disgraced myself thoroughly by asking my hostess what the devil she meant by putting me next to a parson." Then Marjorie, ever deeper in her cups, announced, "To hell with all preachers."

Marjorie wore the brace through April and was barred from typing for two weeks. She regretted the *Cosmopolitan* serialization. "The very worst has happened," she confided to Max. "One of my virgin aunts wrote me that it was 'just dear.' You'd do anything in the world to keep people like that from liking your stuff, because if they like it, you know it's bad. You can understand Faulknerism, and Hemingway's bomb-shell intrusions of obscenity—anything to drive away the fluttering hands and the genteel, ecstatic voices." She lamented *Cosmopolitan*'s edits: "I told them to do their own cutting as long as they didn't add or change. It never occurred to me they'd cut sentences in half!"

Now everyone was impatient for Marjorie's final draft: Scribner's, Max, and Marjorie herself. Toward the end of May 1935, she sent it up to Max, who passed it to the printer—but not without reservations about the book's finale. More changes were required, he said, although they could be made in proofs, and the book, even as it stood, would sell. He added, "But you are not thinking of this book only, nor am I, but of your place as a writer, . . . If you are willing, we can examine those passages carefully once more. It is too fine a book not to have every advantage of thought and work."

Marjorie replied with "relief and despair." The novel was still not unified, and she could point out "every chapter, every paragraph, every sentence, every word, that's melodramatic or off-key or false." She begged Max to think for her—she was all played out. Ten days later, she apologized and got down to professional business: contracts, jacket blurbs, design, and her pen name. She had asked Whitney Darrow, Scribner's business manager, if she could drop "Rawlings," and he had said no, likely because she was already well known by it. In that case, she decided, she would go by Marjorie Kinnan Rawlings, not Marjorie K. "There are lots of three-name writers who don't seem handicapped by the length," she observed.

Max sent Marjorie galleys for *Golden Apples* and his most comprehensive critique, addressing matters large and exquisitely small. "The question of treatment comes even down to the use of words," he wrote.

"For instance, there is one place where you say Claudius *strode* about the room. I would change the word to *walked*." Marjorie made "copious" deletions and rewrites, never mentioning that she had caught malaria. "How can I do such sheer *bad writing*, when I know better?" she asked. She complained about her new author photo. "I have no great urge to see my face smirking from the back of the book-jacket. There's something offensive about female authors at best. . . . If the picture is fairly good-looking you feel the work can't be sincere. If it's ugly, or a bit stark, or terribly earnest, it turns your stomach. . . . Tom Wolfe's picture was effective because his face expressed some of the ecstasy and torment of his work. I'm no genius, and my picture, to my notion, looks like nothing but another she-writer."

Chapter Eleven

What About a Novel About a Boy

1935-36

W HEN *GOLDEN APPLES* WAS out of her hands, Marjorie journeyed to visit her brother in Alaska. Arthur, impatient to see
his sister, had proposed several itineraries the previous winter. "What in
hell have you named this second brat that's caused such long and overdue
labor pains?" he'd asked.

But he had read part of *Golden Apples* in *Cosmopolitan* and written to congratulate her—and update her on his own peripatetic life. His
troubles had begun before Chuck and Marjorie moved to Florida. After
graduating from the University of Wisconsin with a degree in Commerce, he had spent time in New York and Michigan, then finally fled
"the Traphagen regime," as well as a local girlfriend, to start fresh in the
wilds of Los Angeles. Right away, he fell for a woman who didn't return
his affection ("Try as I would, I couldn't reach the well-known first
base") and either summoned or was tracked down by the Michigan girlfriend, now rebounding from another relationship. Arthur Kinnan and
Luca Collins married in 1925, and produced two daughters: Marjorie
Lou and Barbara Claire. "Gross foolishness—admitted, Marj," Arthur
wrote to his sister. "Once in it, I did the only thing left to do. Tried to
make a go of it." In one letter, a "treatise"—he could be as loquacious as

his sister—Art poured out details summarized thus: He and Luca were a horrible match. He was the responsible one, earning a salary, buying a house, doing chores, while Luca was uneducated, slovenly, "colorless, and uninteresting." At least their firstborn daughter, Marjorie Lou, was "as pretty as they come, healthy, lovable, and SMART. She will no doubt live up to the name she was given. She is Kinnan through and through."

By the end of 1930, Art and Luca had divorced, Luca having primary custody of the girls. Arthur's business teetered as the Depression continued, but he managed to salvage it "from the wreckage." (It is unclear what his business involved at that point, but he moved to Seattle.) In 1932, Arthur remarried, and soon afterward he, a boating enthusiast like Chuck, and a member of the Queen City Yacht Club, bought a new thirty-two-foot cruiser, the *Winikin*, named for Winifred, his new wife. In September 1933, *MotorBoating* magazine reported that the *Winikin* "started her career nicely," with a Class II third place in the Olympia-Nanaimo Cruiser Race.

Yet Arthur's business continued to suffer. He and Winifred, having settled in Seattle, wanted out. Luca caused them problems "principally through the children, of course." He hoped to take a job in China with an aeronautical engineering company. Then, almost as quickly as they had married, Arthur and Winifred separated. As Marjorie prepared to visit him, the full truth came out: Winifred had been Arthur's original California love—the one with whom he could not get to first base. While married to Luca, he had encountered her again. The pair rendezvoused behind Luca's back until the divorce was final. But when Arthur discovered that his second wife had enjoyed several lovers in the interim, he became obsessed with her past and broke the tie, blaming himself.

MARJORIE LEFT CROSS CREEK by train at the end of July 1935, stopping briefly in St. Louis, a part of the world she found "awful," she told Max, though the people were "peculiarly sweet and child-like and friendly. The mid-west accent, after many years' absence, hits as strange and staccato as some foreign tongue." She spent two days at the Grand Canyon, taking the fabled mule trip down to Phantom Ranch. The steep, narrow descent frightened her, given her recent fall, but "I had the comfort of knowing that if I broke my neck again, it would be among noble surroundings!" To prepare for the long trip her brother had planned—a

six-day voyage from Seattle up the Inside Passage on the *Winikin*, then
a couple of weeks in Alaska, hunting and fishing—she read a book by
the writer, actress, and suffragist Elizabeth Robins: *The Magnetic North*
(1904) is a fictionalized account of Robins's journey to the Gold Rush
camps of Alaska in search of her brother Raymond. Marjorie knew
Raymond Robins, an economist and writer, and his wife, labor leader
Margaret Dreier Robins; the couple had retired to their Florida home,
Chinsegut Hill Manor House in Brooksville. Marjorie, with Dessie
Smith Vinson, had visited them in 1934. Perhaps Margaret Robins had
loaned Marjorie the book. When Marjorie wrote Margaret an appreciation of *The Magnetic North*, she mentioned Dessie, whose marriage was
in trouble. Dr. Vinson might be a fine surgeon, Marjorie observed, but
he was unreasonably jealous. The Vinson marriage did not survive, and
neither would Dessie's next marriage—in fact, over the course of her life,
Dessie married six times.

In late September Marjorie returned to Florida, having missed the
great Labor Day hurricane, the first storm on record to strike the United
States as a category 5, beginning in the southern Florida Keys and moving gulfside to Cedar Key, just seventy miles west of Cross Creek. The
death toll was 407. Citrus groves close to the Gulf Coast suffered, but
inland, at Ocala and Gainesville, there was little damage.

Otto Lange wrote, offering to meet Marjorie in Jacksonville, filling
her in on more environmental news. "Your beloved Ocala will give you a
shock. Hell has broken loose and all the devils are out," he warned, referring to the controversial Cross-Florida Barge Canal, a 107-mile project
intended to connect the Gulf and Atlantic coasts. The idea had been
discussed for years. Towns along or near the route saw business advan-
tages, while opponents feared heavy environmental losses, particularly
to the state's aquifers. Marjorie might expect harm or even ruin at the
Creek. But ground had been broken as part of President Roosevelt's economic recovery program. "The forward-looking American businessmen
of the great city of Ocala are smacking their lips," Lange wrote. "Yours
for the Rotarians, Kiwanis, Lions, Knights of the Round Table, bigger
and better, upward and onward! Let joy be 'unrefined'!" He went on:
"Blue Spring, Orange Springs, Withlacoochee, Ocklawaha, will all be
done for."

"You proved yourself the best businessman of the lot, though you did not intend it," he added. "You made money out of the scrub, which nobody else ever did, and now they never will." Eventually, protestors achieved a work stoppage, but the project remained in play for more than fifty years.

GOLDEN APPLES WAS PUBLISHED October 4, 1935. The next day, reviews started to appear, mostly positive. Critics mentioned the difficulties of interweaving characters' stories throughout—not just those of Tordell, the privileged Englishman, and Luke and Allie, the orphaned Crackers Tordell employs and dominates, but those of Dr. Albury, a kindly, oracular doctor; Claude, the doctor's odd, disturbed son; and Camilla Van Dyne, an accomplished grove owner who, like Tordell, holds a measure of financial and social status in the community. Percy Hutchison of the *New York Times* wrote that *Golden Apples* had one defect: it lacked unity. It "ends in midair." Yet he sang Marjorie's praises for rendering the hammock and orange groves as fully and organically as the scrub in *South Moon Under.* "The near-Chaucerian dialect of the southern poor white is not an annoyance, but a delight," he wrote.

Henry Seidel Canby, the former Yale English professor who had chaired the Book-of-the-Month Club's editorial board and co-founded the *Saturday Review of Literature*, observed: "There is a tenderness in Mrs. Rawlings's novels of Florida that may outlast the psychopathic hate with which other Southern writers have lifted the despised Cracker into literature. Her books explain, what is a mystery in others, why the poor white loves his soil, why, indeed, he is worth writing about at all except as a psychological phenomenon. Florida, a country made distasteful by its advertising, becomes again in her stories the land that stirred Bartram's imagination, and through him, Coleridge." Marjorie had a gift for the idyllic, but she was not a sentimental writer. The novel's thesis, Canby proposed, was that "not even love can protect against injustice and frustration."

"It is a sound thesis," he observed, "yet I wish Mrs. Rawlings had not labored it." Within the story and through the characters, he suggested, the thesis was implicit.

RICHARD TORDELL NEVER becomes one with the hammock and the groves; instead, he defiles his new environment, impregnating young

Allie, who worships him, undergoing a whipping from outraged neighbors, and cynically marrying the girl—his servant. It is the kindly Dr. Albury who often belabors Marjorie's cosmic viewpoint, by attempting to instruct Tordell. "Peace and ecstasy aren't ends in themselves, to be hunted like quail or run to earth like foxes," he says. "They're byproducts." And: "A man, by himself, is nothing. He's a wretched mass of nerves and misery and fear, always on the defense. He must, he simply must, abandon himself, lovingly, to something more enduring than he. Something that has existed before him, that will continue after him, when he as an individual has come and gone." Later, musing about Tordell, Albury thinks, "In his love he takes and doesn't give. The answer is not less love, but more." Albury has paraphrased Thoreau: "There is no remedy for love but to love more."

Of the early national reviews, Marjorie was most pleased with Canby's. He understood what she was trying to do, she said. "But no one makes note of the one point that was most important to me. That is the struggle of a man against a natural background. . . . How can people miss it? I was afraid my 'message' would be too blatant! Yet everyone is concerned with the characters, the plot, the technique, the 'background,' using the word in the theatrical sense." She accused Max of being too easy on her. "You have too much sympathy with the torment of the writer's mind. A writer was born to be tormented. It is his destiny. You should torment us still further, when you see as surely you must see, the inadequate thing emerging."

Now, in anxious hindsight, she identified again her work's flaws, described to Max what she would have done differently, and how. She complained of "the hell of publishing exigencies; of personal ambition, which makes you want to 'produce' rather than a more natural process of allowing a work the proper time to develop as a unified whole." If only she could have put *Golden Apples* aside for a year or two and come back to it. Yet admiring reviews accumulated, some calling the book better than *South Moon Under*. Scribner's seemed happy with the press and the sales, though by the end of the year, the new book was slipping off the lists.

In a personal letter, fantasy novelist and gentleman genealogist James Branch Cabell, one of Marjorie's new St. Augustine friends—the Virginia author wintered there—told Marjorie that *Golden Apples* was "a grand book" but criticized the balance of characters, concluding with a remark Marjorie must have hated: "Tordell is excellent—that is, as any male character can ever be when a woman writer draws him from the inside." (Marjorie, who had idolized Cabell for his 1919 novel *Jurgen*, later admitted to him, "Often I cross out a phrase, knowing at once that you would throw up your precise hands in horror.")

Max admitted that booksellers in some quarters reported a reaction against what they called "poor white" literature and they blamed it on novelists like Faulkner and Erskine Caldwell. "It is ridiculous to put your book in that class and we fought against it, but Americans seem to have a tendency toward classification in the book business," he wrote. Marjorie might have taken a moment's comfort in a letter from one of her old Wisconsin professors, who had looked up from his German scholarship long enough to notice that his former student's second book had received a "most encomiastic" review. He had not been aware of her notoriety before then—might he be excused? After all, he remembered how she sat in the front row, a superior student whose picture he recognized right away: "You have not changed at all (I presume if I may be presuming enough, that the boyish figure of yore is a trifle rotund), and the same sort of quiet mischief and the same two hundred candle power of the lantern of the hobgoblin in your eyes are still there, and I sincerely hope the goblin will keep swinging his lantern!"

AFTER GOLDEN APPLES, Marjorie considered going on "in the Florida vein in one form or another, a little longer," indicating that she envisioned someday writing outside the grove, the scrub and hammock. "One hates to be localized. Yet there is still much fascinating material here." It was a practical thought, as if she had suddenly stepped back from the pots simmering on the stove and considered another source of heat. It was also typical of "the cauliflower aspect" of her nature. She needed transplantation, but of what sort—the setting of her imagination or that of her life? Or both? She had a fleeting notion to write an Alaska novel, with a year's stay there to get it done. It wouldn't materialize, though the notion might have relieved pressure from the project she had, in a significant sense, already begun—the "boy's book."

By early November, Max was again nudging her about it—not a "juvenile," but an adult literary novel that would fully reveal life in the region, even though its protagonist would be a young boy. Marjorie had made notes for it at Cal Long's home two years before, when Cal had told her how, as a boy, he had been forced to shoot his pet deer. But she still held little enthusiasm for the project. The Florida book she felt compelled to write was something she called "Cross Creek: A Chronicle." It would be a nonfiction assemblage of separate pieces, some already drafted, quiet in tone, and all with an "out of the world flavor, catching, I hope, the quality that has made me cling so desperately and against great odds to this place." She did not want to write a personal memoir, although the work, written in the first person, might one day be regarded as one.

Of the pieces she had in mind for the Cross Creek book was a narrative about 'Geechee, or Beatrice, a young black woman who, soon after Chuck left the Creek, had heard that Marjorie needed help and had shown up one day, unannounced, insisting she be hired. It is Marjorie's first fully formed portrait of a black worker. 'Geechee intimidated Marjorie. "She seemed impossible," Marjorie wrote. "She looked capable of murder." But Marjorie couldn't refuse her. 'Geechee had come from an area near the Ogeechee River in Georgia. Marjorie described her as lioness. Her face had been scarred and one eye blinded in a fight, and she had served time in jail.

For several months, 'Geechee cleaned house devotedly. Once mutual trust was established, she approached Marjorie about her companion, Leroy, who was in Raiford Prison for manslaughter—unfairly, she said. She urged Marjorie to get him out, and after a series of attempts, Marjorie obtained, through well-connected friends, parole for Leroy, provided she gave him a job. When he arrived at the Creek, Marjorie threw a wedding for him and 'Geechee and instructed him on grove work. The pair lived in the tenant house behind Marjorie's home.

But instead of hewing to his job, Leroy relaxed under his wife's care and wages, and complained about living so far from town. He grew sullen, and Marjorie, afraid he might threaten her, called the prison to take him back. The superintendent said there was no room. Stop risking your peace and send him away, the man said. Leroy will get picked up for something else. One day, according to Dessie Smith, who happened to be at the house helping Marjorie hang a curtain, Leroy started an argument with Marjorie about the use of her truck. It was Marjorie's only vehicle at the time, and she refused to let him borrow it. Leroy, standing outside the latched screen door, pulled at the handle, Dessie rushed out and threatened him with her pistol, and the two women ordered him off the property.

'Geechee accompanied Leroy out of the area but returned to work for Marjorie. The women got along very well. 'Geechee's good humor made her popular with guests. But after a time, Marjorie discovered that her housekeeper's happy mood was fueled by liquor—'Geechee had been helping herself to Marjorie's stores. Drink was the only thing that lifted her heart, 'Geechee said. By Christmas 1933, she had disappeared.

In 'Geechee's wake, Marjorie hired a couple to work around the farm and gave them the tenant house. But a year later, after she broke her neck in the horseback riding accident and was recovering in Tampa under Dessie's care, she admitted that she would need a nurse at Cross Creek and wondered if 'Geechee might be found. Plant City, twenty-five miles from Tampa, was 'Geechee's last known home, so Dessie spent a week combing the area for her. "I went to all the honky-tonks . . . and asked these colored people if they knew of a girl by the name of 'Geechee that had a big scar across her face," Dessie recalled years later. After several days, one fellow asked, "What do you want her for?" Dessie explained Marjorie's situation. "Well," the man said, "you come here tomorrow at 1:00 and maybe I will have found her for you."

Dessie met the man and followed him and a companion through two citrus groves to a large, dilapidated house. The man said he thought 'Geechee was there. Dessie hollered, ""Geechee!" and out she came running."

'Geechee agreed to help Marjorie and returned to the Creek sober, but she started drinking again, stirring up the household, losing the physical steadiness Marjorie depended on. Finally, 'Geechee confessed that she would never lose her taste for alcohol. "I know I got to go," she said. "I ain't no use to nobody and I can't help it." Marjorie paid her, and she left for her mother's. By the time Marjorie departed the Creek for Alaska, 'Geechee was gone for good.

The account of 'Geechee, as well as other Cross Creek pieces, whole or sketched, gave way to the boy's book in December, when Marjorie again visited Pat's Island in the Big Scrub. Cal Long had died, and his widow had left. The old house was uninhabitable. Yet in wandering about the place, Marjorie could imagine her boy character playing at a nearby sinkhole—a great concavity, lush with greenery—and by the end of 1935, the project was restored to her. She proposed "The Sink-Hole" as a working title for the book. The location was "grown up in dogwood and holly and bay and magnolia, that would have meant something very fascinating to a boy."

AFTER THE PREVIOUS winter's freeze, Marjorie's crop was down, though she considered her net return "fair" under the circumstances. She hunted again with Otto Lange. Their outings often ended with dinner and drinks at Cross Creek. "What a joy and a relief these days together are to me," Lange wrote in one note. "I hope you get as much pleasure and happiness out of them." In another letter to Marjorie, recounting a rainy business trip from Jacksonville to Gainesville, he asked, "Did you feel me thinking of you riding through the storm on the train last night?"

In March 1936, Marjorie admitted to Max that she hadn't been writing. "It is useless for me to try to get any work done in the winters here. . . . The strenuous hunting season, the comings and goings of people, the activity of grove work and orange picking, all combine to shatter the stillness and solitude I seem to need for writing." She grew impatient for hard work. Otto Lange might have been the recipient of that impatience, as two weeks later he wrote to Marjorie that she had "convinced me that I must be the mean, selfish, stuffy character you have so often charged me with being. I simply am not in your class and cannot measure up to what you require in a man, to give him your real respect and regard." He followed this letter with another note, presumably a reply to one of hers. He had missed her, but he begged her not to write "one of your vitriolic and abusive letters; to begin with, I shall never read any letter from you again, and in spite of it I would still be very much attached to Diana."

One of Marjorie's patterns during her separations from Chuck had been to soundly criticize him in one letter and apologize profusely in the next. That this pattern surfaced with Major Lange might be seen as a measure of their intimacy. They might have been too close for her comfort—Major Lange was married, with children. Or she might have wanted to retrench, now that winter was over and the boy's book was calling to her. In lashing out at the man closest to her, she reclaimed her focus and solitude. Armchair psychologists have wondered if Marjorie's mood swings indicated bipolarity; on the other hand, a sensitive artist consumed by work may simply want to get on with making the book or painting or symphony, to the exclusion of most everything else—and those closest to them might bear the brunt of their frustration. However it went, there exist no more letters that year from Major Lange.

MARJORIE WAS WELL INTO planning the new novel and reading voraciously, resuming exchanges with Max about books he sent, books they both had read. In May, she begged him for Thomas Wolfe's new release, *The Story of a Novel*, because she wanted to know how her editor entered a writer's mind while "keeping a necessary detachment."

The Story of a Novel is Wolfe's personal account of how *Look Homeward, Angel* and *Of Time and the River* got written, with Max Perkins as guiding midwife. Perkins had cut 90,000 words from the first novel, and struggled with Wolfe for two years to keep the second in check. In his opening, Wolfe confesses, "I am not a professional writer; I am not even a skilled writer; I am just a writer who is on the way to learning his profession and to discovering the line, the structure, and the articulation of the language which I must discover if I do the work I want to do." There follows, in fewer than one hundred pages—a remarkable feat for Wolfe—a saga of artistic production, with its hot and cold spells, fears, doubts, and distractions. Perkins recognizes Wolfe's gift but works assiduously, intuitively, to shape it, temper it, rein it in. Putting it mildly, Wolfe tended to overwrite, insisting that he needed more time— six months, then six months more—to fully explore his material. Max finally said time was up—else Wolfe would have spent his life on *Angel* and failed to publish it. Of *The Story of a Novel*, Marjorie wrote, "It's unbearable—its honesty—its fierceness—its beauty of expression."

"He is so young!" she exclaimed to Max. "When a little of the torment has expended itself, you will have the greatest artist America has ever produced." Referring to her editor, she reflected, "When all of us are done for, the chances are that literary history will find you the greatest— certainly the wisest—of us all—"

Chapter Twelve

The Widening Circle
1936-37

MARJORIE'S TWO SUCCESSFUL NOVELS and a place in the Scribner's pantheon attracted admiration and friendship from other notable writers, among them the poet Wallace Stevens, who spent winters in Key West. When he made his annual pass through central Florida in 1936, Marjorie threw a dinner party in his honor at Cross Creek; the menu, as always, featured dishes of local ingredients, including milk, cream, and butter from Dora, her prized cow. If Marjorie hadn't prepared all of the dishes by herself, she had closely supervised their execution. Her meals were served on the screened veranda in good weather, inside the farmhouse dining room before the fireplace when it was cold. Her table was set with linens, silver, and fine china; her maids wore clean, pressed uniforms, with headpieces, to serve. "We eat leisurely, and sigh when we think it is wise to eat no more," Marjorie wrote. Sometimes she gathered her house staff to sing and play the harmonica for her guests. The night Stevens came to dinner, the liquor flowed, as usual. Marjorie remembered that Stevens was "disagreeable and obstreperous, got drunk, read his poems with deliberate stupidity."

Robert Frost wintered in Florida, too. In 1935, after his doctors recommended that he spend the cold months in warm climates, Frost and his family vacationed in Key West, where he encountered, with some friction, Stevens. In 1936, the Frosts wintered in Coconut Grove, near Miami, and in December 1937, Robert and Elinor Frost rented an apartment in Gainesville. He would lecture at the University of Florida and speak at other universities. Frost was so enamored of the area that he began shopping for a permanent residence in Gainesville. Marjorie did her part, inviting the Frosts to the Creek, establishing a warm friendship. One evening, she and Norton Baskin, the easygoing Marion Hotel manager who had attended her divorce party and become Marjorie's constant companion, entertained the Frosts, along with University of Florida English professor Clifford Lyons and his wife, Gladys. At Frost's request, Marjorie read "Benny and the Bird Dogs," and "Mrs. Frost laughed so hard the small rocker she was sitting on tipped over," Clifford Lyons remembered.

But the celebrity writer spending all seasons in the state was Hemingway (born in 1899, three years after Marjorie), who bought a home in Key West and lived there, more or less, from 1931 to 1939. Marjorie met him early in the summer of 1936, while on a big-game fishing trip in Bimini with one of her sporting friends, Mrs. Oliver Grinnell, the widow of a well-known angler and an accomplished sportswoman— widely known by the nickname "Bill"—in her own right. *MotorBoating* magazine had recently described Bill Grinnell's twenty-hour battle with a giant swordfish, temporary relief coming only in the middle of the night from her boat captain. "At fifty-five, Mrs. Grinnell can fool any fish at the other end of her line into thinking that a husky young athlete is doing the pulling. She fought and pulled this swordfish the entire day until after dark. . . . It was five o'clock that morning—twenty hours after the fish had been hooked—that she brought it to gaff." Mrs. Grinnell had written the introduction to a recent book on big-game fishing, which Hemingway had contributed to. He happened to be in the Bahamas at the time and paid a call to her yacht, *Oligrin*. For Max, Marjorie described the encounter with her fellow Scribner's author:

> The man astonished me. I should have known, from your affection for him, that he was not a fire-spitting ogre, but I'd heard so many tales in Bimini of his going around knocking people down, that I half-expected him to announce in a loud voice that he never accepted

introductions to female novelists. Instead, a most lovable, nervous and sensitive person took my hand in a big gentle paw and remarked that he was a great admirer of my work.

The day before Marjorie left, Hemingway fought a 514-pound tuna for nearly seven hours and, coming into port with the giant fish, was greeted by a huge crowd. In attendance, Marjorie wrote Max, was a "fatuous old man with a new yacht and a young bride" who'd declared, based on nothing, that tuna fishing was a cinch. "Hemingway came swimming up from below decks, gloriously drunk, roaring, 'Who's the son of a bitch who said it was easy?' The last anyone saw of him that night, he was standing alone on the dock where his giant tuna hung from the stays—using it for a punching bag."

Marjorie continued,

There is, obviously, some conflict in Hemingway which makes him go about his work with a chip on his shoulder, and which makes him want to knock people down. He is so great an artist that he does not need to ever be on the defensive. He is so vast, so virile, that he does not need ever to hit anybody. Yet he is constantly defending something that he, at least, must consider vulnerable. It seems to me that there is a clue to it in the conflict between the sporting life and the literary life; between sporting people and the artist.

The sporting people are delightful. They have your soul. You feel clean and natural when you are with them. Then when you leave them, you are overcome with the knowledge that you are worlds away from them. You know things they will never know. They are somehow blunted. . . . They enjoy life hugely, yet they are not sensitive to it.

Marjorie thought that, in spending so much time among the sporting crowd, Hemingway felt obliged to hide "the agony that tears the artist" and pandered to them in his work, marring his beautiful writing with "a flippant comment or a deliberate obscenity. He injects those painfully foreign elements, not as an artist, but as a sportsman, and a sportsman of a particular type."

Max agreed with much of Marjorie's assessment. "It is an odd thing, but he has always felt that in being unable to play on a college football team he was deprived of his birthright," he replied. "He would have been a magnificent player, of course, but probably both college and football would have ruined him as a writer."

A few weeks later, Marjorie summoned the nerve to write to Hemingway herself. Two remarkable letters reveal how she strove to match or at least meet the hypermasculine author's tone, as she did with no one else—and to offer (no doubt unsolicited) writing advice. In the first letter, she invited him to stop in at Cross Creek. "I have a big, sloppy, easy-going place," she wrote, "have a better time at my own parties than anyone else, bake birds of all sorts in sherry so that you'd wonder why I wasted my time doing anything else, and like other people's offspring better, I'm sure, than I'd like my own. You'd be free here from annoyance of any sort, and it would make a good stopover for you. And if I should happen not to be here, the farm-menage, sloppiness and all, goes on whether I'm here or not."

She'd been inspired to write him after reading "The Snows of Kilimanjaro," published in the August *Esquire*. "My God, man, that's writing," she exclaimed.

One of the most stirring stories of our time, certainly—I can't conceive of oblivion for it. Tears you to pieces, of course—but writing is no good that doesn't. If it's not impudence to say it, it made me feel awfully good about you and your future. I can't put my finger on it—of course, for one thing, I don't know you, except as I know anyone whose work has meant something terrific to me—but I have a feeling of your having taken some sort of hurdle in your own mind— being done with something that was bothering you—being ready to be free. Your sports writing has been gorgeous—you couldn't write anything that didn't burst with vitality and color—but the people who would get the biggest kick out of it aren't, to me, the people you should be writing for.

. . . Is there any conflict in yourself between the sportsman and the artist? It's none of my goddamn business—but there must be. To me, you are pre-eminently the artist. Yet you'd probably rather do the spectacular as a virile male. It's the same with me. I don't consider myself an artist, but I grope for it, touch it now and then.

Hemingway replied from Montana with questions, which she answered. Yes, there were turkeys near her place, in the swamps along the Ocklawaha. "They are not much hunted in season," she explained, "because the local hunters are rather a lazy lot and don't have the patience to track them and roost them. They have been wiped out, though, in whole sections, by the backwards people who kill them anytime for food—perfectly legitimate, to my notion, when they have wisdom and conscience to respect the breeding curve and leave 'seed'—and by the illegal deer hunters who stumble on them on their prowlings."

She guaranteed good quail shooting, as well as ducks: ringnecks, pintails, scaup, mallards. And she wished for a good bear hunt, declaring that she liked to follow a

smelly, garrulous old Cracker through the swamp and the scrub and the hammock.

I like the birds in the thickets, the water snakes in the clear brown creeks, the sudden openings into a still and forgotten place, dark and clean with live oaks. A while ago I was two hours on a stand, about 30 feet in the air up a pine tree. It was in a red bay thicket, and the bays were tall and young and in bloom. They were all around me, and red birds came and preened themselves so close I could have touched them. At sunset a quick shower moved through, and the moon rose, and the bay leaves were like wet jade. Last winter two of us in the Everglades trailed five big bucks all day, from before sunrise until twilight. Through the cypresses, through sloughs and ponds, across the open patches of pine woods and palmettos. They stayed in a bunch, and we jumped them twice and never saw them. The second time, they slipped out through a long silver slough, and white herons circled, and I found an orchid, perfect, no bigger than my little fingertip, and it seemed to me that we were phantoms, following phantoms. And that's the kind of pleasure I get from hunting—never the kill. The hunting, for me, is only the motive for being in the places I like.

Once more, she invited Hemingway to visit the Creek. "I think you'll like it here," she wrote, "I know you will. Can only hope you like me. I made up my mind in a split second that I liked you." Hemingway didn't take her up on the offer, but the two would meet up again.

THE BAHAMAS VACATION had offered Marjorie distance on the boy's book, which she realized would be a substantial novel, not a story or novella with a quick turnaround. For new material, she had hunted bear twice with Barney Dillard, one of her informants for *South Moon Under*. Some of Dillard's experiences, like rattlesnake bites and hunting the infamous bear Old Slewfoot, would make it into the new book. More characters were slipping onto the stage. They would "make their own plot" as she wrote, but the tale would still be seen through the eyes of the boy, and "the unit I had [once] conceived of as the story will make a perfectly grand climax." The unit was Cal Long's unforgettable story of being forced to shoot his pet deer.

When Max sent a lukewarm response, Marjorie reminded him of his letter nearly three years earlier, in which he had suggested a full-bodied book. She described her growing stores of material from Dillard, and mentioned meeting Herschel Brickell in Blowing Rock, North Carolina, where she had recently given a talk. Brickell, one of the era's leading promoters of southern writers, had encouraged her to write long, as she desired, as short books were priced close to the amount of long ones, and there was no reason to be stingy with her material—readers wanted it, he said, and would appreciate it.

Her scope and intent for the boy's book, then, was "all settled," but she wouldn't be specific about it. "If I try to express in a few sentences in a letter what I mean to do, it has a paralyzing effect—making the stuff congeal in a quickly-said form," she told Max. Addressing the notion of a divided audience or a divided voice, observed in Hemingway, she said, "It is only since *Golden Apples* that I realize what it is about my writing that people like. I don't mean that I am writing for anyone, but now I feel free to luxuriate in the simple details that interest me, and that I have been so amazed to find interested other people."

THROUGH THE REST OF the summer of 1936, Marjorie immersed herself in the new book. "None of the fear and torment of Golden Apples," she reported to Max. In a letter to journalist Ernest Meyer, an old college friend, she confessed, "Now I think I have discovered my weakness: it is a tendency to clutter the text with gaudy colors that somehow mock reality, like a Maxfield Parrish print. I must work under my own mental thumb screws, hold myself in check when I want to gallop."

She finally wrote to Edith Pope, who had extended her hand three years before, explaining that she had been determined not to read Edith's writing, just as she and another Florida author, Edwin Granberry, who taught at Rollins College, had been determined not to read each other's, for "peace of mind." Encountering a few pages of Granberry's work, Marjorie had been "overcome with the beauty of his style, and thought, 'Why do I write about Florida when someone else, writing about it, can write like this?' "Yet," she continued to Edith, "each of us has something to say in his own way, and we could all write about the same tree and the same river, and the results would not be recognizable. But I do think it is just as well we go our own way."

Marjorie was so trained on work that the news that Chuck Rawlings would marry a twenty-six-year-old woman didn't faze her, despite Anne Rawlings's desperate letter to Marjorie, hoping again she'd take back her son. Around the same time, one of Barney Dillard's fifteen children questioned Marjorie's motives: Might she be working on something that could profit them, monetarily? This would happen more than once, as people unfamiliar with publishing imagined that Marjorie had grown rich overnight with *South Moon Under*. She was, and always would be, an outsider, no matter how hard she worked to fit in, and later on, when she did achieve financial success, her position in the community would be sorely tested. But now, Dillard set his children straight about Marjorie's research toward her next book. "She's interested in the old days and the old ways," he told a wary son. "Why, I never heard a woman cuss like she cussed this morning when we went out to Juniper Springs and she found the government had cleaned out the Springs and put up picnic tables." More research yielded unexpected materials. On a fishing trip with friends, Marjorie explored an abandoned house on Lake Kerr and discovered in its attic a day book from a few years before *The Yearling*'s dates (1870–71). She used the supply log as a model for a shopping list.

In August, Marjorie turned forty. For some reason, she had distanced herself from her old friend Dessie Smith, informing Chuck's aunt Ida Tarrant, "She has accepted my withdrawal for she doesn't bother me anymore. Gives me a funny look, but prefers evidently not to make an issue of it, which suits me, as you hate to come right out and hurt anyone's feelings." One wonders if Dessie was eclipsed by Marjorie's newer, wealthier sporting friends. (In an account more than fifty years later, Dessie blamed a falling-out on Marjorie's drinking, depressive moods, and refusal to testify in Dessie's divorce trial—though it's not clear which divorce.)

In September, Marjorie decamped to Banner Elk, North Carolina, to recover from another bout of malaria and to escape the grove business, the mosquitoes, and the heat and humidity—the general "drugged lassitude" one succumbs to in summers in the Deep South. She left her property in the care of Kate and Raymond, the black couple who had come to work after 'Geechee's final departure. Raymond was a dependable grove man, Kate had learned housework quickly, and Marjorie trusted them, mailing their weekly pay from Banner Elk, where she had rented an attractive mountain cabin with a view, walking distance to town. "Brought my Proust and my pointer," she wrote to Max. "Perfect company for work!" By now, she was playing around with other titles for the boy's book, one of which was *The Yearling*.

In late September, Max asked Marjorie to look in on Scott Fitzgerald, who in July had taken a room at the Grove Park Inn, in Asheville, to recuperate from conjoined depression and alcoholism. (His wife, Zelda, was being treated for schizophrenia in nearby Highland Hospital.) Scott's progress at Grove Park had stalled early on when he'd broken his right shoulder in a diving accident and been forced to wear a cast elevating his arm. A longtime alcoholic, he had, like Marjorie, begun his habit in the freewheeling 1920s; for him, it had become a debilitating addiction by the '30s; during that decade, he was hospitalized for alcoholism several times.

His literary reputation had also declined. After the success of *This Side of Paradise*, the sales of subsequent books had disappointed. Even *The Great Gatsby* had barely registered with the public. The *Saturday Evening Post*, which had regularly published his stories, had begun turning down his work, which increasingly addressed subjects like illness and personal failure—inappropriate for the *Post*'s readers. In 1935 he began bottoming out, confessing his illness and despair in three introspective essays published early in 1936 by *Esquire*. Later printed together as *The Crack-Up*, the three installments ("The Crack-Up," "Pasting It Together," and "Handle with Care") were not well received by peers like

Hemingway, who felt Scott's confession was self-indulgent and unmanly. As if that weren't enough, the *New York Post* sent journalist Michel Mok to interview Scott in Asheville, and the result, a mean-spirited piece titled "The Other Side of Paradise: Scott Fitzgerald, 40, Engulfed in Despair," appeared on September 25, the day after Scott's fortieth birthday. Max had written to Marjorie as soon as he'd read the article.

Marjorie had seen the *Post* interview and replied with shock and sympathy for the troubled author. "I don't see how any journalist could do such a cruel thing. It might easily be the last straw for Fitzgerald. . . . I know how that state of mind creeps up on you and I have had to fight it myself. It comes usually when one's personal background is unstable or unsatisfying or empty. Nothing, no work, takes the place of the right human contacts." Of course, she added, Scott had "wallowed in self-pity" and was only interested in himself. The Grove Park Inn, she felt, was a terrible place for him. The expansive, expensive stone hotel, with its mountain view and wealthy clientele, was devoid of anything "sound and vital."

She agreed to attempt a meeting with Fitzgerald, although she questioned its value, and she asked Max to tell her what, in her, would be helpful. Max replied that there was nothing in particular, "but I thought that something might develop that would enable you to speak directly." He agreed that Scott was self-centered and, thus, took no pleasure from the countryside, people, or animals, to his detriment. Others, like Marjorie, could derive strength from simple surroundings.

Toward the end of October, Marjorie planned a journey to Pisgah Forest Pottery, a center important in the Arts and Crafts movement, so she wrote to Fitzgerald, suggesting that she stop in Asheville. She had admired *The Great Gatsby*. "It simply took me off my feet. You have what must actually be a painful insight into people, especially complicated people," she wrote. "I don't understand people like us—and what little I do terrifies me. That's why I write, gratefully, of the very simple people whose problems are only the most fundamental and primitive ones. I have probably been more cowardly than I'd admit, in sinking my interests in the Florida backwoods, for the peace and beauty I've found there have been definitely an escape from the confusion of our generation. You have faced the music, and it is a symphony of discord."

Marjorie joined Fitzgerald in his Grove Park rooms on a Saturday afternoon. Her lengthy report to Max maintained that Scott had not been drinking liquor, thanks to his watchful nurse, and that they had "only sherry and table wine, and talked our heads off," lifting their glasses to Max. Scott had been angry about the *Post* article and felt duped by the reporter, who had offered his own sob story first to gain Scott's sympathy and draw him out. Now, though, Scott had settled down about it, and wanted to talk about Hemingway's recent put-down of him in "The Snows of Kilimanjaro." In it, the main character "remembered poor Scott Fitzgerald" and his fascination with the rich. When he discovered that they weren't a special race, "it wrecked him as much as any other thing that wrecked him." Scott didn't seem bitter about it and agreed with Marjorie that Hemingway's strike was part of the author's "sadistic maladjustment." The two men had previously corresponded about Scott's personal revelations in *Esquire*, Hemingway damning him, Scott defending the effort to openly express pain.

Marjorie admitted that Scott was deeply distressed but felt that he was, at the root, all right. She, as well as other writers, experienced black times—Scott's just received more publicity. They had disagreed about personal expectations, as to how life would go. Marjorie expected highs and lows, neither to last indefinitely. Scott expected the highs to go on and on. "You're not as much of an egotist as I am," he told her. "His point of view lets him in for much desperate unhappiness and disillusion," Marjorie wrote.

The visit lasted more than four hours. In the end, Marjorie felt she had been of little help to Scott, but, she added, "there is a most helpful stimulation in talk between two people who are trying to do something of the same thing—a stimulation I miss and do not have enough of, at Cross Creek." Her isolation was, after all, not the ideal writer's life. She was close to extraordinary material but far from her literary tribe. Back in the Banner Elk cabin, she immediately reread *Gatsby* and wrote Scott an effusive tribute:

> The book resolves itself into the strangest feeling of a crystal globe, or one of the immense soap bubbles we achieved as children, if it could hold its shape and color without breaking — — It is so beautiful, it is so clairvoyant, it is so heart-breaking — —

Please, how can you talk of security when the only security is the loveliness of the dream? And you are right to think that anything can be mended, and life can be cut to order, like a diamond — — But turn about is fair play, and you must give life the same privilege — to mend and change you, and to cut new facets —I suppose you know that nothing is wasted — — The hell you've been through isn't wasted — — All you have to do, ever, is to forget everything and turn that terrible, clear white Light you possess, on the minds and emotions of the people it stirs you to write about — — That's your security — —

As for her own writing in North Carolina, Marjorie continued her deep engagement with the boy's book, and concurrently grew fond of, and fascinated by, a twelve-year-old boy from a nearby orphanage who cut wood for her. The boy, Dale Wills, visited often, and Marjorie became so attached that she considered adopting him, until she learned that he had a mother who boarded him at the orphanage. The situation inspired her to write "A Mother in Mannville," an autobiographical story told by a woman who, like Marjorie, has come to the North Carolina mountains to write and hires a boy from the orphanage to cut wood. The two grow close. The narrator explains her attraction to the boy: he has "integrity."

"The word means something very special to me, and the quality for which I use it is a rare one," Marjorie's narrator explained. "My father had it—there is another of whom I am almost sure—but almost no man of my acquaintance possesses it with the clarity, the purity, the simplicity of a mountain stream." One day, the boy tells the author that he is not really an orphan. He has a mother in Mannville who sometimes sends him gifts; he sees her only in the summer. He elaborates, convincingly. Horrified, the writer intends to locate the mother, to find out why she would place this nice boy in an institution, but she grows distracted by her work and doesn't get around to it. On her way out of the mountains, she stops by the orphanage to leave money for the boy's birthday and Christmas presents, telling the spinster in charge that she's afraid of duplicating things his mother might give him. The spinster says she doesn't understand—the boy has no mother.

"A Mother in Manville" was accepted by the *Saturday Evening Post* for its December 12, 1936, issue. Also in December, *Scribner's Magazine* published the second of Marjorie's Quincey Dover Cracker tales—her raconteur side let out to play. In "Varmints," Quincey unspools a yarn about two men, Jim and Luty, who share ownership of a "droop-eared, sway-backed, wise-looking, tobaccy-chewing, rum-drinking, trompling son of a donkey" named Snort. When Snort falls dead in her sweet potato patch and neither Jim nor Luty will have anything to do with the beast, Quincey is forced to bury Snort herself. "Now I weigh a sight more'n two hundred and I ain't modest about it," she announces. "But ary person who thinks digging a hole deep enough to bury a mule, on a hot day in the blazing sun, is fairy's work, for a woman who weighs more'n two hundred, had ought to get in the same fix."

BESIDES HER VISIT with Scott Fitzgerald, Marjorie was obligated to family and friends that fall. Chuck's aunt Ida Tarrant had visited Cross Creek the previous winter and liked it; while Marjorie was in North Carolina, Ida decided to move from Cincinnati to Ocala. Now Marjorie felt pressured to return to Florida sooner than she wanted. And her brother, Arthur, writing to Marjorie in Banner Elk in October, expressed interest in a Florida hunting trip in late November. He would drive three thousand miles for it.

In his letter, Arthur confessed another motive: "I am not coming to hunt unless you call hunting a lovely charming, educated, refined, gracious and wealthy widow, divorcee or maiden lady for wife #3." He wasn't joking—he was in "a cloud of trouble." There were complications with both former wives now, and his business was still on the skids. He needed his sister's advice, to "sit around with you over our cups and see if the two of us can't find a solution to my bad mental attitude." He promised to honor her work schedule, "or, if you refuse to rest, in typical Kinnan fashion, until your work is done, just put me in line with some of your lovely wealthy ladies." He wouldn't be a bother—he'd give her a hand around the place.

When Marjorie got back to the Creek, she was met by loss and disarray. Her chickens, all fifty-four of them, were gone. Kate said "varmints" had gotten them. There no was food in the icebox or pantry, though Marjorie had sent money ahead for provisions. Her locked liquor cabinet was empty—someone had gone through the attic to raid it. The house hadn't been kept clean. "Spiders swung comfortably in every corner," she wrote. Restraining her temper, Marjorie gave Raymond the keys to her truck so he could drive into town for food. But he didn't return that night, and Marjorie was forced to follow his trail, fire him, and retrieve the truck.

Because Arthur would arrive soon, Marjorie kept Kate on, on a trial basis. Kate said she had a new sweetheart, a promise of stability. In the early days of Arthur's visit, everything went well. He remarked on "the ease and smoothness of this life." But when he and Marjorie left for a weekend to hunt deer, all hell broke loose. Sister and brother returned to a neglected farmhouse and grounds, and in the tenant house they discovered Kate, her new sweetheart, and Raymond in bed, drunk. A frantic scene commenced, and in the end, Kate, Raymond, and the sweetheart departed forever.

For a while, Marjorie kept busy replenishing the chicken flock, milking the cow, driving the grove truck, and hiring a new grove manager and housekeeper. During the turnover, she appreciated the help of the Mickens family matriarch, Martha, "a woman of intelligence, clean, hardworking, and a good cook." Marjorie was glad, at least, that Arthur's visit had gone well, and that he had backed her up in the tenant house scene. He'd also enjoyed a fishing trip with Bill Grinnell and watched his sister land a sailfish.

But while Florida fascinated him, he had been ready to leave after the turn of the year, in January. Florida "lacks the rough ruggedness of the Northwest," he wrote his sister. Apparently, she had floated the idea of moving out his way permanently, but Arthur felt that Marjorie might do better to stay at Cross Creek. "A Mother in Mannville" had proved that she didn't have to travel far for new material, he observed. No matter what the setting, she had a gift for understanding the human condition.

After he left, Marjorie opened her home to old friends from Wisconsin and Louisville, the Hardys, who sought respite from the Ohio River flood that had begun in January. The waters inundated Louisville long into February. Though she didn't expect it, the Hardys' experience would compel her to rethink the new novel.

Chapter Thirteen

The Yearling

1937-38

In July 1936, Marjorie had refused to describe the new book for Max. In August, she had been "perfectly delirious with delight." "You and I are going to love the book," she told him. From Banner Elk, she exclaimed, "I do not know when I have ever enjoyed my material so much, unless it was in Jacob's Ladder." By November, from Cross Creek, she could summarize the story: a critical year in the life of a boy, beginning with innocent play, ending with the death of his pet deer—innocence lost. "I assure you the fabric of the story will carry it," she wrote. "I have no fear of it at all and I shall be careful never to sentimentalize."

Yet early in 1937, after a hiatus—long-term visitors, work on her property, reading "A Mother in Mannville" for Rollins College's Animated Magazine—Marjorie found her pages wanting. She threw out most of them and returned to the first chapter, to deepen the characters, make them "so real, so familiar," that everything befalling them would hit close to home. The Hardys' experience had caused the shift. "The Louisville flood meant nothing to me until I found that the factory and beautiful home of my dearest friends were under water, and I was unable to contact them," she explained to Max. "The whole sweep of water and devastation became at once a true and unbearable thing." Perhaps the

secret of effective fiction, she suggested, was to create characters so realistic that "anything they do becomes vivid and important."

Now Marjorie's relationship with *The Yearling*, officially so titled,
was past the honeymoon stage and in the trenches. In February she was
"on the point of exploding with frustration." In March, she saw that
much of the discarded material could be used later in the manuscript.
In April, she was interrupted when relatives stopped in and one of her
housekeepers had a minor operation. And Arthur had written to say he
was afraid he'd be "back on your hands, at your expense." He'd sunk a
thousand dollars into his boat to sell cruises to Alaska, but no one had
signed up. He was deep in debt and liquidating his assets. If he didn't
draw income soon, he'd use up his modest capital.

ARTHUR'S NEWS BROKE Marjorie's gait. "I lost my hard-won abstraction again," she confided to Max. "Last night I sat on my porch in the
moonlight with no other light, waiting for the maid to bring me my supper tray. I heard her stop in the living room and say aloud to herself, 'I
don't know where Mrs. Rawlings is.' I thought, 'Sometimes I'm not sure
myself—.'"

Max urged her to submit pages, no matter how rough they were. In
late May, Marjorie announced that she was driving to New York with
Mrs. Grinnell, who had offered her a room at her Long Island estate,
which had a view of the Great South Bay and Fire Island. The change of
scene might feed her writing, Marjorie thought, but as it turned out, her
hostess tended a heavy social schedule, and the guest from Florida could
not help but participate. "I really think she [Mrs. Grinnell] is a lonely
soul and puts up with many of these parasites as a panacea to her solitude," C. Blackburn Miller, a fellow guest whose name could be found
on the *Social Register*, confided to Marjorie. (Miller, another of Marjorie's admirers, imagined her "in a hammock on a moonlit verandah with
the night winds softly soughing in the foliage.")

In early June, she met Max and Thomas Wolfe in New York, and the
three painted the town, starting with drinks at Chatham Walk, an outdoor café, and moving on to a steak dinner, more drinks, another dinner
(Chinese), and finally, toward dawn, Fulton Street oysters. In the midst
of their spree, Marjorie brought up the subject of suicide, and Wolfe,
well-lit, thought she was urging him to do it and made a fuss. "I wished

I had argued about something simple, like transcendentalism," she told Max. From Mrs. Grinnell's, Marjorie sent her editor an incomplete draft of *The Yearling*, with notes on things to come. They discussed it on the phone, and Marjorie followed up with a letter. "Why didn't you tell me how sappy The Yearling was?" she asked. Rereading it, she was tempted to "drop it in Mrs. Grinnell's private canal where her gardener dumps the too-full-blown roses."

WHILE IN NEW YORK, Marjorie heard from Clifford Lyons, now head of the University of Florida's English Department, asking her to deliver a lecture to an Imaginative Writing class once a month. (The first guest lecturer, in residence at the time, was John Crowe Ransom, the venerable agrarian and editor of the *Kenyon Review*.) Expecting *The Yearling* to be done by the fall semester, she agreed.

She also dropped a line to Otto Lange, who was thrilled to hear from her. "I've missed you woefully," he replied. It seemed some person or event had previously severed their tie. "It is a good thing that both of us were rapped over the knuckles a bit during the past two years," he wrote. He brought Marjorie up to date on his family and his health. He had undergone a physical, and his doctors suspected heart problems. "That last night at your house," he admitted, "it was pain in my heart that woke me up and caused me to sit up, but naturally I was not going to mention it to you." All he needed was sleep and some rest from nervous strain. He had recently been transferred, and invited her for a "real visit" at Fort Benjamin Harrison, his new post northeast of Indianapolis, offering her his private study and a tour of the area.

Marjorie did not make the trip. In a letter to Julia Scribner, she confided that the one professionally exceptional man she had been in love with, whose work seemed valuable to her, was married, and she had been obliged to admit that he could not become unmarried, to marry her. Besides, *The Yearling* and its fortunes would consume her into the next year, and Norton Baskin was her exclusive partner now, his qualities as a southern gentleman—sociability, even temperament, helpfulness, loyalty—edging out any available choices. Norton was the perfect companion for the high-strung writer, a man comfortable in public situations, agreeable at home, with a quick yet subtle sense of humor and a storytelling talent that Marjorie appreciated and that endeared him to her friends. As a friend put it, "He was the quiet one. But pretty soon Norton would start telling stories, and pretty soon, Norton's got an audience."

BY OCTOBER 1937, Marjorie had returned to Cross Creek, finished *The Yearling*, and was editing: "lots of blue pencil, and a change here and there of tone, rather than revision." She gave her first creative writing lecture to students at the University of Florida, and Clifford Lyons suggested another for November, more focused: "On the Relationship Between Fact and Fiction."

Marjorie didn't write a formal paper for that talk, but she carried a cohesive sheaf of ideas, examples, and anecdotes headed "Scratched for babbling."

"I hope you don't mind my using notes," she began, explaining, "My mind is like a grasshopper." Then she launched into her topic, saying, "The question most frequently asked of fiction writers is: How much of this is true?

"The relation of fact to fiction, from a practical standpoint, is the whole basis of literature," she asserted in her notes.

> Life, and living, are the source of all fiction except sheer fantasy. Even the great invented works, such as Faust, have their source, if not in true people, at least in ideas and emotions that are true. . . . The writer takes his initial inspiration, [and] is fertilized by the creative germ, according to his own response to people and situations of his own experience or imagination.

Sometimes a real person inspires the writer to build ideas, emotions, and story, around a character, she noted. Or a writer might create characters to express ideas, emotions, situations, incidents. But even to real-life characters, the writer "adds his own touches, for his own purposes, to characters he has known." She had done this with Uncle Benny in "Benny and the Bird Dogs."

"The physical description of Uncle Benny is my own invention," she explained. "It better fitted the quality of mind I wanted to catch than the true Uncle Benny's actual appearance. Yet that quality of mind is true, so that anyone who knows the true Uncle Benny says, 'Why, that must be Fred Tompkins.'"

"Neither approach, from the character to the story, or from the story to the character, is more valid or more artistic," she reflected. "Hemingway works almost entirely from true characters, out. Thomas Wolfe is as autobiographical, as biographical, as Hemingway, yet in most of his work he begins with the universal. He works from the outside in, leaving you usually to draw your own universal or cosmic conception from his presentation."

Marjorie considered Wolfe the greater artist, because Wolfe's conceptions were broader.

As for facts themselves, they are not "an open Sesame to good writing."

"It is a common error to believe that travel, adventure, contact with many kinds of people will automatically provide the writer with material," because in the end it "depends on the writers' ability to sort them into himself," she cautioned. "It is tempting to think that if something in real life is compelling, all you need to do is to get that character or that incident down on paper as it existed," but it isn't so. "Sometimes, the material for a story or a book or even a sketch, simply is not there."

Dealing with facts, she said, is like dealing with dynamite. "I don't mean some character will recognize himself and come running for you with buckshot, although that is a minor consideration. I mean that fact is dangerous material from the artistic standpoint." Facts are unreliable and treacherous. That is, a writer's judgment of their artistic value is unreliable and treacherous.

Referring to memoir or autobiography, she noted, "It takes a far greater artist to write artistically of himself than of other people. We are fascinating to ourselves, and doubly dangerous, artistically."

She also remarked on a seeming paradox: "Strangely enough, facts used literally in fiction often do not carry a conviction of truth. Something about them, when used for an imaginative purpose, strikes a dissonant note." To use facts well takes "good taste, good judgment, and most of all, experience."

"You are lost if you cling to them too desperately."

ON DECEMBER 2, Marjorie expressed *The Yearling* to New York, with a note: "Hope you find the book reasonably good." The "boy's book," set on and around Baxter's Island (Pat's Island, in real life) in the 1870s, was finally finished, its central characters—young Jody Baxter and his parents, Ezra ("Penny") and Ora—alive on the page for the course of a year marking Jody's coming of age. Like other Crackers in Marjorie's fiction, the Baxters struggle to support themselves on a remote patch of land, tending crops, raising livestock, and hunting, and although Jody seems to enjoy an idyllic childhood, he increasingly witnesses and participates in the hard labor, physical and emotional, of forging a decent existence. The Forresters, a rough clan nearby, antagonize the Baxters, though their youngest, a crippled boy named Fodderwing, who loves animals, is Jody's friend. A central event involves the hunt for Old Slewfoot, an infamous, destructive bear.

The path to Jody's adulthood begins when Penny is bitten by a rattlesnake and shoots a doe for her liver, to draw out the snake's venom. Against his parents' misgivings, Jody is allowed to take the doe's orphaned fawn for a pet, and the pair become inseparable. Fodderwing names the fawn Flag. But as Flag matures, he feeds on the family's corn crop, endangering their winter stores, so to survive, the Baxters must destroy Jody's pet. Penny Baxter orders his son to shoot Flag. When the boy can't summon the strength, Ora "Ma" Baxter attempts a shot, wounding the deer, finally forcing Jody—out of necessity, compassion, and grief—to complete the task. He rebels and leaves the farm, but not for long. He returns to his family, initiated into adult life.

Max offered only minor quibbles. "The truth is the book is so very fine . . . the whole flow and development is wonderfully successful," he wrote. Indeed, the story and its pacing, accomplished within Marjorie's glowing tapestries of the natural world, are wholly satisfying. Max immediately engaged Edward Shenton, a prolific book illustrator and a house artist for *Scribner's Magazine*, to create headpieces for the chapters, and two days before Christmas, he wrote Marjorie again: "After completing such a book which shows no signs of effort, but certainly must truly represent an enormous amount of it, you ought to have a merry Christmas and a happy New Year, and I hope you may."

As 1938 DAWNED, author and editor tweaked *The Yearling*'s galleys, and when Marjorie finished her part in January, she said she would take one more look, "with as cold an eye as possible, to eliminate as much as I can of the flaccid quality to which you and I are both so sensitive. Isn't it odd that a writer can put down things that he would not tolerate in another's writing?" She observed that in the writing process, "the boy became a very real boy, and less of a symbol of the transition from childhood to manhood, which was the thing I wanted to express." She had moved from the idyllic to the realistic, and "whether the quality of actuality is more valuable than the idyllic quality is perhaps a debatable question. But I do see the story, within myself, poetically and I am afraid there is no getting away from it."

The Yearling was approaching published form. The *Saturday Evening Post* turned down serialization—a financial disappointment but a relief, too. Marjorie hadn't wanted to dole out the book in pieces. She complained again about an author photograph and objected to the omission of "Kinnan" from ad copy. "I always regretted not having used just Marjorie Kinnan to write under," she told Max, "and I want the middle name used always where it shows."

BY THE TIME *The Yearling* was published, in March 1938, the world was teetering on the brink of Hitler's demands, which would lead inexorably to World War II. In Florida, the *Palm Beach Post* tried sounding a light, local note, complaining of Hitler's decree to save fabric by shortening all German men's shirttails by two inches. "It looks even worse for American cotton growers than it did awhile back," the unnamed editor wrote, alluding to the boll weevil's recent devastation in the American South, including north Florida. Orange growers struggled, too—a hard freeze had troubled the Citrus Belt during the winter of 1937–38, thinning Marjorie's crop. "I fired my young grove two nights in succession," she reported to Max.

> It was very beautiful. There was a fatwood fire in the center of each square, that is, one fire to each four trees. The light from the fat pine is a rich orange, and the grove seemed to be full of bivouac fires, as regular as a geometric design. They illuminated the sky to a Prussian blue, with the palm tops against it. Facing away from the fires, the light gave my low rambling house, the orange trees and the palms around it, a flat silver-gold wash, most theatrical. The cold sky was absolutely sequined with stars. It was so beautiful that it was almost worth what it cost me.

Marjorie was up four nights with her nine-man crew, keeping them in "food and coffee and liquor, and two of the boys sang almost all night long." She saved the young trees but mistakenly assumed the mature fruit had survived, and just before Christmas, inspectors condemned some of it. She asked Max for a $1,000 advance on *The Yearling* to cover her bills. "I really should have fifteen hundred," she added. One of her workers had split open his foot with an axe, and she'd taken him to her doctor, covering the costs. "This sort of thing does not bother me," she remarked, "for I have increasingly the feeling that nothing tangible belongs to us. I have supported, with work and assistance, several poor neighbors, all summer and fall, people who are too proud to go on relief and anxious to work, and it seems to me that it doesn't make a scrap of difference whether the few hundred dollars involved are in my pocket or theirs."

A FEW SPEAKING ENGAGEMENTS turned up just before publication: a talk for the Florida Historical Society on the creative use of Florida material, and another appearance at Rollins's Animated Magazine, where she read from *The Yearling*. Hamilton Holt, president of Rollins College, paid her many compliments: "I have never read such art in character delineation. You have made the characters speak for themselves and have never acted the part of the Greek chorus in explaining them," he wrote in one letter. Later on, he added, "The fact is, you are a very remarkable woman and I wish I knew better what goes on inside your head. Perhaps you will let me find out sometime."

Financial relief appeared: the Book-of-the-Month Club named *The Yearling* as its April selection. In New York, Max and his wife, Louise, arranged a celebratory tea. Marjorie went up by train and made the rounds of press, literary folk, and friends. The novel had drawn the highest praise. Charles Poore of the *New York Times* observed that the novel did not follow a formal plot but achieved its coherence and vitality in "the skillful counterpoint of dramatic wilderness incidents and acute homespun characterizations." He quibbled a bit over tone: "Occasionally, in speaking of Jody, Mrs. Rawlings has the fond air of an Amy Lowell contemplating the young Keats. But her sensitively written accounts of his inner life, his private forays in the country, and his feelings of despondency or elation when things go right or wrong, are beautifully done." Marjorie's sensibilities saved her book from being either "a sentimental threnody or a soil-saga."

William Soskin of the *New York Herald Tribune* compared Jody to Tom Sawyer, Huckleberry Finn, and the "lesser members of the fraternity of young boys in American literature"; Jody was possibly "the most charming one in the entire national gallery." Soskin concluded, "Out of this landscape of life in the Florida scrub, woven closely with unforgettable portraits of native people in their kitchens, in their churches, in ceremonies of birth and death, in their tragedies and their virile battles against the elements, Mrs. Rawlings draws a story with a tragic climax—that of the end of youth."

In the Sunday *New York Times Book Review*, Edith H. Walton echoed Poore, noting that although *The Yearling* contained dangerous and tragic scenes, Marjorie did not rely on high drama. "The thing about *The Yearling*—its great claim to distinction—is that it is able to make so much of simple homely events," she remarked. "The zest of a hunting expedition, the stir of a Spring in the forest, a suddenly glimpsed dance of grave, stately cranes—it is out of material as humble as this that the texture of the book is woven." Walton praised Marjorie's ear for dialect and lack of patronage toward backwoods folk. "*The Yearling* is nothing so narrow and limited as a 'local-color' novel," she wrote.

IN NEW YORK, Marjorie spoke on the radio and met new people, continuing her transformation from private writer to citizen of a significant artistic world. On the way back to Florida, she briefly visited Lois and Ed Hardy in Louisville, and Otto Lange and his family in Indianapolis. She'd recently congratulated Lange on a promotion. He still missed her. "The hunger of one person for another, truly congenial, mentally, spiritually and in a physical sense is a rather poignant agony, but I should know that I must not tell you this," he had written earlier that year, with resignation. He'd offered news of his work, travels, and reading, but said he couldn't help remembering a moonlit night at Cross Creek, in a soft wind "and that magnificent old Orange Lake stretched out below us." When Marjorie agreed to visit, he wrote, sounding a familial tone, "We all want you as soon as you can come." They would keep in touch, from a distance.

Marjorie Kinnan, four years old

Ida May Traphagen Kinnan, Marjorie's mother

Arthur Frank Kinnan, Marjorie's father

Marjorie as Pierrette in a Union Vodvil performance, junior year, University of Wisconsin

Left: Marjorie with Charles Rawlings, c. 1919. *Right:* Arthur Houston Kinnan, Marjorie's brother.

The farmhouse at Cross Creek

Top left: Marjorie with her cat and hunting dogs, 1930s. *Top right:* Marjorie interviewing Julian Bauknight, early 1930s. *Bottom left:* Dessie Smith Vinson. *Bottom right:* Zelma Cason as a young woman.

Will and Martha Mickens

Marjorie crabbing, 1930s

Left: Piety and Leonard Fiddia, inspirations for the characters Piety and Lant in *South Moon Under. Right:* Marjorie hunting with Norton Baskin.

Maxwell Perkins, 1930s

Martha Mickens and Idella Parker in the farmhouse kitchen

Julia Scribner Bigham

The farmhouse staff entertaining Marjorie, Norton Baskin
(to her left), and guests.

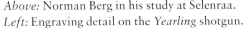

Above: Norman Berg in his study at Selenraa.
Left: Engraving detail on the *Yearling* shotgun.

Left: Marjorie Kinnan Rawlings in her garden. Photo by Alan Anderson. *Right:* Wedding of Marjorie Kinnan Rawlings and Norton Sanford Baskin, October 27, 1941.

Novelist Ellen Glasgow

Norton Baskin, American Field Service

Marjorie signing books for servicemen, 1942

Zora Neale Hurston, 1938,
by Carl Van Vechten

Right: Marjorie outside
the cottage at Crescent Beach

Below: Marjorie's home in
Van Hornesville, New York

Left: Portrait of Marjorie
Kinnan Rawlings, c. 1947,
by Albert Stadler.
Right: Marjorie Kinnan
Rawlings, January 1, 1953,
by Carl Van Vechten.

By the time Marjorie returned to the Creek, *The Yearling* had shot onto the best-seller lists. Reorders poured in. In late April, Carl Brandt sold the film rights to Metro-Goldwyn-Mayer for $30,000; this was followed by sales of foreign editions. Congratulations arrived from old friends, teachers, librarians, fellow writers. Marjory Stoneman Douglas wrote, "It is so lovely, so finely felt, so beautifully unified and sustained," and she sympathized with postpartum slump: "I find myself wondering if you had the reaction you did after *South Moon Under*, a sort of dullness and depression, as if there was nothing else to look forward to, after success. I do hope not, or at least, only briefly. I can see it is nothing more important than a pendulum swing."

But particularly touching were responses from young boys. To one, who confided problems with his father, Marjorie replied,

> I feel that you must be a generous and unselfish person, to have analyzed the situation between yourself and your father as you did. It is true that we all respond to sympathy and understanding, and having a fuss made over us, and feeling that others are truly interested in what we are doing, and are anxious to work with us. The trouble with the world today is that there is so little cooperation, so little unselfishness. If all of us try to understand one another, we should find that the other fellow is as lonely as we are, as anxious for love and sympathy. Then there would be no more quarrels, no more wars.
>
> I should like very much to have you write me again, telling me how you were getting on. I am hoping that your father has understood your attitude and that you have grown closer together. I wonder if it has ever occurred to you that grown people can be very shy? Parents often do not feel sure of their children's love, and hesitate to make friendly advances to them. So they respond more easily to children who make it plain that they do love them.

Chapter Fourteen

Pulitzer

1938-39

WITH HER PROJECTED ROYALTIES and MGM contract, Marjorie now had a financial problem in the plus column, and for practical reasons, she contacted Otto Lange, who recommended tax strategies and investments yielding a good annual income. He had reread *The Yearling* and suggested a rendezvous in Nashville: "Wire me at Ft. Knox." But there is no evidence that she took him up on it. Marjorie was all business, and she might have fallen ill. By early June, she was on her way to St. Joseph's Hospital in Tampa to have part of her lower intestine removed. After years of periodic discomfort, she had finally been diagnosed with diverticulitis—it's possible that she had been born with a diverticulum (an abnormal pouch at a weak point in the intestines)—a condition exacerbated by alcohol consumption. The situation was grave enough for her to write Max, explaining her condition and naming her brother, Arthur, executor of her estate. Norton Baskin would take charge of her affairs if she was in for a long recovery. Max replied with shock and a provisional farewell: "Even if I had never seen you, and we had done everything by letter I should be profoundly concerned because the privilege—which is what it was—of cooperating with you as an Editor has been one of the happiest and most satisfying experiences I have ever had—and ever shall—and I am most grateful for it."

But just as the letter reached its destination, Marjorie's strategy changed. "The Three Musketeers" had persuaded her to get a second opinion, and now she was in Riverside Hospital in Jacksonville, receiving treatment and instead of surgery, dietary instructions. She could regulate her condition herself, Dr. T. Z. Cason told her. Though following a bland diet was a tall order for a high-strung woman given to smoking, drinking, and lavish cooking, the proposed surgery could have been disastrous. "If you'd gone through with it, you'd have been cavorting with the angels just about today," Dr. Cason said. The mortality rate for the surgery was about 40 percent. That fact reminded Marjorie of something Robert Frost had told her the previous winter: "Statistics don't mean anything. A doctor goes peacefully to sleep because he has only lost one patient out of ten. 10% is nothing. The deuce it isn't. It's 100%—I'M DEAD!"

MARJORIE NEEDED A VACATION, and when Bill Grinnell invited her to fish in Bimini again in July, she accepted. Mrs. Grinnell's goal was a five-hundred-pound blue marlin, so the women "fished hard in all kinds of weather," hoping to achieve it. Afterward in Miami, staying in Mrs. Grinnell's luxurious Everglades Hotel apartment, Marjorie was interviewed about *The Yearling* by a reporter who noticed that she was "extremely nervous" and another who described her appearance: "She wore a cotton print dress and low-heeled shoes and her stockings were pushed down to her ankles—revealing severely sunburned legs. Her face, neck and arms also were sunburned from the pilot boat trip which took six hours and during which she had to sit atop an empty gasoline can." It hadn't been much of a vacation.

NOW MARJORIE WAS inundated with requests for magazine stories and articles. She balked: "I cannot and will not write to order." When a good fee was offered, she might acquiesce, but post-*Yearling*, post-hospitalization, she took on just one such project: a long letter about her Traphagen grandparents' farm in Michigan—its beginnings, and her memories of it—for the centennial edition of the *Holly Herald*.

Marjorie opened with a tribute to Louis Bromfield's *The Farm*, wishing she had written such a book about the Traphagen acres, regretting that she had failed to collect her grandfather's stories before he died. Yet her own detailed memories unfurled gracefully. At her grandmother's table, she recalled "poached eggs so fresh they quivered with their newness." Her grandfather was said to spend so much time with a nearby Native American tribe—probably that of King Fisher, the decorated chief who'd heard Fenton's first piano—that locals remarked "Abe Traphagen is half Indian." And the farm's apple orchard she compared to her orange grove in one long, rhapsodic sentence: "From the time the apple blossoms covered the trees like pale careless bouquets, through the long green summer, up to the cool fall, when the fruit hung like lanterns, shining red of Baldwin and snow-apple, wax-green of Greening, golden of sheep's-nose and of banana apple, burnished gold of the russet, and into the snowy winter when the bare gray trunks and limbs were as lovely as a Japanese drawing, the orchard was a thing of grace and beauty."

Three weeks after Bimini, Marjorie was in Riverside Hospital again for dieting and observation. She was running a temperature—it's unlikely she had stuck to spartan meals with Mrs. Grinnell. Norton continued to lift her spirits, writing from the Marion Hotel in Ocala and visiting her in Jacksonville. He offered domestic reports of his own, and her farm, describing business at the hotel, work at her grove, and news of Chuck's aunt Ida Tarrant, whom he kept entertained, for he, too, had adopted her. He encouraged Marjorie's "water diet." If that didn't help, he wrote, "We will switch back to Barklay's." He was watching out for her in every way, as he would continue to do in all the years forward. His summer letters to her, the first she saved, were signed with love.

While recuperating, Marjorie received word that Thomas Wolfe had fallen ill with pneumonia. "He was all alone wandering about the Northwest, and he is in some sort of a private hospital," Max informed her. Wolfe had recently defected to Harper's. Max cited several possible reasons, but he stressed the idea that the expansive writer, often driven by his unconscious, probably needed to detach from dependence on his editor and publisher—which Max, though sorry to lose him, approved. ("That is what he must do, if he is to become a really great writer.") Though the whole thing had been bitter business for Max, it freed him from "a burden that I never realized was so great until he was gone."

Yet he continued to worry about the writer. A few weeks later, Wolfe sent Max an anguished but prescient letter. He "had a 'hunch'" having "seen the dark man very close," and though he did not make his instinct explicit, one can read between the lines. Wolfe wasn't sure he would live much longer. "If I get on my feet, I'll come back," he wrote, adding, "Whatever happens—I had this 'hunch' and wanted to write you and tell you, no matter what happens or has happened, I shall always think of you and feel about you the way it was that 4th of July 3 yrs. ago when you met me at the boat, and we went out on the café on the river." The New York memory marked the summer just after *Of Time and the River* was published.

DURING HER WRITING HIATUS, Marjorie approved Scribner's idea to publish her collected short stories and enjoyed reactions to *The Yearling*. One of her favorite responses came by way of a hunter who had studied the book and written to Barney Dillard, praising its authenticity. Marjorie had worried that readers like the hunter would find mistakes. "I know you think I put too much emphasis on the importance of fact in fiction," she wrote Max, "but it seems to me that this type of work is not valid if the nature lore behind it is not scientifically true in every detail." She was relieved that *The Yearling* made the hunter "so hungry for the scrub that he was ready to throw over his job and get back to it."

Marjorie kept up with new releases, including Scribner's expensive twelve-volume limited ("Virginia") edition of Ellen Glasgow's novels. Max had asked Glasgow to write prefaces for each one. Marjorie wanted to read these pieces, and Max sent her the proofs. A quote from one of the prefaces was a lifesaver, Marjorie thought. Glasgow, she wrote to Max,

> said that the writer must wait between books for the well of the subconscious to fill. I haven't been able to understand why I couldn't get to work, when on the surface at least I thought I wanted to. I have not felt much psychic exhaustion and not too much physical enervation, in spite of the hospital's treatments etc. having taken a good bit out of me—but the work just would not come.
>
> I do not believe a writer can go ahead with a new piece of work until he is entirely free of the old. And as long as one book is in the

news, and is selling, and being talked about, so that everywhere the writer goes, questions are asked about and comments made, and letters come in every mail about it—the writer is not free. I have to feel forgotten, and very private and isolated, to submerge myself in a new thing.

Marjorie continued to fill the well, reading, while a new friend, Macmillan trade manager Norman Berg, emerged to play a significant role in her writing life. Berg, from New Jersey, had been transferred to Atlanta in 1935 to manage book sales in the southeast, a job that included public relations and talent scouting. 1935 happened to be the year after the young Georgia author Caroline Miller won the Pulitzer Prize and France's Prix Femina Américain for her first novel, *Lamb in His Bosom*. Like Julia Peterkin's South Carolina novel *Scarlet Sister Mary*, which won the Pulitzer in 1929, *Lamb in His Bosom* was based on the author's observations and experiences in the rural South. Miller described how she gathered her material—much like Julia Peterkin and Marjorie had. "I'd get in the Ford and ride about the country and talk to the people," she said in 1933. "I'd buy chickens and vegetables from them, and they'd tell me about their lives, in the language which even today preserves many of the picturesque and graphic figures of speech which their ancestors used. These people are obscure, but they are an important part of our history. Their forebears fought in the Revolution, and in the Confederate army. They are loyal Americans, patriotic citizens, and people of high moral character."

It's easy to understand why Norman Berg had been sent south—there had to be more storytellers in the region, and he, a literary man as well as a bookseller, might attract them. Besides managing the Atlanta office, his job required travel to other cities, including Jacksonville and St. Augustine, a winter vacation destination for an increasing number of writers, such as James Branch Cabell and Van Wyck Brooks; the Oldest City was also the ancestral home of the literary Benét family. And Florida, like other states, would soon swarm with writers and researchers contributing to the *Federal Writers' Project Guide to 1930s Florida*, among them Zora Neale Hurston.

Almost immediately, Berg assisted with MacMillan's first gold strike in Atlanta, Margaret Mitchell's *Gone with the Wind*, published in 1936 and awarded the Pulitzer Prize in 1937. Norman and Marjorie probably met through Carl Bohnenberger, the Jacksonville librarian who had reviewed *South Moon Under* and helped Marjorie with her research for *Golden Apples*. (Bohnenberger had since died, in an auto accident in 1936.) Marjorie sent Norman a brief update on her canceled surgery in Tampa, so it's fair to say they'd been in touch for a while.

Later that month, Marjorie wrote to Berg, describing the Tampa-Jacksonville saga. "It was a close squeak," she concluded, "and my three friends unquestionably saved my life." She thanked him for the roses he'd sent: "They are the cool white sort, almost a green white. They were all in bud—two dozen or more, short stemmed, so that they are in a glass rose bowl and not sticking stiffly in a high Vahz—and as they open they pass from an assortment of tight circular layers to a full-blown effect with large yellow stamens almost like the Cherokee Rose." But more tellingly, Marjorie commented on a book Berg had sent: the Irish writer Francis Stuart's novel *The White Hare*, published by Macmillan in 1936, a coming-of-age story about three young people and the mysterious bond between a girl and a twelve-year-old boy, symbolized by a white hare. The young boy character and Stuart's depiction resonated with Marjorie. The author had done "the neat trick of leaving wide avenues open to the reader's own imagination. No completely described character is as convincing as one with shadowy but fine outlines, so that we may add our own minds to that of the writer," she replied to Berg. "Did Carl [Bohnenberger] ever talk to you of 'reader duty'? By that he meant the obligation of the reader to give himself, mind and soul, to the honest writer so that he should be open to receive everything offered."

An ongoing literary conversation, established in person, by telephone, or both, had moved to the page.

AT THE CREEK, Marjorie took closer control of her grove business, even as she convalesced. She had canceled a second set of lectures for the fall of 1938 at the University of Florida, due to her health. And she faced the sad news of Thomas Wolfe's death on September 15, just short of his thirty-eighth birthday. Max sent her what he called "the last thing that Tom ever wrote"—undoubtedly the "hunch" letter. Marjorie grieved for Wolfe and the loss of his further work, reflecting, "His very touching letter to you shows a chastening and mellowing of that great half-mad diffusive ego, that would have been a guarantee of the literary self-discipline we all so wanted from him. It seems that each of us can go only so far in wisdom and insight, and then for one reason or another, we are done. . . . It is not strange that so vibrant and sentient a personality as Tom knew or guessed that he had come to a great wall. He must have felt far beyond most of us that withdrawing of the cosmic force from his individual unit of life."

As if Wolfe's death energized her, she visited Louisville in the fall, then crossed over to Atlanta to meet *New York Post* book critic Herschel Brickell, to whom she'd sent a glowing review of *Gone with the Wind;* he would be in town. She was introduced, possibly by Brickell, Edwin Granberry, or Norman Berg, to Margaret Mitchell and her husband, John Marsh. The women found they had much in common, and in early December, after Marjorie returned from giving her "Fact and Fiction" talk at the University of Chicago, Margaret wrote about a lawsuit she'd filed against a Dutch publisher pirating *Gone with the Wind,* warning Marjorie to watch for the same problem with *The Yearling.* "As you know, the United States is one of the few civilized nations in the world which do not belong to the Berne Convention for the protection of authors," Margaret reminded her. Indeed, ZHUM, the Dutch publisher, did have its eye on *The Yearling.* Marjorie wrote to the firm herself, and informed Max, "I reminded them that a writer put in long years of unprofitable apprenticeship, that a success, such as that of The Yearling, was an accidental boon that might not happen again, and that a writer must gather in all monies possible from such a success, to assure his future financially. I mentioned that I was of Dutch ancestry from two lines, and it pained me to have injustice come from such a course." ZHUM sent her a check for $100.

At Christmas, Margaret sent Marjorie another note, thanking her for a crate of holiday fruit and expressing astonishment: "I had been told you had a grove, but I never actually took it in because it did not seem possible that anyone could write such grand books and run a business, too."

SHIPPING HOLIDAY FRUIT to friends was a pleasant diversion. Marjorie was generous each year with her Cross Creek neighbors, too, offering treats from her kitchen, clothing, and toys. She loaded her car for deliveries throughout the scrub—a Lady Bountiful the children would remember fondly. This season, Marjorie also supervised major repairs on the farmhouse for termite damage, almost "running the termites down, one by one." Her household staff needed stability. To retain her housekeeper, Martha Mickens's daughter Adrenna, she hired and trained Adrenna's new boyfriend, B. J. Samson, to work in the grove—even planning and paying for their wedding, as she had for 'Geechee and Leroy.

Marjorie's grove receipts, however, disappointed her; going prices in the 1938–39 season were low. Despite the state's new regulatory agency, problems with overproduction remained, exacerbated by the fruit's limited shelf life. She was still adjusting to her new diet, checking with a Gainesville doctor twice a week. And Charles Rawlings stopped by one day, alone, having sent a messenger to ask if Marjorie would see him. She felt it easier to accept than refuse, and afterward, she noted that Charles's feelings for her hadn't changed—and neither had hers for him. "He looked just the same, but his face rather lined. Don't know what he's done with his second wife," she remarked in a letter to Bee McNeil. She had known that a post-divorce meeting "would happen sooner or later," and remarked, "I'm glad it's over with." Bee replied, "I should think Chuck *would* keep gravitating back to see you. He doesn't seem to be writing very much. There was a long spell when he hadn't a thing in the *Post*."

ROBUST SALES AND PUBLICITY for *The Yearling* continued into 1939. Lee Keedick, whose lecture bureau booked literary lights as various as H. G. Wells and Edna St. Vincent Millay, urged her to take on a two-month lecture tour in the new year. Marjorie wasn't keen on it, and Max argued against it—her time was too valuable for that. Lecturing, he pointed out, is "very exhausting and unrewarding, and would take you away from what is truly important." But, countered Marjorie, "$8000 for 8 weeks worth of work looks like a lot of money to anybody at Cross Creek." She finally passed it up. For all her storytelling talent, Marjorie could be shy, reticent. Public speaking, performing, drained the introverted writer. Then came an invitation from the Southern Women's Democratic Association, wanting to honor her with a $100 prize for the best book of the year by a southern writer—provided she attend an award luncheon in person. Marjorie was annoyed. If these women weren't sincere enough to give her the award in absentia, why should she bother? She was fighting for writing time. Earlier, her friend Edith Pope had sent her the perfect invitation: "We can guarantee no parties, and no people you don't want to meet."

More correspondence poured in. Rollins College asked if she would accept an honorary doctor of literature degree at a ceremony in February. Of course she would. Irita Van Doren, book editor of the *New York Herald Tribune*, invited her to speak at a book and author luncheon in New York, hosted by the American Booksellers Association. Marjorie declined the honor and the journey, "pleading need of noninterruption." The National Institute of Arts and Letters informed her that she had been elected to membership. Fine. All it required was a thank-you note.

A predictable request surfaced: sometime back, Arthur Kinnan had asked for a loan. His "hot prospects" for Alaskan adventures hadn't panned out, and both ex-wives had been after him for support. "I refuse to let them lick me, but it sure takes conniving and resourcefulness," he'd confided. "Of the latter, I'm nearly depleted." Besides Luca and Winifred, he was probably dodging creditors. "If you get any mysterious inquiries or otherwise sit tight until you hear from me. Hope I'm not taking too much for granted." His sister sent him $4,500 from *The Yearling*'s royalties.

MARJORIE WAS STILL TRYING to maintain her domestic situation. Every time it felt settled, something happened to unsettle it. At the turn of the year, life at the Creek exploded again when a neighborhood grove man, Henry Fountain, pumped B. J. Samson full of No. 5 shot. Fountain, married to Adrenna's sister Sissie, worked for Marjorie's neighbors, Tom Glisson and W. R. "Old Boss" Brice. Why Henry shot his new brother-in-law wasn't clear—and never would be—but their white employers stepped in as the responsible parties, Marjorie covering Samson's hospital bills, Tom Glisson escorting Henry to jail. As the drama unfolded, Marjorie confided to Max, "I am of course much upset about it, not only because of the chaos to the work and my comfort, but because they are good decent colored people and my girl and I are devoted to each other."

There followed several rounds of backwoods justice and intrigue that could be boiled down to this: even though Henry had shot an unarmed man for no apparent reason, more (white) people wanted Henry back at the Creek than wanted newcomer Samson—the hamlet couldn't hold both of them now—and Henry's employers, Tom Glisson and "Old Boss," especially, wanted him back. Old Boss got a friend—a judge—to release Henry from jail, and together, he and Glisson hired Henry a lawyer. According to Marjorie, the trial was a farce performed by seasoned actors, black and white. When she objected vociferously, the judge held in her contempt and ordered her to pay court costs. She refused.

While Samson recovered from his bullet wounds in a Gainesville hospital, Adrenna stayed with an elderly relative nearby. The day Marjorie picked up Adrenna to return her to the Creek, the relative insisted on meeting Marjorie, who recalled the interaction:

> The old woman, who I had happened never to have seen, came marching out to my car with what seemed almost like belligerence. She was an immense but handsome and immaculate woman of the old-school type I thought no longer existed. She called, "That the white woman?" My girl said, "Yes." The old woman shouted, "I want to see her face." I thought I had done something that had displeased her. She came to the car window and looked directly at me for some seconds. I said, "Good morning," and she made no answer. Finally she said slowly, "I want to look in the face of the white woman, got such sympathy for the black one." She nodded her head. She said, "I got you in my prayers. Say your name." I said, "Mrs. Rawlings," and she repeated it. She said, "When I take the case to the Lord, I want to carry your name natural." And she turned and marched away.

"I had the uncanny feeling of the tangible value of such purposeful meditation," Marjorie reflected. But it seemed not to help in the current situation. After the trial, Samson left the area, Adrenna went her own way with another man, and Henry returned to work. Tom Glisson blamed Marjorie for the troubles. She had failed to perceive the Creek's unwritten laws about Negro employees, who were, by old-timers, still treated much like property. And her defense of a black man who'd been wronged by another proved she might be even more of an alien than anyone had thought. Did she even understand Negroes themselves? Marjorie was, still, an outsider. She sought another grove man and housekeeper, and again, Martha Mickens offered interim services. She and her husband, Old Will, who had moved to Gainesville during the uproar to escape family pressures, were welcomed back by everyone at the Creek, and moved into a new addition to Marjorie's tenant house.

MARJORIE'S DESK HELD piles of work: new stories for the volume Scribner's planned, a dramatization of *South Moon Under* she would soon jettison. She considered the life of planter and slave trader Zephaniah Kingsley, not for a biography but a novel—she had been researching him, on and off, since completing *The Yearling*. Around the same time, N. C. Wyeth was engaged for a color illustrated edition of *The Yearling;* he visited Marjorie, who showed him the novel's settings. Young Andrew Wyeth, twenty-one, accompanied his father, making watercolors outdoors. One of a marsh scene especially impressed his hostess, but when the young man quoted his going rate—$150—Marjorie turned it down. "The Scotch in me rebelled against that price for an hour's work from a twenty-one year-old boy, which is an asinine way to look at it!" she admitted later.

Following the Wyeths' visit, Marjorie's English publisher, C. S. Evans of William Heinemann, made a trip to Cross Creek. Marjorie assumed he was coming on business, to meet his American author and tour *The Yearling*'s country. But "he didn't give a damn about any of those things—he was simply having himself a Florida vacation," she complained, having knocked herself out showing him the territory and driving him to Daytona Beach for the speed trials. Evans stayed on for six days, lounging in her sunny garden. Her spring flowers were on the way: African daisies, gerberas, snapdragons, and 'Fluffy Ruffles' petunias—these last so prized she had shot a neighbor's hog for rooting around in them. To hurry Evans along, she hinted strongly that "my doctor was much concerned about my avoiding nervous strain."

After her guest left, Marjorie had her house mostly to herself, clear for work. Max sent new books. Among her favorites were British wildlife painter Peter Scott's *Wild Chorus* and Faulkner's *The Wild Palms* (originally titled, by Faulkner, *If I Forget Thee, Jerusalem*). This time, she paid Faulkner a huge compliment: "He is a magician." But, she added primly, "It is a pity he deals in black magic. It is hard to dissociate his real power from the morbid eroticism that holds you just as when you were a child and peeked in doctor's books."

ON THE LAST DAY of April 1939, Marjorie picked up Aunt Ida in Ocala and drove toward Columbus, Ohio. She would leave Ida with friends in Cincinnati and go on to Columbus to address several hundred women journalists at Theta Sigma Phi's Matrix Table dinner. Aunt Ida's friends lived in Cincinnati's Northside neighborhood, well beyond the central city, and with no directions, the women got lost in the slums. Marjorie finally put Aunt Ida in a cab and took herself to the Hotel Gibson, downtown. "Fell into bed more dead than alive," she wrote Norton Baskin.

The Gibson, Cincinnati's most luxurious hotel, was full of conventioneers and classical music lovers attending the Cincinnati May Festival. With all the regular rooms filled, Marjorie was given a suite "big enough to have a party in." The next morning, room service delivered coffee, a pack of Pall Malls, and a newspaper. She took the paper back to bed, snapped it open, and turned the pages, moving past the May Festival news to stories on the war in Europe, defense spending, and Adolf Hitler, then past a report on the National Congress of Parents and Teachers, in town that week, and an article on a new line of citrus jellies, jams, and marmalades from Florida. Farther on, on page 17, below a photo of two Methodist bishops, she noticed a curt, journalism-centric headline: "Pulitzer Awards Are Won by Four Newspapermen." It was an AP wire story with no photos. She scanned to the end. *What do you know*, she thought. The Pulitzer Prize for the most distinguished novel of 1938 had been awarded to Marjorie Kinnan Rawlings for *The Yearling*.

Marjorie felt surprised, then detached, as if the honor were no more remarkable than a kitten left on her back stoop. To Norton, she wrote, "Saw the Pulitzer announcement in my morning paper. I'm glad for Scribner's sake. Publishers get an awful kick out of these things." To Norman Berg, she commented that she couldn't take "any of those things too much to heart."

"An award over a bunch of mediocre books doesn't mean very much," she continued to Berg, "and where should I have been if *The Yearling* had come out the same year as *The Grapes of Wrath*? My God, what a book." When she reached Columbus later that day, a reporter asked her if she expected to become "the darling of the book shops." "Hell, no," she replied, "I'm going back to Cross Creek where people don't give a damn."

IN MANSFIELD, OHIO, the next day, the *News-Journal* offered an account of Marjorie's Matrix Table appearance. Nine hundred women had attended. Headlined "Author Amazed, Reads She Won Pulitzer Prize," the piece described Marjorie's reaction to the award ("I wasn't exactly excited, but I was amazed") and her evening gown: black crepe with a sequined off-the-shoulder bodice and two big orchids. The outfit, wrote the reporter, seemed foreign to a writer who had made her home in Florida's backcountry, who "takes a shotgun and goes out and shoots the neighbor's hog because it's been eating her bird mash and ruffled petunias." Decorators had honored the author's books, installing a crescent moon on the window behind Marjorie, strewing piles of golden apples along the table, and planting a life-sized fawn of carnations in front of her place setting.

In her address, Marjorie described her relationships with her neighbors in *The Yearling*'s country, adding she'd been asked how she knew a small boy's mind so well. "I think it's because the minds of boys and girls are the same until about 14 years," she explained, after which the sexes develop differently. "The bridge from adolescence to maturity is frequently made through some spiritual or emotional jolt and in *The Yearling*, Jody made the bridge when he was forced to kill the thing he loved most." Had Marjorie wanted to, she might have pointed out that the social roles of boys and girls also change at puberty, and that girls, she well knew, faced challenges in the wider world that boys did not.

Chapter Fifteen

When the Whippoorwill

1939-40

FROM COLUMBUS, Marjorie drove down to Louisville for Derby Day, May 6, "a lot of drunken fun." She visited friends and was honored by members of the Juniper Club, a sportsmen's organization based near Ocala, at a dinner on Derby Eve. Back home, she worked on the new stories and responded to a suggestion from Max: that she write a nonfiction book about her region of Florida: "a book of description and incident which would put the place, and the life, and the beauty of the country and all, before a reader." She could work on it occasionally, as relief from imaginative work, he said, and include anecdotes she had shared with him over the years.

Max was describing *Cross Creek: A Chronicle*, the book Marjorie had already conceived of, hinted at, and intermittently begun. She was glad he had brought it up. The Zephaniah Kingsley novel was not "properly shaped" in her mind. "It would be absurd to begin it until it is as clearly defined as 'The Yearling,'" she wrote. "I learned from that, that it works out best for me to know exactly what I want to do, even though that makes the actual writing a thousand times harder, and almost joyless. . . . Yet the final result is bound to be better."

For the Cross Creek book, she meant to create a "succession of sketches," most of them "coordinated episodes, almost complete stories," except that they would be true, with only "a faint coloring or pointing up here and there for dramatic or harmonious effect." The whole might be unusual, formally, but she was sure of its integrity.

Yet for the time being, Marjorie would work on short forms, which aligned well with responding to a backlog of mail from readers: requests for signed books, requests for advice on buying land in Florida, descriptions of readers' pets, musings about gophers, ducks, and lubber grasshoppers. A northerner was surprised that a Yankee could render the South as he knew it. A southerner asked why she didn't install an electric fence to keep hogs out of her garden. And so on. She was pressed by other *Yearling* matters: press interviews, the question of royalties on the Wyeth edition, news that MGM planned to film *The Yearling* on location the following spring. In late June 1939, *Reader's Digest* approached Scribner's about abridging part of *The Yearling*, and in a long letter to her publisher, Marjorie refused, explaining the drawbacks of abridgment:

> I think it all comes down, basically, to the *effect* of style. My style, for better or for worse, is my own. All my writing life I have struggled for a compromise between a lushness that is natural to me, and an admiration for stark simplicity. No one knows how many composite sentences I have broken up into shorter direct ones, like the convict of hard labor "making little ones out of big ones" on the rock pile. But the short, simple and direct sentences by themselves are monotonous and without color, and so, with a conscious effort toward a certain *rhythm*, I allow myself to explode, deliberately, into longer and richer sentences, definitely poetic, that come as a reward to myself and to the reader for our asceticism.

In reducing *The Yearling* to its basics, she explained, an editor would rely on short, plain sentences to move the narrative, as if writing down to a juvenile audience. "I cannot visualize it with any appeal to the adult mind. The overall effect would be "painful sentimentality."

She argued, "I feel that I cannot allow myself to be judged, as a creative writer, by this emasculated version." Substance would evaporate, she felt. "Take away from me that substance, and you have negated all that life has beaten into me."

FOR AUGUST, Marjorie rented an oceanside bungalow on Crescent Beach, south of St. Augustine. It even came with a butler. Here, she would enjoy complete isolation, as opposed to Cross Creek, where her usual, accepted distractions—house, grove, employees—had been complicated further by invasions of tourists, making their way along backroads to the Creek, stopping in front of the farmhouse to gawk, sometimes walking right through the front gate in search of *The Yearling*'s author. "I hate to have to run from my own home," she told Max, "for you know my feeling that we never run from conditions or circumstances but from ourselves, as Wolfe did, so that actually we make no escape. But there are times when it doesn't hurt us to yield a bit, as long as we are not deceiving ourselves too greatly."

At her new retreat, she walked the pristine beach with Pat, her pointer, swam in the sparkling Atlantic, fished in silence. Norton Baskin visited, and Edith and Verle Pope came down from St. Augustine for dinner and bridge. Halfway through the month, Marjorie had drafted two stories, surmounting the inertia accompanying every new project. This time was different, though. Now, she told her editor, "I have been forced to wonder whether, *subconsciously*, I had been working all my life toward what is known as 'success,' and since *The Yearling* was undeniably that, whether something in me was satisfied. It would embarrass me to believe this, yet if it is true, it is necessary to admit it—and go on from there." Max reassured her with the "Ellen Glasgow theory." She only had to wait for the well to refill. The ego theory might be true of some people, he said, but not "real writers." And he rightly reminded her that health problems had robbed her of more energy than she realized.

ALONGSIDE THE NEW STORIES, Marjorie addressed matters of the heart. Not halfway into her beachside stay, she wrote a long, awkward, but ultimately clarifying epistle to Norton, her steady companion. "When a woman has wanted more of a man than he has wanted of her, it puts him on the spot to talk about it, and is very humiliating for the woman," her opening ran. She recounted how, when their relationship was new, he'd seemed afraid of her, aloof, whereas she wished he'd spend more time with her. But "something told me you really did care for me and things would work out." And they did, she affirmed. "There could hardly be a more loveable companion."

She wanted marriage, while he, she believed, did not, though he'd told her once that he did. By Norton's account, Marjorie had said she wouldn't marry again after making a mistake with Chuck. Yet Norton had continued to bring it up, halfheartedly, because she wasn't entirely against it. "I am not concerned with the legal or social or ethical aspect of it," she explained now. "It is just that I am convinced that the greatest good can be had of life when a man and a woman who love each other and are happy in each other's company, live it together.

"I loathe living alone. I need more solitude, more privacy, than most women, but even I can get all I want in the course of a day. My work does not satisfy me as the end and aim of my life." Marjorie wanted "the solid base of a joint life," but she believed Norton did not. This conflict was "the thing that makes me flare out at you in my ill or drunk unguarded moments." Would he come to want the same thing she wanted? His work might make it impossible, she thought. "I not only could not live the hotel life, but I think there are very few instances where a wife fits in it." When she was younger, she could have adapted herself to a man's life, but not now.

"If I could make up my mind to break with you entirely and set out on a deliberate and somehow shameful manhunt, I would not be so tormented," she lamented. "But I love you too much and appreciate too much the large measure of happiness that we do have, to be able to do it."

There is no record of Norton's response, but a week or so later, the matter was tabled when Marjorie's diverticulitis flared up again, as it often did when she was under pressure—this time emotional—and he insisted she see Dr. Cason in Jacksonville. X-rays at Riverside Hospital revealed part of her colon "in rags and tatters" and a diverticulum all but punctured. She was restricted to liquids, had another attack, and stayed into early September. Her doctors advised her to consult a specialist. She was to spend the month resting, and in early October see Dr. Charles M. Rankin in Lexington, Kentucky—convenient to Louisville, where she would give a lecture. Bedridden, she focused again on revisions and sent four new stories to her agent. The *Saturday Evening Post* snapped up a Quincey Dover story, "Cocks Must Crow," and "The Enemy." The *New Yorker* accepted "The Pelican's Shadow," and *Collier's* took "In the

Heart." By now, she had purchased the Crescent Beach cottage from its owner, Ralph Poole, one of the founders of Marineland, the new tourist attraction a few miles south. She relished the day she removed Poole's name from the mailbox and applied hers. This spot, a seventy-mile drive from Cross Creek, was her new retreat.

Marjorie took to the road on October 1 to participate in the 1939 Kentuckiana Institute Week, events sponsored by the Louisville *Courier-Journal* and the *Louisville Times*. The Louisville Woman's Club Auditorium was packed for her event, and those who couldn't find standing room were forced to go home. "As quietly as a hostess entertaining in her own living room," Marjorie spoke of her career, mentioning the local confusion that arose when she used some of her neighbors' given names in early work. Now "people are constantly asking how much of a book is true or false," she said. Asked about writing out of a particular region, she said, "I don't hold any brief for regionalism, and I don't hold with the regional novel as such. If people really are just as quaint as all get-out, write an essay about them for the National Geographic, but don't make a novel about them unless they have a larger meaning." Her remarks, probably similar to those she offered at the University of Chicago a week later, held the gist of "Regional Literature of the South," a paper she was writing for the upcoming annual luncheon of the National Council of Teachers of English in New York.

Marjorie summed up her Louisville and Chicago sojourns for Max: "I always come back from Louisville feeling like the Queen of Sheba. Unfortunately, I came home via my lecture at the University of Chicago feeling like the lowliest of Sheba's slaves." In Louisville, she'd been shown southern hospitality; in Chicago, it was all cool business. Percy H. Boynton, a professor of English literature at Chicago, told her he had "never seen an audience so spellbound," but, she said, "the poor devils probably hadn't been talked to by a human being since Robert Herrick's day, and they simply wouldn't leave. I finally told them I wasn't going to tell any more stories and they might as well go home." In another version of the tale, she opened her Chicago presentation with a formal address, and then "a wave of pity came over me, and I thought, 'Why, you poor, frozen bastards, you've had the living hell educated out of you,' and I made my technical points hurriedly, swapped the bread of information for hyacinths for the soul, and went to town."

In Lexington, Dr. Rankin clarified Marjorie's intestinal situation. There would be no operation unless complications forced it. She would continue with a bland diet and go to bed on liquids if she suspected an attack coming on. If offered forbidden food, she should ignore it or, if pressed, announce that she didn't like it. Yet the doctor offered leeway on alcohol. "Said not to ever let anyone tell me a highball was bad for me!" Marjorie crowed to Norton. "Said a couple of highballs were the best thing in the world for this condition! What a doctor!"

MARJORIE WORKED AT the Creek for most of November, revising stories and examining the proofs for the Wyeth edition of *The Yearling*. Margaret Mitchell warned her about possible pirating of *The Yearling* in Japan; this had happened to *Gone with the Wind*. Mitchell had written to the Japanese publishers, who had sent her a kimono "with a bird of Paradise on it as a royalty for the first 100,000 copies" and a "three-foot Japanese doll in a glass and red lacquer case" for the second hundred thousand. They asked Mitchell for a picture taken with the Japanese doll, for publicity.

Marjorie contacted Brandt & Brandt. "With [Mitchell's] passion for law-suits and the Japanese gift for evasion, there's no need for us to try anything," Marjorie wrote. But she asked for the Japanese publisher's address so she could "maybe wangle some porcelain etc. out of them for the modern beach cottage I've bought."

By the end of the month, Marjorie was ensconced at the St. Moritz in New York, preparing to address the English teachers' annual luncheon. In the paper, published a few months later as "Regional Literature of the South," she observed that the term "regionalism" was commonly understood as "ruralism," because all cities are thought to be alike.

> Yet the customs of travel, the mode of life and of thought of natives of New York City are so specialized that a book written about New York City with the passion for detail and the odd patronizing condescension brought to many studies of remote rural sections would be truly a piece of regional writing. It would be tempting to write such a book, for the New Yorker's acceptance of the subway and his taxis and his cliff dwelling seems as outlandish and worthy of note as an Alabama poor white's acceptance of mules, drought and the

boll weevil. The truth is that the congregating of a high percentage of the American population in urban centers and the fluid nature of that population have within a generation made any stationary rural group, maintaining its own customs, a matter for wide-eyed contemplation.

"Regional writing done because the author thinks it will be salable is a betrayal of the people of that region," she argued. "Their speech and customs are turned inside out for the gaze of the curious." A valid approach, she asserted, is that of the sincere writer "who has something to say and who uses a specialized locale—a region—as a logical or fitting background for the particular thoughts or emotions that cry out for articulation. This approach results in writing that is only incidentally, sometimes even accidentally, regional."

The best writing, she felt, bears "a profound harmony between the writer and his material, so that many of the greatest books of all time are regional books, in which the author has used, for his own artistic purpose, a background that he loved deeply and understood. Thomas Hardy is a compelling instance." The South, she thought, had so far produced "tons" of regional writing, but very little regional literature— that is, very little literary *art*. She believed that Ellen Glasgow's work would—or at least should—stand the test of time, as would Julia Peterkin's *Scarlet Sister Mary*. *Gone with the Wind* would have to wait until the "tumult and shouting" fueled by the film subsided.

The paper was splendid and intellectually precise, but Marjorie did not deliver it to the crowd. She simply handed the manuscript to the council secretary, faced the audience, and gave an informal talk, describing her early, market-driven efforts to sell short stories and the changes that came over her as soon as she moved to Florida. One day in the scrub, she said, she found herself "for the first time since leaving her father's farm to go to college, in full spiritual harmony with her environment." Not only is such harmony essential to personal happiness, she told her listeners, but "it is necessary to the novelist, who must look upon his people and surroundings with humility and love."

Marjorie stayed on in New York, lecturing at Columbia University, visiting Scribner's and Carl Brandt, attending the theater, socializing. With her doctor's blessing to drink, she freely imbibed. "Went to the

Christmas punch tasting meeting yesterday afternoon of the famous Wine and Food Tasting Society at the Sherry-Netherlands, and oh God," she wrote Norton. "Thought I was being discreet and just sipping, but when my hostess and I ran into some jolly company, including that famous Pierre, of Pierre's, and we agreed the champagne punch was the best, we settled down to a little right steady tasting." There followed dinner, where she had "three cocktails, and wine with dinner, and a long drink later in the evening, and the man who brought me home thought some ale on the way would be a good idea—." Morning brought a terrific hangover.

Home at the Creek, Marjorie dropped a note to Max:

The grove and the farmhouse are as lovely as I remembered them! Each time I go away and come back, I wonder if I will see them with more exact or exacting eyes, and find them ugly or inadequate—and it never happens.

Yet I did really have a good time in New York. The trouble is, that a part of me is drawn to the sophisticated life, to the *thinking* life as against the simple emotionalism of my relation to this place, and it takes some time to draw back again.

MARJORIE'S LIFE WAS now irrevocably split between city and country. Almost as soon as she returned to the scrub, she and Norton were bound for Atlanta by train, for the premiere of *Gone with the Wind* (December 15, 1939). Norman Berg provided tickets to the big night at Loew's Grand Theater. "We expect to have a swell time," Marjorie wrote to Norman, "and you mustn't let us be any kind of a nuisance. We can amuse ourselves for hours with our bottle." The couple spent several "more or less riotous" days in Atlanta, having been forewarned by Margaret Mitchell, who'd wanted to slip down to the Creek but couldn't because "the town is in a frenzy and social and civic festivities are being planned, our work has been doubled and there is no chance to get away until after the premiere is over," she wrote Marjorie. "By that time we will be so tired we will not want to go anywhere but will jerk out the telephone by the roots and thankfully stay home."

Marjorie looked forward to the events. She would attend a special luncheon at Rich's Department Store for three southern women Pulitzer winners: Julia Peterkin, Mitchell, and herself. She would greet Victor

Fleming, *Gone with the Wind*'s director, who would also direct the first attempt to film *The Yearling*. Film stars Vivien Leigh, Clark Gable, and Olivia de Havilland appeared in the spotlights on opening night, though Hattie McDaniel, who would win an Oscar for the role of Mammy, and Butterfly McQueen, who played Prissy, would not—white organizers in Atlanta, fearful of criticism or worse, cautioned against it. Loew's was all white. McDaniel was even left out of the program book. Black citizens could see *Gone with the Wind* four months later, in a "colored" theater.

AFTER MARJORIE RETURNED home from Atlanta, she edited and ordered stories for the spring 1940 release of *When the Whippoorwill*, as she had decided to call the collection. She insisted that "Cracker Chidlings" be omitted. The accounts in it were "almost straight journalism," she decided, "and the difference in style could not help but puzzle a reader." They also gave her "a terribly embarrassed feeling. They have no pretense at artistry." The nonfiction book she was working on, *Cross Creek*, was her chief obsession, though at one point Max suggested, oddly, that she write "a real juvenile" book about a girl in the hammock country. "I'll be damned if I'll write a juvenile about a girl in the hammock country," Marjorie shot back. "I did Allie in *Golden Apples* and she made me sick at my stomach."

AROUND THIS TIME, Norman Berg gave Marjorie a copy of Steinbeck's first novel, *Cup of Gold: A Life of Henry Morgan, Buccaneer, with Occasional Reference to History*. Norman, like Max, had been supplying Marjorie with books, not just those published by Macmillan but titles he had read and wanted to share and discuss with her. He visited Cross Creek fairly often, on the way to or from business in Jacksonville or St. Augustine, and he sometimes stopped to see Marjorie's adopted aunt Ida in Ocala, too.

By now, Norman and Marjorie had developed a close relationship, having much in common. Both had strong personalities. Of Berg, a granddaughter said, "He was hard on people, strong, opinionated." "Feisty and opinionated," echoed one of his protégés in the book business. From time to time, Norman annoyed or angered good friends, including Marjorie—and it's fair to say she did the same with people close to her. Conversely, both were generous with friends and family. Both enjoyed quantities of liquor. Both were hunters and dog lovers, and both owned farmland. Soon after he and his wife moved from New Jersey to Georgia, Norman purchased fifteen acres of an old dairy farm in Dunwoody, north of Atlanta, where he could keep and train bird dogs. The barn he turned into a home, stuffed with books, and the farmer's cottage became a guesthouse, where authors like Margaret Mitchell and Marjorie sometimes stayed. Norman and Marjorie were especially fond of novels of the earth, specifically Knut Hamsun's masterpiece *Growth of the Soil*, which Norman was known to push on others, a must-read. He named his Georgia farm Selenraa, after Isak Selanraa, the novel's protagonist. Norman, twelve years Marjorie's junior, was probably the closest male friend to her in spirit. They were a "we" to the end of her life. The two were moved by a speech in *Cup of Gold* that wise old Merlin (borrowed from the Arthurian legend) delivers to the adventurous fifteen-year-old Henry Morgan. Morgan, not unlike fifteen-year-old Dominic in Francis Stuart's *The White Hare*, has announced that he will go to sea.

> "You are a little boy. You want the moon to drink from as a golden cup; and so, it is very likely that you will become a great man—if only you remain a little child. All the world's great have been little boys who wanted the moon; running and climbing, they sometimes catch a firefly. But if one grows to a man's mind, that mind must see that it cannot have the moon and would not want it if it could—and so, it catches no fireflies."

Marjorie wrote to Norman about it:

> There is no alternative but wanting the moon and catching fireflies. But it is one hell of a nuisance. If they aren't going to let us drink from the golden cup, they oughtn't to make us want to— Odd, the different things different people ask of life. The poor ask to be fed and housed and clothed. . . . Those of us who have that and are capable of asking something better, catch the fireflies, sip from the moon—and are still hungry and thirsty. I myself have held the moon in my hands and I have a whole bottle of fireflies—and I still beat my hands against the cosmic Wailing Wall. It is our blessing and our curse.

In early spring, Norman underwent a divorce, and Marjorie sympathized with him. She knew what he'd been through, and offered solace:

Dear Norman,

I'm more than perfunctorily sorry about the family cataclysm. I know too well not only the hell you've been through, but the hell you're in for. There is a time in youth when rootlessness is necessary and beautiful. A few seem to continue to want it, or to be unable to accept anything else, but for most of us, maturity requires a certain fortification of ourselves against the loneliness that is, as James Boyd [a historical novelist and friend] said, "the terrible discovery of maturity." Of course, the fortifications, whether of place or person, are treacherous, through no fault of their own, but the need to establish them is very great."

When the first attempt, made in such good faith, fails, as it did with you and me, one is more conscious of the lack, the need, than before. Freedom from the pain of the daily unhappy living is relief. It is also a vacuum. Out of that emptiness, the most appalling mistakes seem reasonable. What happens, I think, is that we who are idealists read into others the qualities that we long to find. Then when the truth hits we have a fresh sense of betrayal and frustration. Search—the illusion of discovery—rejection—it is a disturbing business.

However, it is all to the good that you made the break before more futile years had gone by, and life will have infinitely more meaning without the steady torment of bad home conditions. Good luck.

At one point in their relationship, Norman offered Marjorie an extraordinary gift: an L.C. Smith 20-gauge, double-barreled shotgun he had sent to a Chilean artisan in South Carolina for special engraving. It is decorated exquisitely, extensively, with scenes from *The Yearling;* Marjorie's initials are applied in raised gold. It's not clear when Norman presented the gun, but eventually it came back to him. It might have been the same gun she referred to at the end of 1946 when she wrote, "I present you the gun, with pity for your perverseness. It is a bitch of a shotgun, as you have found. I had it cut down for me, and perhaps

you could add another rubber pad. You are MORE than welcome to it."
Three years later, preparing for a dove hunt, Norman mentioned that he
would use "your" shotgun. "I'll be thinking of you," he wrote. "I prize
it very much."

Berg, who outlived Marjorie, left the shotgun to one of his protégés,
author Pat Conroy, who described it as Berg's treasure, "the key to his
combative and sometimes unhappy life." Conroy believed that the shotgun was "the wedding ring he [Berg] always wanted to give the love of
his life, Marjorie Kinnan Rawlings." A few months after Marjorie con-
soled Norman over his divorce, she referred to him as "a rejected suitor."
One imagines that he had offered the shotgun, pled or at least hinted at
his case, and Marjorie had refused him, citing the age difference, the
freshness of his divorce, and her relationship with Norton Baskin. Or all
three. Or perhaps Marjorie felt that two positive charges ought to keep
some distance.

AFTER MARJORIE ADDRESSED the Miami Beach Woman's Club mid-
February, an MGM film crew arrived in the city, searching for a local
boy who could play Jody in *The Yearling*. "The youngster who wins
the part will have an assignment second only to Spencer Tracy," an
announcement read. Boys aged ten through twelve—and their eager
parents—flocked to auditions. In Atlanta, Margaret Mitchell read that
screen tests would be held there, too. "How smart of you not to let them
start at Hawthorne," she wrote to Marjorie, referring to a town near
Cross Creek. "Of all the nightmares we went through, the Atlanta talent
hunt for Scarlett was the worst."

At the Creek, Marjorie hosted Charles and Vera Scribner and their
twenty-one-year-old daughter, Julia, who stayed on for a week. When
Julia returned to New York, she wrote to Marjorie, detailing her journey, speaking of books, and expressing happiness over their new connection: "I would like to tell you in poised but glowing prose how very
happy I was with you (and I don't mean just 'having a good time'), how
much I miss you and how lonely I am when I think of something I would
like to talk to you about, or see something I think you would enjoy, and
most of all, how proud I am of your friendship." She shared some office
gossip from Scribner's: the tale of a *Gone with the Wind* premiere cocktail party where Marjorie supposedly lowered herself into a chair just as

Margaret Mitchell was about to sit there, and Margaret fell on the floor, was injured, and was taken away to the hospital.

"The story about Margaret Mitchell and the chair and the accident and me is the most amazing canard I've run into in a long time," Marjorie replied. At the premiere, she had been in Mitchell's proximity once, when they posed agreeably for a women's press club photo. Nobody toppled or went to surgery. She, too, appreciated the new friendship. "I have really missed you terribly," she wrote in reply. "I can't tell you how much I enjoyed you. Aside from the great bond of the same diet, the same antagonisms and the almost identical profanity, I think you are a grand person."

Julia sent her a package of books, including Isak Dinesen's *Seven Gothic Tales*. She had read it when hunting in Vermont and thought it fascinating. "My mind would get so far off its beaten track and so lost that it took me a couple of hours chasing partridge across the New England hills before it came home and integrated with the body of Scribner, the mighty huntress." For Julia's twenty-second birthday, March 26, Marjorie asked Charles Scribner, who delegated his secretary, who delegated Julia's cousin George, to determine which classical record albums Julia might like the most. Marjorie's gifts, Beethoven's Fourth Symphony and Franck's Symphonic Variations, were just what Julia wanted. "The 4th from now on is Beethoven's Cross Creek Symphony," Julia wrote. Marjorie replied that she had arranged with Victrola to send Julia ten dollars' worth of new operatic and symphonic records a month.

SPRING CAME TO FLORIDA. Visitors—strangers as well as friends—swept down from the north: "the long steady stream of callers and visitors has left me feeling rather drained," Marjorie grumbled to Max. In mid-March, an advance crew from MGM arrived in Silver Springs to plan the production of *The Yearling* in the Ocala National Forest. Locations had to be "seasoned" by planting corn and other crops. A deer, a bear, bulldogs, and a hound had to be recruited. Scouts searched three counties for the right hound and found fine specimens, but they were "entirely too handsome," according to the movie men. "We want an old sister with scars across her nose and chewed-up ears almost dragging to the ground." They still hadn't found a boy to play Jody. The search team had left Florida and moved to other southern states; more than a thousand boys had been interviewed. Additional testing companies would be sent to the Northeast and the Midwest. "The boy must be twelve years old, tall and thin for his age. He must have pathos to his face and a Cracker drawl to his voice," read one announcement.

At the end of March, *When the Whippoorwill* went to press, and Marjorie set out for the kind of lecture tour she'd sworn never to undertake: four women's groups in four cities—Shreveport, Nashville, Chattanooga, and Tallahassee—in twelve days, by car.

"I am furious at myself for leaving now, for Florida is sheer perfection," she complained. "My flower garden is a mass of the choicest flowers, the orange grove is in full bloom, and I am getting buckets of cream from the two perverse cows, who came fresh within two days of each other, after I had battled the wrong bulls and tried to make a match with the right one so that one cow would be six or eight months ahead of the other."

Yet she enjoyed at least part of the journey, relishing for Norton a thoroughly southern dining experience at the Battle House Hotel in Mobile: "Ate in the vast dining-room with its mammoth pillars like the Temple of Karnos [Karnak probably intended] with only two other tables occupied—one by a wizened young aristocrat (obviously), the embarrassing end no doubt of a long proud line, who chatted with the head waitress though his mother had been sending him down here to eat his dinner to get rid of him, for years and years."

Another diner talked straight Alabaman: "'Mah Mothuh is jus' as Ami'cun as the day she was bohn.'"

From Mobile, she drove to New Orleans for lunch at Galatoire's and prowled the French Quarter, picking up English Sheffield serving dishes "much too nice for the way I live." That night in Natchez, she was forced to buy a double room, as the hotels didn't offer singles "this time of year." "It seems that this 'time of year' in Natchez means the garden pilgrimage to the homes of the impoverished elite, who, I am sure, scrub the portal, and quite rightly, after the tourists have come and gaped and gone—"

At the Creek mid-April, Marjorie found fresh copies of *When the Whippoorwill*. She didn't expect it to sell well but thought *Cross Creek* would succeed "if I can beat it into shape." She was eager to read Hemingway's forthcoming novel *For Whom the Bell Tolls*. Charles Scribner said it was the best Hemingway had done, that the author attributed it "to

being happy while he worked." He had written it in 1939, while still married to his second wife, Pauline, but mostly living with war correspondent Martha Gellhorn, with whom he'd covered the Spanish Civil War.

"I have wondered and wondered about that," Marjorie replied. "I
don't get as much work done when I am happy, but the work done in a
tranquil or ecstatic mood is very possibly a little sounder than work done
out of suffering."

Chapter Sixteen

Today's Woman

1940

W HEN THE WHIPPOORWILL was doing all right—doing "excellently, even in these troubled times when people can hardly put their attention on anything but the war," Max assured Marjorie. Germany had invaded Poland the previous September, sparking World War II in Europe. Denmark and Norway had recently been attacked, with France and the Low Countries soon to be assaulted. Still, books got covered in the press, and reviews for *When the Whippoorwill* were plentiful and favorable. Most critics dwelled on the merits of "Jacob's Ladder" and "Gal Young Un," praising also the Quincey Dover stories. Marjorie had brought back *The Yearling* territory in shorter forms, they said. She was a master of the vernacular. The *New York Times* observed that her work had steadily improved, "not so much in deeper knowledge [of the Cracker life] as in her own attitude toward it. Mrs. Rawlings is less and less inclined to emphasize their quaintness at the expense of their humanity." One journalist, pushing the collection during summertime, claimed that short stories were easier to read in hot weather. The review Max thought exceptional came from the *Atlantic Monthly*. Marjorie's stories were "as good reporting of life in the United States as we have today. They *are* stories. Not folklore. Not sociological tracts. Not a personal desire to shout the sourness of these sour times through puppet characters. In this Mrs. Rawlings is nearly unique." The critic compared her to Mark Twain and wondered why religion hadn't appeared in her work. "But finicky criticism of Mrs. Rawlings is no game to play. She is one of the two or three *sui generis* storytellers we have, and we'd better thank God for her."

Margaret Mitchell took up one of the *Atlantic*'s points: "You are just a born story-teller and all of us readers are very lucky because you are willing to let your stories stand on their own feet without dragging in all the extraneous sociological stuff that the bright young Leftwingers think should be included in any story about 'the underprivileged.'" Her appreciation came with a bottle of perfume. James Branch Cabell, writing from Poynton Lodge, his vacation cottage on Chesapeake Bay, expressed himself with typical formality: "I do not kindle, somehow, quite so ardently your accurate knowledge of flora and fauna, or your keen sympathy with the underprivileged, or, in general, the sturdy and noble aspects of your nature. It is when you become more genial and— be it whispered—dally with the obscene, that I revel in your great talent unrestrainedly." Sculptor Malvina Hoffman, a friend of Marjorie's, sent her compliments, and Marjorie replied, "Dear Malveeeeeeena: It was grand of you to write me about the stories!" But her thanks took a sober turn: "With the nightmare that has overtaken the world books seem an awfully ephemeral thing. Sculpture, as always, seems more permanent— yet bombs can raise hell with that, too. The eternal verities are the only thing to cling to, and one wonders what is eternal, and what is real—."

PREPARATIONS FOR *The Yearling* film continued. In late May, MGM reportedly bought up all the decrepit fences from country dwellers, replacing them with new pickets. "They thought there was a trick to it," said a forest ranger, "until the movie people started peeling off bills." Crops planted earlier around the set would be ready in June, but the right Jody still hadn't been found. At one point, an MGM rep, having seen photos of Marjorie, remarked, "Don't be surprised if a screen test follows. You should have played Ma."

As MGM's crew angled for a start date, Marjorie entertained herself and others. In Jacksonville, she heard the Philadelphia Orchestra under Eugene Ormandy and was riveted by a performance of Tchaikovsky's

Fifth Symphony—a reminder that she had, indeed, been living in a backwater. "My hair literally stood on end, and knives went all through me," she wrote to Julia Scribner. "Thought I'd lost the capacity to respond to music but realized I just hadn't been hearing good music." In May, poet Bernice Kenyon Gilkyson, Max's editorial assistant, and her husband, novelist Walter Gilkyson, came to dinner at Cross Creek. (Gilkyson would dedicate her 1951 collection *Night Sky* to Marjorie.) James Branch Cabell fully entered her orbit, embarrassing her by asking, "How does it feel to be a great writer?" "I couldn't tell whether he was pulling my leg," she wrote Max. "Cabell is so frightfully sarcastic and a best-seller must seem such a horrible thing to him, that I felt dubious about his feelings." To Julia Scribner, Marjorie complained, "People have popped in unannounced at Marineland. If there's much of that sort of thing, I'll have to look for a further outpost." Norton recalled, "A stop-by for lunch at the beach cottage took three or four days out of her writing, because she had the idea that they were coming, had to prepare, and then there was the day that they were there. It took her a full day or two to get back into the mood of something. She enjoyed it very much. She liked people." But, he added, "I'd rather chop cotton than work the way she did."

Sometimes, instead of entertaining at home or at Marineland, Marjorie and Norton took guests to Jim's, a hangout on the water with an iron roof and a sand floor. Here Jim, a black man, roasted oysters—all you could eat—on a steel pan covered with seaweed or Spanish moss. Diners brought their own butter and liquor, and they had to make reservations in person, because Jim had no phone. Neither did he offer toilet facilities. The nearest ones were the dunes.

One of Marjorie's drop-ins was Owen D. Young, the founder of RCA, a lawyer, a diplomat, and the recently retired chairman of General Electric. He had been *Time*'s 1929 Man of the Year. Now he devoted much of the year to dairy farming on family property in Stark, New York, where he'd grown up, and wintered near St. Augustine. He and his wife, Louise, had built a home, called Washington Oaks, on the water, just south of Marineland. Young became involved in an effort to establish a national park on Anastasia Island, between the Matanzas River and the Atlantic Ocean, and discussed it with Marjorie. Part of the lovely barrier island had already been developed, with local taxes accruing to St. Augustine, and the developers stood to gain if the land was protected;

their projects would increase in value. There was even a question of condemning oceanfront properties like Marjorie's. Young felt the remaining wild acres and beachfront should go untouched. For Marjorie, proximity to the Youngs, and their interests in land preservation and farming, encouraged a friendly personal connection.

In private, Marjorie received more and more requests for book reviews, blurbs, recommendations. Some she took on; others she flat out refused. When the young Stetson Kennedy, who had attended Marjorie's lectures at the University of Florida and collected Florida folklore for the WPA, asked her to review his book *Palmetto Country*, she turned him down. But Kennedy persisted, obliging Marjorie, who had not seen his book, to clarify: "I prefer to review, or to comment on, only a book about which I am genuinely enthusiastic. If I do not feel a great admiration for a book, especially one by a fellow Floridian, I prefer not to say so. To attempt comment on a book by a writer whose beginnings I have known, puts me on the spot." Critical comment, she felt, should come from disinterested readers.

THE WAR IN EUROPE CONTINUED. The Netherlands had just surrendered to the Germans. Belgium would follow shortly. In early June, Max admitted that the blitzkrieg was hurting book sales, but he told Marjorie not to think about the war, "for it does no good," and at the Creek, he suggested, it could be possible to forget about it.

Only that wasn't so. Not far from the Creek and Crescent Beach, the St. Augustine Airport was undergoing substantial upgrades for possible military use, as many other Florida airports were. In fact, the entire state, with its mild climate and vast, vacant lands, had seen explosive growth in airports throughout the 1930s—they were a popular WPA project. Of the more than two hundred in Florida, two of the largest airports, Camp Blanding and the Jacksonville Naval Air Station, were within a short drive of Marjorie's homes. Camp Blanding was named for General Albert H. Blanding, with whom Marjorie played bridge.

The fear was palpable. One day at the beach cottage, Adrenna Mickens spotted a fishing boat carrying a large group of men and called out to Martha, "Mama, you reckon that's the Germans?"

Up and down the coast, people watched the sea. Marjorie admitted that the war cast a shadow, no matter where she was. "The Ivory Tower long since became the Leaning Tower, and finally crashed to earth," she wrote Max. "It does disturb my work, for it is hard to present my simple matters of the moment in personal writing, even though one knows that in the long run it is those things, and not empires, that have an element of the timeless. I am more depressed than I can tell you." A week or so later, she and Norton had a terrible fight, and she blamed herself. Her apology to him was long, and ran headlong into some of the same qualms she'd had the previous summer: she wanted his company more than he wanted hers; he misinterpreted her affection for him as no more than the vain pleasure of having a man to "dance attendance"; he feared regimentation, even as she wanted a nontraditional arrangement. But in closing she allowed, "It's possible that I'm asking of a man that he act as a buffer for me against the strange despair that hits me and that I can't seem to lick. Only I've hoped that a man I could care for would be glad to help me. But I suppose there are some battles that we always have to fight alone."

IN RESPONSE TO THE WAR, Marjorie agreed to write an article addressing the "American way," part of a larger project syndicated by the mainstream Newspaper Enterprise Association. Its use is unknown, but reflecting on it in July, she wrote privately, less guardedly, to Max,

> There are so many things that I feel had no place in such an article— that democracy, actually, is a failure—the very individualism entailed makes for chaos—and above all, the fact that individual and national and racial greed and selfishness make the whole outlook entirely hopeless. The only point I could emphasize was that, we do really believe, whether we practice it or not, in a basic kindliness, and consideration for the rights of the individual.
>
> We've all been concerned with what we thought was coming to us, rather than what we could contribute to the general welfare.

Of democracy, Max replied, "You cannot have it without a very strong sense of the thing now detested, 'duty,' and a sense that material success is a lower form than that of service." In his youth, he said, wealth was soft-pedaled. It wasn't the point. Businessmen working only for wealth were looked down upon. The schoolteacher, the newspaper editor, the clergyman, the doctor were the truly important and respected citizens. But times were changing, he lamented.

IN JUNE, Marjorie invited Julia Scribner to visit the beach, describing how their days would go: rise between seven and eight a.m., walk with Pat, swim, eat breakfast, read the paper. Marjorie would work in the morning while Julia read. Then lunch, talk, more writing, reading. At the moment, Marjorie said, she was "stuck at the creek" for ten days, because she had loaned the cottage to Norman Berg and his new wife, Julie, for their honeymoon.

Marjorie was annoyed with herself, and with Norman. Sometime before, she had apparently declined Norman's advances, and she must have suffered some regret, griping to Julia, "When he went off on a fresh trail and found him a wife, he decided I was his best friend and calmly asked for my cottage. Why I should provide another woman with a honeymoon I don't quite see, but I hated to refuse, since even much-married people don't do it very often. But it is very stuffy inland, and I entertain the kindly hope that before their time is up they will be cutting each other's throats."

When Marjorie returned to Crescent Beach, she found a grateful note from Norman, saying the cottage had been his Shangri-la. "Was quite disappointed to find the cottage in very good shape," she wrote to Norton, who must have seen through her huffy report. "Had hoped for a mess so I could get real mad."

She explained, "I've looked back and tried to figure just when he clamped himself on me to such an extent. All he did was keep showing up and I was polite to him, and now here we are." Two weeks later, the newlyweds came through again to see Marineland while Julia Scribner was visiting. Marjorie entertained them at the cottage, everyone drinking to excess. When the couple sent Marjorie a pair of expensive vases in gratitude for the cottage, she replied with a stiff note: "I was very much distressed. They are of course very lovely here at the cottage, but you should have done nothing of the sort."

JULIA SCRIBNER'S VISIT deepened the women's friendship. Marjorie considered Julia a daughter. The young woman appreciated a straight-shooting mentor. In the years to come, the women shared hours of conversation, in person and on the page. At the moment, Julia was concerned about marrying—meeting the right person—and fulfilling a potential she knew she had, apart from marriage, but could not define. Marriage was on Marjorie's mind, too, as she fretted over her relationship with Norton Baskin in the aftermath of Norman Berg's wedding. "Marriage," Marjorie wrote Julia in August, "is a little like death—if you're of a loyal and earnest nature, it lasts so long—. And once an unfrivolous woman is in it, she tends to make the best of it, as I did, and suffers in silence. Marriage should happen only when there is absolutely no question in your mind. I know that it is possible to become very attached to someone with whom you were not originally terribly in love, but it is much better and safer to start out with a good margin of feeling!" It seems she was referring to Norton, who had first been a friend, like a brother, rather than Norman, with whom she had shared an intense connection, early on. At the same time, she might have been loath to repeat anything resembling her relationship with Chuck, though more than two decades had passed since she'd married him.

IF ANYONE WISHED TO mark the complicated, ultimately triumphant years since Marjorie's fevered first wedding and entry-level publicity job in New York, one could do no better than peruse the September 4, 1940, issue of the *Christian Science Monitor*, whose cover bore the tall headline "Today's Woman" and an enormous oval photograph of Marjorie. Now forty-four, she is shown seated on the Cross Creek lawn, leaning against a tree, attired in a pressed floral shirtdress and a pair of stylish two-toned shoes—a departure from the unsupported frocks and pumps with socks she wore around the house or the canvas pants, high leather boots, and narrow-brimmed hat she sported on hunting trips. She is caressing Pat, scooched halfway onto her lap, and gazing softly at the camera. Here, Marjorie is "seen in a leisure moment, in the garden of her Florida home." She appears as placid as a belle, as if her hands have never yanked a cow's teat or gripped a 20-gauge shotgun—nothing like the perspiring cake baker young Neal Smith had met five years before. "Understanding, deeply kind, shrewdly observant, Mrs. Rawlings has given us, in the portrayals of Penny and Jody, two of the finest pen portraits in American literature," the description reads. The pages inside contain a hymn to Marjorie's rustic home and natural setting, with commentary on a delicious meal served by Martha Mickens—"a kindly, colored mammy"—with dishes Marjorie had taught Martha to make: crab à la Newburg, fresh potatoes, little beets, biscuits with jelly and country butter, chilled pears and cake. "Cooking is my one vanity," Marjorie told the *Monitor* reporter, as she had told many others. "I get as much satisfaction from preparing a perfect dinner for a few good friends as from turning out a perfect paragraph in my writing."

The reporter pleaded, as had those before her, for writing advice, and in reply, Marjorie "looked steadily at her hands resting on her white dress . . . one was keenly aware of the activity in her mind. 'Writing is hard work,' she said, simply and forcefully. 'You can be taught technic; but no one can teach you to write. You must teach yourself. Must work hard. Must write to please yourself, and be your own severest judge.'" The article covered the same ground others had, with a final question about current world conditions. Marjorie had recently read and admired José Ortega y Gasset's *The Revolt of the Masses*, which, among other things, foresaw the rise of consumerism and the primacy of crowd mentality over expertise. She told the reporter that she believed the current problems were caused by "an excess of national greed," which carried the seeds of its own destruction. "In these cataclysmic times all we can do is to hold tightly to the timelessness of living and loving and working," she said.

SOMETIME AFTER THE "Today's Woman" feature appeared, Marjorie, weary of fawning profiles, wrote a parody titled "Yesterday's Woman: An Exclusive Interview with Lollie Pop Twitter." She shared it with members of her inner circle, including Norton and James Branch Cabell, who must have roared. Here, Marjorie had her imaginary reporter/pilgrim approach the Creek reverentially by car and ask directions of a local.

"Mrs. Rawlings?" I asked hesitantly. "Which way to the writing seat of Marjorie Kinnan Rawlings?"

I knew instinctively that the man I addressed was one of her beloved characters.

"Who?" he said. "Oh. That bitch. Fust I knowed she done it with her seat." He looked at me curiously. "She expecting you, lady? She shore as hell will shoot the pants off you if she ain't. But it's your business. Four miles west."

The reporter arrives at "the shrine I sought." She smells fresh fertilizer. A black-and-white bird dog lifts his leg on her. "An old colored mammy" answers her knock.

"She's here, Missy. She's havin' one of her fits. She was right drunk last night. Tain't her fault. She's as pure as a lily. She jest got low-down friends, comes out here and gits her drunk."

A low voice spoke behind me.

"Don't mind me," it said. "Come right on in and raise hell with my next masterpiece."

I turned and held out my hand. She knocked it aside and looked into me, through me, with that understanding that permeates all her work, and as I soon found, all her doings. She cut a deep blue eye at me. A mean eye if I ever saw one—.

Mrs. Rawlings is a big butted woman with a shuffling step and uncombed hair straggly about her neck. I saw at once the source of the beauty of her writings.

A brief conversation leads to this:

"Tell me," I said, "one word of advice to aspiring writers."

She stared into space and scratched her fanny.

"Tell them," she said, and all the nobility of her literature was in the words, "tell them never to finish anything they can't begin."

"And you," I asked. "How best do you work?"

"Tight as a tick," was her answer.

I sensed now whence came the nebulous fineness of her first novel, "Half Seas Over," her second, "Rotten Apples," and that great classic, "The Blasted Buck."

IN SEPTEMBER, Marjorie sent Max sample chapters and sketches for *Cross Creek*. They were rough, but it was time to show them. "There are so many pitfalls to avoid," she admitted. "The style cannot be facetious.

There must not be condescension or patronage as to the people written about." She worried about the episodic form but knew a connected narrative wouldn't work. Consecutive, chronological history would require dragging in extraneous personal details—such as her marriage and divorce. She was wary of the autobiographical impulse, remarking later that "the great flaw of most autobiographies [is] a listing, for personal satisfaction, of utterly dull details." One should instead write with the "abandoned subjectiveness of a Rousseau, or the same selective objectivity of fiction."

With *Cross Creek*, she could work with social interruptions; this was unlike her labor on the novels, which required more sustained thought. One interruption came during Julia's visit, when Marjorie took her to dinner at Marineland's restaurant and spotted Hemingway and Martha Gellhorn. The pair, who would marry a few weeks hence, joined Marjorie's party for drinks, and everyone met up at the cottage afterward for an evening of talk. "He is obviously in a much better frame of mind than when I met him in Bimini," Marjorie observed, "and we all liked Martha immensely." Although the Hemingway-Gellhorn marriage would end in 1945, the women remained friends and kept in touch. At one point, Marjorie gave Martha use of the Cross Creek farmhouse to write.

Max sent Marjorie an extended critique of the *Cross Creek* samples, saying the book would come together if she viewed the aggregate as a whole. The materials needed development; they couldn't be simply a succession of pieces in chronological order. "It could and even must be organized around episodes which should be developed to stand out as the big events in the novel do," he advised. "And all these episodes should also serve to develop a sense of community, to contribute to building up a total picture of the scene. I think that the book should be a narrative varied somewhat by description, and by reflection—to use a figure, it should be a single piece of string with knots in it, the knots being the episodes, but each connected with the other by incidents etc."

Some characters, he proposed, might recur—the reader could look forward to seeing them again. "As matters stand, there aren't enough knots for the string." He suggested a seasonal arrangement, dividing the book into four groups of knots. All Marjorie lacked, he counseled, was confidence.

Aside from the manuscript, Max questioned Marjorie's impulse to write about current events, as she had in the "American Way" piece, and reminded her to stick to her creative vocation. "There are lots of people who think a good writer can turn her hand to anything," he said. "It isn't true, and we know it. You, as well as I. But there is this pressure, and I hope you will resist it. What you mean comes from your writing, and don't let anything tempt you into the lists of controversy."

IN OCTOBER, Marjorie traveled to Madison to speak at a benefit for the University of Wisconsin Alumni Association scholarship fund—and to enjoy a round of honors. The trip was like a homecoming—the "Representative Woman" made good. She was feted at the president's mansion, given a luncheon by the *Badger* yearbook board and a tea at the Theta house, and inducted into Phi Beta, the national honorary speech and music society. Later there was another tea and a picnic, and finally, the Frank Lloyd Wrights entertained her at Taliesin. Surely, the ghost of Ida Kinnan hovered about the entire week, thrilled by her daughter's celebrity, impressed by her wardrobe, though the girl was no longer a Maxfield Parrish beauty but a heavy-hipped middle-aged woman. Yet Marjorie knew the magic of good tailoring, as did Norton, who had helped choose her wardrobe, and Ida would have envied her daughter's taste, as well as the money she had earned to indulge it.

At the *Badger* luncheon, Marjorie was asked if she thought people in different parts of the country were fundamentally different—the sort of question the less-traveled might ask. "Yes," said the peripatetic guest, "people reflect their background," and she called up the poor Florida Cracker who would share his last bite of corn bread, contrasted with the stingy Maine farmer who holds tight to his belongings. Another question: Had any of her professors expressed an opinion about her talent? Marjorie spoke of William Ellery Leonard, who had warned that her overblown vocabulary would ruin her as a writer and suggested that she ought to try composing without any adjectives or adverbs. She had risen to the challenge, she said, and the result was her first story published in the university literary magazine. At one of the Wisconsin events, Marjorie offered her "Fact and Fiction" talk. A woman in attendance—channeling Ida or, perhaps, any newspaper's social columnist—described the scene: "There was an excellent turnout—the stage was beautifully decorated—

and it was all very exciting. She spoke in the most delightfully informal way—without notes, a stand, or anything to detract."

At the formal banquet, it was announced that the actor Fredric March, a Wisconsin classmate whom Marjorie originally knew by his real name, Freddy Bickel, had sent a droll appreciation: "Now that we are in our declining years, I sit reading Marg's books and I envy her. For while she can write about 'yearlings,' I must continue to try to look like one." One classmate wrote admiringly of Marjorie's appearance: "She wore a perfectly beautiful gown of heavy white brocade with a tailored fitted jacket with short sleeves and three gorgeous brilliant buttons down the front and a corsage of orchids. During dinner, she caught sight of me and waved and smiled in a very friendly manner. Imagine!"

Other classmates offered memories, one describing the Marjorie of 1914 as "a pretty, well-dressed, and demure little damsel from the Nation's Capital," "always quietly attentive, always well-prepared, and never pert." Others remembered her differently. Marjorie "was the bravest thing in school and would talk right back to her profs while the rest of the class shivered for fear of being called on." And: "Some of the Thetas pledged to earn $5 each in order to buy new furniture for the Theta house. Some of the girls sweat blood earning their five bucks, but Marge wrote a short poem—four lines for *The Smart Set*—and five dollars came back by return mail." But the most shocking report, from several sources, was that "Marjorie Kinnan was the first Wisconsin co-ed who had the hardihood to pioneer the use of bright red lipstick." All agreed that she had been exceptional, and no one was surprised by her success.

Chapter Seventeen

Good Women, Marriage, and a Memoir

1940-42

IN THE LAST MONTHS OF 1940, Marjorie was at her typewriter in the woods, struggling with *Cross Creek*. She found it nearly impossible to avoid what she considered "personal" touches, whereas she'd intended a removed chronicle. But a memoir is by definition personal—the past seen through the author's particular lens—and she could hardly avoid revealing herself as narrator-character, though she often wrote from a collective "we." Work went slowly. There had been a freeze at the grove, the ugly remains mirroring her mood. If she escaped to the beach cottage, she told Max, her workers would fight among themselves, "and I have only now gotten them straightened out after my summer's absence." The usual inconveniences both annoyed her and fired her sense of humor. One day, she killed a moccasin snake in her bathroom, first by heaving a Sears & Roebuck catalog at it, then by beating it to death with a copy of *The Yearling*. "Don't mind me sputtering," she wrote. "I have learned that I always feel this way when I'm working something out, but God it is torment."

The good editor reminded her: "Of course you need not be strictly bound by fact. In such a book you can move things around rightly so long as you give the poetic truth. But you know all about that, anyhow."

ALTHOUGH MARJORIE sometimes ran into trouble supervising her workers, she found that in day-to-day business, their interruptions didn't bother her—they were the background, and sometimes the foreground, of her life, and not as distracting as an adoring fan barging in from the road. Still, she longed for a dependable, long-term domestic right hand—which, in Marjorie's case, meant as much a "personal assistant" as a "housekeeper." She'd lost Adrenna Mickens some months before, the gap closed temporarily by Adrenna's mother, Martha. Martha was a godsend, but not capable of everything her boss required. That fall, Marjorie had the good luck to hire Idella Thompson (hereafter Parker, as she was known for much of her adult life), who would stay with her for most of ten years, earning the compliment "perfect maid."

A native of nearby Reddick, Idella had attended the Daytona-Cookman Collegiate Institute—a high school that eventually became Bethune-Cookman College—and earned a certificate to teach in black schools. She had taught for three years before dissatisfaction set in. The pay was inadequate, the supervision overbearing. Like other blacks who traveled around, picking up seasonal work or, if they were fortunate, finding steadier employment with wealthy whites, Idella cast about for something else and found a position with a family in West Palm Beach, where she learned to prepare and serve sophisticated dishes. She stayed for five years, perfecting her skills, until a boyfriend made trouble, forcing her to leave. Back in Reddick, Idella found a job with the well-to-do Camp family in Ocala, but before the arrangements were finalized, Marjorie, who'd heard about her, snatched her away while the Camps were out of town.

The story goes that Marjorie pulled up to the Reddick house one day in her cream-colored Oldsmobile, tooting her horn, brandishing a cigarette with her free hand, asking pointed questions, as if Idella were already hers. When Idella stated that she planned to work for the Camps, Marjorie said, "Oh no, Idella, you don't want to work for Mrs. Camp. She's hard to get along with," and wrote a check to retain her, saying she was about to go to New York, but she'd be back. Soon, another check came to Idella from New York, which seemed to seal the deal, dumbfounding the young woman and worrying her mother, who was afraid to see her daughter go to the Cross Creek–Island Grove area. Idella's mother had heard that black people in Island Grove had "mysteriously disappeared" over the years. It was "a white man's town."

Nevertheless, Idella packed her maid uniforms and was ready when Marjorie returned. In her memoir, Idella recalled that Pat owned the back seat of the Olds, so Marjorie told Idella to sit next to her in front, disregarding standard practice: blacks always sat in back. Marjorie "spoke fast, the words sort of tumbling out. She smoked as she drove, flicking ashes out the window more often than she needed to." Idella was nervous the entire ride. Marjorie was "driving fast and swerving every time she looked at me." But Idella liked her.

When the women got to the farmhouse, "what seemed like a whole lot of black people came running up from out of the woods," Idella recounted. They were Martha and Will Mickens, Little Will, and Little Will's girlfriend, Alberta. All would share the two-bedroom tenant house: the Mickens clan on one side, Idella on the other. Will filled her in on the local scene: W. R. Brice, known as "Old Boss," had always ruled the Creek until Marjorie (sometimes called "Old Miss" or "Missy") moved in and the two began to feud. One such clash had occurred two years before, when Brice's grove man, Henry Fountain, shot Marjorie's grove man, B. J. Samson, and the victim was forced out of town. But, said Will, "when Mrs. Rawlings lit a cigarette and showed those catlike eyes, and almost every other word was a curse, well, everyone would listen."

Soon after she began to work at Cross Creek, Idella asked to read *The Yearling*—she was the first housekeeper who could have done so—and as she did, she reached a deeper understanding of the writer who struggled to guard her time and routine, even from herself. "My new darky maid is too good to be true," Marjorie wrote Julia Scribner.

As soon as Idella learned what to expect and do at the Creek, Marjorie left for Jacksonville with Norton and Cecil Clark for a football game—and afterward, she quaffed her first Zombie at Marineland's Penguin Bar. "They shouldn't call it that, for Zombies are the living dead, and the drink is the resurrection of the prone," she wrote Julia from the Creek. She had been ill and gone to the Jacksonville hospital again for "low metabolism, no hydrochloric acid in stomach, a dash of anemia. I have a whole carton of pills and pellets to keep track of," she reported.

News of Scott Fitzgerald's December 1940 heart attack and death in Hollywood sobered her. He had spent the last years of his life in the movie capital, working as a scriptwriter—one of his projects was an unsuccessful draft for *Gone with the Wind*. Max was one of the handful of mourners who attended Scott's funeral in Bethesda, Maryland. "He suffered by having become too wholly identified with the age he gave a name to," Max reflected, referring to the Lost Generation. "It was Hem who promulgated it, but Gertrude Stein who first uttered it. Scott's despair didn't come upon him until the depression began and then it was more a matter of drinking and personal disaster."

Marjorie responded, saying that Scott's life was more tragic than his death. His success had come too early, and he had valued "the wrong things." Even so, she added, "it was not fair to attribute to him personally all the shallowness and stupidity of the people he wrote about. The very fact that he could write about them with that bitter irony, put him beyond them. But people in general are totally unable to detach the person of a writer from the products of his thinking."

In the new year, Marjorie's story "Jessamine Springs," the brief tale of a lonely itinerant preacher's attempt at non-churched fellowship, appeared in the February 22, 1941, *New Yorker*—an answer to the *Atlantic* critic's comment about the lack of religion in *When the Whippoorwill*. She was still making headway with *Cross Creek*, although she took a break to read a short story at Rollins College, as part of the fourteenth Animated Magazine. The story she chose, "In the Heart," published in *Collier's* the year before, begins with a situation like B. J. Samson's: an incoming Negro worker, Black Bat, is shot by one already in residence, and the shooter is protected by "the courtesy often extended landowners in our section, whereby the local law puts the seignorial rights over Negro workers ahead of such meaningless abstractions as justice." But instead of leaving town, Black Bat, a physically imposing fellow who has miraculously restored and nurtured the white narrator's tattered garden, returns to his job because, he says, "all them little young things in that garden hongry for Black Bat's hands."

Marjorie's dramatic reading drew thunderous applause from the outdoor audience of some seven thousand, and it must have provided a light touch, considering the political stars sharing the podium: Archduke Otto of Austria, who had escaped to the United States; Nobel Prize winner Maurice Maeterlinck, who had fled Paris; and explorer and documentary filmmaker Osa Johnson, whose memoir about life with her late husband, Martin Johnson, had just been published, with material about their time in Africa; the northern part of the continent had lately turned into a battleground. Only the popular romance writer Faith Baldwin, whose escapist fiction sold like penny candy during the Depression, and a local humor columnist who went by the name Colonel Cloudburst shied from serious talk about the United States' position on the war.

A few weeks later at her typewriter, Marjorie stalled out. Re-creation, revisualization of people, places, and events, took a great deal of concentration, and she went into "a temporary paralysis." The principal problem was time, she said—time as a trajectory that, recalled, enriches, refines, and shapes understanding. If she told a direct, day-to-day narrative, she believed, the details would hold no meaning. "It may have taken many of the years I have been here for enough details, with point to them, to accumulate about any one person or family," she explained to Max.

She clarified the challenges in writing a memoir of place. "It is not enough for good anecdotes to be told, either humorous or moving. The sense of knowing a particular place and people with an almost Proustian deepness and intimacy and revelation, with my own feeling about things back of it, is what I want." She needed to "call less on facts and true details" and project herself "painfully and slowing into years and scenes and feelings that I have actually forgotten, and must re-create."

She struggled, as she always had, with her compulsion toward work and the "guilt" that shadowed it. "I suffer from it all the time," she confided to Julia. "I never feel that I have earned my leisure, or a vacation, or anything. . . . I don't know where the guilt comes from, except that anyone with lots of mental energy knows secretly how much more he could get done than he does." Marjorie's aunt Grace Kinnan, a retired milliner who had run her own shop, noted that compulsive work ran in the family and lectured Marjorie about it. "Why? Why?? Why??? cannot a <u>Kinnan</u> take things easy and get <u>pleasure </u>out of living?" Grace cried out in a letter. "Madeleine [a relative] killed herself, so did your blessed father. <u>We all do!</u> Darling, you are young enough to make yourself <u>slow down</u> and live slowly and make a joy of living."

AFTER IDELLA ARRIVED at the Creek, Marjorie encountered another woman necessary to her writing life: Ellen Glasgow, the venerable Virginia author whose novel prefaces Marjorie had begged Max to send her three years before—the writer who had pointed out the need to let the subconscious rest, so that the well could fill, between books. James Branch Cabell, Glasgow's neighbor in Richmond, must have encouraged the meeting, for Glasgow had not cared for Marjorie's writing at first, commenting to her friend Irita Van Doren, "the Southern peasants in *South Moon Under* and even the Florida swamps, all seemed to me to be made of wool." But the women had been in touch after *The Yearling* was released. Ellen had invited Marjorie to visit on her way to Ohio in 1939, saying that the new novel "seems to me to be a perfect thing of its kind." Marjorie couldn't accept then, but in the spring of 1941, frustrated by her work on *Cross Creek*, she might have sought Ellen for inspiration with some urgency, since Glasgow, of delicate health since youth, had recently suffered a series of heart attacks. Glasgow had also been in the news. Her eighteenth and final novel, *In This Our Life*, had been published to admiring reviews in March.

Their meeting in Richmond was a success. Cabell told Marjorie that she had scored "a tremendous hit" with Ellen. "She informs me that you both, figuratively, let down your hair and babbled out your pasts to each other without any auctorial embellishments." Among the women's common interests was a love of animals. Three months later, Marjorie had an extraordinary dream about Ellen, and described it for her:

> The reality of a dream can never be conveyed to another, but you came to live with me. I was away when you came, and on my return, to one of those strange mansions that are part of the substance of dreams, you were outside in the bitter cold, cutting away ice from the roadway and piling it in geometric pattern. I was alarmed, remembering your heart trouble, and let you inside the mansion and brought you a cup of hot coffee. You had on blue silk gloves, and I laid my hand over yours, and was amazed, for my own hand is small, to have yours fit inside mine, much smaller. You chose your room and suggested draperies to supplement a valance. The valance was red chintz

and you showed me a sample of a heavy red brocade of the same shade. I told you that from now on I should take care of you, and you must not do strenuous things, such as cutting the ice in the roadway.

Glasgow replied, saying that the dream letter had brought a "thrilling sense of friendship and sympathy." Since finishing *In This Our Life*, she said, she had felt "as if I were drifting in an icy vacuum toward something—or nothing." She cherished most "the way you brought me in and told me I must do no more cutting of ice in the roadway. And the warmth of the red curtains and the valance!"

"Ever since you came to see me, so strong and warm and vital, I have felt very near to you, and you have had your own chosen place in my life, just as I had in the house of your dream," she wrote Marjorie. *In This Our Life* won the Pulitzer the following year, an acknowledgment of her long career.

After Richmond, Marjorie continued on to Washington, D.C., for the Women's National Press Club annual Flatiron (as opposed to the Gridiron Club) dinner at the White House, hosted by first lady Eleanor Roosevelt. (It is likely that Marjorie had previously met the first lady, through either Martha Gellhorn or Margaret Mitchell, as Roosevelt had asked *Gone with the Wind* producer David O. Selznick to cast her own maid as Mammy. Marjorie invited her to the Creek that spring, but she visited an uncle in south Florida instead.) The WNPC had been founded in 1919 to support women journalists. Mrs. Roosevelt joined in the 1930s when she began writing newspaper and magazine columns. Among the guests this year were playwright Clare Boothe Luce, actress and singer Mary Martin, Margaret Mitchell, and roving Associated Press reporter Sigrid Arne, among other things a superb analyst of the New Deal and, incidentally, a former girlfriend of Jim Rawlings's, one of Chuck's brothers. In the White House, Marjorie was given the Lincoln Bedroom, with Lincoln's bed. "I simply don't feel good enough to sleep in it," she confessed to Norton in a letter written on White House stationery. But, she noted, "the vast room is comfortably shabby . . . there is dust on the marble-topped center table—so I feel almost at home." The newspaperwomen adored Eleanor Roosevelt, she observed. "And it is not that they are being diplomatic, for they say the most indiscreet and disreputable things about the great and near-great."

She added, "The dinner tonight promises to be a delightful brawl."

As was customary, the dinner featured a theatrical send-up of world affairs. According to Hearst's International News Service, "The White House and its friends and enemies, the Capital's fearfully swank society, and other institutions and events peculiar to the governmental seat were given a fine and needed dash of slapstick on the backside." Afterward, Marjorie admitted to Norton, she "did your trick of being the last one at the party," eating and drinking with friends until two a.m.

THAT SUMMER, the *Woman's Home Companion*, a popular magazine that published the likes of Willa Cather and John Steinbeck, ran Marjorie's "The Provider," the story of a shy railroad fireman who grows attached to two children and their mother living along his train route in rural Georgia. Over many months, he builds an elaborate fantasy about their lives, and how he might become part of their family, but the only concrete step he takes is tossing coal out to the children in winter. Eventually he loses his job over the spent coal. But his fantasy leads him on—to the house where the children and their mother lived, which he discovers they have vacated, then off to a neighboring state, where he believes they have moved. "Surely a man in his loneliness and his great need might cross that bridge. Surely he could find his own and come to them," the narrator concludes. "The Provider" may be Marjorie's most effective "lonely man" story. It reflected her ongoing obsession with home: Where is it, who is it, how does one find it, recognize it? Twelve years before, Cross Creek, Florida, had answered some of these questions for Marjorie, but not all.

Soon after "The Provider" appeared, Norton Baskin, with the help of Verle Pope's eye for properties and a $20,000 loan from Marjorie, began negotiating in St. Augustine to purchase the Warden residence, an imposing castle-like mansion Norton envisioned as a boutique hotel, the first he would own himself. Built in 1887 for Standard Oil partner William G. Warden, the manse and its lavishly planted grounds had been the scene of countless social events, but the family had vacated it years before and was giving it up. As the contract moved forward, another agreement was under hot debate: a marriage. In September, Marjorie and Norton finally "had it out." She had "sputtered" about something, and Norton had, according to Marjorie, turned on her. "You changed instantly from my sweet Norton to someone with whom I could not possibly be close," she complained.

"I make no excuses for my 'fits,' " she stated. "I am ashamed of them. But I exercise as much control as is possible for me, and when I make a trivial fuss, or really boil over, I simply cannot help it. My temperament is what it is, volatile and high-strung—and you may use any other adjectives you want to. My virtues—if any—come from exactly the same temperament as my faults, and each is a part of the other. I couldn't write books, I couldn't have a warmly emotional nature, if I were a placid pond. A man who was right for me would never be upset by my fits, and certainly would not hate me for them."

Now her heart was "a chunk of ice." Norton was no longer her sweetheart. Nevertheless, she added, "regardless of our future personal relations, the hotel deal is still a business deal."

By the end of the month, Marjorie was ill again. She confided to Julia Scribner that Norton and Edith Pope had talked her out of seeing a psychiatrist. Edith said Marjorie would never write again if "normalized." Norton was afraid she'd be completely changed. "They convinced me my moods of depression are not manic-depression, but physical exhaustion," she wrote.

She traveled to Columbia-Presbyterian Medical Center's Harkness Pavilion in New York, underwent tests for stomach and colon trouble, tried to rest. The coordinating doctor, Dr. Dana Atchley, would gather the test results to "see the whole picture." The effects of emotional disturbance were clear. To Max, Marjorie wrote, "I am to ease up on nervous tension. The diagnostician said I had an engine too big for the chassis." To Norton, she remarked that the doctor was a friend of novelist John P. Marquand's and poet Stephen Vincent Benét's. "He knows you don't get books out of contented cows."

Dr. Atchley elicited from Marjorie a lengthy self-history, in keeping with his view that "a well-trained and perceptive internist can successfully manage many of the emotional disturbances that trouble an average patient," as most are due to "environmental stresses." In his book *Physician: Healer and Scientist*, Atchley described a busy executive who collapsed of a minor infection and, finding it hard to resume his job, amended his life to avoid an "exhaustion neurosis," which might have described some of Marjorie's complaints. Doctor to well-known women

artists—his patients included Katharine Hepburn and Greta Garbo—
Atchley had an "alert, open watchfulness" that "never lets you rest or
stop at a half truth or an oversimplification or pat answer," according
to Anne Morrow Lindbergh, his patient, close friend, and, for a time,
lover. Atchley's watchfulness "is applying to the search for truth the pre-
cision and objectivity of a scientist and the delicacy of discrimination of
an artist—also of course, the dedication of a monk." Marjorie reported
that he drew from her "the things that I could identify as having disturbed me. He clarified so many things for me. Will have to tell you when
I see you, as it's a long story," she wrote Norton. There is no record of
the "long story," although Marjorie said Dr. Atchley had identified "the
source of my peculiar, spasmodic belligerence to you—and I had to wonder, as I know you must have, whether it meant that I was trying to reject
you." To Dr. Atchley, she had posed the question of marriage—whither
yay or nay—and described Norton. The good doctor asked her what the
hell she was waiting for. Her intended sounded perfect for her.

Marjorie put it to Norton: "I'm giving you a chance to either run like
everything or to propose to me! Think things out from your point of
view, decide what you *really* want, and we'll figure from there." Norton
wrote, "As you know, I have been ready and willing for some time but
want you to be sure that it is what you want. I don't mean that I want you
to assume the responsibility for its success because I realize the necessity
for adjustments and understanding. . . . I had long ago decided that any
adjustments I would have to make would be a thousand times worthwhile. Nothing would make me happier than to be married to you and I
sincerely think that it will work out fine."

Three weeks later, on October 27, 1941, with Aunt Ida and Verle and
Edith Pope as witnesses, Marjorie and Norton were married at the St.
Johns County courthouse in St. Augustine. It had been eight years since
the couple had met. Norton gave Marjorie a gold ring made from half
of his mother's gold ring, which had been large enough for Norton and
his brother to divide it. Ellen Glasgow probably spoke for all of Marjorie's friends when she wrote, "It is just right that this marriage should
bring you the serenity you had lost in all those years of distress and disappointment and mistaken endeavors. Everything you say of Norton
Baskin makes me feel that you have made the one and only decision that
could mean happiness for your future life, and security for your growing

work. I wish you both every good fortune. I not only wish it; I believe it."
Although Marjorie and Norton were both too busy for an extended honeymoon, they took a trip to Miami a few weeks later so Marjorie could
introduce her husband to Marjory Stoneman Douglas. They spent a day
with Douglas in her Coconut Grove home.

MARJORIE'S STRUGGLE to resolve her relationship with Norton had run
concurrently with her struggle to finish *Cross Creek*. In mid-September,
she had sent a draft to Max, with reservations. She knew that the styles
between serious and humorous events varied—would he indicate where
the breach was too wide? Also, didn't she sound a little preachy in some
spots? She was concerned about her neighbors' feelings. "I have used true
names in practically every instance," she explained. "I have tried not
to put things so that anyone's feelings would be hurt. These people are
my friends and neighbors, and I would not be unkind for anything, and
though they are simple folk, there is the possible libel danger to think of."

"What really binds the book together is its author," Max replied. "It
is with the author that one becomes identified." Marjorie would later
explain to a friend, "No actual autobiography ever is the true individual.
In writing of ourselves, we shade ourselves almost as much as we do an
imaginary character—often quite unconsciously." Max offered numerous suggestions for fine-tuning. "As to the question of libel . . . I don't
think any of the people of the book would bring a suit, but you are the
one who must be the judge. If they did, it would not be done because of
any injury, but out of meanness, which is not indicated to be in them."
He singled out two characters he thought "grand": Martha Mickens and
Zelma Cason.

Soon after the wedding, Marjorie shipped the *Cross Creek* manuscript to Scribner's—and suffered another abdominal attack. "It has
been such a funny pain," she wrote to Norton from the Creek—for the
couple, though married, would often live apart when she was writing. "It
flutters about in the middle, then ripples over to where my appendix used
to be, and shoots into a meteoric sort of pain, like a rocket going off.
Then it ripples back again and explodes on the other side like a smaller
rocket. Then it settles down to a steady chewing in the middle, like a
crab feeding itself with those harsh sharp mandibles." She blamed the
episode on catching a cold or swallowing a lemon seed. "If only I could

make pearls of such things, as an oyster does with an irritating grain of sand, what a valuable person I should be!!" Yet the book was successful. In less than a month, *Cross Creek* was in galleys. "I think you are most blessed to be able to give people such a book as this, and they are blessed thereby," Max said. In *Cross Creek*, he indicated, Marjorie had gathered a rich, varied record of her thirteen years in the hamlet and made her finest work of nonfiction: a fluid hybrid of personal essay, nature writing, folkways, and anecdote.

Two days after Max wrote, Norton's new hotel, having undergone a costly renovation, was opened to the public with a Sunday open house and cocktail party heralding "a brilliant new chapter in the role Castle Warden will play in St. Augustine, as a gracious hostelry just north of the ancient City Gates," a local reporter proclaimed. Verle Pope, who had just won a seat in the Florida House of Representatives, greeted guests and introduced them to Norton, who was in his element, shaking hands, inviting people to mingle—being, as he once described himself, "this gregarious hotel man whose whole life depended on people—on being around them and entertaining them." After the introductions, "we sent them up to Marjorie." For the grand opening was not just a chance to see a grand dame of St. Augustine architecture revived but an opportunity to meet the grand dame of Florida writing, who was now in residence—part-time, anyway. During the Castle renovations, a top-floor penthouse, away from the hotel's public rooms, had been designed for the newlyweds. Here, Marjorie would receive guests and stay with Norton, when she wasn't writing at Cross Creek or Crescent Beach. At the Castle, Norton protected her from curious tourists. "She was a bad judge of people," he once said. "She would meet people and they would want to become close friends quickly. I would just get rid of them." His standard line: "Marjorie's busy right now and she's not going to be available for the next two or three months."

That Castle Warden opened on December 7, 1941—the day the Japanese bombed Pearl Harbor, drawing the United States into the war—didn't strike anyone as a personal ill omen. It seemed that everything was in its place: Marjorie had finished *Cross Creek*, Norton had his own elegant hotel to run, and the pair had, after years of friendship, romance, surety, and misgivings, gotten married.

But a week after the Castle's doors opened, Marjorie received a disturbing letter from Max. Previously, the two had discussed issues of libel in *Cross Creek*, and Max had dismissed the possibility. Now, as he read the galleys, those concerns arose again, and he advised Marjorie to "change some names, if they are real names. It would do no harm, and it would be safer." Marjorie replied that she was making "a great many minor changes and deletions" to avoid problems. "It is simply impossible to tell how people will accept being written about," she explained to him. "The Negroes, Snow, Old Boss, the Glissons, the Bernie Basses, Zelma the census taker, are perfectly all right." (Later, she pointed out that a libel case by a Negro against a white would never "reach a southern court.") Marjorie said she would take one chapter to the neighbor most likely to object to his portrayal. "Please question drastically anything you think is dangerous, as it is always possible to make a point without being offensive," she implored Max. "I didn't know that fictitious names obviated this danger. I thought that if anyone was recognizable in his own neighborhood, he could still claim libel." Although the neighbor to whom she showed his chapter gave his approval, Marjorie's fears failed to recede completely.

By February, all of the revisions were in, and the Book-of-the-Month Club had taken *Cross Creek* for its April 1942 selection, along with John Steinbeck's war novel *The Moon Is Down*. Dual selection was rare, and the books—one a personal, bucolic narrative of a sleepy corner of the Deep South, the other a pro-democracy tale mirroring the Nazi occupation of Norway—seemed to represent opposite environments: a stable, throwback world, and an invaded, even annihilated one. Both books would be praised on their literary merits, but it might be said that *Cross Creek* appealed to readers hungry for a reassuring look backward, while *The Moon Is Down* raised controversy over Steinbeck's opinions of the current war, and the future. They were fraternal twins of the times.

Of Marjorie's new opus, Katherine Woods, in the *New York Times Book Review*, wrote admiringly that the book "could have been written only from a born novelist's sensitiveness and skill. *Cross Creek* is one of those unclassifiable books which weaves the threads of personal experience and observation and acquaintance into a far-spun texture beyond the writer's individual existence or surface contact." The book excelled as a work of "integrated re-creation." Lewis Gannett for the *New York Herald Tribune* opened with: "They say that the staunchest Southerners are Northern-born. They love the South as Southerners do, but they see it with the freshness of unaccustomed eyes. *Cross Creek* is written with an intimacy beyond fiction, with that 'true love and exasperation' which bound Mrs. Rawlings to her neighbors. It is, almost, a collective autobiography." *Time* magazine's critic described *Cross Creek* as a prose poem, but added, "Like all her books, *Cross Creek* is saved from too much floral fragrance by her deep sense that, under the exuberance of sub-tropical growth, violence lies always coiled and ready to strike."

Time's reference to coiled violence was prophetic. Sometime in April, Marjorie visited her old census companion Zelma Cason, who now worked in St. Augustine, and presented her with a copy of *Cross Creek*, inscribed, "To my good friend, Zelma Cason, with affection, Marjorie Kinnan Rawlings." In a shocking gesture, Zelma flatly refused it, claiming Marjorie's description of her in the book was humiliating—and some of her friends thought so, too. Stunned and hurt, Marjorie began to cry, defending what she and others thought was a "cute and attractive picture," but Zelma insisted she'd been wronged. The women talked it over, and Marjorie left, certain the rift had been mended.

The book, excerpted in the *Atlantic*, and later condensed—by Marjorie—for the Reader's Digest edition, sold exceedingly well. Scribner's first run numbered four hundred thousand copies, three-quarters of them for the Book-of-the-Month Club. In June, Marjorie reported "very heavy fan mail—much more so than on *The Yearling*." Some readers were either naïve or nervy. One Kentucky woman asked Marjorie to send her a scuppernong grape vine, some chufa plants or seeds, and a four-foot magnolia tree with it roots wrapped in damp moss. Send them collect, the woman insisted; she would be glad to pay the shipping bill. Most letters praised "Our Daily Bread," a long, mouth-watering chapter on Cross Creek food and cooking, with meditations on rural Florida breads (hush puppies, biscuits, corn bread), vegetables (mustard greens, okra, swamp cabbage), fruits (mango, papaya, pineapple, orange, banana, pomegranate), and meats (alligator, rattlesnake, turtle, crab, blackbird, bear, venison, duck, squirrel), confirming Marjorie's notion that a cookbook might succeed on the heels of this memoir. She'd brought it up as soon as *Cross Creek* appeared. Max thought the idea splendid: "a very appealing little volume" that Marjorie could easily assemble before launching a longer project. They discussed the book's form: it would contain rather lengthy commentary, and Marjorie could share more Cross Creek stories related to food. She would test the recipes and offer complete instructions, down to the correct quarter teaspoon of salt.

Chapter Eighteen

Wartime, Zora

1942

WITH *CROSS CREEK* OUT in the world and a cookbook confirmed as an encore, Marjorie could spend more time in St. Augustine. From Castle Warden, she described for Max how she was adjusting to the Oldest City: "I had thought—and hoped—that perhaps I had wrung dry the backwoods section and living, but there is something there from which I cannot seem to tear away. . . . My husband is so completely lovely a person, and it grieves me to see him grieved when I simply have to clear out and go back to the Creek." She added, "Actually, there is a whole new literary field before me in the old town of St. Augustine, and I really hope that in time I shall be able to sink myself into it."

She was correct about the literary scene. In winter, St. Augustine continued to draw authors from the north, and now that the war was driving writers out of Europe, the ranks swelled intermittently throughout the year. In January, Marjorie wrote to the Nobel Prize–winning author Sigrid Undset, who had survived a harrowing escape from Norway in 1940 and, over several months, had made her way to Sweden, Moscow, across Siberia to Japan, and, finally, to San Francisco. In the United States, Undset had undertaken lecture tours arranged by Carol Brandt for Colston Leigh's speakers' agency and made a temporary home for herself in a

Brooklyn apartment. She was acquainted with Alabama writer Hudson Strode and his recent book *Finland Forever*. Strode had forwarded to Undset Marjorie's invitation to visit Cross Creek and St. Augustine, and Undset replied with compliments for *The Yearling*. She would like to meet Marjorie and visit citrus country.

Undset's winter travel schedule was built around her new book, *Return to the Future*, an account of her flight from Norway to America. In February, she would speak at Rollins College's Animated Magazine and receive an honorary doctorate of humane letters. Marjorie attended, then drove her new friend up to Cross Creek. Undset stayed for several days, marveling at the pleasure of fresh oranges. "A brown girl goes out every morning and picks what is needed for the day," she wrote to her sister Ragnhild. "One feels one has not tasted oranges before." Marjorie and Sigrid went on to St. Augustine and Castle Warden, where Norton arranged for his chef to serve a special dinner in the restaurant. Over drinks, Sigrid told guests of her experiences with the Nazi invasion so compellingly that everyone lost track of time. Finally, Norton ran back to the kitchen to apologize to his patient chef—who, it turned out, had been listening through a cracked-open door. "Please don't hurry her," he told Norton. "The later the better. She is very interesting."

Marjorie and Sigrid bonded quickly and deeply. Besides a love of the literary arts, both were interested in horticulture. Both were politically engaged. Both had managed—and departed from—difficult marriages. In St. Augustine, they enjoyed long talks at the Shrine of Our Lady of La Leche at Mission Nombre de Dios, the grounds thought to have been the spot where the first Spanish conquistador landed in St. Augustine, in 1565. The peaceful chapel invited prayer; the surroundings, quiet conversation. Undset had been raised a secular Lutheran, then come to adulthood as an agnostic, but after World War I, she had turned to the Catholic Church and converted in 1924, four years before she was awarded the Nobel Prize for her *Kristin Lavransdatter* trilogy. Her conversion—and her subsequent leaning toward more "Catholic" materials—had triggered moral outrage in predominately Lutheran Norway. That Marjorie, who claimed no religion other than a belief in cosmic consciousness, became one of Sigrid's closest confidantes speaks to a shared regard for mystery.

When Undset returned to Brooklyn, with a flowering blue spiderwort from Cross Creek, she wrote to Marjorie of the political work she, as a representative of Norway, was called to do—"speaking at 'Rallies' and writing articles to order. And now they have booked me for Radio talks. In a series which is called, of all things, 'The Spirit of the Vikings,'—and we over in Norway had ceased a long time ago to be especially proud of the deeds of our Viking ancestors." Yet, she remarked, "among the Americans of Norwegian descent the mouldy Viking romanticism is still alive." A few weeks later, she reported that her house in Lillehammer was now occupied by Gestapo officials. Her older son had served in the military and died in the war, early on. Undset thought him lucky, to have missed the devastation. "Every week almost I learn that one or the other of our best writers are in concentration camps, in Norway, in Germany, or Poland. I wonder how many of them I will ever meet again." Sigrid and Marjorie corresponded through mid-1949, the end of Undset's life. Of Undset, Marjorie wrote to Julia Scribner: "There is a woman. I felt like a small wave washing against a piece of medieval architecture."

At Castle Warden, business was slower than Norton had antici-pated, as the war took an unexpected toll on the state. Difficulties began on the night of February 19, 1942, when the German submarine *U-128* reached Florida waters near Cape Canaveral, about 125 miles south of St. Augustine, and torpedoed the oil tanker *Pan Massachusetts*, the explosion lighting up the sky near the headwaters of the St. Johns River. Two days later, the *U-504* joined in. Two American tankers went down in flames. As more armed subs arrived, more defenseless tankers and merchant ships exploded and sank, and survivors swam for their lives through fire and oil toward ruined sand. A blitz along Florida's Atlantic shipping lanes—from Fernandina Beach, north of Jacksonville, to the Keys—was on.

At first, hotels and other tourist operations along the coast refused to lower their lights—it would hurt business, they said—and with no exter-nal authority demanding a dim-out, the gay winter parties continued, as if no one a few miles out to sea had burned up in a firestorm. But the brighter the lights, the easier for a German sub to spot a cruising ship, and in mid-May, a dim-out was finally ordered along the Florida coast.

That month, eighty-six vessels were sunk in the territory, reportedly the work of only six U-boats. In June, Marjorie wrote to Max: "We have the dim-out and are very close to the war in general."

As the flow of northern tourists slowed, due to gas rationing and danger along the coast, Norton installed a new cocktail lounge at the Castle to attract a growing clientele of army officers and their wives. Later, he would say that it became the unofficial officers' club. Both he and Marjorie served as fire wardens and plane spotters. Norton signed up for night duty with the Coast Guard's horse patrol. They, like everyone else, had procured ration books for meat, sugar, canned goods, and other foods. The list of rationed items would grow to include automobile parts, shoes, coffee, butter, jellies, and more.

It would be months before American forces coordinated an effective defense and the German subs backed off from Florida, but the dim-out must have eased the situation for Marjorie, who retreated to Crescent Beach, bearing down on what would be titled *Cross Creek Cookery*. To Edith Pope, she wrote, "I simply associate Castle Warden with fun and cannot work there. Norton hangs his head like Topper [his dog] and looks very abused, and I feel as though the book were coming, not out of my life's blood as usual, but out of his."

"It is faintly spooky at the cottage alone at night, what with all the roads closed, and the thought of spies landing," she went on. If a Nazi investigated the light from her cottage, she planned to cry out, "Ach! Meine Freunden! Heil, Hitler." (Or, being nervous, she allowed, she would more likely squeak, "Mes amis! Comment-allez-vous?") "But as Norton points out, they will probably not react as I have planned, and then what do I do? I should be furious if they shot me or trussed me up before I could get in my counter espionage."

MARJORIE'S FIRST ATTEMPT at the cookbook had seemed too sophisticated to Max. Now they agreed on a homier, "Cross Creekified angle," with a casual narrative and characters like Martha Mickens and Idella Parker. Marjorie even included ten of Ida Kinnan's recipes, though she had long surpassed Ida as a cook and hostess. She had just given a dinner for friends, and she listed the dishes for Max: iced honeydew melon with lime juice, roast wild duck, wild rice, carrot soufflé, fresh lima bean croquettes, whole braised small white onions, tiny cornmeal muffins, kumquat jelly, celery hearts, fresh mango ice cream, devil's food cake. Feeding her wild mallards cost twice what was required to feed two mules—yet after all the work and expense, she hated killing the ducks, and was relieved of guilt only by their rate of reproduction; the flock had to be thinned. Marjorie achieved the best flavor from her mallards by feeding them skim milk, clabber, grain, and greens.

For dessert, ice cream was served at nearly every dinner, courtesy of Marjorie's sainted cow, Dora, described thusly in *Cross Creek Cookery:* "She gives no great quantity of milk, her disposition is vile and we dislike each other, but I joyfully swap her the most expensive twenty-percent dairy feeds, and allow her to nibble on my coral honeysuckle and my oranges, and raise fine cow-pea hay for her, in return for her cream. It rises to a depth of three quarters of an inch on a shallow pan of milk. It is as yellow as buttercups. It is so thick, when ladled off into a bowl or pitcher, that it is impossible to pour. It must be spooned out." One of Marjorie's most precise introductions to a recipe was that for crab à la Newburg; it describes secret springs in the Big Scrub where the choicest blue crabs could be hunted. Those upwellings, she explained, were connected by streams to the Atlantic. Huge ocean crabs often found their way to the mineral waters, which sweetened their meat. Marjorie and her cronies hunted them at night in a rowboat, equipped with flashlights and a long gig for plucking the crustaceans straight from the clear runnel. Another daring dish was red-winged blackbird pie, as shooting the birds was illegal, "which I discovered probably just in time to save myself a term in the penitentiary." She included it in *Cross Creek Cookery* because other small birds could be substituted. Less daring was the recipe for Minorcan gopher stew, requiring gopher turtle meat. For a time, she kept a pen of turtles who would give their lives for her table.

IN THE SUMMER OF 1942, Marjorie was invited to speak at historically black Florida Memorial College in St. Augustine. One of the summer session instructors was Zora Neale Hurston, author of *Their Eyes Were Watching God* (1937); she had recently moved there to complete her memoir, *Dust Tracks on a Road*, covering her childhood in Eatonville, Florida's first all-black incorporated city. The women became acquainted, and when Marjorie returned to Castle Warden, she told Norton she'd "met the most wonderful woman."

In fact, she had immediately invited Zora to tea at their Castle Warden apartment. But as soon she told Norton about it, she grew flustered, regretting the offer, and suggested she meet Zora elsewhere, not at the hotel, which was segregated, and where white regulars might frown on a fashionably dressed black woman passing through the lobby and perhaps withdraw their business. Norton, however, assured Marjorie that the invitation could stand, instructing a trusted black assistant—who balked at first—to watch for Zora at the appointed hour and "get her through this lobby the fastest you ever seen and get on the elevator, and get her up there." The hour came, but neither Norton nor his assistant saw anything of Zora. Marjorie's guest had foreseen the situation, entered the hotel through the kitchen, and found her way to the apartment. When Norton checked with his wife on the hotel phone, she told him what Zora had done and invited him up: "We're having tea and having more fun than you've ever heard of," she told him. "And if you've got any sense, you'll come on up here."

To Edith Pope, Marjorie described Zora as

a lush, fine-looking café au lait woman with the most ingratiating personality, a brilliant mind, and the fundamental wisdom that shames most whites. She puts the full responsibility for Negro advancement on the Negroes themselves and has no use for the left-wingers who consider her a traitor, nor for the "advanced" Negroes who belong to what she calls the fur-coat peerage. She says she doesn't like spirituals "with their faces lifted" and wants to establish a Negro Conservatory of music that would depart entirely from white tradition and develop Negro music from its own roots.

She says that both "advanced" whites and "advanced" negroes make a mistake in handling the negro problem with kid gloves, each afraid of the other.

What Zora told her squared with the assertion that, as one Hurston scholar put it, Zora "staked out a conservative position on race that grew from her fierce pride in black institutions and her suspicion of any mask unless it were her own." Zora, who throughout her life had to negotiate race, sex, and class to achieve artistry and serve her ambition, wore many masks, and as friendly as she and Marjorie became, she no doubt modulated her behavior, observing the southern code of manners, notes the critic Hilton Als, in which blacks adopted "theatrical modesty and duplicity" to manage their inferior position. Marjorie might have found ease in a point of view that piled responsibility for the oppressed onto the oppressed. Yet the meeting challenged her perspective on race—her ambivalence, her tendency toward what James Baldwin would call "the lie of their pretended humanism."

As a child in Washington, D.C., Marjorie had known a mixed but largely segregated neighborhood. The Kinnan family housekeeper might have been black or Irish. At the Creek, Marjorie mostly adopted the racial attitudes common in that time and place. Her workers were second-class citizens, needful of management, discipline, and even common sense. "Mrs. Rawlings, kind as she was, never asked her workers to do anything," her "perfect maid," Idella Parker, remembered. "She *told* them." She talked *at* them, not *to* them. In letters prior to meeting Zora, Marjorie often referred to her workers as "niggers." Yet she was considered liberal by her white neighbors. She paid her black workers more than the going rate, provided more medical, legal, and personal support than was customary, and extended unusual privileges, like the use of her truck for a Saturday night in town. She complained about some employees' lack of commitment to her (manifested either in routine mishaps or decisions to leave the Creek) but appreciated and depended on those who understood and grew close to her—as close as could be achieved, given their unequal standing in the society of the times. Marjorie afforded everyone a measure of human dignity, as when she defended B. J. Samson, eliciting appreciation from black neighbors and derision from whites.

But beyond the Creek, Marjorie moved in elite white circles, such as the academic crowd at the University of Florida, where, the year before, a Negro student at historically black Bethune-Cookman College had applied to the master's program in business administration, troubling the waters in Gainesville. The state attorney general, Tom Watson, addressed the question, saying the student was by law entitled to attend a state school "in the absence of other and adequate provision for the training desired," and, practically speaking, separate dormitory, dining hall, and classroom space "could be provided and marked for negroes, separating them from the white students." A university official remarked that the student would have to pass qualifying examinations that stumped many white applicants—implying that the Bethune-Cookman applicant might not make the cut, anyway. And, for some reason, he didn't. It would be seventeen more years and many lawsuits before the University of Florida admitted a black student.

Marjorie's ambivalence is apparent in "Black Shadows," a chapter in *Cross Creek*, in which she highlighted several of what she termed "reasonably accurate" clichés about Negroes: they were childlike, carefree, religious "in an amusing way," liars, undependable. Yet she called these clichés superficial, pointing to the Negro population's African heritage, the unspeakably difficult adjustments to slavery and, since Reconstruction, to "so-called civilization." The Negro is "left to shift for himself for the most part instead of being cared for," she wrote. She was on the fence, which is why meeting Zora gave her "quite a jolt" and made her feel "rather small"—so small she wrote about the encounter in the voice of her new pointer, Moe, to Edith Pope's dog Patrie. Referring to herself, she wrote: "By all her principles, she [Marjorie] should accept this woman as a human being and a friend—certainly an attractive member of society acceptable anywhere—and she is a coward. If she were on her own if she would do it. She feels that she cannot hurt her husband in a business way. But her pioneer blood is itching—"

BY THE END OF JULY, Marjorie had closed in on finishing the cookbook manuscript, even as German subs threatened her beach. Passes were required to access the ocean roads leading to her retreat. Marjorie had installed blackout shades, and she found it "rather creepy alone here at night, with no traffic on the beach highway, convoys going by, bombers overhead, and the thought of the saboteurs who land on isolated beaches." Submarines had been spotted. She told Max, "We hear mysterious explosions out at sea and never know the cause."

Max loved *Cross Creek Cookery*. Marjorie was glad, but she was more concerned with the mail flowing in from servicemen who had read *The Yearling*—which had stayed on the best-seller list for two years, through February 1940, and was still going strong—or *Cross Creek*, which had been touted in ads as "America's No. 1 best-selling book of nonfiction." How many libraries did soldiers and sailors have access to, Marjorie wanted to know. She wished to send them copies of her books.

She knew that *The Yearling* and *Cross Creek* had reached soldiers and sailors since the start of the war, when Americans began donating thousands of books, via campaigns led by the American Library Association and other agencies, through the Army Library Service. The Nazi book ban had galvanized donors, as had President Roosevelt, who famously wrote in 1942, "A war of ideas can no more be won without books than a naval war can be won without ships." In 1943, the army and the Council on Books in Wartime (a group of publishers, librarians, and booksellers) agreed on a series of what were called Armed Forces Editions—cheap, pocket-sized paperbacks, easy to tote and less expensive to ship than full-sized books. When the project ended in 1947, nearly 123 million books, comprising 1,322 individual titles, had been printed. *South Moon Under*, *The Yearling*, and *Cross Creek* were among them, and as soon as they appeared, Marjorie's mail increased manifold. She answered every letter—sometimes with an assistant's help—and continued corresponding with a few readers who engaged her about topics beyond her own work.

Now the war was bringing Norton some good fortune. The Coast Guard had claimed the grand Hotel Ponce de León for a training school, leaving the smaller Castle Warden as an alternative for military visitors and the usual winter trade—which was actually booming, as the Florida Chamber of Commerce encouraged visitors to snap up rooms not used by the military. Money poured into Florida as industrial projects tied to the military expanded. Jacksonville's shipyards alone employed more than thirty-five thousand men and women, most coming from north Florida and rural Georgia, until labor shortages, caused by the draft, forced a broader search. That year, the federal government requisitioned all canned and processed citrus for the American military and allies—a boon for growers like Marjorie, but also a headache, since many grove workers were taking off for better jobs in the war industries. In some cities, such as Gainesville, "idling" men who could not prove they were gainfully employed were arrested—a tactic to ensure productivity.

Marjorie worried that Norton would be drafted, even though he was almost forty-one and the upper limit was then thirty-six. He had applied to officers' training school but, lacking a college degree, had been deemed ineligible. As a couple, they contributed as they could. One weekend, they entertained seven army doctors from Boston who were serving at Camp Blanding. They fished for blue crab on Saturday, and on Sunday, Marjorie served crab à la Newburg, plus plain crab with mayonnaise, baked sherried grapefruit, raised rolls with guava jelly, carrot soufflé, tomato aspic with artichokes, peach ice cream, orange cake, and "a good Burgundy." "That meal was a symphony," one of the grateful doctors proclaimed.

Among the servicemen who wrote to Marjorie was Alexander P. Haley, who was serving in the Coast Guard on the USS *Murzim* and teaching himself to write short stories while off-duty. "May I commend you on having become one of my favorite authors—for having done to the Florida backwoods what Damon Runyon did to New York?" he said by way of an opening. He offered lavish praise for *Cross Creek* and *The Yearling*, and revealed his aspirations: "I hope, too, that I'll someday be as efficient as you at portraying people whom I have known and wish to use in plots. You see, I am a writer too, but, as yet, definitely amateur. . . . Like Aunt Martha [Mickens], too, I am colored, though that, rather than hindering, spurs me." Later, as Alex Haley, he would write two of the century's most notable books: *Roots* and *The Autobiography of Malcom X*.

AFTER THE JULY MEETING with Zora, Marjorie's understanding of race relations began to shift significantly, though not without the interior conflicts, the steps forward, back, and sideways, that monumental change entails. That she had been urged to break custom by her Alabama-born husband, who invited Zora to visit via Castle Warden's front door, led to the couple's discussions about racial prejudice and Negro rights for many months to come.

Marjorie and Norton were not alone in this. Their changing views corresponded with a civil rights movement among educated whites as a whole, sparked by the war. Nazism had forced some white Americans to own up to and examine their racist policies and behaviors, while across the sea in the armed forces, men and women of many ethnicities served together, shoulder to shoulder, softening some racial divisions. As the United States emerged to lead the "free world," it would have to embrace civil rights reform as bedrock—both as proper ideal and as defense, for as the Cold War began, Soviet propagandists keen on locating America's weaknesses found an easy target in racism, particularly in the South, where lynchings continued. It was no accident that the NAACP's membership ballooned in this period, or that the Congress of Racial Equality, founded in 1942 by fifty people, black and white, grew steadily.

Sometime afterward—1942 or 1943—Marjorie wrote an undated letter to syndicated "southern liberal" Alabama columnist John Temple Graves in response to one of his editorials, very likely his robust piece that appeared in the September 20, 1942, issue of the *Miami Herald*. Titled "Negroes' Role in War Crisis," it ran a full half page, a condensed version of a longer, much-talked-about essay published that month in the *Virginia Quarterly Review*. Graves's central arguments supported segregation, not integration, as the greater boon to Negroes' advancement. He was typical of other southern "liberals" of the era, who decried extreme oppressions, such as the Klan, lynching, and poll taxes, and often supported New Deal economic programs. But they drew the line at Jim Crow.

Graves especially criticized Negroes and liberals like Eleanor Roosevelt for making racial equality an issue during wartime—because, he lamented, America couldn't address both problems at once, and winning the war was more important. As well, Negroes had to make sure they stayed on the good side of southern whites who might support moves toward equality, meaning: Blacks, step lightly—if at all. Neither "side" was "ready" for integration, Graves and his colleagues said. Besides, integration and true equality would never be achieved. He might have been responding to the new Double V campaign announced earlier that year in the *Pittsburgh Courier*, a nationally circulated African-American newspaper. One *V* stood for victory overseas, the other for victory over racism at home. The campaign generated discussion everywhere. Marjorie agreed: anyone who served in the armed forces deserved equal rights when they returned to Pittsburgh—or Atlanta or Tallahassee—and those rights included freedom of social movement.

Marjorie responded to Graves with a passionate manifesto. Whether Graves received it is unknown, but the author's position—or the position she personally strove for—is clear:

I am afraid that it is utterly futile to try to make you see the point of view of a Southern "liberal" who goes so much further than you in interpreting Southern liberalism. But I must speak my piece. I know how sincere you are, I know of your integrity, I know that you are convinced of your broad-mindedness, and that you must feel you have gone a long way since your early prejudices. To a degree, you are indeed fighting the good fight, and I applaud you.

Yet in a recent column, you urge "justice" and "opportunity" for Negroes, while insisting on the pattern of segregation. This is where we part company.

How can I say it, how can I open your mind and heart to the psychological and actual fact that "justice" and "opportunity," however far they extend into education, politics and economics, are a cruel and hypocritical farce, as long as the artificial barrier of "segregation" is maintained. Don't you see, can't you see, that segregation denies a man or woman something more important than "justice" or "opportunity," and that is self-respect, freedom from being made to feel subtly inferior, from being, after all, and finally, an outcast. Most of us now know enough of psychoanalysis to understand the devastation worked on even the character of the dominant white Nordic male, that top-dog in the world of today, when he is made early to feel inferior.

You have been honest enough to admit that part of your own timid psychology, and that of such semi or pseudo-liberals as Hodding Carter, derives from a preponderance of Negroes in certain sections of our mutually beloved South. I do not remember your ever having said so, in so many words, but I assume there is an unexpressed fear that if segregation disappeared, for one reason or another, the masses of Negroes in their heavily populated districts in the South would "take over," with appalling results.

I have no idea of your age, but this fear amused me, for I am of an age to remember the Suffragists, or Suffragettes, picketing the White House to try to get "Votes for Women." The great argument against "Votes for Women" was that once allowed "equality," women would "take over," men would become slaves, and the country ruined. It is not only obvious, but shameful, that since women were given "equality" they have not even done their proper share towards solving national and world problems, to say nothing of "taking over." I prophesy that the same thing would happen among the Negroes if there were no segregation, they would go on about their own affairs as before, and would do very well indeed if they took a greater interest than before in government and general problems.

As to "social equality," no one has given a better answer to that than Eleanor Roosevelt, who said quietly, "Why that's something that can't be legislated. It is something you have with your own friends." And as long as we have our blessed democracy, we can all choose our own friends. There are circles in which I should not be welcome, there are folks I should not invite to my home, not because of "race, color or creed," but because we have nothing in common. This will hold good forever.

I myself began with an acceptance of segregation. . . . I can only tell you that when long soul-searching and a combination of circumstances delivered me of my last prejudices, there was an exalted sense of liberation. It was not the Negro who became free, but I. I wish and pray for your own liberation. It is almost a religious experience. No man is free as long as another is enslaved, and the slavery of the spirit is more stringent than that of the body.

AROUND THE TIME she engaged with racial questions, Marjorie stepped into a public role as an environmental protector. In mid-September, she embarked on a two-week, five-thousand-mile research trip through Louisiana, Mississippi, Tennessee, and the Carolinas with a U.S. Forest Service team, investigating treed lands and the timber industry, taking notes for a *Collier's* article promoting conservation in American forests. The project was timely, and probably solicited. The Great New England Hurricane of September 1938 had cost the country millions of trees. A three-year salvage operation managed by the Forest Service with the help of the Civilian Conservation Corps had recently finished recovering seven hundred million board feet of timber. Concurrently, timber sales, lagging during the Great Depression, had begun to rise, as building in towns and cities resumed. And now that the United States had entered the war, the army and navy, Marjorie learned, were using at least one million board feet a month—much of it coming from national forests, where lookouts on coastal preserves were going up for monitoring enemy aircraft. Earle H. Clapp, acting chief of the Forest Service, had tried unsuccessfully for federal regulation of timber use in private forests, and he sounded a wartime alarm for preservation. "The scarcity of natural resources and their control by the very few may pave the way through widespread human misery to despotism and dictatorship; while an abundance of natural resources, accessible to people generally, makes for democracy and freedom," he wrote.

Julia Scribner, who had volunteered for Civilian Defense Corps work in New York, joined Marjorie on this whirlwind research trip, and by the end, the two were exhausted. But Marjorie had gathered more than enough material for a conservationist's rallying cry aligned with Earle Clapp's. "Trees for Tomorrow," published in the May 8, 1943, issue of *Collier's*, opened with the scene of a young Mississippi boy standing in front of an abandoned lumber mill. "It has destroyed his future in his own country," Marjorie wrote. "American greed and American thoughtlessness have destroyed the community itself. The tall steps behind him lead—nowhere."

On the Forest Service tour, she had seen how plenteous virgin forests attractive to the first settlers had been ruined by development and clear-cutting. Thriving communities turned to ghost towns once the trees were gone and absentee investors turned out the lights. In the South alone, she reported, cutting had exceeded annual growth by three billion board feet. "The war demands," she informed her readers, "are the final tragic note."

Yet she pressed on with a positive reminder, straight from the farm: "Trees are not like a gold mine. They are not like a coal mine. They are not a vein of platinum to be worked out. Trees are a crop." She praised growers in national forests, industry, and private lands who approached tree use and generation practically and scientifically. She called for a national law to control cutting. Trees belonged to everybody. "They are my trees and your trees. They are our trees."

Her summary point echoed the heart of her creative work: "On this earth, man and the products of earth are bound together."

After the piece was published, Marjorie received a long letter from a congressman serving on a committee investigating the lumber industry.

If he provided her with confidential information, would she write more articles? Although she wished to be helpful, she declined. Perhaps someone else would take up the cause.

AFTER THE FOREST TRIP, Julia Scribner wrote Marjorie morosely about "this disappearing-into-the-void-of-marriage business," and Marjorie blamed it on Julia's feeling that their old closeness had been broken, presumably by Marjorie's new married state. If Julia had stayed longer, Marjorie said, and been at the cottage or the Creek, rather than on a forest tour, she would have gotten over it. "As you grow older," Marjorie wrote "you will learn what is perhaps the greatest tragedy of human life: that we are each of us unutterably lonely, and no friendship, no passion, no marriage, ever joins any one of us so completely and permanently to another human being that we can avoid that loneliness."

She then amended that somewhat:

> I don't say that the perfect union of one sort or another is impossible. I still believe in it! Presumably, the Brownings had it—yet I wonder. One finds it temporarily in a passionate attachment. I myself have hoped that I would find it in a quieter sort of thing with Norton, if I was patient enough. At the moment, the horror of his life makes it impossible. Yet I feel that if I stick it out, there may be sort of a twilight peace, for Heaven knows, he is the loveliest human being I have ever known.
>
> I have had more than my share of love in my life, more men who loved me than is really decent, and looking back on them it seems that if I could combine this from one, that from another, this from one way of life, something else from another way of life, I would have that completion that all of us who are sensitive long for.

She advised Julia to accept loneliness and "be grateful for moments of completion," and to understand that if and when she married, she would find that "it does not cut you off from the need of other kinds of friends." She added, "Some rather stupid women, and some rather dull men, seem to find all they need in marriage, but they are people who do not ask very much."

In mid-November 1942, *Cross Creek Cookery* was published to wide acclaim. In early December, Wilma Lord Perkins, editor of the *Fannie Farmer Cookbook*, gave it a holiday boost in the *New York Post*, admiring how Marjorie's recipes were "interwoven with brilliant vignettes of Cross Creek characters," as well as "engagingly told anecdotes from Cross Creek life." Lewis Gannett, for the *New York Herald Tribune*, noted that "the Army seems to have been responsible for *Cross Creek Cookery*. Men in the service read the chapter on food in Mrs. Rawlings's *Cross Creek* in Hawaii, Australia, Ireland and Egypt, and wrote nostalgically of things they intended to eat when they got home. Some of them—yes, men!—asked for recipes." Mary Meade in the *Chicago Tribune* addressed her review directly to Marjorie. The new cookbook had made her terribly hungry, she complained, and "only a dinner with you and Idella at Cross Creek" would cure it.

In the wake of the cookbook's publication, Marjorie agreed to appear with illustrator Bob Camp—one of her old musketeers—at a war chest luncheon in Jacksonville, and thought to take a copy to Zelma Cason, whose recipe for ice box rolls claimed two pages. "Only the expert dare attempt the baking of Zelma's rolls," writer cautioned reader. On this visit, Marjorie believed that, seven months after the disquieting *Cross Creek* presentation, Zelma would be cordial to her. The outburst over the former census taker's portrayal must have been a passing mood, she thought; certainly, the whole matter had blown over. But it hadn't. When Marjorie handed her the cookbook, Zelma refused it. Something was terribly wrong. Marjorie couldn't fathom what it could be.

Just as *Cross Creek Cookery* appeared, Norton was called for military service and reported for a preliminary physical examination. "Actually, I think he is pleased at the prospect," Marjorie told Edith Pope, whose husband, Verle, was serving in the Army Air Corps. "He has not been happy on the sidelines and I respect him for his attitude. Of course, that's where women play such a hellish part in wars. They 'respect' men for going out and killing other men and getting killed. If women once <u>en masse</u> rared back on their dew-claws, men would find some other way of settling things. We are so pleased with ourselves, and we are so primitive and stupid."

After the exam, however, draftees over thirty-eight years old were rejected, so at forty-one, Norton didn't make the cut. In the new year, he would investigate volunteering for the American Field Service. The holidays passed with few changes, though it was Marjorie's first Christmas away from the Creek. Castle Warden hosted parties, Marjorie wrote to servicemen, and everyone watched the sea.

Chapter Nineteen

Lawsuit

1943

T HEN CAME A SURPRISE, and one of the great tragedies, of Marjorie's life: a lawsuit instigated by Zelma Cason, who suddenly, publicly claimed that Marjorie had defamed her by way of an eighty-four-word description in *Cross Creek:*

> Zelma is an ageless spinster resembling an angry and efficient canary. She manages her orange grove and as much of the village and county as needs management or will submit to it. I cannot decide whether she should have been a man or a mother. She combines the more violent characteristics of both and those who ask for or accept her manifold ministrations think nothing of being cursed loudly at the very instant of being tenderly fed, clothed, nursed or guided through their troubles.

In Gainesville on February 1, 1943, Zelma filed an eleven-page declaration on four counts: two claims for invasion of privacy, one for libel, and the fourth, exploitation for financial gain. The first count stated that Marjorie had violated a friendship by using material from intimate exchanges, turning Zelma's private life into a public one. The second claimed that Marjorie had used Zelma's name without prior consent. The third count, for libel, alleged that Marjorie had damaged Zelma's reputation in the community. The last, the "profits" complaint, stated that Marjorie had commercially exploited Zelma; thus, Zelma deserved a share of the book's income. In all, Zelma demanded $100,000 in damages. Norton was also named in the suit; in Florida, a husband was jointly liable for his wife's wrongful acts, so the case was officially titled *Cason v. Baskin.*

The "invasion of privacy" claim was the first of its kind leveled against an author.

The next day, wire services announced the lawsuit from coast to coast. "It is charged that in *Cross Creek* Miss Rawlings cheapened Miss Cason's name and made her 'notorious,'" one report read. By Sunday, February 7, *Tampa Tribune* book columnist E. D. Lambright had come to Marjorie's defense. "Let's turn to the book and see how Miss Zelma is damaged $100,000 worth," he challenged, and he proceeded to point out that not only did Marjorie refrain from giving Zelma's last name, but there was no evidence that she had maligned her neighbor. "In truth," he concluded,

> Miss Rawlings is rather complimentary—depicting the census taker as knowing all the inhabitants of the district, industriously doing the enumerating job, befriending the under-privileged natives, charitably bestowing upon them medicines and other necessities, joking with some and sympathizing with others. She does write of "Zelma" as an "ageless spinster," which is a testimonial of youth and virtue, and as "resembling an angry and efficient canary," which is a testimonial of industrious activity. Instead of suing her for $100,000, I think Zelma, whether real or fictional, owes Marjorie Rawlings a letter of thanks, for presenting her in a very favorable light before thousands of readers of a "best seller."

MARJORIE WROTE TO Phil May, her attorney, in Jacksonville. "I think the Declaration is one of the funniest documents I have ever read in my life," she said. "I laughed out loud all by myself, which I seldom do." Zelma's claims to inconspicuous behavior was "a riotous one to come from a woman who cusses a blue streak in front of assorted people, and in a voice so loud that she is famous for its carrying quality." And now this supposedly modest woman wished to call national attention to herself, even though "she admits herself that the portrait is 'clearly recognizable' to friends and acquaintances."

Marjorie offered other peoples' descriptions of Zelma's character and suggested witnesses, including Fred Tompkins, the Uncle Benny character in "Benny and the Bird Dogs." Fred had been pleased by his portrayal and had found it "an honor to be interesting enough to be written about." She drew May's attention to a passage in Zelma's declaration mentioning the early days of their friendship, when Marjorie was "neither wealthy or famous." It signaled a narrative Zelma and her attorney might push as hard as they could: one woman had climbed above the other and taken advantage of her friend down the ladder—and even of the place where they both lived. Signing off, Marjorie wrote, "I thought in the beginning that poor Zelma's reaction was one of exhibitionism and venom, but as I read the declaration, I think the hope of 'collecting' is the main motive."

Max told Marjorie not to worry. He'd shown the offending passage to Arthur Train, a lawyer and an author of legal thrillers, who'd said, "If it were in New York, it could easily be laughed out of court."

But in small-town Florida, the story might be quite different.

For representation, Zelma had hired Kate Walton, a University of Florida Law School graduate and a tenacious litigator; she worked at the firm run by her father, J. V. Walton, in Palatka, a community between Cross Creek and St. Augustine. Walton was among the first five women admitted to the Florida Bar. For the next five years, with Walton's support and encouragement, Zelma would grip her perceived insults like fetishes. Why? In north-central Florida, theories about her motivation abounded: she was still nursing a grudge from the women's rift ten years before; she'd been teased by friends and strangers; she was jealous of Dessie Smith's more agreeable portrayal in the book and of Marjorie's friendship with Dessie, as well; Zelma's brother—Marjorie's doctor— had egged Zelma on; Kate Walton had egged her on; Zelma aimed to gain a handsome settlement from the once-struggling author who now owned two homes and a healthy share in a St. Augustine hotel. Over the time it took to resolve—or exhaust—the case, Marjorie, blindsided by the whole matter, was continually puzzled, suspecting one motive, then another. No one ever figured out exactly what drove Zelma, although Phil May learned too late in the ordeal that Zelma had initially been pleased with her part in the book. Something had flipped her switch.

Zelma hadn't been the only Cross Creek resident ruffled by their portrayal. Even though Marjorie had checked with several people before the book's publication, she inquired of others' feelings after the book was out and learned that a few subjects felt uncomfortable with the exposure, though not enough to complain. More people than not expressed appreciation, and many thought Marjorie's picture of Zelma authentic. Later, J. T. Glisson, who grew up at the Creek, said of Zelma's profile, "It's probably the most perfect description that's ever been written about anyone. It was deadly accurate."

At one point early in the process, Marjorie, together with Dr. T. Z. Cason, visited Zelma at the family's home in Island Grove. The Casons' mother greeted them. Zelma took some time to appear. When she did, Marjorie told Zelma that she was puzzled by the whole thing. They'd been friends for a long time, and couldn't they discuss it, come to a friendly understanding? But Zelma said little except "Talk to my lawyer." On February 26, Phil May claimed Zelma's declaration was unsound, and argued for its dismissal. A hearing was scheduled for April 20, in Gainesville. In advance, May sent the judge, John A. H. Murphree, a copy of *Cross Creek*. It would be helpful if he read it, he told him.

MARJORIE ENDURED ANOTHER diverticulitis attack and returned to New York for care. This time, she required a hysterectomy and developed an infection; she had to remain in the hospital through mid-March—nearly a month. Yet in her letters to Norton, she relayed her good spirits. "Had my abdominal X-ray yesterday," she reported one day, "and was relieved, in a way, to have the doctor say, as he watched the barium percolate, 'You really have a dandy diverticulosis. There's certainly enough here to cause all your symptoms.' . . . I had begun to think they thought I was just another neurotic." At one point, John P. Marquand, who'd won the fiction Pulitzer the year before Marjorie (for *The Late George Apley*), was in the next room. The Brandts, who were his agents, too, visited him with "a huge jar of Martinis and what a racket," Marjorie wrote. They stopped by to see her. "I refused a drink, naturally."

Numerous other friends and associates visited—it seemed she was holding court in the Harkness Pavilion—but Norton was her steadiest companion, through the U.S. Postal Service. Marjorie signed her more ribald letters to him "Dora Rolley," referencing her dairy cow. His grove report lifted her spirits; finally, after fifteen years, the farm was making enough for her to live on, without writing income. She pondered anew how she and Norton, with three homes between them, would arrange their disparate lives together. "I know only that I love you—and that I cannot live at the hotel," she mused. "But long visits ought to be lots of fun. And then when I go to the cottage for the summer, it will be grand."

"You know I will cooperate in your living arrangements but please plan your visits here long and often," her husband replied. Norton kept her posted on business at the hotel, where, after a few drinks, some people offered opinions on the lawsuit. A doctor hinted that T. Z. Cason had been behind the whole thing and suggested that if a private detective were to expose "certain medical practices" in Dr. Cason's career, he could be "brought to his knees." The next day, one of their acquaintances reported that Zelma was showing people her autographed copy of Cross Creek ("to my good friend, Zelma") "to prove she is *the* Zelma." "If she does things like that," Norton said, "I think we can let Phil go," for certainly Zelma's exhibitionism would defeat her purpose. Of Zelma, another friend said, point-blank, "You know she would settle for $8000." Norton thought it sounded like a proposition. The friend pressed him on it; Norton reminded him that Zelma had wanted a court hearing, and gotten it. There was nothing more to say.

In other news, Dessie Smith stopped by the Castle in a new army uniform, bound for the Women's Army Corps. In contrast, Diana Vreeland, photographer Louise Dahl-Wolfe, and a group of models for *Harper's Bazaar* arrived in St. Augustine for a photo shoot and dined at the Castle. "The models are pretty enough, but mere babies," Norton commented. One of the models was the young Lauren Bacall, soon to make her film debut with Humphrey Bogart in Hemingway's *To Have and Have Not*. Norton had held back one piece of news, lest it upset Marjorie: two soldiers had stolen her car, driven it to Jacksonville for a holiday, and left it there. It took the state highway patrol and police departments from five towns and cities to track it down.

WHEN MARJORIE WAS well enough, she went to the home of friend and fellow Scribner author Marcia Davenport for supper with Max and Wendell and Edith Willkie. (Marjorie had supported Willkie's 1940 bid for the Republican presidential nomination.) Back in Florida, she found evidence that her grove had been ruined by a weeklong freeze: "It looks as though fire had swept through." It wasn't a total loss. Some of the crop could be used for juice or pulp. Idella revealed that she had been married in West Palm Beach prior to coming to the Creek, and needed to go back for a divorce. A property complication arose when "Old Boss" Brice's son-in-law bought the grove land between Marjorie's and the Glissons'. A new survey was planned, and Marjorie supported it, as all three parcels ended "together in a tangle of swamp and marsh." Once again on edge, she got angry with Norton for allowing a woman friend of theirs to use their Castle apartment ("the height of indiscretion"), admitted that he must have done it out of kindness, but insisted that he was courting a scandal. "I am *furious*, but I love you," she wrote. Now she experienced some unexpected bleeding—should she see a Jacksonville doctor? She was "about to go nuts again" over her correspondence. Julia Scribner had written another despairing letter, and Marjorie, on sure footing with her young friend's complaints, suggested,

You are an artist, and probably the key to your torment lies in the fact that so far you have found no valid or even satisfactory outlet for that artistry.

If you will look up again Thomas Wolfe's *The Story of a Novel*, you will find his admission of this same suffering—actually, a sense of nakedness, of shame, that overwhelms one who has torn the words from his guts and then cruelly sent them out into an irrevocable daylight where they are doomed to wander for any dolt to observe their pitifulness, their inadequacy and the embarrassing blood with which they drip. The one compensation is that those who are not dolts see beyond the blood and tatters and take the wanderers to their hearts for the sake of the breath of life that is in them.

Marjorie scolded Julia for her "masochistic desire to feel that your torment is so unique. It is unique, of course, in the sense that each individual, fortunately, is unique." Yet, she allowed, "the agonized groping of the sensitive individual to make sense out of a totally inexplicable universe is unique"—and so, that individual is doomed to a certain loneliness. There is comfort in knowing that "there are a hell of a lot of suffering souls in the same boat."

She refused to soothe Julia. Above all, the privileged young woman would have to channel her agony into something constructive. "Let it out of its cage and use it." Furthermore: "Don't use the war as an alibi for putting it off. Your rage about the sins of war and the sins against man is a good and righteous rage. Use that, too. Every such individual rage is a vital part of the great sweep of human hope. The slow spreading of that rage is the yeast in the cosmic bread."

OVER ALL OF THIS, the lawsuit hung. Finally, on April 20, the long-anticipated hearing took place. Judge Murphree and the attorneys spent three hours at it. Afterward, Phil May felt it had gone well for Marjorie, since Kate Walton had leaned heavily on the "invasion of privacy" counts, rather than the libel charge, and a right to privacy was not judicially recognized in Florida. The young judge, not yet forty, wouldn't enter uncharted waters, May thought. Now all they had to do was wait for Murphree's ruling.

Zora Neale Hurston offered Marjorie a moment's reprieve with an enthusiastic response to *Cross Creek*, which she had just read. "Twenty-one guns!" she exclaimed to open her letter. "It is a most remarkable piece of work. You turned your inside light on that community life, and it broke like day.

"Whether it pleases you or not, you are my sister," she continued. "You look at plants and animals and people in the way I do. You are conscious of the three layers of life, instead of the obvious thing before your nose. You see and feel the immense past, what is now, and feel inside you something of what is to come. Therefore, you are not pacing the cell of the current hour. You are free, because you have made your peace with the universe, and its laws. You are deep and fine."

One of the most gratifying parts of the letter must have been Zora's approval of Marjorie's Negro characters, front and center in three chapters:

"Taking Up the Slack," which introduced Martha Mickens as an ongoing, binding presence; "'Geechee," the story of Marjorie's wayward, maddening house girl; and "Black Shadows," the account of numerous employees, including the sagas of Kate and Raymond, and Adrenna and B. J. Samson.

"You did a thing I like in dealing with your Negro characters," Zora wrote.

> You <u>looked</u> at them and saw them as they are, instead of slobbering all over them as all of the other authors do. They talk real too, and act as I know them. You have done a remarkably able thing with the Negro idiom. It is <u>so</u> accurate. I am so sick and tired of that blackface minstrel patter that is put out as Negro dialect. I am not objecting to the bad grammar but the lack of imagination. <u>You</u> catch this thing as it is. You note the "picture talk" that's something of a linguistic hieroglyphics. I am tickled to death with you, Sugar. I love your description of the women's behinds. "Box" and "shingle" and they fit the thing so beautifully. You were thinking in hieroglyphics your ownself.
>
> You have written the best thing on Negroes of any white writer who has ever lived.

IN EARLY SUMMER, Idella Parker left Marjorie's employ and moved with her sister to New York, where a cousin and another friend from Reddick had found work more lucrative than anything available in Florida. She had left Marjorie for short periods before, spending weekends with her mother, delaying her return. Now, after two and a half years at the Creek, she found Marjorie too difficult to bear and made a dramatic break. "As the years went by, the troubles compounded and got worse," Idella later reflected. "And it didn't take long for her troubles to cause me to have troubles, too."

Idella had known from the start that Marjorie was moody and a chain smoker but hadn't realized how much she drank. Describing Marjorie's writing table—the typewriter, the large, filled ashtray, the vase of fresh flowers—she added, "On the right-hand side of her typewriter was a brown paper bag. It was awhile before I realized that she had an open flask of whiskey in that bag, and she drank from it liberally while she worked." In New York, Idella rented a room in Harlem with her sister, two blocks from the Apollo Theater, and found a good job with a well-heeled family on Long Island. Cooking for a northern table took some adjustment, but she soon proved herself, preparing a ham as Marjorie had taught her.

MARJORIE HAD LITTLE TIME to respond. In early July, Norton, who had enlisted in the American Field Service, was called to the New York headquarters to be sent overseas as a volunteer ambulance driver. Marjorie accompanied him to New York, and along the way, the couple contracted a bronchial flu. If Marjorie hadn't "all but held up the St. Regis Pharmacy" to get a prescription Dr. Atchley had phoned in, Norton might not have sailed. When he left, she had no idea where he was bound—India? the Middle East?—wherever the British Army was. Right away, Marjorie underwent another diverticulitis attack, and the good doctor was ready with belladonna and luminal, with which he had been experimenting. The New York stay begun in the Gotham Hotel ended in the Harkness Pavilion. "It works divinely," Marjorie wrote of the new remedy to Edith Pope. "I will be able to get over the attacks quickly, and without pain."

Marjorie hadn't understood why her easygoing husband, who would turn forty-two in October, wanted to serve in the war. In a letter, he had tried awkwardly to explain his motives: "I could hardly hope for you to understand my feelings about the service when I don't understand them myself. I just have a lot of things I want us to do after it is all over. They are such silly and selfish and inconsequential things as far as the world is concerned that I feel that I must do something now to earn the right to enjoy them. Mix this up with a lot of other conflicting emotions and ideas and you have a mess. That's me!" It hadn't helped much. Marjorie was terrified that her perfect husband would soon be lost to her. "They [the American Field Service drivers] work in the front lines and in the last war their casualties were twice the rate of regular army casualties—which of course makes me feel just swell," she informed Norman Berg. But she wouldn't try to stop him. "A man has to make his own decisions about things like that. I think it is infinitely more heroic for a man of Norton's temperament to do such a thing, than for most kinds of men. And he will do a calm, good job, no matter how he suffers inside."

———————

TOWARD THE END OF her New York stay, Marjorie tracked down Idella's Harlem address and wired her, asking her to visit the hospital. Idella waited until after Marjorie's checkout date to call, sure she would be gone, but to her surprise, Marjorie was there. Still, Idella wouldn't come to the hospital—she was too ashamed to face Marjorie. "I feel a little better in knowing that she does, or did, have a certain affection for me," Marjorie wrote Norton. "But I shall have to mark her off, at least for the time being." At the Creek, Marjorie hired Martha Mickens's daughter Sissie to take Idella's place. The training challenged both of them. Sissie couldn't read, and one day, Marjorie found her gathering a pile of written material, thinking it was trash, when it included notes for a book, correspondence marked "Urgent," and other manuscripts. Marjorie told her to throw out only what was actually in the waste basket.

The matter with Idella simmered. In October, she wrote Marjorie that she missed the Creek, and in November, Marjorie replied, offering a generous raise that, considering the lower expenses at Cross Creek, equaled what Idella was making in New York. It was settled: Idella would return to Marjorie after New Year's.

ALL THIS TIME, Marjorie agonized over Norton's fate—not to mention his whereabouts—and the lawsuit, which would not be easily resolved. For the duration of the case, Marjorie would fuel her own anxiety, obsessing on details and writing or calling Phil May with ideas, theories, anecdotes—some helpful, many not. She had little knowledge of legal procedure or strategy. The matter generated plenty of gossip around the Creek. A few people in St. Augustine wondered aloud why Norton had shipped out so soon after his marriage. One matron had told him "what people are saying—that you're going off like this just because you're so desperately unhappy!" and advised him to stick with his marriage for ten years, see if he wasn't comfortable with it by then.

A third obsession, claiming first place when the other two stood at temporary rest, was a new novel. James Branch Cabell, who had just finished a book about the St. Johns River with Alfred J. Hanna, wondered if Marjorie was "not chilled, or, as it were, gummed up, by knowing that nowadays one cannot hope to find anywhere an intelligent audience? That to me is the worst part of war: it begets an imbecility so universal that when I am shaving, I cannot but regard myself with distrust." But Marjorie was optimistic. In June, she had told Max that the unwritten book felt like a whole, completely shaped. There seemed "a certain inevitability about it." The protagonist would be based on her Michigan grandfather, Abram Traphagen. "It would not be a farm book, nor a 'novel of the soil.'" The farm would simply be the background," she explained. The cast of characters represented "a cross between Dickens and some of the Russian novels." A keynote of the book would be "the consciousness of the principal character of the cosmic set-up."

Marjorie had been researching her ancestral history sporadically since the early 1920s; the "Jenny" fragment from her Rochester years was probably an outgrowth of this interest. "You asked me once if I ever thought of using the details of my childhood, and I said that I should do so only objectively and creatively, and it would be so in this," she wrote Max. "The things one has known and loved lend themselves to richness of detail, I think." Max met with her in the hospital during her New York trip to discuss the novel, and from there, Marjorie traveled to Michigan for Traphagen family material provided by her aunt Ethel Riggs, her mother's sister. There were boxes of family letters dating to 1822, farm ledgers, and account books. Marjorie enjoyed deriving personalities from these, and she was delighted that one female relation wrote of the 1869 American Equal Rights Association convention (which birthed the National Woman Suffrage Association), "On this subject, I myself am greatly in its favor, and mean to exercise every privilege offered me."

Abram Traphagen, her maternal grandfather, emerged as a more articulate character than she'd imagined, but he still fit the profile of the "frustrated artist and man of thought" she intended as her protagonist. The most meaningful find was a receipt for *Smith's Illustrated Astronomy*, a book intended for public schools, which her grandfather had surely read. It contained lessons, diagrams, maps, telescopic views. Marjorie would track down a copy from a Chicago rare book dealer, "for it will give me just the slant I want on the principal character's thoughts along cosmic lines. It does seem a strange coincidence, doesn't it?" she mused to Max. Still, she added, "I know that my bones will have to go through a duck-press to squeeze out the essence of the thing I want to do." Also, she learned that her grandmother and great-aunt had written poetry of the sentimental, religious sort. "I had thought that all the annoying urge-to-expression came from the intellectual Kinnan side," Marjorie remarked, "but find I am doubly damned."

A MONTH AFTER Norton shipped out, the lawsuit briefly claimed Marjorie's attention. On August 9, 1943, Judge Murphree dismissed Zelma Cason's declaration, giving Zelma and Kate Walton fifteen days to amend it. During this pause, Marjorie received a letter from Zora, whom she had written, mentioning Idella's defection and the difficulty of starting a new book. Zora replied with an enthusiastic desire to help, in a tone similar to one she used with other friends and benefactors, black and white: "How I wish that I were not doing a book too at this time! I would be so glad to come and take everything off your hands until you are through with yours. I know just what you need. You are certainly a genius and you need a buffer while you are in labor. Idella is much less intelligent than I took her to be. What a privilege she had! Well, it is inevitable that people like you will waste a lot of jewelry by chunking it into hog pens. Even though I am busy, if it gets too awful, give a whoop and a holler and I will do what I can for you. I really mean that. I am already looking around for somebody who would really do for you permanently." She offered her own news: she was living and writing on her houseboat at Daytona Beach. The *Wanago* was jammed with books and papers, but it offered solitude, and her fellow boat owners were cordial. "Not a word about race," she added.

Deeply moved, Marjorie immediately wrote to Norton, not knowing when or where he would receive the letter: "The Negro writer, Zora Neale Hurston, has done one of the most beautiful things I've ever known. After several months, in which she must've thought I had taken offense at her letter about "Cross Creek," I wrote her a good letter. I am ashamed to say that I alibied about taking a river trip with her, telling her I should love to (which is true), but that I was deep in work on a book."

In truth, Marjorie had only put the first words to paper in August, but with the lawsuit simmering and the public eye trained on her and her husband, she was reluctant to travel openly with a black friend. Such an act, in that time and place, would certainly prejudice a critical segment of the public—such as the Cracker Floridians who might sit on a jury—against her.

"When she and I have finished our present books," Marjorie explained,

> I shall take the trip with her if it costs me the lawsuit and you your business, not, God knows, in any spirit of condescension but with a desire to learn and to know. Her offer settles in my mind all doubts I have had about throwing myself into the fight for an honest chance for the Negro. The mass of people, black or white, is always found to be the hoi polloi. The rare, choice individual is the one who carries the torch and nothing much stands in the way of such an individual. And of course, when the individual is big enough, as she is, and as Dr. Carver was, any deep South obstructionism, any Jewish-radical "fight for rights," is a candle before a great wind.

A few weeks later, from somewhere in India, Norton responded: "The offer from Zora Neale Hurston was certainly a touching one and I am sure was just as sincere as it sounded. I can certainly understand why and how she could do it but it tends to make a body ashamed of his selfishness."

AFTER JUDGE MURPHREE OFFERED Zelma Cason and Kate Walton extra time on their declaration, client and attorney announced that they would stick by their original document, sure that the "invasion of privacy" claim would hold up. But Judge Murphree decided it did not, and on September 1, he ruled in Marjorie's favor. It seemed a celebration was in order. But on October 19, Kate Walton filed an appeal with the Florida Supreme Court. The show would go on. Philip May encouraged Marjorie, reminding her that, though the case was expensive, *Cross Creek* was receiving plenty of publicity because of it. Publicity "is not nearly sufficient to compensate for the unpleasantness and expense," she replied.

Although the lawsuit weighed heavily on Marjorie, her correspondence with Norton rarely referred to it. Preparations for the appeal would take time. "It shouldn't worry us, because the higher she [Zelma] goes, the less chance she has of winning," Norton commented. Marjorie replied with new information: months before, Zelma had told Ida Tarrant that she planned to sue Marjorie, saying, "I'm going to get some of her easy money. And I'm going to sue Norton too. She needn't think she can make over everything to him and get out of it." Now Phil May would come to Ocala for Aunt Ida's testimony. Jim Rawlings offered to testify for Marjorie, remembering how Zelma had administered her own douche to her female dog after a male dog had opportunely visited the Cason property. Later that fall, Marjorie visited Zelma's mother, bearing a bottle of sherry. She told Norton, "I have always enjoyed her—we talk about our cows and the difficulty of getting a bull at the proper moment and our gardens and the weather etc. We had the same sort of friendly and rural visit as we have always had, she was glad to see me, begged me not to go. . . . Neither us of mentioned her unnatural offspring. It was good clean fun."

Chapter Twenty

What Is Home?

1943-44

For the duration of Norton's service—more than a year, including training and travel—Marjorie and her husband exchanged substantive letters, he as often as he could manage, she nearly every day. The lag time could be weeks. At least once, a sack of service mail was mistakenly returned to the United States, further delaying Marjorie's outgoing letters. Since a true epistolary conversation was impossible, they responded as they could, describing their days for each other. Norton, immersed in an entirely new experience, infused his reports with humor and wonder.

"We all talk like Hemingway characters," he said of his compatriots, while at sea. "Every now and then an eight-letter words creeps in but you realize it was formed by two four-letter words." On the deck, the men underwent physical training. "I do two push-ups," he reported, "and collapse on the deck more or less in hysterics." After landing in India, the men took a train to AFS headquarters. "The terrain was as different from Florida as it could possibly be, but the growth was just as lush, and very much like Cross Creek growth. Some of the most beautiful flowering trees you ever saw." Norton complained of mosquitoes, but he found pleasure in the headquarters library, where symphony concerts were given twice a week. Movies were shown. There was a racetrack nearby. He was reading a great deal, and he commented on his choices. Virginia Woolf's *To the Lighthouse*, he said, was at first "as obscure as some of the more obscure Gertrude Stein but now I am fascinated with it."

Norton began his field training in the fall of 1943 with a motorcycle class. The major in charge told the men that their lives in the AFS "would be replete with boredom about 90 percent of the time—with discomfort about ten percent—and only on rare occasions would we be in any danger." Norton was afraid that this meant they wouldn't get close to the lines. "This place seems absolutely unconscious of the fact that there is a war on," he wrote. He studied motor mechanics in preparation for ambulance duty. During his off-hours, he explored his surroundings: the palatial Victorian stucco homes of India's nobility, "with lots of lattice work and gingerbread trimming." He observed the flights of parrots, rode a bicycle up a mountain to a Hindu temple, took a boat to a botanical garden. He heard traditional Indian music, which, he told Marjorie, "leaves the impression that the instrument being played is being taxed to the breaking point and is complaining under the strain. You feel like correcting every note." One night, he and his friends were in a holy city (which he could not name) during a religious festival. "Four of us roamed the narrow streets of the bazaar section in absolute delight. The only light came from millions of tiny candles that outline each little shop. The people were in high good humor and most friendly. There was no drinking at all. The only drunks we saw belonged to a faith foreign to the celebrants."

Marjorie's letters were feast or famine for him—they came in clumps or not at all. "Don't even think that anything that happens to you is too small for you to write about," Norton told her. "I would even enjoy discussions of your torment in relation to the cosmic unconscious." And: "Don't ever put off writing me when your mood is mental or temperamental because if all your letters were all sweetness and light I would know you were going through some horrible transformation and I wouldn't like it. Stay as sweet as you are and no sweeter."

By mid-October, Norton was behind the wheel of an ambulance; he described an instructional drive for Marjorie: "You are given a truck and an Indian who does not speak English and told to drive anywhere and be back in two and a half hours. The drives are beautiful and the Indian sits and sings native music all the time. The water buffalo on the highways are definite hazards. They are much less skittish than our Florida scrub cattle and never seem to move and look in the same direction."

The primitive conditions challenged him. When he came home, he planned to "retire to the bathroom for about three weeks. . . . The usual three fixtures will be my Trinity and I shall worship at each shrine in a never-ending rotation. . . . I have never before had any desire to write a book but now I have and I will call it, "My god, have you seen the latrines."

Four months after his departure, he confessed, "I think that if I did not write you often I would go nuts." Writing "increases my feeling of having someone of my own, and it is awfully important to hold onto you. If you were not there, there would be no incentive to go through with my part in this god-awful foolish war."

He also grew introspective: "For probably the first time in my life I am living inside myself and I have seen much better houses. I am afraid that too much time has been given to furnishing the porch with suitable gliders and swings and welcome mats, and not enough time spent on deep leather for the study, the library and the den." It upset him, he explained, because he prized his self-sufficiency. "Having been so gregarious that it was a vice, I have nevertheless always felt that there was a storehouse inside me which I could enter whenever I wanted to and that there I could be perfectly happy." Now, he related, "I have entered the storehouse and find it just about as livable and comfortable as a cold storage room would be."

He added, "I still feel the need of one person and that person is you. I tell you, I will never be separated from you again."

MARJORIE ADDRESSED Norton's "cold private storehouse":

If you have really never been in it before, I can tell you that yours is not the only one that is cold and empty—they all are—that's the hell of it. Mine is not a house, or a room, but a deep black pit. There is *never* anything in these places. Yet because they are isolated in time and space, they are almost the only places into which important things are free to enter. If you stay in long enough, you go mad, or blow your brains out—but if you wait patiently, you become aware of something that is like a cross between phenobarbital taking effect, and the first drink after a hard day. You become a tightly-strung instrument for the play of forces that are around and beyond us. Sometimes the tune is audible, so that you can seize on the definite ideas or emotions—and anything good that a writer does, comes this way—and it is why a writer is obliged to go alone into this void. Sometimes there is nothing that can be expressed or identified, but you are left with a surge, a lift, that can come no other way, for the circumstances of daily living, the mass of people, make an impenetrable barrier to this so delicate thing that comes on velvet feet in the hush of solitude.

And as you have found, it is only one person you want when the sadness is too great. I think it was in "Golden Apples" that I said, "For to comfort any mortal against loneliness, one other is enough." And I think it is only in the happy relations of man and woman that the comfort is found.

MARJORIE'S REPORTS FROM the Creek or Crescent Beach detailed what was being planted, harvested, or cooked, who was or wasn't working efficiently, who married, who died, who visited, what property was under dispute, who said what to whom about the lawsuit, how she was or was not dieting, how slowly her work was going. Norton's manager, Douglas Thompson, kept Castle Warden running, but occasionally some business fell to Marjorie, and Norton regretted the additional burden for her.

Marjorie clipped magazine and newspaper articles for Norton, fretted over tax returns and war shortages, continued her plane-spotting shifts. She was worried about Julia Scribner: "She is in a perilous neurotic state." Dana Atchley wanted Julia to see a psychiatrist, but she refused; she needed to guard her spiritual privacy. Marjorie, the armchair psychologist, thought nothing was wrong with her young friend that "a good man couldn't cure." Not surprisingly, Marjorie was drinking a great deal. Though there was a national liquor shortage, she had been able to get what she wanted. In late October, she admitted, "I have been unable quite to get back on the wagon since my recent fall—I take a lot of drinks before supper—I am down to gin—." She was studying the New Testament. She wondered why the Jews hadn't recognized Jesus, while the Gentiles had taken up Christ's teachings.

She was listening to symphony concerts on the radio. She was binge-reading: Edith Wharton's *The Age of Innocence*, Rousseau's *Confessions*, *The Education of Henry Adams*, *Ulysses*. Her first description of Joyce's masterwork ran: "It is a magnificent thing, and completely lucid and intelligible." But a day or two later: "It went into the stream-of-consciousness unintelligibility of 'Finnegans Wake.'" She blamed *Crime and Punishment* for her depressed mood. Norman Berg sent Arthur Koestler's psychological novel *Arrival and Departure*, prompting her reply: "Where has Koestler been, and where have I been, not to have known his work before? The book has bowled me over." She noticed that Norman's business card now read, "Southern Editor and Trade Manager," "so he is evidently carrying his point toward becoming a Max Perkins," she wrote to Norton. "I'll be damned if he can ever get me to leave Scribner's." She read Roi Ottley's *New World A-Coming: Inside Black America*, noting, "I have forced myself to take the final leap about Negroes." On an uplifting note, Sigrid Undset sent her *Happy Times in Norway*, her memoir of prewar life.

Henry Fountain, Sissie's husband, died, and Marjorie transported his family and friends to the funeral in the National Cemetery in St. Augustine. Dessie Smith visited the Creek with five other WACs, "a tough bunch of pistol-packing Mamas." Marjorie went hunting with her grove manager, Chet Crosby. Norman Berg wanted to stop by the Creek during a swing down to Jacksonville, but, given the lawsuit, Marjorie was afraid that his presence—a man other than Norton spending the night—might ignite gossip. He visited her at Crescent Beach instead. Smoky, her cat, died. In late fall there was a freeze at the Creek, affecting the farmhouse pipes, the ground, the citrus trees. At one point, Marjorie looked into fostering three little boys from the Children's Home Society, but she found the requirements too regimented—among other restrictions, she had to promise to take them to church.

MARJORIE'S OBSESSION WITH home, uprooting, and homelessness, flared up in Norton's absence. In August, she had written: "I am toying with the idea of making a year-round home of the cottage. . . . There is no hope of ever <u>living</u> at the Creek. All I need is a <u>home</u>, sufficiently remote from people and town. The distance will be nothing after the war."

A week later she had a "homeless" nightmare: "For a long time I have been awakening at about three or four o'clock in the morning and going into a black abyss," she confessed. "This goes back long before you embarked for parts unknown. . . . It is usually preceded by a nightmare, customarily the one in which I am homeless, and wandering around in strange places looking for an abiding place." In the recent nightmare, "I was celebrating Christmas all alone at the Castle Warden and feeling properly forlorn. The scene changed, and I was at the Creek, and feeling equally frustrated. My mother was there, and I cried out to her, 'Help me get out of this awful place!' Now, psychoanalysis would undoubtedly trace some connection whereby some sort of betrayal on the part of my mother made me feel without ground to stand on, while at the same time leaning on her," she told Norton.

"I wish I could figure out what the hell it is I want, what the hell I am afraid of, and what the hell I am fighting," Marjorie wrote. "It seems to me that I want one of two things: roots in the earth, a home life that radiates from that earth, or an absolutely gypsy-like existence without ties, without dogs or cats or material belongings." She believed she could live either life but could not tolerate the vague back-and-forth. She hoped she and Norton could find a solution together.

A MONTH LATER, she was still having nightmares about homelessness. "Something of my old desire to keep moving on has been on me," she explained to Norton. "It seemed to me I could leave Florida behind forever." In some dreams, she was trying to arrange her belongings in a new room or apartment. In others, she was missing trains that would take her home. "It is all probably Freudian in that I have never had a true home since my father's death, yet I have understood and outgrown my childish attachment to him," she wrote, invoking Thomas Wolfe: "We are all lost, and you can't go home again. And I can't accept it. Somehow, surely, even in maturity, one should be able to be at home."

As Marjorie reflected, she dug out the *Blood of My Blood* manuscript, written about fifteen years before. "There were so many unhappy details in the book, and the picture of my mother was one of such tragic futility, that it made me feel very badly," she confided to Norton, with the remorse of distance. "This style . . . made me almost literally ill. If I could ever have written that badly, I don't see how I was ever able to improve. And then, I wonder, God, have I?"

BY THANKSGIVING, Norton's unit had arrived at its official outpost. Soon, he was making runs: one twenty-mile trip a day, five hours, out and back. "I thought I would get great satisfaction out of being of help to the sick and wounded," he wrote. "Sort of a whole [Florence] Nightingale feeling. Far from it. My first patient had a badly fractured leg. Every time I hit a bump pains shot through me as if I were the sufferer. I realize now that mentally I was carrying both patient and car on my shoulders."

On Christmas Eve, he was sick of "the waste and the horrors of war," was "against the snobbishness and caste system in the military set-up. And against anything that separates people who shouldn't be separated. I'm homesick and I miss you terribly because I love you so much."

A FEW DAYS BEFORE Christmas 1943, Marjorie wrote Zora to confirm her Daytona Beach mailing address. She wanted to send her friend a holiday box of oranges and pecans. Again, she expressed frustration with her writing, and Zora responded immediately, driving the hundred miles from Daytona to the Creek on a mission to give Marjorie a boost. When Zora arrived, Marjorie was in Gainesville, Christmas shopping for the Cross Creek families. Martha and Sissie invited Zora to wait. Marjorie described Zora's visit for Norton:

> Well, I had the most mixed emotions. I was so touched by her doing it, as I was touched by her offer to do my housekeeping while I worked —and it was supper time, and it was nighttime and bedtime—and dat old debbil prejudice fair stuck a needle in me. I was ashamed, and I was worried, and I thought this would probably be the evening Mrs. Glisson would come up to ask me something, and the word would go out [that Marjorie had a black guest], and I would lose the lawsuit!
>
> Meantime, Martha and Sissie had fallen *fatuously* in love with Zora—and Zora herself had arranged things with such modest tact

that I felt like a dog for having any qualms. Martha came over to say that she had supper ready for Zora. I said no, I wanted her to have supper with me. And I thought, "Watchman, what of the night?"—and Zora had already been invited by Martha to spend the night over there, and had taken her bags over there, and was taking it for granted that she would sleep there—and if I was a bitch about it, Zora would never have blinked an eyelash. It was all so quietly and gracefully done to spare me any embarrassment, if I proved the sort who needed sparing! And I thought of the tenant house already crowded to the rafters, and my empty house, and I thought, damn it, now is the time for all good men to come to the aid of a moral principle! So I said that I didn't want to be selfish or disappoint Martha, but I had so much more room, and would Jack please bring her bags over here to the back guestroom. And I have never in my life been so glad that I was not a coward. I had to hurdle an awfully wide ditch! I was amazed to find that my own prejudices were so deep. It has always surprised me that my thinking is so Southern. But I felt that if I ever was to prove my humanitarian and moral beliefs, even if it cost me the lawsuit, I must do it then.

That night, as Zora slept in the guest room, Marjorie had a nightmare in which Norton rescued her.

I had gone to a Negro football game where "high whites" were to be, and I was going with the Negroes as a moral gesture. And it was going to cause me trouble with the lawsuit, and was going to make a pariah of me, and I hated it, but the die was cast. And when I reached the boxes, and a Negro came out and fervently welcomed me and I felt quite ruined, lo and behold, you were suddenly by my side, and were shaking hands with the Negro, and I had the most wonderful feeling of your standing by me. In the nightmare, you were a dean of a college, and it was going to make trouble about your job, but you were there beside me, making the gesture with me.

After Zora left the next day, Marjorie pronounced, "She is entirely at home in both the white and the Negro world, and any citizen of the cosmos should be so at home, and I am way ahead by the experience. We had a fine time, and by the time she left an hour ago, I had gone a long way."

The same day, Marjorie wrote Norton breezily about domestic matters, opening with "Dearest I am whipped down by three little nigger babies." She had been eating lunch, gathering strength to set out 170 flower plants she'd just bought. Then: "I became aware of chirping like that of sparrows, and went back, and there sat Sissie's three little black birds on my back steps, waiting to be called." There followed a humorous account of the children helping Marjorie with the plants, all three calling her "Mama," because they knew they were to mind her.

That was one of the last letters in which Marjorie employed the N-word. In the months to come, as she wrestled with her prejudices, her xenophobia, she would occasionally refer to everyone on the farm, black and white together, as "the family."

ON CHRISTMAS EVE, another lawsuit arose: a woman who had published an article about losing a pet deer accused Marjorie of plagiarism and infringement of copyright. The matter could be batted away easily, but on Christmas Day, Marjorie, having certainly downed a drink or two, drove out to see a friend, failed to signal a turn, and caused the car behind her to collide with her—tires, fenders, and a bumper hit the dust. A day or two later, she received a copy of Zelma's brief for the supreme court appeal. The last point listed, she explained to Norton,

> was that I had been "unjustly enriched" by the book at Zelma's expense, her personality having "a substantial sale value," and so she should be repaid "to the extent of the enrichment."
>
> So I got out the goddamn book and counted up the characters, and there are 120 identified by name, and many of them occupied much more space than she did, and I figured for Phil that on a pro-rata basis she might possibly get as high as $25, but if we counted the Baptist and Methodist ancestors, whom I mentioned, and Hawaii, which I said had lost most of its horticulture since 1910, because of the Mediterranean fruit fly, Zelma owed me money!

A week later, Marjorie had an intestinal attack. To protect her health, Phil May suggested that she apologize to Zelma ("on conditions which she imposes") and pay her a certain amount of money or else follow up on personal information that might nip the whole thing in the bud. Marjorie's talents were far too great to waste on a victory over Zelma, he said. But Marjorie, wouldn't, couldn't, back down.

IT WAS NO WONDER she couldn't move her new novel forward. The lawsuit business, daily letters to Norton, correspondence with soldiers, and her consistent output to Julia Scribner, Edith Pope, and Max commanded several hours a day. With Norton, the question of how and where to live together or apart after the war continued to surface, without resolution. They would figure it out when he got home. For herself, Marjorie kept pushing hard at the question of racial discrimination and Negro rights. It was as if Zora's visit at the end of 1943 had determined what, aside from everything else, would be her chief obsession in the new year.

One day she broached the subject of the "Negro problem" with Idella, who had returned to the Creek. Idella explained the riots she'd witnessed in Harlem weren't about race but class. Marjorie shared their discussion with Norton: "The rioters were the lowest class of Negro hoodlums, who went wild and decided to 'get theirs,' and smashed in shop windows promiscuously and stole. They raided the grocery stores the Negroes dealt with, so that there was no food for anyone in Harlem, and when they stole from the dry cleaning and laundry establishments, they were stealing the clothes of colored people. She said that the better element was more distressed than the white people could possibly be, for they realized it reflected on, and set back, the whole Negro race."

At the top of Marjorie's reading list was *Strange Fruit*, Lillian Smith's best-selling new novel about an interracial romance in Georgia; it ends with the murders of two men, white and black, the black by lynching. Smith, a white author born into a prominent Jasper, Florida, family and who had studied and traveled widely, claimed that her novel was not about the "Negro problem" per se. "What I wanted to do was to show how people develop or are warped by the segregation patterns that exist. They may be political, racial, religious, economic, or cultural," Smith told the press. For Marjorie, *Strange Fruit* was "so devastating and accurate a study of the Southern town and of Negro-White relations. . . . For a white lady to do that in Georgia is certainly exciting and all hell is going to pop." And hell did. The book was literally banned in Boston and from shipment through the U.S. Postal Service, until Eleanor Roosevelt persuaded her husband to intervene.

About the issue, Marjorie wrote to Edith Pope, who replied, "Southerners don't want to think on a subject on which subconsciously their consciences are unclear; they don't want to think it through because they don't want to have to realize that morally their position is indefensible. Either you have justice for all, or you haven't justice; nobody wants to know it. The more sure they are they're doing wrong, the more they'll band against you." A week later, Scribner brought out Edith's novel *Colcorton*, which revolves around an old Florida plantation family's shameful secret: a black grandmother, who had tainted the "line." The knowledge warps the lives of Abby Clanghearne, who isolates herself in the old home, and her brother, Jared, who turns to drink. It is set in Palm Valley, a once-rural coastal swamp area between Jacksonville and St. Augustine where farming, cattle raising, logging, and moonshining— the same occupations Marjorie wrote of—were prevalent. The novel drew excellent reviews and comparisons to Marjorie's work.

WHEN JULIA SCRIBNER VISITED in late winter 1944, she and Marjorie asked Idella to take them to a black church—an effort to step inside the black community, to understand it. The women found "an old shack of a church," and Marjorie gave Idella three dollars for the pastor, with a request to hear some singing. "It seemed awful to walk into someone's church and buy their songs," she wrote Norton, though she wasn't sorry to have played the cultural tourist—it was a start. The music wasn't as good as expected, and "the testifying was definitely in the unknown tongue." A day or two later, Marjorie took Julia to a cocktail party in Ocala, drank too much, and when a guest made a racist remark, Marjorie held forth on "moral principles" until everyone except Julia turned against her. A friend told Marjorie, "You have never been hated in your life as you are hated here tonight."

About this incident, Norton wrote to his wife, "You will gain nothing by trying to convince the hidebound Southerner. Their beliefs on the question are firmly congealed and they are determined to keep them intact. . . . Trying to argue the question with them merely increases their hate of the movement and plants the idea that the problem is getting out of hand and something has to be done." And that something, Norton suggested, was more violence against black people.

A week later, Marjorie dreamed that Norton had just come home from overseas and the two attended an interracial meeting with whites, blacks, and people of mixed race. When someone addressed a black attendee as "Sir," a southern white woman protested. "And you got up," Marjorie wrote her husband, "and with great formality shook the hand of the very black man and announced, 'One says, "Sir" to any man who behaves properly.' The white woman made a speech about the repulsiveness of black bodies." The dream ended when Norton and Marjorie left the meeting for Castle Warden.

The next day, Idella took Marjorie and Julia to another church, one where Idella's uncle played the piano for a choir of eight, including Idella's father. "They don't shout like the sanctifiers do," Marjorie observed. "The choir sang quite respectable hymns from a book, but one of the preachers 'lined out' some that are not in the books, and that is when everybody really went to town." She noticed in particular an older woman in the congregation, "slim and very erect, with the most delicate, finely chiseled features and bright sharp eyes." The woman had a deep voice, with "a strange, pleasing harshness, like some great nightbird in the swamps." Idella entreated the choir to sing "The Old Rugged Cross," one of Marjorie's favorites. A few days later, the three women, plus Martha Mickens, attended another sanctified church, this one in Hawthorne. There was no preacher, just a small congregation, "but they really did their stuff," Marjorie wrote. "At times the vibrations actually hurt my eardrums. One enormous black Negress made a really lovely talk, and said that 'Singing is the coming of an angel.' That is a hard phrase to beat in any language."

Marjorie had begun reading Gunnar Myrdal's new two-volume study, *An American Dilemma: The Negro Problem and Modern Democracy*, an extensive analysis of the racial divide; it might have influenced, in April, her advice to Idella about income taxes. Idella wanted to pay hers, but Marjorie asserted that no one would catch her if she didn't. A taxpaying citizen should have the right to vote, Marjorie said, along with all other privileges. She was well aware that the Fifteenth Amendment, passed nearly seventy-five years before, was routinely circumvented in the South, through white primaries, poll taxes, literacy tests, long residency requirements, and other obstacles. She was upset that blacks were drafted in wartime: "You can't force men into military service for their country, without giving them the same rights as anyone else," she wrote Norton. And she was furious with Florida's liberal populist senator Claude Pepper, who, like John Temple Graves, held the position that a post-Depression "new economy" need not guarantee social equality. Supposedly, everyone, black and white, would benefit without having to rub shoulders. After the lawsuit was over, Marjorie said, she intended to "go all out on the question of Negro rights."

A few days later, she was horrified by a court decision in Montgomery in which Arthur A. Madison, a Negro lawyer who had initiated a case for sixteen black citizens who had been refused voting privileges, was disbarred by way of an old statute preventing attorneys from defending anyone pro bono. Soon afterward, Norton's mother, in Union Springs, Alabama, sent a photograph from *Life* magazine showing Negroes registering to vote; she had jotted, "We haven't had <u>that</u> here yet." Union Springs had, however, seen an altercation between a white clerk and a black customer—the clerk was nasty and the customer surly in return. "Why <u>wouldn't</u> the Negroes say 'and the hell with you'?" Marjorie wrote in response to the story. "On the other hand, with hate having built up over so long a time (even though that hate is the fault of the whites), there is certainly a respectable fear on the part of the whites, if the backward Negroes came into power in such a section. Of course, they are backward because we have held them back."

When the Newspaper Enterprise Association syndicate asked Marjorie to contribute a piece on the war, something "close to the heart," she wrote about a conversation she'd had on the train to Michigan the previous summer. A black lieutenant and two white lieutenants sat down together in the dining car, and Marjorie asked a sergeant next to her how men in the services felt about fraternizing with Negroes. "He said, 'Lady I'm from the South myself, but all I can say is, if a man's good enough to die for his country, he's good enough to live in it.' 'The Southern Soldier and the Negro,'" she told Norton, "was rejected as 'too controversial.'" She was offered another try, but she refused: "I could not provide any starry-eyed platitudes." Marjorie felt the United States had been hypocritical, trying to "stop other nations from doing precisely what we intended to keep on doing to the Negro."

It was one thing to take a stand on paper or at a party, another to recognize personal, deep-seated prejudice, occasionally revealed in her own language and behavior. A few days later, Marjorie admitted a revulsion to black skin—like the white woman in her dream about the interracial meeting. "I still have to fight a lingering prejudice, and when little black Martha [Sissie's daughter] touches me, as she loves to do, I cringe. But if one recognizes it for a prejudice and a hang-over from one's prejudiced training, it will pass." A week later, she explained that she was making herself "get over the creeps" when little Martha put her hand on her arm, and added she had always felt uncomfortable touching other women, even those she was fond of. "I get over the necessary embrace on arrival and departure as quickly as possible," she told Norman. She thought it might stem from the repulsion she felt for her mother.

Somewhere in India, Norton had just finished reading *Strange Fruit;* he had found it "marvelous," but it had evidently inspired an anxious dream. He and Marjorie were attending a large meeting of Negroes at the Florida Normal and Industrial Institute (in St. Augustine) as the only white people present. Afterward, the school's president asked Norton to say a few words, and he declined, assuring them that Marjorie would be the better speaker. But Marjorie pushed him forward, and he spoke, winning the approval of Idella and Zora. Yet Marjorie was furious at him, and he couldn't tell why.

Marjorie's nightmares continued to plague her, too: she searched for Norton in a terrible jungle; she couldn't find a home. Her mother usually appeared in the homeless dreams. She awoke from one realizing that she had depended on Ida "for a certain spurious sort of approval, which I have never had from anyone since."

IN MARCH, Marjorie had another car accident. She and Julia Scribner were heading into Gainesville for a movie, and at a bend in the road, the women saw one of the Brices' mules galloping toward them. It had run away, and Hugh Williams, Brice's son-in-law, was driving it home. Marjorie claimed she was going no more than twenty-five miles an hour. "I cut as far to the right as possible," she told Norton, "and the mule swerved into my path, I slammed on the brakes, but mule and car met, with utterly disastrous results to both." The mule piled up over the car's hood; the windshield on Marjorie's side was "frozen spray." "The glass held, or the consequences to me, at least, would have been serious. The whole front of the car is mashed to metal pulp. The mule was killed instantly."

As soon as Julia got home to New Jersey, she wrote a stern, heartfelt letter to Marjorie about her mentor's drinking problem. "I don't believe I have ever been as scared in a car as I was on two days with you," she said, and she described two events, including the mule incident. "I don't think you realize this change in your reactions and that's why I must tell you."

And she did: "I can't explain exactly what you do, but your judgment seems all wrong and you drive with very atypical carelessness. . . . I can tell you I was really frightened, so much so that I was madder at you than I ever hope to be again, because I really thought you were going to land me in the hospital with a broken something for no damn reason but you wearing off your nervous mood."

Marjorie took two months to reply, finally apologizing but also defending herself: "With all due admission that I drink too much, I do not believe I am a menace on the public highways, for I have been driving, drunk and sober, for twenty-five years, and if my reflexes were too unreliable, I should have had some sort of accident long before this—and have not." She added that she drove "with deliberate slowness when I have had a good many drinks."

In April, a worse catastrophe unfolded in St. Augustine: a guest at Castle Warden fell asleep with a lighted cigarette, starting a fire in her room. It spread all the way to Norton and Marjorie's penthouse, where a good friend of theirs, Ruth Pickering, was staying. An attempt to rescue Ruth failed; she was overcome by smoke and died. (The smoker died, as well.) The Associated Press distributed the news. Ruth had been a longtime winter resident of St. Augustine, and her funeral was held at the damaged hotel. Norton was overcome with sorrow and guilt. He was sick about Ruth and felt responsible for the "worry and nervousness" he had heaped on Marjorie. "This is truly one of life's darkest moments," he wrote from India.

"I shall never feel the same about the castle," he added. "I wish to God I could sell it."

Norton's letters, which usually detailed the grim events of war or the exotic settings he visited on leave, began focusing on his health, as he'd suffered, on and off, with afflictions caused by stress and a foreign environment. By the middle of the summer of 1944, close to the end of his service year, at the point when British forces evicted the Japanese from Burma, he lay in a hospital suffering from carbuncles (a staph skin infection) and what turned out to be amoebic dysentery. He had lost fifty pounds. He was finally transferred to a British hospital in Calcutta, and although given extensive treatment and rest, he was still too ill to travel. In October, he anticipated flying home, if someone would deem him able. Marjorie couldn't stand any more disturbing or provisional news—always belated—and contacted an old friend from Ocala, Louise Somervell, who had married General Brehon Somervell, commanding general of the Army Service Forces in Washington. General Somervell requested that the army put Marjorie's husband on a hospital plane as soon as possible. On October 29, Norton landed in Miami. The next day, he was flown to New York, where Marjorie awaited him, and was taken to the Harkness Pavilion by ambulance. He remained there for the final weeks of recovery, under Marjorie's watch.

Chapter Twenty-One

On Trial

1944-46

ALTHOUGH MARJORIE HAD set aside her novel over the long year, she worked on three short stories, each inspired by her obsessions: Norton and the war, the question of home, and racial conflict. All three would appear in the *New Yorker* in the coming months. "The Shell" is a tragedy set in an area like Crescent Beach, where a naïve young wife awaits her husband, Bill, who is fighting overseas. Word comes to the unnamed woman that her husband is missing, and failing to understand what that means but remembering that her husband had told her to "watch the sea, for he would be there," the young woman wades into the ocean to look for him. An undertow delivers her to the sea creatures. Yet her death is unintentional because his wife is, Bill says, "a moron, the way a wild rose is a moron."

"Miriam's Houses" is set in Brookland, the Washington, D.C., suburb where Marjorie was born, and is narrated by Helen, a woman recalling a childhood friend named Miriam who, with her mother, moved frequently to different houses in the neighborhood. Helen is fascinated by their moves, and because Helen's mother sees in Miriam a genteel child worth associating with, the friendship is encouraged, and Helen's mother attempts to make the mother's acquaintance. But Miriam's mother is wraith-like, evasive. A meeting never occurs. As for a father, Miriam says hers is either away on business or so occupied that he only comes home to sleep. Remembering the situation years later, Helen realizes that Miriam's mother had been a streetwalker, and not even a good one. "And my prudish mother had never guessed," she observes, just as Marjorie's mother, Ida, had not caught on to Mrs. Nolan, their Hammond Court neighbor of the ermine coat, black velvet hat, and egret plume.

The third story, "Black Secret," was drawn from a family story in Norton's hometown, Union Springs, Alabama. A little boy named Dickie overhears his mother and a friend gossiping about liaisons between black women and white men. A secret wafts over their talk, but he can't grasp it. When the women change subjects, Dickie's favorite uncle, Baxter, who owns a cotton plantation, is mentioned in admiring tones. The women adjourn, and Dickie is sent to get a haircut at the barbershop, in the black neighborhood. As he submits to Black Robert's scissors, he overhears the other customers, white men, chatting about a "high yellow" girl who had married a white man in Chicago, revealing that the girl's father is Dickie's Uncle Baxter. Dickie is suddenly sick, and Black Robert understands why. He gives him a penny for an ice ball, and Dickie runs down the street. "The cyclone was on him," Marjorie writes. He clutches the penny, which is "wet and sticky with sweat from the black hand and from his own." "Black Secret" was included in the O. Henry Memorial Award Prize Stories of 1946.

Marjorie took on more long-form journalism, as well. To the October 1944 issue of Transatlantic, a wartime magazine, she contributed "Florida: A Land of Contrasts," which details the state's history, from Ponce de León to commercial development. "At the moment, Florida is a vast, armed camp," she wrote, and she warned: "It remains to be seen whether the Florida of Bartram will survive, or the Chamber of Commerce will kill the goose that lays the golden egg." A few months later, she wrote a piece for Florida's Representative Joseph Hendricks; it was entered in the Congressional Record. "Florida: An Affectionate Tribute" praises the state's natural beauty in gorgeous prose, cracks a joke ("Take the lies of California, and in Florida they are the truth"), then lists ruinous activity around the state and shakes a finger: nothing and no one but human beings are responsible for the damage.

MARJORIE'S PUBLIC ADVOCACY for Florida might have bought her some sympathy in the lawsuit, but it wasn't enough to hasten the process. In February 1944, Phil May had argued on her behalf before the Florida Supreme Court and expected a quick decision on Zelma Cason's appeal. But nearly six months dragged by with no word, and in August, to Phil and Marjorie's dismay, the court adjourned without addressing *Cason v. Baskin*. On November 24, 1944, a month after Norton returned to the United States, the Florida Supreme Court finally addressed the case and reversed the first judgment, which had been in Marjorie's favor. Of the four original counts, only one, "invasion of privacy," survived, but it was enough to send the case back to Alachua County. This was the first time the court had recognized privacy as a civil right, "for breach of which an action for damages will lie." And even though the court felt that Marjorie's portrait of Zelma "portrays plaintiff in a favorable light and evinces real admiration for her," it judged that the depiction was also an intimate sketch and Zelma might be entitled to some damages. Still, the court admitted, the free speech ideal might hold sway, and if Marjorie could successfully argue that the public was served by eighty-four words in a literary work, she might win the case.

Right away, Phil May petitioned the Florida Supreme Court for a rehearing, but it was denied after New Year's. In February 1945, he and Marjorie decided that since the trial would take place in Gainesville, with a local jury, their team would be well served by the addition of a local attorney. They settled on a strategic choice in an accomplished lawyer who would have made an excellent character in a Marjorie Kinnan Rawlings novel—one who had, in fact, played a nameless role in *Cross Creek*. When Marjorie's grove worker B. J. Samson had been shot by Henry Fountain (the man working for Old Boss Brice and Tom Glisson), Sigsbee Scruggs had defended Henry, winning one for the locals, and humiliating Marjorie. Now she was more than willing to set aside that old hurt for a man who had excelled at debate at the University of Florida and then, once in practice, had invested in real estate to the extent that he could afford to defend the poor, black and white. He knew the Creek well and would likely attract backwoods information and support. Plus, he had a gift for selecting sympathetic jurors. When he accepted the case, he told May in a letter that another "character" in *Cross Creek* had contacted him about bringing suit and he had refused, "upon the same legal basis you are now defending." His interest had been piqued for some time.

In March, attorney May responded to Zelma's invasion of privacy charge, focusing on the higher court's ruling that writing in the public interest trumped the right to privacy. May argued that Zelma was a public figure, in both her professional work and her general deportment, and *Cross Creek* was, after all, a great work of American literature. In June, he and Kate Walton argued their sides before Judge Murphree. May gathered that Walton was bent on driving Marjorie out of Florida, ostensibly so the author would stop demeaning the state, and that Walton, May suggested privately, "feels that autobiographies and biographies are not to be written unless the author pays all the characters whom she portrays in the book"—a ludicrous point of view that would, if ever honored, break the backs of so many authors and publishers. Marjorie realized this. One of her motives for fighting Zelma, rather than quietly settling, was to defend the rights of all writers—many of whom had been watching the case closely since it was first made public.

In August, the judge struck some of the defendants' pleas, obliging them to streamline their arguments. Marjorie and her attorneys collected more information and sought depositions and potential witnesses for the upcoming public show. To highlight her delicate health, Marjorie asked Jacksonville's Riverside Hospital to tabulate her admissions over the years. (Between January 1931 and December 1941, she had been admitted to the hospital five times and treated by the outpatient department six times.) She contacted some possible witnesses herself.

HIS HEALTH RESTORED, Norton returned to work at Castle Warden. Marjorie tried returning to her novel. She supervised a hog killing at the Creek, even though Martha Mickens felt it was the wrong time of the moon. She continued to take part in public life. At Florida A&M College in Tallahassee, she was the principal speaker for a two-day celebration honoring the distinguished educator and activist Mary McLeod Bethune. Bethune, born of slaves, had, among many accomplishments, founded Bethune-Cookman College and the National Council of Negro Women, and she had recently headed the Division of Negro Affairs in the

National Youth Administration. Her political and social network was vast; she enjoyed the support of Eleanor Roosevelt, and she knew Zora. That Marjorie was offered the lead role among many black speakers is notable, reflecting her increasing public support for civil rights, as well as the fact that Bethune's own advocacy wasn't limited to black citizens— she often spoke and acted on behalf of all women and their rights to equality, no matter the race. Marjorie's address, "A Floridian's View of Mary McLeod Bethune," is lost to history, but afterward, she wrote to Edith Pope, "It was a fascinating experience and I am more than ever ashamed of the people who try to hold the Negroes back."

Marjorie also lent her voice to the war effort, appearing as a guest panelist on the popular radio quiz show *Information Please*, hosted by Clifton Fadiman. During the war, the show broadcast from various cities to promote war bonds. Marjorie took part in Atlanta on April 2. The next day, she visited a new veterans' hospital and spoke to men in the officers' ward, among them double amputees. She was exhausted by the disconnect between public pleas for war bonds and the reality of human sacrifice. "I am out of patience with sentimental appeals to buy bonds, as if we were being asked to contribute to a worthy charity," she said in a statement regarding the Seventh War Loan Drive. "It is more or less reasonable to feel a slight glow of self-satisfaction when giving generously to an orphan home or a blind beggar. But when we buy war bonds, most of us feel no more nobility, no more sense of sacrifice, than when we turn a stream of water on our house that is blazing." It appeared that the war's end might be in sight, and on May 7, 1945, the Germans surrendered unconditionally. Yet war with the Japanese continued; Marjorie's statement was printed later that month.

As Marjorie awaited the courtroom trial, several of her closest friends registered significant shifts. Julia Scribner, after years of ennui and persistent headaches, announced abruptly she was engaged to be married. The news took Marjorie by surprise. The women had discussed Julia's possible future for years, Marjorie trying to play matchmaker, theorizing that Julia was "clinging to the safety of childhood and refusing to enter into adult life, with its responsibilities and disagreeableness." She thought Julia's migraines were subconsciously generated and urged her see a psychiatrist. Julia replied, "You make it sound like an acute pathological condition which I think is overplaying it a bit" and pointed out that psychological theories abounded. "Surely they all exaggerate, like the doctors who blame all ills on vitamin deficiency, or vertebrae, or allergy." Julia's fiancé was a man Marjorie had never met: Thomas Bigham, an Episcopal priest who had stayed in the Scribner home the previous year. He taught at the General Theological Seminary in New York. "I think university life shall suit me very well," Julia wrote.

Norman Berg, who had served in the marines and worked the South Pacific as a war correspondent, was coming home, and he brought his wife to Crescent Beach for a second honeymoon. Marjorie also invited Sigrid Undset to visit, but her friend was returning to liberated Norway. She, too, was concerned with where "home" might be, and her predicament was more profound than Marjorie's. Sigrid would not return to her house, she said. The Nazis had used it up; the furniture was gone. There was much resettlement work to be done, well beyond her personal situation. Marjorie sent her a generous assistance check, and a few months later, Undset reported how it was to be spent: one-third would go toward the education of children whose parents had been killed in the war or on the home front. The rest would go to rebuilding the three northernmost provinces, "where the Germans destroyed everything with true German thoroughness." The challenge, Undset wrote, would be to acquire and transport building materials, household goods, and clothing. "The people of the North cling to their homes, or the sites of their homes," she explained. Those who had been evacuated rushed right back after liberation "and now they refuse to budge."

THE CREEK WAS in disarray most of the year. Idella had left again, Martha Mickens taking the baton—with, understandably, less vigor. To give her a break, Marjorie spent an extended period at Crescent Beach. Perhaps this was the time when she observed a group of boys from St. Augustine repeatedly looting turtle nests on the beach at night. Angry, Marjorie decided to fool the boys, protect the eggs, and have fun, too. One day, she asked Norton to gather some croaker sacks, a spade, and a thermos of martinis. Shortly after dark, the couple went down the beach, tied the burlap bags around their feet, and dragged them up from the shore to the dunes, creating trails mimicking a mother turtle's. At the end of each trail, they dug a hole sized for egg laying and covered it up with loose sand, the way a turtle would with her flippers. Then they climbed higher on the dunes, poured themselves martinis, and waited for the boys, who usually appeared around ten p.m. Again and again, the boys were stymied by the false trails and fake nests, as the Baskins, stifling laughs, moved farther down the beach, creating new trails and toasting their success.

Marjorie was also concerned about Max, who had written that he was laid up "with the most idiotic and utterly unknown ailment. I am absolutely well, and just can't get around. And what's more, I keep getting worse, and worse, and worse." He was glad the *New Yorker* had accepted her new stories, but he wanted more humor from Quincey Dover, imagining a book-length collection. Marjorie sent him one story the *Saturday Evening Post* had rejected, and he agreed that it was not successful. Gregarious Quincey had run her course and Marjorie was, whether she knew it or not, approaching the end of her short-story run. In the fall of 1945, Brandt & Brandt managed to sell a sentimental tale, "Miss Moffatt Steps Out," to *Liberty*, a general interest magazine, after the *New Yorker* turned it down. Two years later, G. S. "Gus" Lobrano, the *New Yorker*'s fiction editor, contacted Marjorie. They hadn't heard from her in a while. "And I hope the day is very near when you'll miss us as much as we miss you," he wrote. But the only other new story she published, "The Friendship," a slight morality tale featuring a young boy, went to the *Saturday Evening Post*—a good fit.

In November, from Virginia, James Branch Cabell sent word that Ellen Glasgow's health was declining quickly. Glasgow had written nothing in two years and had reached "an advanced stage of melancholia." She was starved for literary contacts and would benefit from a winter in St. Augustine, Cabell thought. Marjorie should urge her to come down. "You and I could acquire merit by discussing literature with her on, say, alternating Thursdays," he suggested. Marjorie begged Ellen to come, imploring her to finish the autobiography she was writing, lamenting her own lack of progress on the new novel. Ellen replied that she wasn't strong enough to travel. "Go on with your book," she wrote. "Do not give up. You have great gifts." Four days later, November 21, 1945, Glasgow died. The following March, Marjorie wrote Cabell: "At the time of Ellen's death, I felt no especial shock. I was prepared for it, or so I thought." But when, for a retrospective, the *Atlanta Journal* asked to publish Ellen's response to Marjorie's dream of her, she related, "the most overwhelming sense of loss came over me, and I was physically faint, and it seemed to me that I could not endure it. I could not bear it for her not to be here."

MARJORIE CONTINUED PREPARING for the trial, fretting over Scribner's passivity—wouldn't the firm come to her defense, guns blazing? Here was an issue important to all writers. But here, also, was an issue over which a publisher, as well as an author, might be sued. The less publicity, the better—for Scribner's. For her defense, Marjorie asked Max for a copy of a letter in which he had encouraged her to develop Zelma's character—"it was in response to that, that I wrote the description of her to which she objected—or pretended to object." Although she saved all of Max's letters, she couldn't find this one, and neither could he. He must have said it in person, he thought, or penciled it on the proof. He did remember asking for more of Zelma.

One cold day at Christmastime, Marjorie paid a visit to Zelma's mother in Island Grove, bringing a gift bottle of whiskey. She described the visit for Phil May: how the women poured the whiskey into jelly glasses and repaired to the bathroom—the warmest room in the old house. Marjorie blurted out that she was still fond of Zelma, that she was sure Zelma still loved her and that Kate Walton was to blame for the mess. "It does seem rather incongruous for a daughter to be suing me for invasion of privacy, while her elderly mother sits on the john and drinks half a jelly-glass of whiskey with me," she reflected.

In New York, Phil May spoke with Scribner's people about their upcoming depositions, and in January 1946, Max's brother Edward Perkins, an attorney, represented Marjorie, taking depositions from Max; Charles Scribner; Scribner's business manager, Whitney Darrow; and four others. Kate Walton was also present to question the witnesses; she was most interested in Marjorie's earnings. The publisher later sent income figures for *Cross Creek* to Phil May, who was assembling witnesses, among them Alfred J. Hanna, a Florida history scholar at Rollins College who would also identify himself as a "Cracker."

In April, Zelma's niece Clare dropped by Marjorie's beach cottage and, finding no one home, left a note. When Marjorie discovered it, she and Norton drove to Clare's cottage nearby. Clare met them at their car. "Please come up and have a drink with us," she said. "There isn't a soul there but Aunt Zelma."

"Realizing that she must have called by my cottage with 'Aunt Zelma's' knowledge, love nor money could not have kept me from going up for a drink," Marjorie explained to Phil May. She and Norton went up, Zelma was cordial, everyone shared some whiskey, and Marjorie shot the breeze with Zelma. Norton couldn't believe it. "He said it just did not make sense for two women who were at each other's throats, to chat so amiably about Cason family matters, and I reminded him that I had never been at Zelma's throat, and was actually glad to see her, and she certainly seemed glad to see me.

"Now the whole goddam business is ridiculous—"

THE TRIAL WAS SET FOR May 20. For diversion beforehand, Norton and Marjorie attended the Kentucky Derby on May 4. A horse named Assault won and would take the Triple Crown. The Baskins were in good spirits. Norton had recently accepted a new job managing the Dolphin Restaurant and Moby Dick Lounge at Marineland, the popular oceanarium and tourist destination a few miles south of Crescent Beach. He could live at the beach cottage full-time, provisionally settling the question of home. Castle Warden, that grand, high-maintenance mansion, would be sold. Marjorie did not approve, but she realized that her inability to live in the hotel was a factor. She could have followed Norton completely fifteen or twenty years ago, but not now, in her late forties. "In the long years of loneliness, with the dubious solace of lovers, working alone, I have become unable to share in a commercial, gregarious life such as that of a hotel," she admitted to Norman Berg.

IN GAINESVILLE and the surrounding towns and hamlets, citizens anticipated the Cross Creek trial as high theater, starring two strong women with colorful personas known to all and a supporting cast ranging from backcountry fishermen to literary critics. Mild-mannered Judge John A. H. Murphree would preside over the stage. Zelma's side featured Kate and her father, J. V. Walton, with E. A. Clayton of Gainesville; Marjorie's side had Philip May, Scruggs, and John T. G. Crawford, May's law partner.

Day one opened with a promenade to the brick courthouse, attracting students, townspeople, and gossipmongers from beyond. J. V. Walton strode forward in a safari helmet; Marjorie and Norton pulled up in a jeep. Zelma, playing the offended flower, covered her curly gray head with a bag to prevent news photographers from capturing her likeness. Indeed, throughout the week, the same photo of a large bag with a woman's arms and a polka-dot dress beneath it ran in the papers, while next to it, one might see different views of a smiling Norton and Marjorie, he in a suit, she in a stylish dress and hat. Inside the courtroom, on days so hot all the windows were pushed open, fans moving the sluggish air, Zelma continued her demure act, producing knitting needles and a ball of yarn. Throughout the proceedings, observers in the packed gallery could hear the clicking of needles. Several times, the yarn ball fell out of Zelma's lap and rolled under a table or chair. Norton gallantly retrieved the grounders. Over the course of the week, a sweater gradually formed in Zelma's lap.

Everyone knew why Zelma claimed to have been wronged: her privacy as an anonymous citizen had been compromised, with, she argued, malicious intent. How would Marjorie's team argue against this charge? The press summed it up: "The defense contends that when Mrs. Rawlings referred in her own phraseology to Miss Cason as a forceful woman with a colorful and interesting personality, her privacy had not been invaded: that she took an active part in community affairs; that Miss Cason has assisted her many years in gathering materials for her writings and had reason to believe that she herself might be a subject for book material. Mrs. Rawlings contended . . . that she wrote about Miss Cason only as a friend whom she believed would relish the resultant publicity."

JURY SELECTION TOOK most of the first day. Except for a Hawthorne turpentine farmer, the all-male jury was drawn from Gainesville and included a candy dealer, a carpenter, an electrical worker, a hardware store owner, and a jeweler. Two farmers were chosen as alternates. (Women were not permitted to serve on Florida juries until 1949.) Potential jurors who disapproved of naming living people in books without advance consent had been released. The electrician was heard to say he wasn't prejudiced against the practice because otherwise, no history books would be written.

On day two, the swearing in of witnesses was completed. Zelma had thirteen, all from the area. Six, counting Zelma, would testify. Astonishingly, Norton had been on Zelma's prospective list, apparently to be questioned about Marjorie's finances, but had been dropped when May pointed out that Norton himself was being sued as the author's spouse. Marjorie had fifty-five witnesses, including farm people, historians, scholars, and, eventually, servicemen, plus six depositions. Even her old friend Dessie Smith, from whom she had distanced herself ten years earlier, came to her aid. Twenty-six people would testify. Judge Murphree described the case as most unusual, since virtually all of the testimony would be opinionative, not factual. Not one jury member had read *Cross Creek* in its entirety, and some hadn't even heard of it before May 20.

Zelma, the first person called to the stand, admitted that she hadn't read the whole book, either—though she knew her own chapter very well. She was a shy, retiring woman, she contended, with a small circle of friends in Island Grove. She was not given to profanity, as Marjorie had written. "I've never used the Lord's name in vain in my life," she said. The publicity she had received "humiliated and mortified her," she claimed, adding that she had been forced to go on a diet for an anxious, ulcerated stomach, though the best cure was filing the lawsuit; she hadn't had any abdominal attacks since that day. What's more, she had weighed 108 pounds before *Cross Creek* was published, and after the book appeared, her weight plummeted. Now she was up to a healthy 120 or 125 pounds—proof that she expected vindication. Her ordeal had included enduring "slurring remarks" from co-workers at the welfare office where she was employed, who, she told the court, "began calling me 'Cross Creek' and asking me where my gun was and things like that." She had turned down an invitation to join the Pilot Club of St. Augustine because she couldn't face public gatherings. Strangers called her on the telephone, approached her in restaurants, asked her how much she got paid to be in the book. "I finally got so I did go to a drive-in stand and eat in my car," she said. She claimed she had received letters from all over the United States and that some had made her so mad that she'd thrown them in the wastebasket. She had thought Marjorie was her friend, but "now I know she was using me as a tool."

Zelma added, "I told her she took a lady and made a hussy out of her in the book." Her statement was published to wide amusement.

But by day three, Phil May had gotten Zelma to admit that she had used epithets like "bastard" and "sons of bitches," even as she insisted that she was a shy country nobody with no anger issues. And he proved that she was not as retiring as she claimed, but a public figure. She was, after all, an employed state welfare caseworker, not a homebound farm woman. Not only had she conducted the area census years ago, she had held office in the Order of the Eastern Star, was a member of the state welfare commission, had worked for the Federal Emergency Relief Administration, and had attended state meetings for all of these organizations. A longtime deputy sheriff at Island Grove testified that Zelma was active in politics, routinely cursed, had a bad temper, and had once called him a son of a bitch. Other stories of Zelma's political intrigues emerged. An observer wrote, "The lawyer was apparently attempting to lift the character right out of the book and show her as she is described in Cross Creek: a cussing, swash-buckling woman who knows her way around the swamps and ranges in rural Alachua County." Three of Zelma's women friends swore they had never heard her curse, but their testimonies evaporated as the week wore on. As well, J. V. Walton's attempt to prove malice, by calling the stepfather of a man who had been properly named in "Cracker Chidlings," fell flat when May objected and Judge Murphree agreed, saying, "We can't try every character in all of these books."

Witnesses for the defense were called. Marjorie's neighbor Tom Glisson took the stand, saying Marjorie had characterized him accurately in Cross Creek and had done Zelma the same courtesy. A woman from Citra said Zelma had denied much knowledge of the case, blaming her attorneys for whipping it up; Zelma had also told her that Marjorie had "paid off" all the characters in the book, except her. A local attorney said he was once "blessed out" by Miss Cason on the St. Augustine courthouse steps about a welfare case. Her attitude was "vigorous and aggressive," he recalled. Others followed him, attesting to Zelma's salty tongue. When Dessie Smith testified, saying that the profanity Zelma used was common in small towns and the backcountry, many in the gallery nodded in agreement.

Cross Creek's value to readers and scholars—indeed, all Americans— was argued. A navy chaplain, recently returned from the Pacific, testified that he had prescribed Cross Creek for homesickness, and a deposition from James R. Peters, a former navy man, now a student at Michigan State, stated that he had been on the USS *Lexington* in 1942 when the Japanese attacked the aircraft carrier in the Battle of the Coral Sea. Before the battle, he was reading his copy of *Cross Creek*, sent by the Book-of-the-Month Club, and though the battle interrupted him, he clung to the book as he dove overboard and was rescued by a destroyer.

In very specific ways, over the heads of some auditors, the book was, according to one reporter, "dissected, analyzed, evaluated, and interpreted." Dr. Hanna of Rollins College cited Marjorie's numerous honors and *Cross Creek*'s value in offsetting garish tourism publicity. University of Florida professor Clifford Lyons was asked by the prosecution to define biography and autobiography and to compare sixteenth-century biographies to modern ones—in an effort to show that *Cross Creek* was not strictly biographical and, thus, not history but something else—possibly malicious or lascivious. But Lyons compared Marjorie to Mark Twain and defined *Cross Creek* as a "regional biography," dismissing the plaintiff's objections to subjects like hog mating and outhouses. "If all inelegant passages were removed from all great works of literature, there would be great gaps," he said. "Even the Bible has some accounts that are bloody and unsavory." Lyons cleverly proposed that Zelma was "a type of person which is very much admired in America; self-reliant, able to take care of oneself in any circumstances, even under conditions which approach hardships." She had the pioneer spirit, as well as "a sense of kindliness. It is a great tradition in American literature; as democratic as the country."

FINALLY, ON FRIDAY MORNING, May 24, Marjorie, the star of the show, and unquestionably the recipient of most of the public sympathy, took the stand. The gallery was packed. Some people had brought lunches—they were in it for the long haul, which would spill over into Monday. On the verge of tears, Marjorie responded to Phil May's opening questions, describing her youthful, market-driven attempts to write, how coming to Florida had felt like coming home. The first financially lean years at the Creek were difficult, as she struggled to learn to live in the backcountry, derive a profit from her grove, and write in her spare time. But, she explained, she had been determined to put formula writing behind her and "go at this new material in an entirely different way."

She would forsake plot and drama—the sentimental stuff of women's magazines. "I was interpreting this lovely country and these people as they appealed to me; and I decided that if that sort of writing was not wanted, wasn't acceptable, I would not try to write anymore."

She described her family background as southern—a disingenuous statement, given her parents' solid midwestern roots (her father left Washington every four years to vote in Michigan)—though it's true that relatives a few generations back could be traced to the South. Her love of farm life, she said, stemmed from her father's farm in Maryland. She described the recent, friendly visit with Zelma at Crescent Beach. The matter puzzled her: what happened offstage did not square with the courtroom business. And she explained that her original portrayal of Zelma had been very slight. Her publisher had encouraged a more extended portrait than the one she had first submitted.

At May's invitation, Marjorie took up a copy of *Cross Creek* and read from the offending "Zelma" description, pausing to comment, line by line. She had used the term "spinster" because Zelma was not an old maid; her friend had had opportunities to marry. "She was a woman who didn't grow old," Marjorie said. She wrote that Zelma resembled "an angry and efficient canary" because "she was small and quick," and as a young woman had golden hair and was efficient and occasionally angry. Defending the line "I cannot decide whether she should have been a man or a mother," Marjorie said, "By that, I meant that her abilities were more or less wasted." If she had been a man, Zelma would have been an executive, an attorney, or a doctor. But she would have made a fine mother, too. "I have never known anyone who loved children as much as she, or cares more for any children, black and white," Marjorie explained. As for "she combined the violent characteristics of both," Marjorie said, "I was thinking of a man being more forceful and using stronger language than some women do." At this, the audience tittered.

Marjorie hadn't worried about named characters in the book except for Mr. Martin, whose pig she'd shot for uprooting her petunias, but she had shown him the proofs, and he had approved them. She had approached others, too, so sensitive was she to her neighbors, but hadn't imagined that Zelma would object to her portrayal, since they had been friends from the census days. But she admitted that the women had had a falling-out in 1933, the year *South Moon Under* was published. According to Zelma, Marjorie had damaged their friendship by complaining to Zelma's family about the census taker's profanity. Yet in Marjorie's account, the rift went deeper. In 1933, Zelma had grown jealous of two of Marjorie's friends, insisting that she break off with both.

Now, thirteen years later in Gainesville, Marjorie testified that she'd asked Zelma's mother and brother to help restore the friendship, but Zelma "came up one day and told me she was through with me. . . . I thought she would get over this flare-up, as she had in similar instances with friends." As the trial continued, it seemed Marjorie's description of the census taker might have been an excuse for Zelma to revive grievances she had nursed for at least thirteen years.

AFTER LUNCH, J. V. Walton led Marjorie through an agility course of inquiries and insinuations, hoping to trip or trick her, but she was just as canny as he—and sometimes cannier. In one instance, she asked him to clarify a question, offering several possible meanings and putting him in the role of respondent. Walton wasn't prepared for that. As Marjorie described it later, "Phil May jumped up and said, 'Mr. Walton, what are you doing?' Walton said most plaintively, 'I'm answering her question.' Phil said, 'Mr. Walton, you don't have to answer her question. She has no right to ask you questions.' The audience howled. Once again, she was asked to explain Zelma's *Cross Creek* portrayal, line by line, and she hewed to her previous explication. When Walton asked what was meant by Zelma's "special brand of profanity," Marjorie replied, "Well, she combined various ordinary cuss words for different effect. Her cussing was different from my cussing or Thelma Shortridge's cussing. It's a matter of style." Was Zelma blasphemous? "That depends on what you consider blasphemous. You might say Goddam or my God with no thought of blasphemy. I think the use of such words today is more free and less literal than in other years."

Marjorie concluded, "It was just common country cussing. Zelma and I would about have to divide the honors on cussing."

Walton asked if she didn't think some descriptions of animal life in Cross Creek were vulgar. "Yes, I would call certain passages vulgar, or earthy. They are part of life at Cross Creek and therefore in the picture," Marjorie replied. She turned the question back to Walton, asking if he had counted the number of lovely passages in the book, but the attorney was silent.

MARJORIE'S TESTIMONY on Friday lasted four hours. On Monday, she was again on the stand, J. V. Walton pressing her further on *Cross Creek*, questioning its literary merit, trying to establish parts of it as "cruel" or "fictitious." He cited an "embarrassing" passage about the mating habits of ducks and drakes. (Marjorie had written that the drakes' "love life is merciless, public and continuous." They are "Rabelaisian, they are Turks, they are Huns. The ducks go for months with pecked heads and lamed legs. They must feed surreptitiously by night, for it does not seem as though the drakes give them time by day.") Marjorie assured him that this was an authentic account of life at the Creek. She was accused of cruelty in her portrayal of a ne'er-do-well, George Fairbanks, the last of a formerly prosperous Florida line, who relied on the community's kindness. He lived in a derelict house, entertained with corn liquor, was tongue-tied because of a cleft palate. In *Cross Creek*, Marjorie had reproduced his speech. Walton presented a letter from an outraged Fairbanks relative. Marjorie maintained that her portrait was harmless and that George hadn't been offended.

At one point, grasping at straws or misunderstanding (willfully or not) the book's form and intent, Walton faulted her for not mentioning either of her marriages in the book—even though Chuck had left the Creek before Marjorie made most of the notes feeding the memoir and Marjorie's marriage to Norton occurred after the book was completed. When Walton asked about her finances, Marjorie told the jury her net worth was $124,000 (equivalent to more than $1.6 million in 2020), but when asked by May if she wrote for money, she answered no. "It is in my blood and bones to write, you might say. I have done it so long; it is the thing I do, that's all; just as another man wants to be a carpenter." She had struggled financially for a full ten years before *The Yearling* was published. May asked her to read passages from *Cross Creek* that best illustrated her love for the hamlet, and she turned in a bravura performance. But that wasn't the end of the show. After Marjorie was released, Phil May produced parts of the out-of-state depositions and had Sigsbee Scruggs take the witness stand, reading the deponents' answers to May's questions. This, too, pleased the gallery, and so the day ended.

On Tuesday morning, May 28, Marjorie took the stand for the last time. Her attorney threw softballs: Had she paid the other characters in *Cross Creek*? Had she apologized to Zelma? No, and no. There had been no reason to do either. J. V. Walton called Zelma once more, also to go over previous ground. The closing arguments that afternoon ran passionately. On Zelma's side, the right to privacy and "objectionable" passages were emphasized; on Marjorie's, literary merit and freedom of speech. Walton spoke last, maintaining that Marjorie's descriptions of mating animals were purposefully salacious to sell books and that the portrait of Zelma was malicious. Judge Murphree instructed the jury, and the six men disappeared. Zelma departed with her knitting, expecting a long discussion. Marjorie and Norton remained. A mere twenty-eight minutes later, the jury returned with its verdict: not guilty.

Chapter Twenty-Two

"I Have Never Felt More Inadequate"

1946-47

CELEBRATIONS ON THE Rawlings-Baskin side commenced. Congratulatory letters poured in from all over. Floridians who hadn't read *Cross Creek* stormed libraries and bookstores for copies. A Miami doctor, sending Marjorie compliments, wrote that he had not read *Cross Creek* because copies were scarce; a prominent news dealer insisted he'd had eleven thousand requests for the book. In Clearwater, the book was "more in demand than silk stockings." The annual sales, which had dipped from thousands of copies to hundreds, began climbing again.

Scribner's hadn't been aware of the trial dates until they were nearly over. Max wired good wishes to Marjorie on the final day, and she wired back immediately that she and Norton had won. Although national wire services distributed updates, mostly Florida papers picked them up. Max read details in copies of the *St. Augustine Record* sent up to New York and forwarded the clips to *Publishers' Weekly*, hoping for coverage. James Branch Cabell had followed the trial via the *Record* and wrote to Marjorie that "it was something past Lewis Carroll's wildest fancies and riotously funny," and he hoped she felt the same. She did. At the end of June 1946, *Publishers' Weekly* ran an article about the trial, and in July, *Time* took it up in a brief note: "Zelma Cason, Florida social worker, felt that her portrayal of 'my friend, Zelma,' had 'taken a lady and made a hussy out of her.' After listening to six days of testimony, a jury thought not."

The lawsuit had cost Marjorie $4,500 (about $60,000 in 2020 dollars), and the final bill hadn't been delivered—it was too soon. Astonishingly, Zelma's attorneys filed a motion for still another trial, to be heard by the judge in mid-July. The hearing would facilitate an appeal. On the street, one might have heard it said that Zelma was not over her hissy fit. To Phil May, Zelma's lawyers matched Santayana's definition of a fanatic: "A person who redoubles his efforts after he has lost sight of his purpose." Marjorie shared the saga with Sigrid Undset, who wrote from Lillehammer, "It seems so crazy to me—how could anybody write one's memoir if it is a punishable offense to mention one's neighbor by their first name. Thank God, we are less finicky here."

She added, "If anybody had wanted to trouble me about *Happy Times in Norway* I would have a lot of cases on my hands."

In September, Zelma and her team filed a second appeal, two days before deadline. The delay was intentional, Marjorie was sure: "I can hear Zelma saying, 'Let 'er sweat,' " she wrote to Norton.

BESIDES THE NEW NOVEL, Marjorie was working on another project for MGM: an expanded version of "A Mother in Mannville," the autobiographical story written in North Carolina ten years before, about a writer in the mountains who grows fond of a boy from the local orphanage. It would be a Lassie tale (with the beloved collie belonging not to a writer but to a widowed pianist) featuring Claude Jarman Jr., who was playing Jody in *The Yearling*. Marjorie hoped to turn the story into a full-length book, possibly a novel, but to work effectively, she had to get out of Florida, away from the trial's backwash, the sultry weather, and the possibility of guests. Late in the summer, Norton drove his wife and her animals to a rented house in Blowing Rock, North Carolina, in the Blue Ridge Mountains. "The mountains give a great lift after a long time at sea-level," Marjorie wrote Norman Berg. Idella, who came up by bus, was happy there, too. For recreation, she and Marjorie attended the movies, and Idella, seated in the segregated balcony, made friends with another woman who rode home with them. Marjorie, the casual anthropologist, described for Norton the

Negro population of nearby Boone: "Most of them mulattoes, with a mountain cast of features!" She noted mountain speech: "git," "kin," "shore," and "I be dogged"—just like country Floridians.

Once settled into a routine, Marjorie gave Henry James another chance (*The American Scene*), having been so annoyed by his style in the midst of the trial preparations. Her reaction this time proved how much the reception of a book depends on one's state of mind. "The James is a revelation," she admitted to Max. "At first, the extremity of the involutions of his style is exasperating. Then you realize you have simply been reading too much stuff that was written as though the authors were rushing to meet a deadline on the MGM $125,000 prize contest. It strikes you with embarrassment that you are forced to go as slowly as James and to think along with him."

She knew about the haste of meeting an MGM deadline, since she was trying to meet one herself. ("The story goes rapidly, awful tripe, but I think all right for MGM," she told Norton.) She managed to produce the commissioned work, temporarily titled *A Family for Jock*. Although the project was fawned over by Hollywood gossip columnist Louella Parsons, Max refused to publish it as a book. As a movie scenario, he thought, it was fine, but it had been written on assignment, not organically—it was not up to her level. Marjorie was relieved. She admitted that she had done it for MGM's handsome fee. The story was serialized as "Mountain Prelude" in the *Saturday Evening Post* the following year (May 3, 1947), and when Marjorie read the first installment, she "could have died with shame," she confided to Max, and she regretted having allowed Carl Brandt to sell it. Later, she wrote to fellow author and Wisconsin graduate Walter O'Meara, "I have paid with my life's blood for that casuistry and compromise. The style, the surface writing, of that long story, ruined, for several years, whatever creative ability I had. I simply could not write deeply." Once again, she cited William Ellery Leonard's warning at Wisconsin: that her vocabulary and her ease on the page could ruin her as a writer.

The "Lassie" movie was released in 1949 as *The Sun Comes Up*. Instead of being a pianist, the Marjorie character was transformed into a soprano, played (and sung) by Jeanette MacDonald. As the story opens, the singer comes to the mountains with Lassie, grieving the loss of her son, who was struck by a car as he chased the beloved dog. The movie script roughly evokes "A Mother in Mannville"—the drama of a lonely woman and an orphan boy who befriend each other—but with the addition of nosy neighbors, a chorus of orphan boys, a love interest, and several opportunities for Lassie to save the day. Instead of sorrowfully driving into the sunset, the woman breaks through her grief and adopts the boy.

IN LATE NOVEMBER 1946, Marjorie met with Max in New York, visited friends, attended the theater. Continuing her interest in African-American artists, she witnessed the Katherine Dunham Dance Company's *Bal Nègre*, a showcase of dancers, singers, and musicians that had toured for nine months before arriving on Broadway. The three-act evening struck Marjorie as one of the most exciting performances she'd ever seen. Like Zora Neale Hurston, Dunham had studied anthropology, focusing on African dance and winning travel grants to study Caribbean forms. (Both women had received support from the Guggenheim Foundation.) Dunham was one of several black dancers who toward the end of the Harlem Renaissance in the 1930s formed companies to enter the concert scene. Her first full-length ballet, a mix of ballet, modern dance, and folk/social dance titled *L'Ag'Ya*, had debuted in Chicago in 1938 and served as Act 2 of *Bal Nègre*. The night Marjorie attended, she sent a note to Dunham backstage; the dancer recognized her name, and the two met briefly after the show. Dunham told Marjorie that *The Yearling* was her mother's favorite book. "The woman is a great American artist," Marjorie wrote Norton. "Miss Dunham has the sweetest, *saddest* face. I had a deep feeling of love for her."

BUT THE YEAR'S crowning event was MGM's December 1946 release of *The Yearling*, seven and a half years after work on the first version of the film had begun. While Marjorie had been embroiled in the lawsuit, MGM had renewed its effort on the project, which had been set aside during the war. The perfect Jody had to be recruited, and instead of issuing a cattle call, the new director, Clarence Brown, whose recent credits included *National Velvet*, disguised himself as a building inspector and toured fifth- and sixth-grade classrooms in eight southern states, searching for the right young actor. In February 1945 he selected ten-year-old Claude Jarman Jr. of Nashville, the towheaded star of local children's theater productions, ostensibly after a screen test requiring the boy to walk into a pen with one hundred deer. "In five minutes the herd was following him around . . . we called off the search right then," Brown said. Jarman was said to be the 19,863rd boy tested. Gregory Peck would play Penny Baxter, and Jacqueline White, an unknown starlet, would play Ma.

Once more, land, buildings, and animals were prepared, and cameras were set to roll in mid-May. MGM hoped for a Christmas 1945 release, but various delays unfolded. Cast members changed. White, too young for her role, was replaced after Brown saw Jane Wyman leaving a Beverly Hills supermarket with mussed hair and no makeup, and hired her. The baby deer had outgrown its part. One journalist remarked that Jody would be cast as a white-bearded old man by the time the movie was done. Not only had the main cast changed completely since its prewar beginnings, but its non-speaking members—caged, penned, trained, and/or filmed—had, by the end, numbered 469 animals, including 126 deer, 9 black bears, 37 dogs, 83 chickens, 36 pigs, 8 rattlesnakes, 18 squirrels, 4 horses, 17 raccoons, 53 wild birds, 17 buzzards, and 1 apparently forbearing owl. "Those movie people are all crazy," Marjorie told a reporter. Gregory Peck confirmed that she never dropped by the set. "She wouldn't come to the place where we were working," he said, "but I hear she's a grand lady."

The Yearling received rave reviews, Oscar talk, and parental approval. Here was a clean, heartwarming drama for everyone, even the children of America's most protective mothers. In January, the film opened in New York for a long run at Radio City Music Hall. Marjorie went back to New York with Norton to see it, celebrating afterward with martinis at Marcia Davenport's. *New York Times* critic Bosley Crowther praised its sensitive portrayals, especially Claude Jarman Jr. and Gregory Peck's. "To be sure, there are two or three moments when the Aurora Borealis is turned on and the heavenly choir starts singing," the critic sighed. "With those we could willingly dispense." Among the film's many strengths was "the feeling which a lonesome lad has for wild things, expressed with such tenderness and eloquence in Mrs. Rawlings' classic work." Screenwriter Paul Osborn received nods as well. *The Yearling* captured seven Oscar nominations, including Best Actor (Peck), Best Actress (Wyman), Best Director (Brown), and Best Motion Picture. It won two: Best Art

Direction (Color) and Best Cinematography (Color). Claude Jarman Jr. was given a special Academy Juvenile Award (past recipients included Shirley Temple and Judy Garland). It is interesting to note that Marjorie recorded little personal reaction to the film. Its commercial nature and the long haul to the screen might have perturbed her, even as it attracted new readers.

In Atlanta, Margaret Mitchell, watching out for her friend, complained that Scribner's hadn't yet issued a movie edition of *The Yearling*. MacMillan had printed a cheap paperback when *Gone with the Wind* was released, she said, and several hundred thousand copies had sold, "and they and I cleaned up on it. I think it's outrageous that Scribner isn't doing the same for *The Yearling*. Why not needle them?" *The Yearling* was reprinted by arrangement with Grosset & Dunlap, which published inexpensive editions of juvenile books. Later that year, Grosset released a movie edition of the novel, with photographs from the film on the jacket.

AFTER *THE YEARLING*'S RELEASE, Marjorie found herself at odds with the Creek, despite her friendly neighbors and the comforts of daily life. "I have never felt more inadequate," she confided to Max in the new year. "The time between books has been so unreasonably long that I feel a true writer would not, could not, have let it happen. I don't mean about 'publication,' etc. but about *working*." Blaming the war and the lawsuit didn't occur to her, as if the two monumental, prolonged situations had numbed her to their impact. Might a small project bring her back? Max had suggested she try a children's book about a little black girl. Marjorie herself had foreseen such a thing in *Cross Creek*: "The Negro imagination is dark and rich. As they grow older, they learn to save it for their own kind, to hide it from unfriendly minds, perhaps, in an alien civilization. But a Negro child will someday make a sad and lovely study for a poet." She considered the idea: "I have found that each of my books has developed out of something I have written in a previous book. Some thought evidently unfinished." She would prefer this to "the *terrible* chore of the book about the spiritual and inarticulate man who derived remotely from my own grandfather."

She set to work, stopping to address grove business and entertain visitors, such as literary naturalist Edwin Way Teale and his wife, Nellie, who had embarked on the first of their four seasonal pilgrimages.

When the couple pulled into Cross Creek, Teale wrote in *North with the Spring*, they found "Mrs. Rawlings had been working late the night before and pages of interlined manuscript, weighted down with a box of Keeboard Redemption Bond [typing paper], were strewn about a low table near the fireplace at one end of the living room. Responding to our concern over her leaving her work, Mrs. Rawlings assured us: 'I always welcome a chance to get back to the scrub,'" and a jolly day of sightseeing and picnicking around Pat's Island and Silver Glen, "that secret and lovely place" in *The Yearling* where Jody made his flutter-mill, began.

However, in his private journal, Teale more vividly and honestly described the day with the *Cross Creek* author, who, although she had invited them, was not so pleased to see her guests. The Teales approached Marjorie's house two minutes before their ten a.m. appointment time, were received by a housekeeper (probably Idella), and were told that Marjorie was not up yet. The couple browsed for about twenty minutes, during which Teale noticed Marjorie's manuscript pages and Remington typewriter, by which sat "a quart bottle of Old Overholt whiskey, two-thirds empty."

Teale wrote, "When Mrs. Rawlings came in, her eyes were swollen and puffy. She seemed extremely nervous. And all day long she lit one Lucky Strike cigarette after another. When we started on the picnic, she carried the bottle of whiskey along. She seemed not in good health, nervously worn out. Perhaps we arrived on a bad day."

He added, "Seven times she told me she had torn up the new novel she is writing, 'and it's still pretty bad,' she said."

Marjorie invited the Teales to ride in her Oldsmobile, the make she preferred because it was not as low-slung as other cars, thus better for sand roads.

"On the way to Ocala," Teale jotted, "she nearly scared me out of my mind driving 75 miles an hour, at times almost 80, with one hand on the steering wheel, and a handkerchief wadded up in it, while with her other hand she fumbled about for cigarettes or the lighter on the dashboard. Finally, she said, 'I hope my fast driving doesn't bother you. I have Goodyear tires—they give you at least a mile to stop in case of a blowout before they go flat.' That helped a little, but not much."

At the Juniper Springs picnic area, the trio found half a dozen cars. Marjorie remarked that she remembered the scrub when it was wild and that she hated crowds—a dozen people scattered over the park seemed a crowd to her. They chose a secluded table, and Marjorie produced a wicker basket stuffed with fried chicken, boiled eggs, potato salad, layer cake, and oranges—proof that, even out of sorts, Marjorie, with Idella's assistance, could provide home cooking and baking to go.

Meeting an author is tricky, Teale observed in his journal:

> What we like first of them is their books—that is what they are like inside. What they are like outside is often different. It is the inside that means the most in the end.
>
> Mrs. Rawlings was different from our conception. She impressed us as being one who had made her own way against everything. Who owed little to her fellow man. Who had been sensitive and hurt, who had struggled harder than most. There was a sincerity about her. Yet she gave us everything but herself. She was cautious and did not trust us entirely. She stalked ahead and let us tag along as we would. She took the choice place at the picnic table. She was generous, but not gracious or thoughtful. We had the feeling of being obligatory charity . . . we never got a common level of friendship or understanding. This of course was too much to expect on a first meeting. Especially from one who has been taken advantage of by strangers.

Teale mused about how he and Nellie were "always at a social disadvantage. We don't drink or smoke, and many people who do probably feel we disapprove of them. There is nothing we can do about this except to be as friendly and cordial as we can. But sometimes probably this is not enough."

Marjorie shared tidbits of her writing life with the Teales. A few weeks before, John Steinbeck had asked her if writing got easier with time, and both had agreed that it got harder. "In good writing, ease and excellence are rarely found together," Marjorie proclaimed. No one else, she added, had tapped the Florida scrub region in literature before she did. She loved Conrad, especially *Heart of Darkness*. She found Proust "strong meat" and could read only one hundred pages or so at a time, though she always returned to him. She read Thoreau for the first time when she was over forty, and thought many people came to him too young. Now she was reading *Das Kapital* by Karl Marx, "to see what all the shouting is about."

After a long day with Marjorie at her most mannered, the Teales were eager to return to their room at a tourist court near Gainesville, but Marjorie insisted that they stay for a hearty country dinner at Cross Creek—an impressive encore. The couple finally left at nine p.m., navigating uncertainly on dark, unlit roads, and crawled into bed around ten, exhausted.

AFTER THE TEALES' VISIT, Marjorie sent Max a draft of *The Secret River*, a story for children about a black child, Calpurnia, written in "pretty much fairy-tale style." Max replied with suggestions for deepening it. One of his ideas pertained to poems Calpurnia writes—he wondered if Marjorie could introduce "a little of the Negro quality" in the phrasing, without using actual dialect. Marjorie balked. In the postwar era's rising awareness of racism and cries for equal rights, including her own awakening and public appeals, *The Yearling* had been called out for offensive language. For example, in January 1946, more than a year before Marjorie drafted *The Secret River*, *The Yearling* had been withdrawn from required reading at the predominantly black Morris High School in the Bronx, after irate citizens deemed it a "poison" book for its treatment of Negroes.

A few months later, members of the venerable National Equal Rights League protested the inclusion of *The Yearling* on a summer reading list for James Monroe High School, also in the Bronx, with the same objections. Offending passages sprinkled throughout the book included "'He's got a foot like a Georgia nigger,' Penny said," and "A black nose protruded between narrow slats. A tiny black paw, like a nigger baby's foot, reached out." In the *People's Voice*, an article headlined "Anti-Negro Book Banned by School" reported that Monroe's principal, Abraham Bernstein, withdrew *The Yearling*, without penalizing any student who had read it. The English teacher responsible for the list admitted that he hadn't known about the offensive passages. He hadn't even read the book—proof of the novel's blanket acceptance.

Upset, Marjorie wrote to the Reverend Frank Glenn White, director of the People's Institute of Applied Religion, which espoused social activism and equal rights in particular, and to the *People's Voice*, addressing her use of "nigger" in *The Yearling*. The newspaper published part of her letter, introducing her as someone considered "a staunch supporter of Negroes." Quoted in the newspaper, she stated:

> I approve with all my heart the policy of laying a taboo on the use of the word "nigger," not because any word is in itself offensive, since all words are only their connotations, but because those who use the word in ordinary speech or casually in print are those who have the wrong attitude, not only toward Negroes, but toward all of life and Christian living.
>
> But in your zeal, you must not see things out of proportion. This is one cause of my weeping for the Negro race, for it is inevitable that intelligent Negroes are likely to be psychologically touchy. As you know, this is not solely a Negro characteristic. Probably ninety-nine out of the hundred human beings, anywhere and everywhere, have been conditioned by circumstances to be touchy about something.
>
> Now it is a great deal to ask of Negroes who have borne up so nobly under inconceivable injustices, not to be unduly touchy. Yet it seems to me extremely important that your race rise to difficult heights and prove itself above trivialities.

Marjorie pointed out that *The Yearling*'s time period, 1870–71, called for the N-word: "It would have been an unpardonable anachronism to have used the word 'Negro' instead of 'nigger' in a book of this date." This was the stronger argument. But in striving to defend herself, Marjorie evidently could not hear condescension in the message: "Don't be so touchy." That message echoed Zora's attitude. In talks with Marjorie, Zora had said Negroes were responsible for their own advancement; in later circumstances, she implied that southern Negroes were whiners. Considered a traitor by many blacks, Zora would ultimately criticize the Supreme Court's decision to desegregate schools. ("How much satisfaction can I get from a court order for somebody to associate with me who does not wish me near them?" she cried in the press.) It's possible that in 1946, Marjorie was taking a few cues from the author who first galvanized her.

James Monroe High School's objections ultimately contributed to the publishing of a "school edition" of *The Yearling*, free of the two offending passages. Other works underwent similar revisions in the 1940s. Agatha Christie's 1939 novel *Ten Little Niggers* was retitled *And Then There Were None* for American audiences; Joseph Conrad's *The Nigger of the "Narcissus"* was summarily pulled from school library shelves. Other books containing the insulting word, such as Harriet Beecher Stowe's anti-slavery novel *Uncle Tom's Cabin* and Mark Twain's *Huckleberry Finn*, were called into question or banned.

Marjorie had not entirely shaken the slur in casual circumstances. She walked a fine line that hadn't been clear to her until recently. Portions of *Cross Creek* contained far more offensive material than *The Yearling*. But to use Negro dialect in *The Secret River* now, even though it had been employed for years by both black and white authors, would be a mistake. She explained to Max that she had avoided dialect because she wanted to give "complete dignity to all Negroes" in the story and Calpurnia was "only accidentally a little colored girl."

"Thinking of them and seeing them as human beings, with the color of the skin as incidental as it is with blonde Swedes and dark Italians, seems to me the most important thing," she continued. Furthermore, she felt that dialect would distract the reader from the story. Max disagreed, reminding her that "the world will be robbed if the phrasings and rhythms of different peoples are avoided. They are part of the wealth of literature. The Irish, the Scotch, and Welsh, for instance, have all their own ways of expression." Marjorie, a master of dialect, knew that very well, but the times had changed. She stuck to her plan and eventually set the project aside—she could not adequately complete it. *The Secret River* was published posthumously with black-and-white illustrations by Leonard Weisgard on tan paper, the characters' race open to interpretation.

That spring, Marjorie had another wreck, turning her car over twice near the Creek. It had been raining, and, unknown to her, the road had been oiled to keep down the dust. Idella, who had returned to the Creek, was with her. They skidded and rolled. Marjorie was bruised, but Idella had two broken ribs. Later, Idella told the story differently. Marjorie had been drinking. Idella asked for the car keys, to visit her mother in Reddick, and Marjorie got mad, "cussing and storming about how I always had to be going to Reddick and so on. She'd grabbed the keys and stomped out to the car, shouting for me and Pat to come on." Marjorie drove too fast, swerving about, and as they leaned into a curve, the car "flipped into the air, and in one awful moment rolled over on its side." A car that had just passed them stopped to help. Marjorie was unconscious. Idella was also taken to the doctor. Her mother was furious. "She kept reminding me that she had told me so, that woman was no good."

Two days after the accident, two of Marjorie's elderly aunts arrived from Phoenix to visit Marineland and commented on their niece's unhealthy appearance. "I had been obliged to tell them lightly of the accident," Marjorie wrote to Norman Berg, but "when one's eye meets one's ass, one really doesn't look one's best." In the weeks following, she regained her strength, despite being bedeviled by a beginning writer who pestered her unsuccessfully to read and comment on his manuscript. "I don't know why I fool with such people," she complained to Norman. "Tomorrow I am having a picnic for a high school writing club from Gainesville! Do, Jesus, strike me dead."

In May, the Florida Supreme Court addressed Zelma's appeal and reversed Alachua County's judgment in the lawsuit. There had been too much extraneous material presented on Marjorie's behalf, they said— her status as a famous writer made no difference, for instance—and Zelma hadn't proved that she'd been injured or that Marjorie had acted maliciously. Still, there was enough evidence to support an invasion of privacy. Zelma was vindicated, but hers was a soft victory. She was awarded no more than unspecified "nominal" costs and damages, not the $100,000 she had hoped for. On Marjorie's side, the leading principle, authorial freedom, had disappeared. In a sense, there was no winner, only two women who had lost. Marjorie wanted to appeal to the U.S. Supreme Court, but Phil May talked her out of it. Filing for a rehearing with the Florida Supreme Court was inadvisable, too—it might send the whole case back for a full trial. May advised a payoff agreement with Zelma and her lawyers, and Norton encouraged Marjorie to "settle the thing and get it over with." But Marjorie voted to continue the fight: "I cannot allow a precedent to be established, if I can help it, that would hamstring other writers."

Kate Walton filed for a rehearing, and in June, it was denied. May suggested that Judge Murphree rule in Zelma's favor for $1.00 plus court costs and be done with it. The matter stalled. It wasn't until the following year that *Cason v. Baskin* completed its death throes. In January 1948, Kate Walton filed a motion to clarify the unspecified costs mentioned the previous year. Marjorie heard that Zora had weighed in on the case privately, having written to a friend, "I could have saved all kinds of trouble if she [Marjorie] had just plain let me kill that poor white trash that she took up so much time with, and who paid her for it by suing her for defamation of character. . . . If you hear of the tramp getting a heavy load of rock salt and fat-back in her rump, and I happen to be in Fla at the time, you will know who loaded the shell." Sometime that spring, a *Miami Herald* reporter suggested the paper might back an appeal by Marjorie in the interest of free speech, but in the end, all parties adhered to what Phil May had suggested the year before: award Zelma the legal victory, a one-dollar bill, and court costs of $1,050.10. On August 9, 1948, the case—a five-and-a-half-year ordeal—was closed.

IT IS NO WONDER, then, that in the summer of 1947, Marjorie accepted Owen D. and Louise Young's offer of a farm cottage in rural Browns Hollow, New York, twenty miles from Van Hornesville, where the Youngs had a home. To write anything at all, she had to get away from Florida again, and the Youngs knew it. Van Hornesville, which Marjorie would claim as her new address, was "almost to Canada and is mountainous," she told Norman Berg. "I am most thrilled about it." The Brown's Hollow farmhouse, which Louise Young had restored with comfortable antiques, stood above a trout stream. One of the Youngs' maids would clean for Marjorie once a week, as Idella had left Marjorie after the car accident and married. The author would have total privacy. As well, upstate New York was a better choice than western North Carolina, the landscape being closer to her tortured novel's setting. In mid-June, Norton drove Marjorie and the animals north. The Youngs welcomed them and handed Marjorie a telegram that had been forwarded from Cross Creek. It was from Charles Scribner. On June 17, Maxwell Perkins had died of pneumonia.

Chapter Twenty-Three

A New Outpost

1947-48

"UNSPEAKABLE GRIEF." This was Marjorie's first and lasting reaction to losing Maxwell Perkins, her editor, mentor, and friend of seventeen years, the gentle force field who had nurtured her work with the respect and sensitivity of a fellow artist, the mind and skills of an exacting wordsmith. He led by suggestion, guided smoothly, a quiet rudder. One of his most extraordinary qualities was his vision of a talented writer's potential and its development over years of output, coupled with the friendly patience to shepherd each writer and manuscript along, from rough draft to publication. For Max, the complete fruition of the work mattered most, not sales, which he trusted would come if the book was good. Three years after Max's death, Marjorie wrote a review of *Editor to Author: The Letters of Maxwell E. Perkins* (Scribner, 1950) for *Publishers' Weekly*, summing up the subtle alchemy his authors experienced: "Several of us who had the privilege of his counsel have asked one another, 'What was it that he gave us?' We agreed that his special gift was his ability, as creative as that of the author himself, to enter into the mind of the individual writers, to understand what that writer was attempting to do and say, to direct all criticism and all help toward the writer's own best expression, whether Max himself agreed or not."

When the devastating news was handed to her, Marjorie wrote right away to Norman Berg, distressed that she had traveled so far to write a book Max would never see, "and on which he could not save me from possible pitfalls." Scribner's fell briefly into disarray. Authors were assigned new editors, who helped relay the terrible news. Marcia Davenport's first reaction, she wrote, was terrible: "panic, the sense of falling off the surface of the earth, rushed over me for the first time in my life." She remembered confiding to her lover, Jan Masaryk, the Czech foreign minister, "Max would be the one loss in life that I could not bear." Charles Scribner told Hemingway, "the best [authors] have decided that it is now up to them to go on writing and do their best, as that would be what Max would have wished." Marjorie said as much to Norman: "I felt inclined to return to Florida. Then I realized how horrified Max would be by such an attitude, for to him only the book mattered." She assured Charles Scribner that no other publisher would lure her away: "The almost indefinable quality of your firm is as important to a writer as Max's editorial judgment. . . . For myself, I feel that I shall only have to work harder, to be even more critical of my own work." Marjorie often dreamed of Max, waking up in tears. In a dream she related to Bernice Gilkyson, who had worked with Perkins at Scribner's, "I went into his office and said to him, 'I have terrible news for you. Max is dead.' He smiled, and I said 'But you are Max. You know better than anyone what this means to all of us.' "

Marjorie took solace in the Youngs' friendship, joining them for meals and parties and touring the area with Louise, who encouraged her to go on a high-protein diet, sans liquor. "Mrs. Young is 'mothering' me like all get-out, and my soul is not quite my own," she confided to a friend. "I am really enjoying it." Marjorie told Norton that she was happy and content, and that if he were there, he'd have to join her on the diet. "There isn't a drop of liquor in the house," she jotted. "I shall keep it that way." The only problem would be "afternoons when I drop in at the Youngs' and he is home and wants someone to take a drink with him. I can probably just sit back and let Louise fight the battle for me." It didn't quite work that way. In time, Marjorie joined Young regularly at cocktail hour. The two had established a warm bond. His personal strength and humility drew her to him, and he admired her work enormously. She found she could speak with him of her struggle to write—a gift, after the loss of Max—and for her, a drink made good conversation easier.

AFTER SO MANY YEARS of climbing onto the wagon and hopping off, Marjorie's tendency or desire to overconsume alcohol must have puzzled many around her, except for confirmed alcoholics like Hemingway and Scott Fitzgerald, and to some extent Norton and friends like Norman Berg, who indulged liberally, socially. As Idella Parker had witnessed, Marjorie drank alone as well as with friends, and after so much time, a series of unreasonable arguments, petty outbursts, car accidents, and illnesses could be traced at least in part to overindulgence, though Marjorie often denied it. Liquor was a strong habit, and one can only guess at the causes behind it. Depression? Frustration? Loneliness? Anxiety? Relief from physical pain? The need to prove herself tough, as she'd attempted to in her letters to Hemingway? Or maybe the source was simple physical addiction, begun during Prohibition, when she was in her twenties.

The reducing diet in Van Hornesville was effective, though. After a month, she could crow to Norman Berg, "I have lost ten pounds already!" She was exercising more, walking the countryside with the Youngs and their neighbors, wading in streams, picking berries, drinking in "deep draughts of peace." She continued, "Ever since I have been here, I have had a feeling of belonging to a wonderful family. I don't know whether it is the people, the climate, the terrain, or a combination, but I feel strong again, and myself. I have not been down in the black pit at all." She was sure she'd return to Florida with a "sound beginning" for her book.

Marjorie's happiness in rural New York seemed so complete that, after barely one month there, she bought a Colonial farmhouse in Van Hornesville, without advance word to Norton, who was having the Crescent Beach cottage refurbished and expanded for their greater comfort. Like the Creek farmhouse before it, the Van Hornesville Colonial needed work—a new roof, plumbing, electricity, and more—but Louise Young assured her that with the low purchase price and the reasonable cost of furnishings "picked up here and there," it was worth it. The house, once a headquarters for Major General John Sullivan during the Revolutionary War, was set on several high wooded acres, with a long view of descending meadowland and Otsego Lake, James Fenimore Cooper's "Glimmerglass." "You will love it as much as I do, when you see it,"

Marjorie assured her husband. "It will make a nice vacation place for us." Norton wasn't surprised by the purchase. He'd even expected it and was glad she got "such a honey." He wrote, "Your castles are a little far flung but the house there sounds just too good to miss and I know it will be a knockout when you get it finished."

Nineteen years after falling in love with a Florida hamlet, Marjorie was falling in love with a New York village. Consumed with renovations inside her historic home and plantings outside the foundation and portico, she aimed at full restoration by her departure in October, so that she could move in when she returned the following summer. She bought antique furniture, made friends with neighbors who tended a dairy herd. She was drawn in further when, in a Cooperstown antiques shop, she discovered an American primitive portrait of Maria Bogardus Schuyler and her daughter Catherine. That her new house stood on part of the original land grant to General Philip Schuyler, another Revolutionary War hero, piqued her interest, but more compelling was Maria Schuyler's maiden name, Bogardus—the same as that of her father's ancestors on his mother's side.

Sure of a connection, Marjorie wrote to a relative who managed the family tree. Yes, Maria Bogardus Schuyler was either an aunt or a cousin, far removed. Marjorie bought the painting. Whereas in Florida she had once claimed, with lean evidence, southern connections, in New York she had material proof of her Yankee heritage. Her allegiances were shifting. Of the painting, she later told Robert Frost that "having felt insecure all my life, it seemed to give me a feeling of having roots." When the Youngs took Marjorie to the races at Saratoga, an Albany *Times-Union* photographer snapped her with Owen Young. The picture's cutline, "Celebrities at Saratoga," announced her stake in the area. Shortly thereafter, Colgate University, in Hamilton, New York, invited her to speak. "Get your work done and COME ON UP!" she exclaimed to Norton.

YET THE CREATIVE WORK she had come to do was barely started. "Sometimes I sit in front of my typewriter for eight hours, and produce only one line worth publishing," she lamented. She was able to complete one of the short commercial projects she was still accepting: an article for Grolier's *Book of Knowledge* 1948 supplement. Titled "If You Want to Be a Writer," it is a question-and-answer piece geared for aspirants. To the question "Should books be planned out before beginning the writing?" she wrote, "For a book, a writer should know in advance his general theme; the final result for which he is heading; a rough outline of the story, as to plot or development; and his principal characters. The rest must be worked out as he goes along. Sometimes a character comes to life and takes over and becomes more important than the author planned, or even runs away with the story. Plot changes usually occur as the characters themselves develop." She knew all of this from experience—and that the novel she wanted to write lacked advance knowledge, an outline, and a full cast of characters. In July, she fell ill with an intestinal complaint.

Norton worried that Marjorie wasn't eating properly, but he wouldn't nag her from afar. In St. Augustine, he fended off rumors the couple had separated—a common occurrence when Marjorie went away for long stretches to write. One night that summer, a visiting gossip stomped into the Dolphin Restaurant, introduced herself to Norton, and demanded to know if the couple had split up. Since she'd heard about it in New York's "21" Club, there had to be something to it, she insisted. Norton replied in his "best Southern drawl" that "where I came from, the affairs of ladies and gentlemen were not discussed in low saloons."

Stymied by her novel, Marjorie played with verse. "One sonnet needs reworking but is not too dreadful, another needs tearing to pieces," she reported to Norman Berg. "Did you see Edna St. Vincent Millay's strange poem in the last Atlantic Monthly, 'To a Snake'?" she asked him. "It is wonderfully *vigorous*." Coincidentally, her husband had just written of another foolish visitor at the Dolphin, a man convinced that Marjorie could make a book from snake information he'd brought. Assuming shared credit, the man believed that he and the famous author could "make a lot of money from it." The papers he clutched "seemed to be a list of snakes which had been stolen from Ross [Allen] and sold back to him by one of his cracker employees," Norton reported, having shown the opportunist the door.

As the summer continued, Marjorie wrote even less, drank more, worried about the new house and where she would ultimately spend her time—five months a year in Van Hornesville and the rest at Crescent Beach? She thought she could wean herself of the Creek, and though Norton disagreed, she insisted she could work well at the expanded beach cottage. After all, her husband had assured her, "Every nail that has been driven has been driven in the hope that it will make you more comfortable, and happy."

Perhaps she was correct about the Creek. Though the grove was still lovely and her neighbors still friendly, the Creek had been tainted by the lawsuit, and it contained, after all, a business, with year-round and seasonal employees, products to be harvested and sold. Most of her best friends would visit anywhere she chose to live. That summer, Julia Scribner and her husband made the trip to Van Hornesville, and Julia came a second time by herself, having set aside updates of her marriage, burgeoning photography career, and infant daughter to comfort Marjorie in the wake of Max Perkins's death. "It must seem hard to write now without his helpful and encouraging criticism to look forward to," she offered, "but surely much of what he wrote you in the past was not just for the moment, and is continuously inspiring you, as only he could be."

By the time Marjorie threw a Labor Day party for the Youngs' family and friends, she was gaining weight and drinking so much that she turned over the liquor she had accumulated to the Youngs. She was reading long and rigorously again: F.S.C. Northrop's *The Meeting of East and West*, a gift from Norman, who, with Marjorie's permission, had stopped by Cross Creek for a night. Norton, usually agreeable, was annoyed by Norman's stop: "I think it damned white of Norman to go by and keep Cross Creek from falling apart. I am sure he would do a comparable chore for any too long unloved lady." He added, "Ain't that catty. I really don't mean it for I am really quite fond of him but sometimes his smugness and patness set me wild." A few days later, Norman visited Norton at Marineland, and the pair enjoyed each other's company over many beers. After Norman left, Ernest Hemingway dropped in. "I enjoyed him very much but should never try drinking with him," Norton told his wife. "He walked out in fine shape and I was left talking to myself." Hemingway inquired about Marjorie's writing. Norton told him it was going badly. The author asked if she was "afraid" of her book, and added, "You know when you have done a tremendous job like Marjorie has, you sometimes get scared and think that you can't write. Hell, you know, if you ever think you can't—you can't—. You tell her that."

IN LATE OCTOBER, Norton took a northbound train to collect Marjorie. Finishing out the cottage, supervising his Marineland employees, and responding to a heavy storm season—a category 4 hurricane had slammed Fort Lauderdale and battered the northern coast—delayed his departure, and as he prepared to travel, Marjorie fell ill again. When he arrived, the couple went to New York to consult with Dr. Atchley. Back at Crescent Beach, Marjorie was "shocked by the new size and elegance of the erstwhile 'cottage,'" estimating it cost Norton a year's worth of profits. She loved her new private studio and made another start on the novel. Only briefly did she visit the Creek, "like a bird in passage." Increasingly, she offered the farmhouse to family, friends, and aspiring writers as a creative retreat or vacation getaway. Martha Mickens would welcome them all. In Marjorie's accumulated mail was a Bible for Martha, a gift from Norman and Julie Berg, who had stayed there several times. "She was more than happy about it—there was a hushed awe— her first Bible—," Marjorie relayed to the Bergs. "Since she can't read, it had never occurred to me to ask if she owned one. She wants me to read a bit from it to her before I leave today."

Marjorie returned to New York, spending most of November at the Harkness Pavilion. A week of tests revealed a need for surgery. Summoning her bawdy persona, Marjorie described one examination "in which you stand on your head and have a locomotive run up your rectum with the headlights on." Between four enemas, she wrote a sonnet. But the problem was not diverticulitis. She had a lump in her side. After that operation, another was needed: to remove benign cysts from her breasts. Julia and Marcia visited, took her out for air and distraction. Norton wrote with good news: Idella was back. Her new husband, Bernard Young, had taken a job at the Dolphin, and the couple now lived in the cottage's new garage apartment. From Phoenix, Marjorie's aunt Wilmer Kinnan, a former schoolteacher, scolded, "I just hope so earnestly that you will try to take as good, I mean as <u>scientific</u>, care of your body as your knowledge and good sense dictate. Just remember that <u>your</u> body is absolutely no different from any other so far as the general laws of health are concerned."

BY THE SPRING OF 1948, Marjorie's thoughts had returned to racial issues, concerns that had receded in rural, white New York. She continued to follow southern columnists like John Temple Graves and Hodding Carter, whose long piece in the *New York Times* on March 21 disappointed her.

For all his surgical perception of the South's reluctance to support equal rights and integration—or its militant objection—he, too, was a gradualist. She was angry with Florida's current governor, Millard Caldwell, a segregationist. "I shall have to make a different attack in my attempts to make Southerners realize what they are doing to the Negroes—and to themselves," Marjorie told Norman. In late April, at historically black Fisk University, in Nashville, she addressed a seminar titled "Writing and Folk Materials," part of Fisk's three-day spring festival of music and art. She told James Branch Cabell she had accepted the invitation for three reasons: "I cannot resist any student audience; I wanted to make my small private gesture (praying there would be no touch of condescension) against that strange myth known as 'segregation,' (and the beautiful pale faces and blue and gray eyes and golden or tawny hair of many of my audience did indeed establish it as a myth); and I hoped to be able to take the final step in my own liberation from prejudice. I can only say that I had succeeded in the last." After three days in the home of Fisk's light-skinned president, Charles S. Johnson, and his wife, she said, "I was no longer conscious of race or color, but only of individuals."

Marjorie's compatriots in Fisk's seminar were Arna Bontemps, poet of the Chicago Black Renaissance, now a librarian at Fisk, and moderator John E. Palmer, editor of the *Sewanee Review*. The festival included concerts, a Haitian art exhibit, scholarly presentations, and, especially interesting to Marjorie, a performance by dancer-choreographer-anthropologist Pearl Primus, whom she might have seen perform previously in New York. Primus had been active in civil rights activities before, during, and after the war, believing in the political power of dance. She had first captured national attention in June 1943 when performing in *For This We Fight*, a pageant written by Langston Hughes and featuring Paul Robeson and Duke Ellington, among others, part of the second annual Negro Freedom Rally in Madison Square Garden. Twenty thousand people had witnessed Primus's fluid athleticism, particularly her awe-inspiring leap, "a jump of almost five feet that sent her soaring high above the rafters." This appearance had launched her public career, but in 1944, she had embedded herself in the South as a migrant cotton picker, "to know my own people where they are suffering most."

At Fisk, she was the star of the festival. Marjorie was drawn to Primus, and Primus to her. Also attending was Edwin Embree, president of the Julius Rosenwald Foundation, which had donated millions of dollars toward educating African-American children in the South and supported individual African-American artists Marjorie knew, such as Zora and Katherine Dunham. Embree was about to close down the foundation, but when he saw Primus perform at Fisk, he decided to award one more fellowship—to her—for research in western and central Africa. A few months later, Marjorie received a formal letter from two dancers—Gloria Smith and Georgianna Stamatelos—representing Primus. The Rosenwald Fellowship, together with the Viking Fund, would support Primus for a year and provide sound equipment, they said, but Primus still needed photographic supplies, and they had started a fund. Would Marjorie consider contributing? Most likely she did, and after Primus set out for Africa in December, the women corresponded.

AFTER THE FISK EVENTS, Marjorie returned to Van Hornesville to supervise the last work on her new house. One night in June, she woke up, "and my book suddenly appeared in its complete focus." She was reading the French physicist-philosopher Pierre Lecomte du Noüy's new book, *Human Destiny*. One of the book's purposes was to apply science and mathematics toward proof of "the intervention of a transcendent, extra-earthly force" that would explain life. It addressed readers who wished to understand how their earthly trials could be "integrated in the cosmic order." Every person has a part to play, the author felt: "He is a link in a chain and not a wisp of straw swept along by a torrent." Marjorie pressed the book on Norton. Significantly, it would inform Marjorie's slow-moving novel, whose protagonist, Ase Linden, wonders about the same things.

Later that summer, Idella joined Marjorie in Van Hornesville. One evening in September, the two had an adventure when Marjorie's cat Uki got stuck in the crotch of a tree well up the side of Mount Tom, nearby. The women heard the wailing cat and set out by car in their bedclothes, Marjorie in a satin nightgown, silk bed jacket, and bedroom slippers. At the foot of the mountain, Marjorie, wielding a dim flashlight, climbed straight up through thistles, timber, rocks, and moss, her dog Moe slipping and sliding behind her. Idella stood guard by the car, holding a candle. When Marjorie reached Uki, the kitty felt brave enough to jump down. "Without much to hang onto, I simply could not walk or creep down, and did most of it on my bare rear," Marjorie related to Norton. When everyone was safely at home, Marjorie was surprised by her bravery. She'd let herself go soft, and was glad to know she could still respond to an emergency.

But in terms of writing, the summer of 1948 was mostly a loss. Urged by Carl Brandt, Marjorie worked on a second Lassie story for MGM, but it came to nothing—the studio rejected it, and so did the *Saturday Evening Post*. Once again, she kicked herself and her agent for succumbing to commercial opportunities. She had another diverticulitis attack—a bad one—and Norton came up to drive the animals back to Florida, while Marjorie paid another visit to Dr. Atchley. Word that Zora had been falsely accused of molesting a ten-year-old boy discouraged her, though Scribner had stepped in to help, advancing Zora a weekly living allowance.

In October, *Seraph on the Suwanee*, Zora's novel about white Florida Crackers, was released, dedicated to Marjorie and Mrs. Spessard L. Holland (Mary Holland, the wife of Florida's previous governor, now a U.S. senator). The reviews were lukewarm. But in a Christmas letter to Marjorie and Norton, Zora referenced none of her recent disappointments, cheerfully explaining the "poor white" idioms she had studied for *Seraph* over in rural Dixie County, a sparsely populated area west of Gainesville, fronting the Gulf Coast. At first, she had thought the Crackers were copying her speech, until it dawned on her that the Africans brought to North America had spoken no English and, thus, had copied the whites. "The expressions for the most part are English, held over from the Colonial period," she wrote. "I began to read English literature and found much of the picture talk there. The black face minstrels of the past sold America on the notion that all colorful idioms originated with Negroes. Just stand around where poor whites work, or around the village stores of Saturday nights. There you will hear something." Her ears confirmed what Marjorie had recognized years before: speech dating back to Chaucer's time.

Chapter Twenty-Four

The Cosmic Novel

1949-1950

I N THE NEW YEAR, Marjorie resolved to redouble efforts on her novel. "I may be at a crossroads in my so-called literary career, but Hollywood is not to blame," she told Norman Berg. She was still smarting from the Lassie project. Writing was more anguish than ever, but "I shall not whore it again if I starve, and if the [new] book is not any good, it will not be because there is a taint on it."

She had spoken with Norman about the novel, to be titled *The Sojourner*, and particularly about Ase Linden, the inarticulate central figure—inspired by her grandfather Abram Traphagen—who would become the "frustrated artist and man of thought." This character would both contain and express her obsession with cosmic consciousness. Norman recommended that she read Scott Graham Williamson's new novel, *A Convoy Through the Dream*, a war story in which a man, Eric Clark, leaves his wife to join the merchant marine, determined to challenge and find himself. It explores the effects of war on men, but more so the internal quest of an individual—a deeply psychological, dreamlike inquiry in the spirit of Conrad. Marjorie loved it. It offered her ideas and inspiration for rendering gentle, quiet Ase's heart and soul.

"I have never read a book where the intangible was so articulately made tangible," she responded. "The book is a great shock. I found myself trembling at going so deeply into the dream reality. It is dangerous, and the beginning of death. This, of course, is what killed Williamson." The author had taken a fatal fall at home on Long Island soon after the book was released. Marjorie loved these lines: "Eric was <u>enjoying</u> the sensation of becoming increasingly lost; he was not certain whether this wandering was into the maze of the world or into the caverns of his own secret being. Whichever it was, he wanted to give way to it, to <u>submerge himself with even the vague purpose of lostness</u> before destiny submerged him without any purpose other than its own geometry."

The old friends grew closer, gradually coming to collaborate on Marjorie's "cosmic" novel. As Marjorie had noted, Macmillan had promoted Norman to editor for the southeast region "in recognition of the increasing importance of southern literature to the cultural development of this country." Rather than refer writers to New York, he worked with them directly, "on the ground, to obtain the best result because of the personal equation involved in the production of books." Certainly, Norman was not Max. Where Max would suggest, Norman might opinionate; where Max would gently follow his author's pace, Norman would, on occasion, crack the whip. But, like Max, Norman Berg admired Marjorie, tended a love for her, and wanted to support her. He was a deep, astute reader and shared Marjorie's interest in metaphysical thought, a boon to her in this particular project. Like no one else, he grasped Marjorie's intellectual and spiritual obsessions.

She sent Norman notes she had made two years before, to give him a better idea of her themes. Among them, and those added later, were sketches of the farm and its setting, notes on Gypsy dialect, farm machinery, and flowers. "It will not be enough for this book to be a 'greater work' than *The Yearling*," she told him, "it must be artistic and unified, or it will not be any good at all. The loftiest and most searching ideas are worthless in fiction if they are only ideas. All the thoughts must be spoken through the fictional characters, and those characters must come to life, and seem important, and must resolve themselves into a coherent pattern, and rise to a satisfying climax as to their own destiny and value."

She finally acknowledged the considerable interruptions to her work over more than half a decade: the lawsuit, Norton's wartime absence, five major operations in five years, and, finally, the death of Max Perkins. But everything could have been overcome, she believed, if she weren't so ambitious for this book.

"Do not ever question yourself as a critic," she assured her friend as she prepared to enlist his help. "You are harsh, you demand too much. But when a piece of work satisfies you, you should not have the slightest doubt of your critical ability, having, as you do, your standards, almost too high." Before she gave her papers to the University of Florida—she was now aware of her legacy—she wanted Norman to read the 178 letters she had received from Max, from 1930 to 1947. Norman was interested, but his primary concern was Marjorie's health. He wrote:

> I am very much worried about you. In January you seemed more composed than I have seen you since the war. You knew exactly what you were attempting to do and had the peace of mind with which to do it. Now you are nervous, worried and fatigued again. Something must be done. You cannot stand much more of the mental and physical beating that you are now taking. Perhaps you yourself do not realize that the life you are living is destroying you not only as a creative artist, but as a woman. I hate to say or write these things, because I love you very much, and I know much of the beauty that is within you, but unless you find some sanctuary and solace for long periods of time, from the environment in which you now exist, you are doomed.

Marjorie knew that Norman was right. She replied, "I cannot blame environment, or the life, anything at all, but myself. I may be fooling myself in thinking that the excessive drinking is the effect, and not the cause, of my mental and emotional disturbance—"

She reminded Norman how much she needed a natural background for work and daily life, and vowed to return to it, to save herself. One day, when she was written out, she and her husband might have a "fine quiet time together"—a true retirement.

But she hadn't been ready for that when they married, and she certainly wasn't now. She knew her need for solitude hurt her husband, despite his understanding. She believed he would be happier if she left for the North. "He said the other day that he could not take much more of my desperation. I have been punishing him as much as myself." Norton's discomfort, she added, wasn't for himself—he was worried about *her*. "He offered to disappear early in the morning and not appear again until I was through working. I could not let him do this, as there is no place for him to go, and he has spent such a huge sum on enlarging the cottage, giving me the studio, to make me happy, and it is the first and only home he has ever had, and he loves it, and it is truly <u>home</u> to him, as Cross Creek is to me." She wouldn't blame Norton for her problems.

Norman proposed that excessive drinking was the effect, not the cause, of her disturbances. And there were three effects of drinking: "to transport you to the dream-reality world; to help you bear the surroundings and people who are imposed on you, and a method of relaxation." He approved of the last one, only.

NORMAN STOPPED BY the Creek to read Max's letters and Sigrid Undset's, and was moved by Undset's descriptions of the war and its effects. Her updates explored living conditions in Norway, the specific ways individuals responded to their changed lives, domestic and political—yet she maintained a broad overview of the Cold War. "We are in the middle of a world conflict between two incompatible ways of life, one whose main representative is the USA, the other the Soviet way of life, and all the medium and small nations have to take sides, willingly or by force," she had written. "How long this tension is going to last, and what will be the out-come nobody can tell at present, I should think." Since Undset had returned to Norway, Marjorie had routinely sent her parcels of food—tinned fruit, coffee, tea, cheese, sugar, rice—and personal items: nylon stockings, soap. In one of her last letters, Undset addressed their mutual interest in the natural world, mentioning prophetically, "I don't know if it is the same on the Western Hemisphere—the glaciers are dying all over Norway, Iceland and the Alpine mountains." The previous summer she had visited the Rondane peaks, where she had hiked as a girl, and found them "entirely gray and dead. My Iceland friends tell me whole valleys have appeared where there were glaciers some ten years ago. They say our climate is slowly getting warmer. We may be able to grow citrus fruit in Norway someday, even if I shall not live to see it." Sigrid Undset died fewer than three months later, on June 19, 1949.

In early May, Marjorie, Idella, cat, and dog drove to Van Hornesville in a heat wave—a "ghastly trip"—but all four were happy to be there. "Everything is too beautiful," Marjorie wrote Norman. "The lawn is green, the lilacs will be in full bloom in another week, the peonies are covered with little bug-like buds, the apple trees in blossom along the roads and flung across the hills are almost too much to bear."

Books arrived from Scribner and various friends, one prize a new first edition of Bartram's *Travels Through North and South Carolina*. Marjorie's well-worn copy had fallen to termites at the Creek. Julia Scribner insisted she take up Paul Tillich's *The Shaking of the Foundations*—her husband thought Tillich the greatest Protestant theologian of all time. In all the years, her devotion to Marjorie had never wavered. "When you brace yourself and give yourself over to labor pains," Julia wrote, "remember I am right there at your shoulder metaphysically, giving you moral support."

MARJORIE FINALLY TOOK up Norman's offer to read her start on the new novel, reminding him that her principal character "is almost inarticulate, and almost everything has to go through his <u>thoughts</u>, which may be making for inarticulacy on my own part. And I keep getting off key."

She confessed, "I am afraid, not of criticism, but of the questions you would ask—where I am going—what is my theme—and my experience with "Golden Apples" was so disastrous, talking too much about it in advance with Carl Bohnenberger—that I dread a repetition."

She admitted that she was deeply depressed: "Oh Norman, I have been in such anguish. I came closer to killing myself than ever before, except once, last Sunday night. I have always felt that without my writing, I was nothing. And the writing was going so badly. But I made myself wait, and now it is going better.

"Sexual failure, lack of happiness, none of it matters if I can say the things I want to say—"

She shared new notes for her project—brief meditations on the meaning of life, of death—initiating ongoing exchanges about her characters' psychological states and motivations. Ase Linden, the quiet country philosopher, has a large family to contend with: his arrogant older brother, Benjamin, who rejects the farm and heads west; his widowed mother, Amelia, who worships Benjamin and discounts Ase, even as he supports her; Ase's lighthearted wife, Nellie, who runs an efficient, bounteous household but doesn't share Ase's depth. Of his four children, the one closest to Ase in spirit dies tragically, leaving three others who are, in various ways, bent toward public success and materialism. Those who understand Ase best are outsiders, travelers: the wandering Indian Mink Fisher, the itinerant fiddler Tim McCarthy, a band of Gypsies. Marjorie reminded Norman that when she sent letters to his Atlanta business address, as she had this one, "I am writing privately, and in trouble." He wired immediately: "I love and need you very much—don't ever leave me!" She mailed him an apologetic card and shared the exchange with Norton, commenting, "Of course, Norman doesn't know, as you do, that no matter how far I go into the abyss, I always claw my way out again."

Norton replied,

Norman's reaction to your letter from the depths was touching and understandable and typical. He wants so much to be a part of you and of course would be supremely happy if he could be of any help to you in an editorial way as well as a morale bolstering way.

And by the by . . . the fact that I know that you eventually claw your way out of the abyss doesn't make me any less sensitive to the agonies you suffer while there. So tell me when you are at rock bottom and I promise not to say "O, you'll come out of it," but will have the feeling when you do come up of having suffered with you.

FOR HER FIFTY-THIRD BIRTHDAY, the Youngs threw Marjorie an impromptu party. She spent the morning of August 8, 1949, writing verse inspired by her childhood, when, on her birthday, her mother would wake her up and say, "You may do anything you wish, today."

"I am trying to relate the gift of a day, in childhood, to the terrifying implications in maturity," she mused. She might have meant mortality, as well. The University of Florida would accept her papers in the spring, inaugurating a new creative writing collection, and now she was drawing up her will—an outline from Phil May had just arrived. She felt weak. At her physical exam in Cooperstown, her doctor found evidence of malnutrition. Idella had gone back to St. Augustine for a time to be with her husband, and though Marjorie had hired a local housekeeper, she had been subsisting on "bread and butter and Bourbon" since Idella left. "I cannot bring myself to cook for myself alone," she told Norton.

Devastating news arrived: Margaret Mitchell had been struck by a car in Atlanta and had not survived. Marjorie was incensed by two photographs in the *New York Herald Tribune:* one of Margaret sprawled on the street, the other of the car's driver, "hands on hips, a smirking grin on his face!" She thought them an "indictment of the human race." The first picture proved how much pleasure people take in other's tragedies, "which accounts for war"; the second "sums up all human stupidity." She was sure the driver would be proud to say "I am the guy who hit Margaret Mitchell." A few months later, John Marsh, Margaret's husband, sent Marjorie a photograph of the two women. Looking at it, she said to Norton, "I cannot help wondering whether you husbands of writers don't derive a greater satisfaction from the <u>idea</u> of us, than from our troublesome reality. Of course, Margaret Mitchell was a better wife than I could ever be."

BACK AT THE CREEK, a late August hurricane had wreaked major damage. "The South seems so shabby, so sad, and somehow rather ominous," Marjorie reflected. "Yet I find myself loving all of it as much as ever." With her husband's encouragement, she stayed at the Creek, rather than spend weekends at the beach. Nevertheless, she failed to thrive, and in late November, another intestinal attack came on. She was homesick for Van Hornesville, "yet the Creek, as always, is comforting," she insisted.

A week before Christmas, Leonard Fiddia's five-year-old daughter, Grace, died of leukemia, and Marjorie attended the funeral at the tiny Fort McCoy cemetery, sitting in the front row with the family. (The Fiddias were the family she lived with in 1931 while working on *South Moon Under.*) During Christmas week, she drove out to visit the Fiddias in the Scrub, her car laden with a fresh turkey and all the fixings, to cook for the family in their old woodstove. Rain hadn't fallen for weeks, the miles of sand road between her place and theirs was slippery, and Marjorie had to dig out twice en route. But the meal was delicious, and "Mis' Piety put her thin old arms around me and said 'This is like old times.'"

Marjorie told Norman, "I don't know what inferiority of character is involved, that I am so happy in elemental places and with elemental people. I do know that so-called 'Success' is a curse."

THE BASKINS SPENT Christmas together in St. Augustine, but were apart on New Year's Eve and the start of the 1950s—he at Marineland, she at the Creek. They had decided separately to quit alcohol, at least for a spell. And then Idella received word her husband was in a St. Augustine hospital. Bernard had been badly burned in their apartment below the Crescent Beach cottage. He had smelled a gas leak, struck a match over the pilot, and been badly burned in the explosion. Norton wasn't home; Bernard hailed a passing car for a ride to the hospital. Marjorie drove Idella over to be with Bernard, and on the way to see Norton at the cottage, she picked up a bottle "and lit into it," she confessed to Norman. "Norton was simply furious at me." When she got back to the Creek for dinner, she had two more drinks before opening her mail: "I was in pretty good shape!"

Among her letters was a note from one of her writing protégés, Gene Baro of Gainesville, confirming that he and his companion, artist Albert Stadler, who was painting Marjorie's portrait, would be over that very evening. "They appeared soon after, and I drank more, and more," she continued to Norman. "We went to the kitchen to fix dinner, Gene doing most of it, and before it was ready for the table, I knew that the energy, equilibrium, and equanimity I had left would just get me to bed!" Marjorie fell asleep. The men ate dinner, washed up, and slipped out, leaving a thank-you note.

Two weeks later, Albert Stadler finished his portrait of Marjorie and brought it over. Her first reaction to the painting was "raucous laughter"; the second, fright. Studying it, she saw

with what art Stad had indeed portrayed a schizophrenic soul. What had seemed a meaningless distortion resolved itself into two faces, two aspects of the one soul. The left side, Stad said later . . . is an "inner mask" that he called "the dreamer." The eye is closed and the effect is soft, even tender, and mysterious. The open eye on the other side, at a higher level, is objective, penetrating, quite cold. The mouth and chin are accurate and bind the whole together. I found this encouraging, as it seems to preclude actual insanity! The composition itself, in line and substance, is striking.

She asked Martha Mickens what she thought of it. Martha, who had known Marjorie since she'd arrived at the Creek, answered,

Ain't got my mind composed, but it means a whole lot to me. The way it's looking direct, just like you fixing to pray. Wish he could have had your hands in it. Your hands has meaning.

Just to stand up and look at it, makes you think way back, way back.

He couldn't have done a better thing.

It brings a half-sorrow to me.

Chapter Twenty-Five

Ferment

1950–51

W HEN NORMAN STOPPED BY the Creek in March 1950, Marjorie showed him some pages and he offered suggestions. Yet afterward, she wrote him a blistering note, accusing him of bad behavior one night at a party. "I should be the last person in the world to complain about your freezing up at a gathering where talk took a frivolous turn," she wrote, "for I go much stonier than you at inane parties."

Norman was back at his Dunwoody, Georgia, farm, plowing and harrowing his land, reading manuscripts for Macmillan after dark. "There is so much to be done," he wrote of the farm chores. "It is hard work and such satisfying work." He added, "Dear Marjorie, we have been friends and Platonic lovers for so many years. . . . I thought that I was being very nice and unobtrusive, even well-mannered, when suddenly I was accused of being bored or what have you. Well, I do not believe I showed it, but you sensed it and that's unfair."

Defusing the situation, as Norton would have, Norman continued with ideas for the novel, questioning Marjorie's treatment of Amelia, the bitter, manipulative mother of the protagonist, Asahel Linden. "It appears that you might be taking out your personal vengeance on women in the character of Amelia, and your personal bondage, being a very passionate woman. . . . How long has it been since you 'was woke up' and the earth shook? This isn't a question, I'm just musing. You know that I love you so; it is alright for me to say these things to you. I just feel that I've missed something! Good! Well, this letter is taking a curious turn, so—"

Norman knew of Marjorie's tortured relationship to her mother and certainly to Zelma Cason. By "personal bondage" he might have been referring to Marjorie's marriage to Chuck or her relationship to her work and its effect on her marriage to Norton. Whatever it was, Norman identified Amelia as a narrow target, not a generously formed character, in a far more personal manner than Max would have, or could have, adopted. Here was a possible advantage to engaging a more intimate friend as editor.

MARJORIE PACKED FOR Van Hornesville in early May, without help from Idella, who had left again, for the fourth time in eleven years—and, in this instance, the final time. For all her public support of civil rights, Marjorie hadn't settled on a comfortable public relationship to her "perfect maid." In April, when Mary McLeod Bethune was honored by children at Silver Springs, which had set aside a "colored" beach and play area, Idella attended and identified herself to Mrs. Bethune as "companion to Marjorie Kinnan Rawlings." Marjorie was surprised when she heard about it. "When I want to make Idella feel good, or in impressing any of her friends, I refer to her as my housekeeper," she told Norton. "On checking the facts, I could hardly deny 'companion' as an accurate description of her job. It was a severe test of my liberation from race prejudice."

Idella detached herself in the same week Norton was forced to fire Idella's husband, Bernard, for lackluster work and "tampering with the bar bottles." Bernard went to New York, and Idella followed him, taking all of her belongings except eight maid uniforms, left hanging in her Cross Creek room. Marjorie was furious at first, and attempted to contact Idella until it appeared the break was permanent. Norton sympathized with Idella, but Marjorie was hurt: "I understand her left-over slave psychology, but I had hoped in nearly twelve years of treating her like a white woman, of talking with her about the reasons for race prejudice—on both sides!—she might have brought herself to tell me something approximating the truth, in leaving me this last time." Nevertheless, the uniforms left hanging in the tenant house belied the "like a white woman" claim. In Idella's memoir, assembled many years later, she described disconnecting from Marjorie as a clean, tidy event: the Baskins took her to the bus station, and they parted amicably. It might have been the last scene, but it wasn't the ending. A year after she left, Idella wrote Marjorie in Van Hornesville, asking to accompany her to Florida for the winter. Marjorie didn't trust her, and after a few more letters back and forth, the matter was dropped. Idella asked once more in the summer of 1953, and Marjorie turned her down.

From Van Hornesville, Marjorie sent Norman a progress report, from which he could tell little, because his dog Pooh ate it. She was trying to determine how much Ase Linden, her introspective farmer, should be attuned to the outside world, in matters such as presidential elections or the local Grange. Max Perkins, she said, had felt an individual's story should be told against a broader background or context, which troubled her, since the novel was mostly the story of Ase's mind. "You see, Ase <u>thinks</u> constantly about all mankind and his relationship to it, his thoughts go farther afield than that, into the cosmos. He has a keen conscience, a terrific awareness of good and evil, and where he muffs it, at the end of his life, is in not speaking for what he knows is good and true, because of his inarticulacy, which is a part of his nature." Marjorie finally claimed a valid reason for abandoning outside context. Simply, mundane details cluttered the life of the mind she was trying to express.

She'd clarified her approach after a recent visit with Robert Frost, who had accepted an honorary degree at Colgate University and afterward come to Van Hornesville for a night. "I love him with the same tearing tenderness I feel for Owen D. Young; my heart turned over when I saw him on the 'honorary' platform at Colgate, with his mortar-board altogether too askew on his noble head," she wrote Norton. When Frost asked what her book was about, Marjorie told him it was "pretty much" the theme of his poem "Revelation," and quoted for him the last stanza:

> But so with all, from babes that play
>   At hide-and-seek to God afar,
> So all who hide too well away
>   Must speak and tell us where they are.

But while she thought Frost's poem spoke of the need for direct communication of similar experiences, she was thinking along the more philosophical lines Norman had suggested. "A mature human being, unless he feels and thinks about himself in relation to the rest of mankind and the world, is not too far removed from an animal," Norman had written, in relation to Marjorie's Ase Linden. "Man must have a conscience that is always pricking him inside and this conscience, I think, grows and gnaws more constantly as the years go by." To which Marjorie replied: "Each of us who knows, recognizes, the good, is at fatal fault when he doesn't 'stand up in meeting' and speak for it. And so, we let wars happen—there are enough of us to make a decent world if we were not individually cowardly and lazy. No indeed, the outside world always matters more to Ase Linden than his own life; he knows the great values."

IN MIDSUMMER, when Gene Baro and Albert Stadler visited her in Van Hornesville, Marjorie had what she called a breakdown. She had been working too hard, "collapsed on them and was quite ill." But it had been a good thing, she told Norman, "as I was getting way off the beam." Her manuscript was close to one hundred thousand words. She went to stay with Julia Scribner Bigham's family in Massachusetts, a bit joylessly; she found the Reverend Bigham's formality uncomfortable. She attended Bach concerts at the Berkshire Music Festival: "It fed my soul." Pearl Primus came to Van Hornesville bearing gifts from Africa: an antique knife, carved elephants, Nigerian bookends. For months, she had written Marjorie about her experiences in Nigeria and the Belgian Congo, and the ongoing quest for racial equality: "The fight has not yet begun . . . therefore it <u>cannot</u> be a losing one." Now she enthralled Marjorie with tales of African cultural groups in the bush country. One of her goals had been to trace the roots of the American Negro. "Some of the African tribes believe that there is a vast Divine out in space, and a touch of that Divine in each individual," Marjorie told Norton. The Youngs had Pearl and Marjorie to their home, and Pearl "held them spell-bound." The day before she departed, Pearl insisted that Marjorie change into casual clothes and do reducing exercises with her, for the stomach and hips—

after which Pearl "went as far as she could in teaching me one of the African dances of welcome."

MARJORIE'S HEALTH WAVERED, still. During Pearl's Van Hornesville visit, she had resumed her old habits and had experienced several nosebleeds. She consulted her Cooperstown doctor, who could find nothing wrong and ordered further tests. "Can't seem to find a doctor who will forbid drinking and smoking," Marjorie remarked to Norton. "You have told me how much better your work goes when you leave it alone," he reminded her, "and I know that none of the beauty of your writing comes from the bottle."

A day later, she took a fall on her house stairs—"was cold sober, going down for cigarettes"—and got "fixed up" by a Cooperstown chiropractor. She had just finished reading Hemingway's new book, *Across the River and into the Trees*, and argued against the author's claim that the book's characters were fictitious. "Shit-fire, honey. He has torn Martha [Gellhorn] limb from limb. The way he has done it indicates to me that he still hasn't gotten her out of his system." Norton, too, was disappointed, and if he were Martha, he said, he would write a personal book titled "Life Is Real but Life Ain't Ernest." The Baskins had last seen Martha two years before, when she spent a month in one of Verle Pope's St. Augustine tourist cottages, meeting a deadline. "Martha is one of the most sex-conscious creatures I have ever known in my life," Marjorie had written Julia Scribner. "Fortunately, she is so absorbed in the manuscript that the local husbands are safe."

NOW MARJORIE FOCUSED ON *The Sojourner*'s ending—specifically, whether or not to introduce a new character. "Hemingway says always to stop the day's work when you're at a going point, so that the next day you can get into the swing again," she wrote Norman. "I have done that just now, although I feel that I want to write on and on." She wished to speak with him about the new character—a young boy who would supersede a beloved lost daughter—and why it might or might not work. She might have been inspired by a local boy of eight or nine who had helped her pick wild strawberries, or even by Buddy Bass from the Creek. ("Blast those heart-breaking little boys—") She admitted, "I am at once frightened and thrilled at being so close to the end of my first draft but the book as it stands is so over-written, that I pray I may not be literally caught dead with it."

In mid-October, Marjorie completed a full draft of *The Sojourner.* Norton came up for a week's holiday, then returned to Florida just in time to catch the end of Hurricane King. The storm damaged inland citrus crops and affected tourism along the beaches. Repairs at Marineland and the Crescent Beach cottage nearly wiped out the memory of his pleasant trip north. Marjorie had begun revising the novel, complaining, "The book is not fluid enough. I make too many awkward jumps in time. Much of the book is dull and plodding, and now I must add even more stupid chapters." She had another car accident, and it made the papers. Norman Berg read about it in the *Atlanta Constitution.*

"I was driving very slowly," she explained to Julia. "Was not drunk, and before I had completed my turn on the highway, going toward Van Hornesville, a car came roaring over the knoll that blocks vision completely at the left turn. What a hell of a crash—. Both cars were totally wrecked." The other driver was a Syracuse University student. He asked if Marjorie was the author of *The Yearling* and told her the book was compulsory reading at college. "This is a very great pleasure," he told her. Darkness fell. Marjorie called the highway patrol to send out a man the next morning. It was determined that the blind spot was dangerous, and warning signs would be posted. All agreed that the young man had been driving too fast, but Marjorie took "a slight blame" for not having come to a dead stop.

She stayed in Van Hornesville through November, revising and growing increasingly moody, even accusing Norton of not adapting his life enough to hers. "With my own doubts about my writing, this has been an extra hazard," she complained. She had decided to subject her ego to his happiness, she wrote, "since you are such a lovely person." She mused about Edna St. Vincent Millay, who had been hospitalized several times for drug- and alcohol-fueled breakdowns, and whose devoted husband had protected her writing life until his death in 1949. Millay, headquartered a hundred miles southeast of Marjorie in Austerlitz, New York, had died just two weeks before, on October 19, 1950. She had fallen down a set of stairs and broken her neck. "Why was she all alone with no help at all, only a caretaker who found her some eight hours later?"

Marjorie wondered. Norton made two attempts at a reply before sending a third. "I have become so conscious of—and please, not complaining—your changing moods that I find it hard to write of my picayunish doings. If I could gauge your mood it would not be so bad." He added, "I thought I might write notation on the outside of the letter with such directions as 'To be read before breakfast' or 'To be read in the light of 'I love you' or even, 'To be read through a Bourbon bottle, darkly.'"

Marjorie shared the last chapters of her draft with Norman, hoping for guidance with the ending. The new character, a young Polish man, made sense. In working Ase's land, Jan Rabaski would carry the farmer's "American dream" forward. Norman approved. By late November, winter had come to Van Hornesville, and Marjorie, still revising, admitted that she needed to leave.

BY EARLY FEBRUARY 1951, Marjorie had finished her revisions and sent the manuscript to Scribner. Right away, Julia wrote to Marjorie: "Daddy called me up when he was about two-thirds through your book and he was so full of enthusiasm. He said he really thought it was some of the finest writing you had ever done—that your writing about the country and life in it was truly wonderful, and he was feeling a better man just from having read it." Marjorie replied dolefully, "I seem not to have written the book I wanted to write, as 'the good earth' has apparently taken over, where I intended it only to be a natural background for the story of this particular man's mind."

She sent a copy to Norman, who read it twice and sent by airmail, special delivery, a thoughtfully worded critique. "There is absolutely no doubt in my mind, and there should not be in yours, that a major novel is here," he wrote. "But because of the very nature of the work, the final laboring of it into a convincing artistic novel is a much more difficult and tortuous undertaking than you have heretofore attempted.

"At the present time it is my humble opinion that the work is wooden, i.e., that the characters do not come to life. Neither do they react one against the other determining and forcing each character to his or her inevitable conclusion." He thought the characters were handled "almost as loosely as lives are really lived, where we are all to a great measure strangers to one another."

He added, "However, in a creative literary work it is essential that the characters never be strangers to the reader and that we see them being bent, twisted, matured toward the inevitable end conceived by the novelist."

Norman explained how Marjorie's characters did or did not succeed, and suggested changes in plot and motivation. Specific page notes followed. The whole was nearly a blueprint for a complete revision—he'd taken the same care as Max.

He mailed his notated manuscript to Marjorie, and she thanked him right away:

> The valuable thing you have done for me is to make me think deeply. I am now in that painful process.
>
> At the moment I am in a state of—not quite depression—more, I should say, an angry ferment—. Angry, that I so mistrusted myself on the book as not to think it through more thoroughly in the very beginning—. Ferment, in that I am facing endless unanswered questions and recognize that I must sweat hotter and darker blood to answer them to my satisfaction, to translate them into the combination of reality and mysticism toward which I am struggling.

IDELLA'S EXIT HAD created gaps at Cross Creek, but conditions slowly improved. Though Martha Mickens, now seventy-five, was failing, her daughter Adrenna, who had worked for Marjorie in the past, had returned, along with *her* daughter, who would also care for Martha. A familial atmosphere prevailed. One day, Robert Frost came for lunch and recited some of his poems for Martha, and she sang for him in return. The following week, Norman ran into Frost in Davison's department store in Atlanta. The poet was shopping for luggage. "I walked up to him and introduced myself saying that you and I were old friends," Norman told Marjorie. "His face lit up and he said, 'I've just been at Cross Creek. Isn't it a fine place. We too are old friends and isn't the liquor good!"

A few weeks later, Marjorie went to New York to discuss revisions with Charles Scribner and John Hall Wheelock, who had succeeded Max Perkins as her editor, but not as her literary mentor. She underwent tests at the Harkness Pavilion and was diagnosed with glaucoma—in the early stages, and controllable. In Greenwich Village, she attended

Pearl Primus's new *Dark Rhythms* show at Café Society, the country's first integrated nightclub; black and white patrons were treated equally. Pearl's mother, brother, and husband, Yael Woll, joined her table. Woll, who was white, was also Pearl's publicity agent. *Dark Rhythms* employed some of Pearl's new African material and costumes. "She is magnificent," Marjorie told Norman. "And amazingly, the not-at-all night club stuff was well received."

MARJORIE RETURNED TO the Creek, reveled in the spring. "God's in His heaven and all's right with the world except the people in it," she wrote Norman.

> No, no, only some of the people—. How I long to live for aeons, in an abstract curiosity, to see for myself which side wins. And despite my abstract questioning and what I have decided is my hypocritical will-to-death, (an immature sulking because life has not been as accommodating as I expected and planned) I believe in my bones and my blood that in the end the angels will whip the devils. Yet why should I say "in the end," for the glory of it is that there can never be an end. At least to my way of thinking.
>
> Again, God, to live long enough to know some of the answers. Even the answer to you.

IN VAN HORNESVILLE, Marjorie worked hard at revisions, buoyed and beleaguered by Norman. He lectured her about her drinking, and she swatted back at him. She complained that her housekeeper's three-year-old girl was a noisy and intrusive child. "All my life I have hated little girls," she harped. "This probably goes back to my memory of myself as a nasty little hypocrite, dressed perforce in frills, and to my long fight to attain a dispassionate sexlessness in writing. There must be a plane, aesthetic, intellectual and spiritual, where there is no sex, as the Bible says that there is no marrying in heaven—.

"I refused to be only a biological female. If I had achieved the normal destiny of a woman, which I indeed wanted, to bear children, I might have felt differently." In August, Julia Scribner gave birth to her second child. "Another girl, damn it," Marjorie remarked to Norton. Yet she had been generous with her young niece, Sally Baskin Hooker, who remembered fondly Aunt Marjorie's gifts: a pretty dress, with a matching purse or hat. At the same time, Aunt Marjorie was "a stickler for manners." The pretty dress must remain smooth and clean.

Norton encouraged his wife to take the revision time she needed. "You must not ever think of me as fretting and waiting to come for you. I do miss you and look forward both to your coming home and my going for you but I really never want to hurry you. Last year you were in such a state that I honestly thought that if you were here I could be of help in a quieting sort of way. I learned that lesson, though. Your unhappiness here last winter was heartbreaking. As long as you love me I shall not feel neglected."

Chapter Twenty-Six

Losses
1952

B Y JANUARY 1952, Marjorie was at the Creek with *The Sojourner.* Her household ran steadily, but the grove was a liability. Chet Crosby, her manager, told her that their picking, hauling, and shipping costs would cancel any profit this year. "I am just about down to my capital, which I don't want to touch," Marjorie wrote Bernice Gilkyson.

She had a nightmare about Chuck's aunt Ida Tarrant, ninety-two years old, who now lived in St. Augustine. "It seems so callous of me not to be near her, to say nothing of the much more important matter of failing you in every respect, but I can't help it, Norton, I can't help it," Marjorie wrote from the farmhouse porch, amid draft pages.

Occasional admirers still rambled rural Alachua County's sand roads in search of the famous author's retreat and, when successful, felt they'd earned unannounced peeks at Marjorie, typing at the rustic table Charles Rawlings had fashioned for her more than twenty years before. One couple drove down from Kentucky, the man priding himself on having lifted Marjorie's hush puppy recipe from *Cross Creek Cookery* and creating a commercial mix. "Said when he read my recipe . . . he realized at once it could be marketed!" Marjorie exclaimed. Apparently, an earlier solution to intruders—having Idella, and now Adrenna, tell people she was not well—hadn't been effective.

Daily, Marjorie was so sensitive to even minor interruptions by Adrenna that by the end of January, she was writing letters under the influence ("Heaven knows to whom or about what") and asked Martha Mickens to pray for her. For a moment she "turned all spiritual and noble," but she admitted to Norton she was "not as repentant as I should be, for if I get this job done, I don't care what it takes, and I should sacrifice you, me, anybody and anything to that end, and I _am_ forging ahead, and that is all I give a damn about."

ON FEBRUARY 11, Charles Scribner died suddenly in New York; he had just turned sixty-two. "The loss, while severe, is not that of Max," Marjorie told Norman Berg. "Charlie was a dear friend. Max was part of my thinking. It was perhaps in losing Max that I became more or less inured to death. After too great a wound, there is scar tissue, and one can never feel in that region too acute a pain again."

Loss piled on loss. After Max's death in 1947 had come the deaths of Sigrid Undset and Margaret Mitchell in 1949, and in 1950, Marjorie's close neighbor, Tom Glisson, had died of accidental poisoning. At the turn of 1952, Marjorie's former brother-in-law Jim Rawlings died in Rochester, his obituary noting that he had "remodeled the home at Cross Creek of famed novelist Marjorie Kinnan Rawlings," who had been married to his brother. Among Jim's survivors was a daughter named Marjorie.

And then, not long after Charles Scribner's death, Marjorie was warned of her own mortality. Within two days of completing _The Sojourner_ revisions, she was caught by a severe coronary spasm one Sunday while relaxing with Norton at Crescent Beach. Thinking it was indigestion, she drove back to the Creek. The pain escalated. She could do little but go to bed, wait for Adrenna to come in at breakfast, and send her to a neighbor who could drive to a telephone at Island Grove. Norton was notified. An ambulance took Marjorie to Flagler Hospital in St. Augustine. There she recovered among sweet-smelling floral arrangements, with a healing view of Matanzas Bay, and was given strict instructions never again to pass a certain limit on physical strength and mental tension—a sensible limit only she could judge. Marjorie made light of it for Julia Scribner: "I had planned a perfectly lovely collapse when I finished my book, rather gauging it for Harkness in mid-April, just in time to luxuriate there and then go to Van Hornesville in early May. I certainly never planned on <u>anything</u> like this."

Smoking was forbidden (again); liquor might be enjoyed in moderation, "but for a year or two it will be easier not to take it at all," she told Norman Berg. For all she knew, the night of the coronary, she was dying, and she was relieved to discover that she hadn't been afraid. "Death seemed cold and dark and lonely, but I seemed to be looking down a straight road over-arched by trees, and the road simply went on with no end in sight, and there was no fear or dread or terror in the thought of going down it."

Norman recalled that the first longhand letter he'd received from her, many years ago, had been written from a hospital in Jacksonville, when she'd thanked him for flowers he'd sent. He waxed philosophical: in order to live fully, he thought, one must learn not to fear death. He sent Marjorie a large box of books, to be devoured at Crescent Beach, where she was recuperating, albeit annoyed by Norton's housekeeper, who seemed "hysterical" to her. A favorite book at the moment was one she and Hodding Carter were urging on the Southern Book Parade, a new book club. The other three judges agreed, and *Shiloh* ("by a Shelby Foote?") was selected for May. "It is labeled a 'novel,' which it most certainly is not. I consider it in the great tradition," Marjorie pronounced.

Norman and Julie Berg visited, and Marjorie's old friend again infuriated her. Addressing him as "Dear Bastard Berg," she fumed at him for shouting at her one night at dinner. He sent more books in apology. "I have survived in spite of you," she wrote ungratefully, noting that her manuscript, for which he had served as midwife, was in final preparation. Norman replied, "We had two bad evenings at the beach, but in all justice you should admit that one was not of my making. When I arrived, there you were tight as a tick and dominating, not dominant. The other evening, I am very much ashamed to have had happen."

Marjorie met her April 15 deadline, and by the end of the month, *The Sojourner* was in press. Yet she continued reworking passages in the final chapters, hoping to submit changes before the printers started on the galleys. She told Norman she had stopped drinking three weeks prior, "and hope and believe this time it is for good." But she had said this before.

THE BASKINS HEADED NORTH in late spring, stopping in New York so Marjorie could meet with John Hall Wheelock at Scribner and have Dana Atchley check her heart. *The Sojourner* proofs went to Van Hornesville, and Marjorie set to work. Dr. Atchley had prescribed Dexedrine to help her stay focused, but she refused to take it—its side effects included insomnia and nervousness, and she wrestled with both already. "I have never been so jittery in my life," she wrote Norton. "Literally thought I would blow up, literally." Norman Berg stopped to read the galleys and sent her a pointed list of suggestions and corrections, with enthusiasm: "I have read the ending at least ten times since I left you and each time I am awed by it. It is almost like listening to great organ music. I do not see how anyone can read it and not feel that here is great writing—that it could only come from a truly great artist."

In the midst of the final corrections, word came that Aunt Ida had had a stroke. Marjorie must have felt that the recent nightmare about her adopted aunt equaled a premonition. She completed her last tweaks and took a train down to St. Augustine. Ida had fallen into a coma, and she died within a week. Together, Marjorie and Norton settled her affairs, spending "two unspeakable days" clearing Ida's apartment. "She had saved paper bags and Christmas cards for most of her 92 years," Marjorie remarked. She took Ida's ashes to a family plot in Cincinnati, as promised. "I amazed myself by going to pieces on Aunt Ida," Marjorie reflected. "It was all <u>so right</u>, but we had been friends for nearly 35 years."

MARJORIE'S LIFE HAD always abhorred a vacuum. Almost on cue, the hornet's nest of her brother's life burst open—not for the first time— saddling Marjorie with a situation as bizarre as the kind she had reported on for the *Rochester Evening Journal* nearly three decades before. A few years earlier, Arthur had announced that he had given up his expedition business in Alaska, telling Marjorie to "be prepared to hear of drastic changes." Would he ask his sister for more funds? What of his daughters? He said he yearned for another marriage—he'd been alone for fifteen years.

"The woman I'm considering has enough fine attributes and few enough faults so I feel I'm not able in the future to do better," he wrote. He wasn't in love with the woman but was "very fond" of her. "Her worst fault is her poverty."

Marjorie begged Arthur not to marry, but it turned out that her brother had already remarried and had failed to notify family members. It was the new wife, Grace, already pregnant, who, without Arthur's knowledge, sent the news to Marjorie, but not to their aunts Grace and Wilmer Kinnan in Phoenix, who had made a home for Arthur's eldest daughter, Marjorie Lou. Wilmer suspected that Arthur had been unhappy from the outset—after all, his new wife was a social worker. "Do you know in general what kind of people 'social workers' are?" Wilmer asked, incredulous. "Have you had any very personal experience with the type of person who makes a 'social worker' and loves the work? She probably has neither means or family. And if she is a good Methodist . . . the good Lord help Arthur."

Marjorie was hurt. She and Arthur had always written openly—why should he hide a *marriage*? She replied to the new wife that she hoped Arthur's "great lovability will compensate for the Kinnan neuroticism." Arthur followed up to explain how, two days after "this very hasty marriage," he wasn't sure if he could "cut it or not." He claimed that his wife's letter to Marjorie had been an act of pain and vengeance. Marjorie was furious. She had thought Grace's letter honorable.

"My <u>objective</u> sympathy is entirely with this Grace," she remarked to Norton. "My blood and bones, of course, cry out with distress for Art, wrong and half-crazy as he may be."

Not long afterward, Marjorie received a much longer complaint from Arthur. His main gripe with Grace was her previous sexual experience, most of which he had known about. "She has had two previous husbands, and he said she gave plausible reason for divorcing them, and for 'a few affairs,' then it turns out there'd been more than she had mentioned," Marjorie told Norton. "He said she shows no outward signs of her immoral nature, shows no coarseness, only he's spelled it 'courseness,' and knowledge of her promiscuity is just too much for him, only he spelled it 'permiscuity.' This is the same trick he tried on the second wife Winifred, having known all about her two affairs before he married her, then deciding he didn't approve.

"I am afraid he is six feet four of adolescence, no Galahad he, but hell bent on having, I presume, a passionate virgin." Arthur Kinnan was fifty years old.

And then Grace Kinnan left Seattle, "raising a whirlwind in the going." Still, a child was on the way, and Arthur felt responsible for it.

THE SAGA HAD just begun. In June 1951, Arthur unloaded more complaints against Grace, who had borne a son they named Arthur Jeffrey Kinnan, called Jeff. From Van Hornesville, Marjorie wrote Norton, "What made me furious in his letter was his selfish and casual remark, 'So, I'm planning to be ready to whisk Jeff away, from here or wherever he may be, get him placed, possibly with you.'" It appeared that Arthur would park Jeff with relatives, settle things with Grace, and return for the boy at his own convenience. But, Marjorie wondered, wouldn't taking Jeff constitute kidnapping? And what of a stable home for him? Marjorie examined all the possibilities, which might or might not involve herself and Norton. Accepting the boy indefinitely would be unworkable. And she was afraid that if Arthur left Grace, he'd "go on the hunt for another woman, this time for a suitable mother for Jeff. And I wouldn't trust him to pick a foster mother for a rabbit."

She begged Arthur not to "whisk Jeff away" and reminded him of a family characteristic: unnecessary hysteria, which she shared. She hoped he'd make the best of things until the boy was school-aged. That would be a better time to divorce, and her brother could hope for custody. And if neither parent proved fit, she and Norton could take Jeff permanently. "That would be worthwhile, and since it would be a <u>stable</u> thing, I could make an adjustment that would not wreck me or my damned writing," she told Norton. "It doesn't help us neurotics to be reminded that our tail-spins don't take place in a self-centered vacuum! Anyway, I did my best."

Marjorie offered to take Jeff in an emergency, but privately she felt that Arthur didn't deserve help or sympathy. "I don't believe this blind family 'standing by'; it only makes the weak weaker. I believe in fighting one's own battles. All of this is his own fool fault, when God knows he is old enough to have known better. He won't live too long, he will burn himself out, and I am more concerned about that little boy than I care to admit." Arthur wrote angrily to Marjorie, rehashing complaints about his wife, then praising her appearance as "just what I idealize in a woman." He had sought advice from two Seattle psychiatrists, who at first thought him perfectly normal and later diagnosed "basic emotional problems which, although not acute, are nevertheless severe enough to warrant a recommendation for prolonged psychotherapy." Marjorie would have urged therapy on Arthur, but Dana Atchley doubted its efficacy. "A lot of it has proved to do more harm than good," she wrote to Norman. Now Grace had taken a job, and Arthur was working at home to care for Jeff. But the marriage unspooled. Grace sued for the house, maintenance, and custody of Jeff. Arthur hoped to move the case from Alaska, his base for conducting seasonal hunting and fishing tours, to Seattle, where he'd have a better chance at custody, but would settle for visiting privileges. He feared that Grace would turn the boy against him, as he said Marjorie Lou's mother had done.

By October 1951, Arthur had reached a truce with Grace and hoped psychiatry would help *her*. He'd applied for a real estate license, intending to make good on Vashon Island, where a bridge from Seattle over Puget Sound might be built, increasing the demand for homes. He was divorcing Grace and had retained a lawyer, who advised him not to run away with Jeff. And he had spent the $500 loan Marjorie had sent him— could she spare more? "I feel more strongly than ever that our father should have been castrated and our mother spayed," Marjorie remarked to Norton.

WITHIN A FEW MONTHS, Marjorie was forced to field frantic phone calls and letters from Arthur, her Kinnan aunts Grace and Wilmer, and Norton, about the fates of Arthur and little Jeff. In the middle of June 1952, when Marjorie was in Van Hornesville, Arthur called Norton from Seattle, saying he and Jeff were accepting Marjorie's offer to stay at the Creek and would fly down to Florida the very next day. Did this trip amount to kidnapping? Marjorie and Norton didn't know what to call it, but later on, the facts emerged: Grace, who had custody of Jeff, had allowed Arthur to take the boy for the Memorial Day weekend, and the pair had vanished, launching a Seattle-based search. When Norton met his brother-in-law's plane at the Jacksonville airport, Norton reported, "There was six foot four of Arthur with a ten-gallon Stetson on and holding the most angelic looking child you ever saw." Norton installed them in a motel near Marineland, and when he met the pair one morning, he found Jeff throwing a tantrum. "Arthur spoke of a psychiatrist because he was so afraid that the tantrums were hereditary," Norton wrote Marjorie. Presumably, Arthur would blame his wife's genes. "Tell Arthur that if tantrums are hereditary, Jeff gets it straight from him," she replied. "Art was famous for them his first few years of life. He would kick and scream to be carried downstairs. Mother would simply <u>drag</u> him down the stairs, and he would turn right around and scramble up again, and kick and scream to be carried down—."

The boy and his father were bone-tired. Norton didn't know what to say to them. Arthur's divorce wouldn't be final until September. The question of Jeff's custody hung in limbo, and financially, Arthur was unstable. He had no job, but he talked of "establishing" himself in Seattle or Madison. (Marjorie: "I kept myself from remarking acidly that Mother is not in Madison—. I have wondered if that is what he is hunting so futilely—the Puritan Mother who impressed it on him that a 'nice' woman is not 'passionate.'") Phil May advised Arthur to forfeit his boat's mortgage, which Marjorie held; the title would then be passed to her. Norton registered more Kinnan volatility when he overheard Arthur verbally abuse the boy in an effort to potty-train him. Yet the same safe harbor Norton provided for his wife, he offered to these two. He found a day nursery for Jeff, giving the youngster a break from the exclusive relationship with his father and giving Arthur a chance to relax.

At the end of July, Arthur and Jeffrey boarded a train for Baltimore, en route to Van Hornesville, and when father and son arrived, Marjorie was aghast. "I have never seen anything so pitiful as that great hulking stricken ruined man, looking twenty years more than his age, nursing so tenderly the beautiful child. Arthur's love for, and obsession with, the boy, is actually terrifying. . . .

"It is all totally mad. . . . Instead of stopping cigarettes and liquor, I have just bought a fresh carton and a fresh bottle—"

Within a week, Arthur had gone to Syracuse, hoping to start a gun business. Now that Marjorie had seen him, she agreed with Norton that her brother would never win custody of Jeff. They worried that Arthur would go bankrupt, especially if he continued running from place to place with the boy. But for the moment, they could let things be. Marjorie was entertaining, cooking, gathering berries in the upstate countryside. She bought a pair of jeans for berrying, "and while I could get them on," she told Norton, "I could not possibly bend nor stoop in them but they will serve for high picking." She had tied up loose ends on *The Sojourner* and paid Robert Frost a visit in Vermont, tucking the page proofs into her suitcase. When the poet asked her "infinite questions" about the book, she offered to read two chapters aloud. "So I did, and the next morning he said I should either have read most of the book, or nothing at all, as he had stayed awake, 'wondering what you're up to and where you're coming out.'" She and Frost discussed their troubles with depression. "I had said to Robert that what kept me going was the feeling that one was obligated to fight in one's small way on the side of the creative, not the destructive, forces, and Robert said 'I've never quite committed suicide. I figure as long as you can <u>make</u> something, if it's only a basket, the whole business is worthwhile.'"

Marjorie next checked on Arthur in Syracuse and was told at the shabby boardinghouse that father and son had been evicted the day before and moved on. "Nice as the man is, and the boy too, I couldn't stand the organized confusion," the landlord said. When Marjorie found her brother, she was relieved to see him a little steadier than he had been. A woman who had cared for welfare children was keeping Jeff while Arthur made his rounds. But it appeared Syracuse wasn't a good choice, and Arthur had decided to go west again, to revive his film and photography business, try selling guns, and finish the divorce negotiations. He finally admitted that he might lose custody of Jeff. It would be nearly unbearable to him.

On the way back to Van Hornesville, Marjorie stopped in Rochester to visit friends and look in on Jim Rawlings's widow, Olive, and the two daughters, including the one named for her. To Norton, she reported, "Marjorie Kinnan (Godamnit) looks like Jim and is quite pretty and is the whole show, the most terrible exhibitionist and as mealy-mouthed as her mother." The girl "was all over me, and asked if she might kiss me, snuggled beside me, announced that I was her great-aunt and that she was named for me, and said, 'You didn't send me anything for my birthday.' As you know, I have never done anything for my namesake. . . . The whole set-up gave me the same sense of gold-digging that I get from Arthur's daughters." She sent a similar account of the visit to her old friend and nemesis Zelma Cason, who had known Jim Rawlings in the early days. Miraculously, Marjorie and Zelma were back on speaking terms.

As if anticipating her need, Julia Scribner sent Marjorie the Book of Common Prayer and a collection of St. Augustine's prayers. "I read night and morning in the Common Prayer and say either the Lord's Prayer or a despairing one of my own, hoping for some sign of grace," Marjorie told her. "It has not yet come but surely it will. I don't understand what I might call my spiritual sterility. It is not a matter of crying, 'I believe. Help thou my unbelief,' for I do believe. But I have a sullenness which I should be unwilling to offer."

Chapter Twenty-Seven

"Down"
1952-53

NINE YEARS TO THE MONTH after *The Sojourner* was begun, in August 1943, it was finished. Julia Scribner acquired a rough bound copy and sent it to Norman. The last time he had stayed at the Creek, Martha Mickens had asked him the title of the new book. He read her the epigraph, a verse from First Chronicles: "For we are strangers before thee, and sojourners, as were all our fathers: our days on the earth are as a shadow, and there is none abiding." He placed a bookmark in the Bible so she could find it again.

Publication was set for January 4, 1953. The Literary Guild of America selected it, but the Book-of-the-Month Club turned it down. Now came the quiet period before reviews appeared, but as was always the case with Marjorie, there would be little time to lie fallow, to let the well fill, as Ellen Glasgow had recommended. Another project was waiting in the wings, and this time it was Glasgow herself. Four months earlier, Norman had written Marjorie about a meeting with Gilbert Govan, a longtime librarian at the University of Chattanooga and an authority on the Civil War. According to Norman, Govan had been singularly responsible for Ellen Glasgow's Pulitzer Prize, and he asked Govan if he thought a biography of Glasgow might be a good idea. Yes, Govan said, and Marjorie should be the one to do it.

Norman knew Marjorie's mixed feelings about biographies, but once *The Sojourner* was out the door, she decided to take it on, and in August, Scribner made her a gift of the last twelve-volume Virginia edition of Ellen Glasgow's work. Marjorie planned to spend at least a month that fall in Richmond, talking with Ellen's friends and family, conducting library research. "I shall not hurry the book <u>in any way</u>," she wrote Norman. Irita Van Doren encouraged her; important contacts in Richmond were enthusiastic. "It seems to be 'in the cards,'" Marjorie remarked, although one obstacle was already clear: at her death, Ellen had requested that her memoirs be published "as soon as might be," but not as long as anyone living might be hurt—which could mean a delay of years. Ellen's completed manuscript, *The Woman Within*, was among her papers. Would Marjorie be allowed to read it? James Branch Cabell, upset about Marjorie's projected biography, acted "as though I intended to rush into print overnight, ahead of the memoirs. I couldn't miss the chance to remind him that of all my friends he alone kept jabbing at me because I took so long to write and re-write *The Sojourner*." Cabell soon came around.

But first Marjorie would take an overdue vacation with Norton in October, setting sail from New York to England and Ireland on the SS *United States*, a new luxury liner. Marjorie had preferred a "slow, cheap boat." Norton looked for a "moderately inexpensive one" and, finding such passages full, booked first class on the *United States*, sparking another long-distance argument with his wife. "I am sure that my fatigue is responsible for my private balkiness," she told Norman. "Probably the quiet ocean trip and the slow driving around those beautiful countries will fix me up."

In Van Hornesville, preparing for the trip, Marjorie thought to petition the Alachua County School Board to allow one of the Mickens children to ride the white school bus to Hawthorne. She explained that the child's mother could work only part-time until February (when Marjorie returned to the Creek) and couldn't afford boarding along the Negro bus route as before. "I believe the state law requires 'equal facilities' in education for white and colored," Marjorie wrote the school board, "but of course a colored bus could not detour for just one child." She assured the board that the child would be "modest and unobtrusive." Her request was denied. In response, Marjorie wrote an account of the story for the *New York Herald Tribune*, which earned her praise from civil rights leaders and embarrassed the school board into reversing its decision.

As well, Marjorie hired Owen Young's secretary to help her clear correspondence, and on the way to meet her one day, she had another car accident. She admitted to Norton that she had "lit out way too fast and skidded around the curve" between her property and her neighbors,' "lost control of the car, went through the Redjives' barbed wire fence and over the stone wall, and took down a telephone pole, snapped right in half. Car motor all right but left fender and headlight well smashed." All telephone service in the area went down, and a neighbor offered Marjorie coffee and cake while the driver of a passing bread truck went for help. Except for a few bruises, Marjorie escaped injury. "My admiration for the Oldsmobile increases with every wreck," she told Norman. "Of course, these accidents are all impulses to suicide, except that I really don't ever mean to do it that way—it is likely to be both painful and messy. There are other more pleasant alternatives, such as running away." Her friend replied, "I know what you write about your automobile accidents is true and some day it might happen, and, of course, there are no answers or solutions because one cannot even run away from oneself."

THE SOJOURNER APPEARED after New Year's. Coleman Rosenberger for the *New York Herald Tribune* summarized the novel thus:

> Marjorie Kinnan Rawlings has written the story of one man's life, and in the telling has endowed it with a measure of significance for every man. Asahel Linden, whose story she tells, was a farmer, living out his 80 years from the 1860s to the 1940s, but the elements of his story are as timeless as the continuing search of mortal men for certitude and understanding and brotherhood. Mrs. Rawlings' talent as a storyteller—her ability to evoke character and mood, to create a narrative of sustained interest—is widely and affectionately known. This talent is abundantly evident in *The Sojourner*.

Paul Jordan Smith of the *Los Angeles Times* compared Marjorie to Thomas Hardy. "Precious to her are those eternal verities that proclaim man's kinship to his earth," he wrote. "The coming year is unlikely to produce a finer novel."

Naturally, references to *The Yearling* appeared. The *Miami Herald*, partial to Florida's famous writer and her Florida subjects, wrote, "She has the gift of identifying her people with their environment so that they seem to grow together, to be a part of the same thing. It gives her work an epic quality that places it on the level of some of the great Russian novelists. But," the unsigned critic opined, "the book is no *Yearling*." Louis Bromfield for the *Saturday Review* praised the new novel but said he missed "the lift of *The Yearling*. It was as if the earlier book were written out of the heart because the author *had* to write it." In *The Sojourner*, he detected parts that read "as if the author felt she must go ahead and finish it."

Every commentator bowed to Marjorie's luminous prose. "Mrs. Rawlings can make a small poem about four kinds of honey on a table," one remarked. But the most craft-conscious critics addressed, in various ways, the challenge of portraying a virtuous character whose only flaw is introversion, or an inability to speak up. Paul Engle, a poet and the director of the Iowa Writers' Workshop, pointed out *The Sojourner*'s roots in traditional sagas—like that of the brothers Jacob and Esau in Genesis, noting, "The book is really as much of a legend as it is a novel." But in Engle's reading, "Ase is so saintly a character, so dedicated to absolute good, that the reader hardly believes in him as a man." Gilbert Highet, in the *Atlantic* disagreed: "Only a skillful and sensitive writer can make such a man come alive as the center of a book." It was "by the way in which others talk to him, by their love or hatred or contempt or loyalty toward him, we discern very clearly what kind of man he is; and as he works the farm year after year and faces the recurrent crises of raising a big family and fighting a selfish mother, we see the land and the people through his eyes, so that, even without his speaking, we can share his experience fully and eloquently." John K. Hutchens, for the *New York Herald Tribune*, took another angle: "Since Ase is no conversationalist . . . much of the tale takes the form of internal monologue, which gives Mrs. Rawlings free rein to write out of her own eloquent vision." Orville Prescott of the *New York Times* ventured one step further: "Sometimes when Ase is meditating on the world and life and time his own identity merges with his creator's and the thoughts expressed seem Mrs. Rawlings', not his own."

Sterling North, in the *New York World-Telegram*, concluded, "*The Sojourner* is a noble attempt to portray with sympathy the meek, who, alas, have not yet inherited the earth."

ALTHOUGH MARJORIE HAD expected comparisons to *The Yearling* and felt she had fallen short of her ambition for *The Sojourner*, she was dismayed by critics who misunderstood the new novel, and ultrasensitive about it. "Although you warned me, and I was somewhat prepared, it is a little hard to take," she wrote Norman. Yet she thought "the complete lambasting I am taking to date is a good omen. There were 'rave' reviews about my lesser books, long ago, books that will die, decently, I hope; and I have held the theory that the best work of most creative people, artists, sculptors, musicians, writers, is not appreciated at the moment of presentation. I am humble about my work, as you know, and as you know also, I have no mock modesty. *The Sojourner* is a major novel, for all its faults. I shall stand or fall on that." She acknowledged a few comparisons to Steinbeck's *East of Eden*, which Norman had sent her after its September release. She'd read it during the Baskins' return passage on the *Mauretania*. ("It is magnificent, more beautifully and poetically written than almost any other of his books beloved by you and me," she'd commented.) But she herself wasn't given to weighing her work against another's. Norman once told Norton that Marjorie was the only author he knew who was "without envy."

Marjorie had expected *The Sojourner* to be much more appreciated across the sea. A critic (signed W.C.G.) for the *Kemsley House Evening News* couldn't have pleased her—or any American writer, including Steinbeck—with his brief, withering assessment: "Another of those long, analytical novels favoured by so many American writers is *The Sojourner*, by Marjorie Kinnan Rawlings. Character dissection down to the last quivering nerve is the formula now becoming familiar in transatlantic fiction, and this one is a dramatic example." Yet a Welshman was among the many readers who admired the book and wrote to Marjorie. "I have never laid down a book with more regret and more gratitude," Geoffrey Marshall wrote.

If I interpret your book and my own life correctly it seems that some people go through life with a burden of love. With a staggering load of love for which they search receptacles. And most of these receptacles resent the intrusion. They are full of other things. Full of yearnings for nylons and chromium plated things which will make the neighbors jealous, and the love which you would dump in their lives like a coal man dumps sacks of coal in the coal box, is not wanted and is resented. And you still have a heart or a soul or something inside you foaming over with the desire to serve and to give and to help and to enjoy the flowers together with.

May your life run full and may the spirit which inspired <u>The Sojourner</u> always and forever abide with you as I will try to have it forever abide with me.

NORMAN WAS TROUBLED by most of the reviews and felt that Coleman Rosenberger had come closest to understanding *The Sojourner*. Still, he wondered why the critic hadn't caught the "man in relation to the cosmos" theme, which flowers so fully at the end. He still believed the novel Marjorie's best, "but," he conceded, "it will be hard for reviewers and the public to dissociate from straight narrative and understand that you are writing something very much more mature and important than the message in <u>The Yearling</u>."

Marjorie would give her book due diligence in mid-January in New York, appearing on radio programs, giving interviews for the *Times*, the *Herald Tribune*, and others, and speaking at the *Herald Tribune* and the American Booksellers Association's Book and Author Luncheon. But she was in no mood to talk about her own work: "I shall brazen it out and fool the boys by talking about the work of other writers!" She spent one quiet evening with photographer and writer Carl Van Vechten and his wife, actress Fania Marinoff. Marjorie and Van Vechten had corresponded for several years, the two addressing each other as "Cousin" after discovering a very distant kinship. This night, Cousin Marjorie sat for Cousin Carl. She liked most, she told Norman, the image "in the Chinese coat facing straight into the camera with the hands somehow a bit Chinese, probably the pose during which you laughed and said, 'You look like the Dowager Empress of China.'"

Norman continued to send Marjorie new, admiring reviews, which she appreciated—and, indeed, the book had "crawled" to the best-seller lists. But by early February, Marjorie was in Richmond, pursuing Ellen Glasgow's life story. "<u>The Sojourner</u> is already part of my past," she told him.

"THE CREAM OF RICHMOND is curdled with malice and indiscretion. They tell me all they know and do not know about Ellen Glasgow and try like mad to pump <u>me</u>," Marjorie wrote Julia Scribner. She had rented a house in the city for the late winter of 1953 and hired a full-time typist, who tapped away in a spare room, at enough distance so that Marjorie— organizing notes, reading materials from the University of Richmond library, copying important correspondence, and arranging interviews— could barely hear the ding of the carriage return. Her idea of "leisurely" research had been quashed as soon as she arrived. Even precious caches of Ellen's letters were a burden—the late author's handwriting was difficult to decipher.

It seemed all of Richmond knew that Marjorie was in town to research Ellen Glasgow. This included Glasgow's close friends (elderly, to be handled "with kid gloves") and the literary figures who invited her to lunch or tea or cocktail parties, granted interviews, divulged memories, gossiped and fibbed. As well, average citizens had read about Marjorie's project in the papers: the famous writer was in residence to write about their own famous writer. In her first week, Marjorie went shopping downtown at Miller & Rhoads department store, where she spoke with another customer. "I said something about filing research notes, and she said, 'Why, you must be Mrs. Rawlings, doing the Glasgow book!'" At the book counter, a saleswoman recommended *The Sojourner*, "and I said I had a copy, as I had written it," she told Norton. "The heads of the department store were called and I was most welcome."

Norton kept the home fires burning. In early February, he briefly entertained Dale Wills, who as a boy, seventeen years before, had inspired "A Mother in Mannville." Wills was traveling in the area and stopped by the cottage, staying for just a few minutes when he learned that Marjorie wasn't there. Other than that, Marjorie's world affected Norton very little. For entertainment outside Marineland, he had bought one of the new television sets, but he found programming thin. "I am happy to report that it is not going to be the time robbing element in my life that I thought it was going to be," he told his wife. "There is so much more on it that is bad than good that you just have to pick your programs." At one point, he grew annoyed with "a horrible country store program" and moved to shut it off, until he noticed his housekeeper and her daughter in the doorway, wide-eyed. "They stayed through a child's program called Howdy Doody which should insult the intelligence of a four-year-old," he said. "I won't get trapped like that again."

Because the couple communicated more and more by telephone, Marjorie was as likely to call Norton as write, often when she had been drinking. "Sorry that you lost a short skirmish to the bottle and hope that you have retaken the hill," he wrote after a call. Another time: "Darling, when you call me in the middle of the afternoon when you have obviously been drinking more or less heavily I freeze up and can't help it. You should know it by now and it isn't a thing I can control. I wish I could. I know that my reaction does not help but there it is."

In mid-March, Irita Van Doren came to Richmond and Marjorie threw a cocktail party for her with eighteen members of the Richmond literati in attendance. In April, Marjorie returned to Florida satisfied, finally, by "the most amazing results" in Richmond and planning to return in the fall. Some of her sources had just begun to warm to her. Even so, she wrote Norman Berg, "I am still on the thinnest ice." Now she turned to a project for the *Los Angeles Times*: a five-part retrospective on her writing life, which ran on Sundays, from April 26 through May 24. Of her published works, she said, "None of my novels has satisfied me. *The Yearling* is probably the most coordinated of my books. Its theme is direct and simple." She was "reasonably satisfied" with three recent short stories. "The short story form permits of a maintained subtlety and a certain roundness," she explained. "Robert Frost said to me not long ago that a piece of creative work has to have roundedness. He said, 'There's big roundedness and little roundedness, but if it comes out rounded it's all right.'" But, she thought, "complete roundness, complete perfection in writing is possible only in a poem, and not too long a poem at that." She predicted that it would take her several years to write the Glasgow biography, but she hoped to follow it with another novel and more short stories. "And that is about all I can say about my life and work thus far," Marjorie concluded.

As the *Los Angeles Times* series was about to go to press, Marjorie wrote to the *St. Augustine Record*, objecting to a racist incident at the beach. The Henry Seidel Canby family, frequent visitors to the area, had brought a West Indian nursemaid for their grandchildren, and one afternoon, the woman went for a swim in the ocean, "unaware of the local custom, whereby colored bathers are expected to go to Butler's Beach several miles south." A neighbor reported her, and a deputy sheriff appeared and arrested her, calling her a "nigger" several times. Canby was as puzzled as the nursemaid and explained the situation to the deputy, who released her. "I myself do not know the nature or legality of the restrictions as to race that apply to St. Augustine Beach," Marjorie wrote. "What concerns me is, not to call it by so harsh a name as brutality, the lack of simple courtesy and good manners on the part of a representative of the Law." Had the officer extended civil questions, and informed the woman that "her presence on this beach, unattended by her charges, was locally unwelcome," a conflict might have been avoided. "It is such a great pity that Dr. Canby will have to report such ungraciousness in our community," she said in closing. She was livid, but she knew her local audience. A polite complaint might be heard here, while an angry one would not.

FOLLOWING THE *Los Angeles Times* retrospective, Marjorie accepted an honorary degree from St. Lawrence University in Canton, New York. Norton and the Youngs accompanied her. Norman Berg chided Marjorie about the honor, as if he thought better of her. "It takes very little time and no effort at all to receive them," she replied,

> and it seems to me that it is as the woman answered to the objection to wearing diamonds in the daytime, "them as has 'em wears 'em." I have had a life-long inculcated respect for the Groves of Academe, and I consider an honorary degree a far higher and purer honor than a book club choice or a Pulitzer prize, for these latter are competitive and relative, while a degree from a college or university of any repute is a detached and academic tribute to a general body of work.
>
> And because of my deep devotion to Owen D. Young, I am especially touched to receive such an honor from his own university.

Norman continued ruminating on *The Sojourner*, having reread it a third time. He still thought it a major work, that no one at Scribner "knew or even knows now what the book is about, nor do I think they believed in it." Marjorie offered him the extra carbon of the second draft of *The Sojourner;* the rest of the novel's materials had already been turned over to the University of Florida. He accepted it, with gratitude.

AFTER THE St. Lawrence University award, Marjorie's family affairs took center stage. Her Aunt Wilmer, seventy-one, had had a major operation, and Marjorie flew to her side. Arthur finally wrote to Marjorie. The business with Jeff was not settled. He and the boy were still hiding out from Grace, and he didn't say where. It had now been more than a year since he'd picked up his son for a Memorial Day outing and fled.

Neither he nor Marjorie knew that Grace planned to hire a private detective.

Dismayed and distracted, Marjorie occupied herself in Van Hornesville by socializing with the Youngs and berrying. Norton was back in Florida. She acknowledged how often she had tested his patience. "The horrible thing that gets me in its grips is of course a form of mental illness. No one knows a thing about it who isn't subject to it, and such another person could scarcely help, except that everybody could cry together," she explained. She had just finished reading Sherwood Anderson's letters, "and he went through the same thing. A great part of it is the writer-not-at-work." Norton tried to be helpful. He was concerned about his wife's eating habits. "I have found some wonderful frozen individual chicken pies which I think you would like. They come in a little foil container and you just slip them in the oven frozen and presto you have practically a full meal. You simply must eat properly. Who told you how to breathe before I took over?"

COME OCTOBER, Marjorie was in Richmond again, this time at the elegant Jefferson Hotel ("where I could entertain the old ladies"), continuing her Glasgow research and the endless socializing it required. "I finished my job of ingratiating myself with the last three 'hold-outs' and was rewarded with rich and sometimes shocking material," she told Julia Scribner. The hotel expense was tax-deductible, she added. She couldn't have known it, but this would be her last trip to Richmond.

In early December, the Associated Press reported that Jeffrey Kinnan had been found with his father on Vashon Island, after an eighteen-month, continent-wide search. "The child was produced on a writ of habeas corpus obtained by the mother after a detective agency told her the father, Arthur H. Kinnan, 53, was keeping him on the island." A hearing was set for December 9. Jeff would remain with caretakers while Arthur worked "as a real estate salesman." At the hearing, Grace Kinnan was awarded custody. The saga was finally over.

Norman visited the Creek briefly that week. "It is almost a year that *The Sojourner* has been published," he wrote Marjorie afterward. "I think you are right about what the book needed, but I seriously doubt that you had the strength for any further revision." He felt that had he pushed Marjorie further, she would have taken her own life: "Your last reserve measure of strength was about used up." The book began slipping in the middle, but "in some unfathomable way," she had pulled it together at the end. "Another six months added and you would've had the book as you wanted it, but even as it stands, it is a credit to you. Time will tell!"

Then he turned somber, reflecting on his recent visit. "I lay awake a good part of the night at the Creek. Somehow it is not as it used to be. You own the place, but now only possessively; you do not live there anymore. You have grown alien to it and only the closeness you and it have known in the past, keeps alive the warm association."

A FEW NIGHTS AFTER Norman wrote, on Friday, December 11, or Saturday, December 12, Owen and Louise Young entertained Norton and Marjorie at Washington Oaks, their home near Marineland. No doubt drinks and dinner were served, and afterward, the quartet enjoyed some hands of bridge. In the midst of what—a deal, a bid, a play?—Marjorie flagged, complaining of a severe headache. Offering apologies, she and Norton departed for Crescent Beach, but soon afterward, Norton rushed his wife to Flagler Hospital. She'd suffered a stroke.

Over the weekend, Norton drove back and forth between the hospital and Marineland, visiting Marjorie and seeing to his work. But by Monday, Marjorie had declined precipitously. Her overall health and habits made her especially vulnerable to a second, fatal stroke. And so it would come.

At the end of *The Sojourner*, Marjorie's quiet, philosophical Ase Linden is flying home from Seattle, having finally found his errant brother, Benjamin, dying in a poorhouse. He folds his hands over the box of ashes on his lap. "More than ever Ase felt that men were not held to earth, and by it, but were crushed there by an imponderable vastness. The tallest trees could grow no taller, not that their roots chained them, or the force of gravity, but because their strength was unequal to the greater pressure. The earth had thrust up its mountains as high as possible, and the mountains were collapsing not from below but from above, as though the kind firm hand of a master pressed on a dog and a great voice said quietly, 'Down.'"

Marjorie died on Monday evening, December 14. She was fifty-seven.

As Norton, stunned, quietly planned his wife's funeral, news of Marjorie's death spread across the country and around the world. Norman and Julie Berg heard about it on the radio. Pearl Primus reportedly fainted at the news. Others read it in the papers via the wire services on December 15. On the sixteenth, a version of the AP story succinctly marked the funeral and Marjorie's time in Florida: "Today she will be buried in the moss-hung Florida swamp country about which she wrote and which brought her misery, happiness and fame." A service was held in St. Augustine at Craig Funeral Home, the rites administered by the rector of Trinity Episcopal Church, the Reverend Charles Seymour. From St. Augustine, the funeral cortege set out on a seventy-mile drive southwest, passing over the St. Johns River, through forests and the lake region west of Palatka, to tiny Antioch Cemetery, near Island Grove. The sky was sunny and blue, the air crisp. About fifty people, many of them Marjorie's neighbors, attended the interment, standing in the sandy soil, among scrub oaks and pines.

The *New York Times* published a long, fitting obituary, praising Marjorie's "skill in reproducing the color, characters, speech, local customs and way of life of the backwoods of Florida."

"It was the Florida of hammock trees and palmetto and alligator hunters that made Mrs. Rawlings famous," the writer commented.

"She did not produce a great deal in twenty-two years, considering the demand for her every line.

" 'Writing is agony for me,' she once told an interviewer. 'I work at it eight hours every day, hoping to get six pages, but I am satisfied with three.' "

No member of the press or the general public knew exactly what contributed to that agony, but those close to her did—what it took to make good on her 1928 promise to write in and about Florida, or quit.

IN THE DAYS FOLLOWING, Norton received an abundance of condolences from near and far, from private folks and public figures who had been deeply affected by Marjorie's books, whether they had read them in English or in one of the many translations published around the globe. At the close of 1953, Eleanor Roosevelt spoke for many in a column remembering Marjorie: "Her novels have brought so many people pleasure that it is a real sorrow to us to think that nothing more will come from her pen to delight us in the future." The outpouring prompted the epitaph Norton Baskin chose for Marjorie's tombstone: "Through her writings she endeared herself to the people of the world."

Chapter Twenty-Eight

Legacy

I choose to call beauty anything that stirs an emotional reaction to such an extent that you're conscious of the spiritual excitement over and above the sensory perception. You see the leeway that definition gives me.

It means that beauty is not absolute but is distinctly relative and that what fails to stir me may constitute beauty for you.

It means too that beauty is more valid, more important, more trustworthy, than truth. Because while we cannot be sure of truth, we know, with our own minds and senses, when we are aesthetically or spiritually stirred, and by what.

The artist is one who tries to share, by giving it concrete expression, the particular form of beauty that has stirred him.

—Marjorie Kinnan Rawlings,
From notes for a talk, "The Relativity of Beauty"

DEEPLY MOVED BY RURAL FLORIDA, Marjorie Kinnan Rawlings found it beautiful, and she strove passionately to express that beauty. In her work, one feels the breeze in the pines, catches the elusive fragrance of magnolia blooms, hears the *cheer-cheer* of a cardinal or the crack of an axe in a forest. The inner lives of her principal characters are rendered with respect, sensitivity, and awe. Their interdependence with nature and each other, describes, in Rawlings's major works, the cosmic web she had sensed since her college days. Cosmic connection was the "private gospel" she wanted so much to preach, the thing close to her heart she wanted to write about.

Most of her work has remained in print over the years. Norman Berg, who founded his Selenraa publishing company to restore access to books he thought worthy of a long life, released new editions of some of her work, including *The Sojourner*, and in 1984, his widow, Julie, republished all of Marjorie's titles. Today, a variety of editions are available.

In her introduction to the 1966 Time Reading Program edition of *Cross Creek*, Shirley Ann Grau affirmed the lasting value of Marjorie's nonfiction masterwork, describing it as a portrait of the author, as well as of the region.

> As you read, bit by bit the character of the author emerges. A complex, curious woman. A woman who loved the earth and the little creatures in it with the intensity of a Francis of Assisi. A woman who could be incredibly patient with drunken Negro hands, trusting them with more responsibility than they could bear. A woman who could turn into a busybody, a bluenosed meddler, insisting on court justice in a jealousy shotgunning, insisting on the inevitable travesty of a trial that everyone else wanted to avoid. A woman who is stubborn, sentimental, kind; at once perceptive and foolish, spiritually troubled, searching for personal contentment. In a way, *Cross Creek* is the chronicle of a modern woman coming to terms with her existence.

THE IDEA THAT portrayals of black people might have hampered *Cross Creek* and, to a lesser extent, *The Yearling* seems not to hold; most readers today understand the importance of context and will tolerate in literature the views, conventions, and language of past times and places. Marjorie's masterpiece, *The Yearling*, suffered more from misidentification as a children's book. The 1946 movie advanced that impression, carrying *The Yearling* into the grade school story hour during the 1950s and 1960s. But since those years—coincidentally matching the period when, after an author's death, the work is often temporarily in eclipse—*The Yearling* and the rest of Rawlings's oeuvre have enjoyed a wide, steady resurgence.

AS MARJORIE'S LITERARY EXECUTOR, Julia Scribner examined her friend's remaining papers for those appropriate to the University of Florida's collection; she was responsible, too, for destroying any other materials she deemed unworthy, for any reason. Among the papers destroyed were personal letters pertaining to Ellen Glasgow. Julia also saw to it that Scribner published *The Secret River* (1955) with illustrations by Leonard Weisgard and, a year later, *The Marjorie Rawlings Reader*, which Julia edited. The *Reader* contains all of *South Moon Under*, chapters from *The Yearling* and *Cross Creek*, *Jacob's Ladder*, which was published as a novella, and several stories.

Marjorie's will held a few personal bequests. Julia received N. C. Wyeth's 1939 painting *The Dance of the Whooping Cranes*, Otto Lange was left the writing desk from Marjorie's porch, and Arthur took custody of Ida's silver. Most of the rest of the author's property was assigned to the University of Florida Endowment Corporation, in trust, with Norton Baskin and Arthur Kinnan to be equal beneficiaries during their lifetimes after certain requests were fulfilled. Arthur's debts to Marjorie were canceled. Martha Mickens was given a small weekly income and use of the Cross Creek tenant house for life. The farmhouse and its land would be used by the University of Florida for various purposes, but both were eventually turned over to the Florida Park Service. Today the house and farm yard are known as the Marjorie Kinnan Rawlings Historic State Park, the upkeep aided by a support organization, the Friends of Marjorie Kinnan Rawlings Farm. Visitors may tour the house, which contains some of Marjorie's belongings, and stroll the grounds, alive with chickens, ducks, bright flowers, and vegetable gardens. In 2007 the park was named a National Historic Landmark.

A few miles away in Antioch Cemetery, Marjorie's gravestone (next to Norman Baskin's and a few steps away from Zelma Cason's) has become a shrine decorated by faithful readers and writers, tended by descendants of the Cracker families she knew—for, after all, she had recorded and expressed the Cracker life, and its folkways, with the greatest respect and care. The Marjorie Kinnan Rawlings Society, established in 1987, maintains the author's literary legacy, holding an annual conference and publishing an annual journal. In 2008, the United States Postal Service issued a commemorative stamp honoring Marjorie Kinnan Rawlings in its Literary Arts series.

Most of the people who were close to Marjorie are gone. Julia Scribner Bigham succumbed to cancer in 1960. Having told family members he'd probably die at seventy, Norman Berg did, indeed, die of a heart attack in 1978, his seventieth year, at a booksellers' convention. Arthur Kinnan continued fighting for custody of his son, Jeff, and finally won. Arthur died of lung cancer in 1961. Marjorie's long-lived aunts in Arizona left their estates to Jeff Kinnan, who lives in Sitka, Alaska. Norton Baskin outlived his wife by forty-four years, tending Marjorie's memory, granting colorful public interviews about life with the author. "She was really three people, at least, and you never knew which one it was going to be," he said in a television interview. "One was as prim as a New England schoolteacher, she was just that straight-laced and prim; and then again she was an absolute bawd, just like a French girl; and—the hardworking, struggling writer and artist. You never knew which one you were going to run into."

Rawlings's work, and who she was, continues to inspire. In 1979, filmmaker and native Floridian Victor Nuñez made a feature film of Marjorie's O. Henry Memorial Award–winning short story "Gal Young Un," and in 1983, Martin Ritt directed the film *Cross Creek*, based mostly on Rawlings's memoir, and starring Mary Steenburgen and Peter Coyote; it also featured octogenarian Norton Baskin in a cameo role. Both films were shot in Florida. *Cross Creek* was nominated for four Academy Awards. Other writers have based poems, plays, novels, memoirs, and documentaries on Rawlings; scholars have gathered portions of her correspondence and other materials into compelling books. (Much of this output can be found in the bibliography that follows.) The University of Florida continues to expand its Rawlings collection, as more letters and other papers are donated or purchased.

Recently, together with environmental author and activist Marjory Stoneman Douglas (1890–1998) and naturalist and activist Marjorie Harris Carr (1915–1997), Marjorie Kinnan Rawlings was dubbed one of "the Three Marjories," forward-thinking women who argued early on for the integrity and preservation of Florida's beautiful natural world. The Marjorie, an organization founded by three women journalists who cover Florida's environmental issues, is among the many groups and individuals working to preserve the state's land, water, air, and wildlife. Rawlings's literary legacy, in the service of beauty, has generated art and action.

The dream is dreamed. It must be built; the intangible loveliness must be made so tangible that critics' teeth will find actual substance to tear into. The memory of the joy is there, the hope sustains you all the way through, but ladies and gentlemen, don't let anyone talk of the delightful life of the author. The moment you put down your title, or, if you write without a title, your first line, you're in for a job of carpenter-work, of bricklaying, of roof-covering, of intricate plumbing.

—Marjorie Kinnan Rawlings, notes for a college lecture

ACKNOWLEDGMENTS

"You are a wonderful example of a shell game with your soul as the pea," wrote Charles Rawlings, Marjorie Kinnan Rawlings's first husband. "God knows which walnut shell you will find it under next. If anyone asks you what you are, tell them that."

Marjorie responded: "You mustn't interpret a mood as a permanent state of mind."

That exchange, discovered early in my research, only hinted at the complexity of my subject, and the work necessary to bring her life to the page. My task was not solitary; it took a village far larger and wider-ranging than Cross Creek to accomplish it, and to each individual and institution who joined and assisted me, I am ever grateful.

First, I owe profound appreciation to the Thinking Like a Mountain Foundation, Steve Daniels, president, for its extraordinary, ongoing support, given in the memory of Dick and Joanne Bartlett. *The Life She Wished to Live* was Joanne's idea. She knew, before I did, that Marjorie and her work would consume me with passion and pleasure over the course of six years, and I regret mightily that Joanne did not live to hold the first copy of this book in her hands.

Florence Turcotte, Literary Manuscripts Archivist in the Special and Area Studies Collections, George A. Smathers Libraries, University of Florida, was the deep, beating heart of this project. Over the years, her guidance and vivid, conspiratorial enthusiasm for "Marge" proved to be a vital engine for my effort. I cannot thank her enough.

As well, I wish to recognize the Rawlings scholars who have contributed so much to the study, interpretation, and organization of materials related to the author's life. Rodger Tarr, in particular, paved the way by gathering and editing four books of Rawlings's short works and correspondence, plus a descriptive bibliography, and a sixth collection coedited with Brent Kinser. These and other resources are listed in the bibliography. Anne Blythe Meriwether's edition of *Blood of My Blood* was invaluable, as were the additional research materials she shared with me.

Special thanks go to University of Florida research assistant Celine Hickey, who selected and gathered materials as I needed them over the years, maintaining her own helpful interest in Rawlings's life. Together with Flo Turcotte, she completed what I referred to as "Team Marjorie" in Gainesville.

Many more people contributed time, expertise, and resources to this project, and it is my hope that I've included everyone in the following.

For institutional research assistance, I am obliged to Mazie Bowen, Special Collections Library, University of Georgia; Neil Budde, executive editor/vice president, *The Louisville Courier-Journal*; Central Library of Rochester and Monroe County, NY, Local History and Genealogy Division; Kenneth J. Chandler, archivist, National Archives for Black Women's History; Jessica Dowd Crouch, archivist, Ernest F. Hollings Special Collections Library, University of South Carolina; Chad Germany, St. Augustine Historical Society; The Getty Research Institute, Research Library, Special Collections, Los Angeles, CA; Barbara Gilbert, Special Collections Research Center, The University of Chicago Library; Paul Haggett, Archives and Special Collections, Owen D. Young Collection, St. Lawrence University; Kevlin C. Haire, assistant archivist, The Ohio State University Archives; Jason W. Hasty, Hargrett Rare Book & Manuscript Library, University of Georgia; Cathy Jacob, operations program associate, University of Wisconsin-Madison Archives; Dean Jeffrey, director of archives and preservation, American Dance Festival; Bill Keeler, Rochester Historical Society; Cindy Knight, Norlin Library, University of Colorado; David G. Null, director, University Archives, University of Wisconsin–Madison; Mahina Oshie, librarian, Special Collections, Seattle Public Library; Pike's Peak Library District; Amy Purcell, associate curator/registrar, Archives & Special Collections, Ekstrom Library, University of Louisville; Valerie Rivers, manager, Marjorie Kinnan Rawlings Historic State Park; Lauren Rogers, Archives and Special Collections, University of Mississippi; Schomburg Center for Research in Black Culture, New York Public Library; Betty Shaw, University of Southern Mississippi Gulf Coast Library; Mark Simon, The Library of Congress; Robert Smith, photographer, Ernest F. Hollings Special Collections Library, University of South Carolina; Johnny Schafer, reference librarian, Howard County Library, Big Spring, TX; Jennifer Skarbek, The John F. Kennedy Presidential Library and Museum, Boston; Elizabeth Sudduth, director, Irvin Department of Rare Books and Special Collections, Ernest F. Hollings Special Collections Library, University of South Carolina; Melissa Watterworth Batt, archivist for literary collections and rare books, Archives & Special Collections, University of Connecticut Library; Victoria L. Thames, library specialist, University of Mississippi.

For advice and private research materials: Dr. Anne Blythe; Ron Bridwell, Bridwell Books, Columbia, South Carolina; Dr. Charles Dew, Williams College; Dr. Alexandra Duckworth, Richard Bland College; Robert Malesky, historian, Brookland neighborhood, Washington, D.C.; Dr. Kevin McCarthy, professor emeritus, University of Florida; Nicholas Meriwether, former archivist, McHenry Library, UC Santa Cruz; Anne Pierce, The Marjorie Kinnan Rawlings Society; Michael Slicker, Lighthouse Books; Dr. Ashley Lear, Embry-Riddle Aeronautical University.

For additional research assistance, warm thanks to Trevor DeJarnett, University of Louisville; Victoria Gao, University of Rochester; Lawrence Jaubert, AIA.

For personal materials, connections and conversations: Royce Bemis, Kathy Brooks, Pat Conroy (1945–2016), Tom Consolino, Mary Z. Fuka, J. T. Glisson (1927–2019), Sally Baskin Hooker, Phil May, Jr. (1925–2019), David Nolan, Nels Parson, Dr. Leslie Kemp Poole; Dr. Ruth Streeter, Sam Vickers, Norman Vickrey. Karen Kushner, granddaughter of Marjorie's close ally Norman Berg, was especially helpful as I worked to describe their friendship. Film documentarian Sonya Doctorian's invitation to assist with her film about Marjorie (*Here Is Home: Marjorie Kinnan Rawlings and Cross Creek*) challenged me to streamline my story lines.

For personal support, and often the idea or connection I didn't know I needed, I salute Pat Alexander, Ana Balka, Shannon Davies, Bonnie Friedman, Emily Fox Gordon, Stephanie Hawkins, Jimmie Killingsworth, Elizabeth Lide, Skip Shockley, and Alice Ann Vanbuskirk.

For rich quietude at a critical time, I am beholden to the Ucross Foundation for a fruitful winter residency. While there, I struggled with writing about Marjorie's racism, and the complicated awakening she experienced after meeting Zora Neale Hurston. When I explained my task to fellow resident Ngwah-Mbo Nana Nkweti, the Cameroonian American writer, she said simply, "Just tell what happened." And so I have, grateful for her insight and clarity.

At a late stage in writing this book, the eminent historian David Nolan of St. Augustine read the manuscript closely and offered invaluable information, corrections, questions, and advice. He, more than anyone, understood Marjorie's life in its cultural context. For his red ink, assurances, and gentle humor, I am deeply indebted.

From beginning to end, this book has been championed by an angel, my agent, Doe Coover, whose lively enthusiasm for the project took it straight to Jill Bialosky and W. W. Norton, the ideal editor and publisher for it. Assistant editor Drew Weitman guided the process thoroughly and gracefully, along with project editor Susan Sanfrey, production manager Julia Druskin, art director Sarahmay Wilkinson, and publicity/marketing team Elizabeth Riley, Rose Sheehan, and Michelle Waters. Copy editors are often unsung heroes; Bonnie Thompson's impeccable work merits highest praise.

The final steps in pushing a manuscript out the door—or off the laptop—are often frustrating and stressful. What has one missed? Is every 'i' dotted? Thank you, Ken Gerow, for encouraging me with warmth, thoughtfulness, and good humor.

NOTES

The following correspondents are abbreviated after their first mention:

MKR: Marjorie Kinnan Rawlings

MEP: Maxwell Evarts Perkins

NSB: Norton Sanford Baskin

JSB: Julia Scribner Bigham

INTRODUCTION

xiii "letters, particularly those of more than casual interest": March 30, 1950.

xiv "This saddens me": Marjorie Kinnan Rawlings to Norman Berg, 1952.

xix "True artists, whatever smiling faces": John Gardner, *The Art of Fiction: Notes on Craft for Young Writers* (New York: Vintage, 1991), 34.

xix "I have an acute need for solitude": manuscript, June 4 (1929?), Marjorie Kinnan Rawlings Papers, University of Florida.

xix "One part is easy to tell": William Stafford, *You Must Revise Your Life* (Ann Arbor: University of Michigan Press, 1986), 3.

xxi "If human wantonness and human greed": MKR, "Florida: An Affectionate Tribute," Congressional Record: Proceedings and Debates of the Congress, vol. 91, part 2, p. 1692.

CHAPTER ONE: ORIGINS

1 "Do not waste one cent, Madam": MKR, *Blood of My Blood,* ed. Anne Blythe Meriwether (Gainesville: University Press of Florida, 2002), 68.

1 "and the world would be at her feet": Ibid., 50.

5 "I find those various": MKR, "Having Left Cities Behind Me," *Scribner's Magazine* (October 1945): 246.

6 "the cauliflower aspect of my nature": MKR to Ethel Beebe, July 28, 1929.

6 "His barns were good and sheltered": MKR, *Blood of My Blood*, 9.

7 "Your Pa's yarns won't buy you any silk dresses": Ibid., 11.

7 "dressed in a frock coat of navy blue": Edwin O. Wood, *Our History*, Fenton Historical Society, http://fentonhistsoc.tripod.com/id79.html.

8 "savagely religious": MKR, *Blood of My Blood*, 27.

8 "The psychology of mis-mating awaits an analyst": Ibid., 29.

8 "an enslavement to convention": Ibid., 26.

10 broke into a Highland fling: Ibid., 34.

10 According to county records: Joe Pickle, *Gettin' Started: Howard County's First 25 Years* (Big Spring, TX: Heritage Museum, 1980), 202.

10 first "Worthy Matron," or presiding officer: Ibid., 246.

10 "Moody's ranch": MKR, *Blood of My Blood*, 35.

11 "exploded with enthusiasm": Ibid., 36.

11 "looped back to show neat ferns": Ibid., 43.

12 "The furniture was decent enough": Ibid., 50–51.

14 "an elderly eccentric": Ibid., 45.

14 "delightful evening at home": Washington *Evening Star*, January 30, 1892, 13.

15 "as time went on": MKR, *Blood of My Blood*, 49–50.

16 The community was segregated . . . the segment continued to grow: Robert Malesky, *Bygone Brookland: Tales from a Storied DC Neighborhood*, www.bygonebrookland.com.

CHAPTER TWO: THE PERFECT DAUGHTER

17 Arthur's birth dismayed Ida: Arthur's birth is recounted in MKR, *Blood of My Blood*, 54–55.

18 "by walking in apparent demureness": Ibid., 64.

18 "I love my little daughter": Ibid., 57.

18 "noble and deserved": Ibid.

18 "utterly useless and indefinable knick-knacks": MKR, *Cross Creek Cookery* (New York, Scribner, 1942), 39.

18 "through the mistaken idea": Ibid., 30.

18 "Receive our thanks our Heavenly Father": Ibid., 2.

19 "old brown Emma": MKR, *Blood of My Blood*, 77.

19 "scenically beautiful . . . Venus's body": Ibid., 70.

19 "richly black and white": Ibid., 71.

20 "He was architect, engineer": Ibid,. 72.

20 "the whippoorwills in the valley below": Ibid., 75.

20 "The air was spiced": Ibid.

20 "had two little nieces to provide for": Marjorie Kinnan [Rawlings], "The Best Spell," *Washington Post*, January 2, 1910. Reprinted in Rodger L. Tarr and Brent Kinser, eds., *The Uncollected Writings of Marjorie Kinnan Rawlings* (Gainesville: University Press of Florida, 2007), 16.

20 "So this morning I went downtown": Marjorie Kinnan [Rawlings], *Washington Post*, January 30, 1910. Reprinted in Tarr and Kinser, *Uncollected Writings*, 17.

21 "pounced on this morsel": MKR, *Blood of My Blood*, 78.

21 "Self-confidence is a great loosener": Ibid., 78–79.

22 "Over her left breast, she wore": Ibid., 102

23 "fancied herself as a high soprano": MKR to Norton S. Baskin, March 15, 1944.

24 "I guess I have the wanderlust": Marjorie Kinnan [Rawlings], "The Traveler," *Washington Post*, September 11, 1910. Reprinted in Tarr and Kinser, *Uncollected Writings*, 18–19.

24 "Ah, gentle reader": Marjorie Kinnan [Rawlings], "A Battle for Life," *Washington Post*, February 25, 1912. Reprinted in Tarr and Kinser, *Uncollected Writings*, 22–25.

24 "The water was thick, thick as oil": Ibid.

26 "We Fweshman do to all de games": Marjorie Kinnan [Rawlings], "The Freshman's Side of It," *Western* (October 1912): 24–26. Reprinted in Tarr and Kinser, *Uncollected Writings*, 42–46.

26 "I don't reckon you ought to talk": Marjorie Kinnan [Rawlings], "A Surprise," *Washington Post*, June 8, 1913. Reprinted in Tarr and Kinser, *Uncollected Writings*, 66–67.

26 "three or four old negroes who I knew": Frank Carpenter, "Chat with Harris," Washington *Evening Star*, December 19, 1896.

27 "Uncle Remus is one of the saints": Ibid.

27 "wildly of his plans": MKR, *Blood of My Blood*, 104.

CHAPTER THREE: WISCONSIN

29 "Somethin' pulls me": "Alonzo Perceval Van Clyne," *Washington Post*, May 10, 1914. Reprinted in Rodger L. Tarr and Brent Kinser, eds., *The Uncollected Writings of Marjorie Kinnan Rawlings* (Gainesville: University Press of Florida, 2007), 68–72.

30 "the enemy's camp": MKR, *Blood of My Blood*, 110.

31 "Miss Kinnan has great natural ability": University of Wisconsin recommendation for admission, June 12, 1914, courtesy of David G. Null, director, University Archives, University of Wisconsin–Madison.

31 "I remember seeing her on registration day": Jean Wardlow interview with Bee McNeill, 1970. Marjorie Kinnan Rawlings Papers, University of Florida.

31 "flicking down adjectives": MKR, *Blood of My Blood*, 120.

32 "the rich, tragic quality of his own being": Leslie Fiedler, *Love and Death in the American Novel* (New York: Criterion, 1960), xxx.

32 "had white hair": Neale Reinetz, *William Ellery Leonard: The Professor and the Locomotive God* (Madison, NJ: Fairleigh Dickinson University Press, 2013), xi.

32 "high laced boots": Ibid., 83.

32 "And I say it can!": MKR, *Blood of My Blood*, 121.

32 "I don't call that encouragement": Ibid., 121.

33 "a shoddy little affair": Ibid., 125.

33 "intellectual bunch": Ibid., 131.

34 Little Southern Woody: Ibid., 137.

34 "I'm full o' vulgar words": J. M. Barrie, *The Admirable Crichton*, 1902, the Project Gutenberg EBook edition, February 28, 2009, EBook #3490.

35 "The two maids prepare the stage": Marjorie Kinnan [Rawlings], *Into the Nowhere* synopsis, Marjorie Kinnan Rawlings Papers, University of Florida.

36 Her transcript cites her withdrawal: Transcript courtesy of David G. Null, director, University Archives, University of Wisconsin–Madison.

36 Kreymborg refused her permission: Alfred Kreymborg to MKR, January 15, 1918, Marjorie Kinnan Rawlings Papers, University of Florida.

36 "had drawn freely upon their imaginations": review of *Lima Beans, Daily Cardinal*, March 6, 1917. Quoted in Tarr and Kinser, *Uncollected Writings*, 87.

37 "every inch of six feet eight virility": Marjorie Kinnan [Rawlings], "The Brute,"

Wisconsin Literary Magazine, January 1916. Reprinted in Tarr and Kinser, *Uncollected Writings,* 89–93.

37   **"Her tiny black eyes had a tendency":** Marjorie Kinnan [Rawlings], "The Captivating Odors of the Kitchen," *Wisconsin Literary Magazine* (December 1916): 87–88, 100, 102. Reprinted in Tarr and Kinser, *Uncollected Writings,*108–15.

38   **"I scarce can see your eyes":** Marjorie Kinnan [Rawlings], "The Mouse Speaks," *Wisconsin Literary Magazine* (January 1917): 117. Reprinted in Tarr and Kinser, *Uncollected Writings,* 115–16. *The Poets of the Future: A College Anthology for 1916–1917* (Boston: Stratford), was edited by Henry T. Schnittkind.

38   **"The cross-roads Calvary shone":** Marjorie Kinnan [Rawlings], "Creation of the Soul," *Wisconsin Literary Magazine* (February 1917): 146. Reprinted in Tarr and Kinser, *Uncollected Writings,* 117.

38   **"Out of the noise, the push":** Marjorie Kinnan [Rawlings], "The Stuff of Dreams," *Wisconsin Literary Magazine* (April 1917): 212. Reprinted in Tarr and Kinser, *Uncollected Writings,* 119–20.

39   **"I believe that every one of us here":** Marjorie Kinnan [Rawlings], "On Poetry and Vachel Lindsay," *Wisconsin Literary Magazine* (April 1918): 169–70. Reprinted in Tarr and Kinser, *Uncollected Writings,* 144–46.

39   **"unwholesome, pernicious, and undemocractic":** *Daily Cardinal,* May 29, 1918, pp. 1, 4. Quoted in Tarr and Kinser, *Uncollected Writings,* 88.

39   **"filled with the usual juvenile despair":** MKR, *Blood of My Blood,* 131.

40   **"I am as acutely conscious":** Marjorie Kinnan [Rawlings], "Convictions," unpublished manuscript, Marjorie Kinnan Rawlings Papers, University of Florida.

40   **"I owe you nothing":** MKR, *Blood of My Blood,* 131–32.

40   **"In the early spring of 1918":** Ibid., 139–140.

41   **"He was adorable":** Jean Wardlow interview with Bee McNeil, Marjorie Kinnan Rawlings Papers, University of Florida, 1970.

41   **"He summed up for her":** Ibid., 140.

41   **"You've got her wanting the things":** Ibid., 142.

41   **"Terrible rot":** Ibid., 143.

42   **He entered Rochester's West High School:** Transcripts courtesy of David G. Null, director, University Archives, University of Wisconsin–Madison.

42   **"I should have been in awe of her":** Jean Wardlow interview with Charles Rawlings, Marjorie Kinnan Rawlings Papers, University of Florida, 1970.

43   **"perhaps the last [war] to be conceived":** Paul Fussell, *The Great War and Modern Memory* (New York: Oxford University Press, 1975), 246.

43   **"universal commitment to the sporting spirit":** Ibid., 26.

43   **"For those eager to harmonize":** Jackson Lears, *Rebirth of a Nation: The Making of Modern America, 1877–1920* (New York: HarperCollins, 2009), 29.

43   **"Lieutenant E. L. Hahn":** *Badger* yearbook, 1918, Marjorie Kinnan Rawlings Papers, University of Florida.

43   **"Hundreds of 'dear departeds' ":** Marjorie Kinnan [Rawlings], "PSI—University of Wisconsin," *Kappa Alpha Theta Magazine* (January 1918): 176–77. Reprinted in Tarr and Kinser, *Uncollected Writings,* 139–40.

CHAPTER FOUR: NEW YORK

45   "This then was the beginning of life": MKR, *Blood of My Blood,* 144.

45   "It was the fall of 1918": Ibid., 144.

46   "Well, you've got the gift of gab all right": Ibid., 146–47.

46 "They tell me contact": Ibid., 147.

46 "Do you know, my dear": Ibid., 146.

46 "They have just been married": Ibid., 147.

47 "He said, 'You have the writer's gift' ": Ibid., 147.

47 "everything about proofreading signs": MKR to Charles Rawlings, September 18, 1918.

47 "go around broke": Charles Rawlings to MKR, October 23, 1918.

47 "They give you the material": MKR to Charles Rawlings, October 10 and 16, 1918.

48 "I'd rather take a little longer": MKR to Charles Rawlings, September 8, 1918.

48 "Chuck sweetheart": MKR to Charles Rawlings, September 8, 1918.

48 "My sweet Christian cherub": Charles Rawlings to MKR, October 6, 1918.

49 "I don't see any way out of it": MKR to Charles Rawlings, October [26?], 1918.

49 "were bitten to the quick": MKR, Blood of My Blood, 148.

49 "I'm unconsciously mixed-up tonight": MKR to Charles Rawlings, October 10, 1918.

49 "She felt as I do": MKR to Charles Rawlings, October 10, 1918.

50 "Can I go ahead with that psycho-analysis job": Ibid.

50 "Remember, inspiration or materials be hanged": Charles Rawlings to MKR, October 11, 1918.

50 "How damnably weak": Charles Rawlings to MKR, October 9, 1918.

50 "You were the stronger of the two": Charles Rawlings to MKR, October 13, 1918.

51 "miles and miles of subways": MKR to Charles Rawlings, October 16, 1918.

51 "Don't worry": MKR to Charles Rawlings, September 13, 1918.

52 "There a little place, like a shrine": Charles Rawlings to MKR, September or October 1918.

52 "You know, I'm coming around to your belief": MKR to Charles Rawlings, October 17, 1918.

52 "we are like a cup": Charles Rawlings to MKR, October [21?], 1918.

52 "We, old moody-and-depressed-and-cynical us": MKR to Charles Rawlings, October 22, 1918.

53 "a trashy story I dashed off": Ibid.

53 "If he felt badly": Ibid.

53 "Sweetheart. There is a God": Charles Rawlings to MKR, October 23, 1918.

53 "The process going on in you": MKR to Charles Rawlings, October 25 and 26, 1918.

54 "You are a wonderful example of a shell game": Charles Rawlings to MKR, fall 1918.

54 "You musn't interpret a mood": MKR to Charles Rawlings, December 20, 1918.

55 "a couple of books and lots of articles": MKR to Charles Rawlings, November 15, 1918.

55 "Why is it 'getting wrong' ": MKR to Charles Rawlings, November 23, 1918.

55 "We're so intensely individualistic, both of us": MKR to Charles Rawlings, December 15, 1918.

56 "Oh my daughter": MKR, Blood of My Blood, 152.

56 "the flight of stairs and the slim broken neck": Ibid., 152.

56 "You were quite right": Charles Rawlings to Ida Kinnan, April 15, 1919.

57 "This strange female creature": MKR, Blood of My Blood, 152.

CHAPTER FIVE: LOUISVILLE

58 "My dear Miss Kinnan": Hazel Deyo Batchelor to MKR, n.d. [1918–19].

58 Marjorie succeeded in selling: MKR, "His Little Cabbage Head," Young's Maga-

zine (May 1919): 252–54. Reprinted in Rodger L. Tarr and Brent Kinser, eds., *The Uncollected Writings of Marjorie Kinnan Rawlings* (Gainesville: University Press of Florida, 2007), 169–73.

59 **"the first time in history a great war"**: MKR, "The Blue Triangle Follows the Switchboard," *Telephone Topics*, March 28, 1919, pp. 312–13. Reprinted in Tarr and Kinser, *Uncollected Writings*, 154–56.

59 **"An enforced independence"**: MKR, "Women as Constructionists," *New France* (1919): 434–35. Reprinted in Tarr and Kinser, *Uncollected Writings*, 156–59.

60 **"I only mean that there is something vital"**: MKR, *Blood of My Blood*, 159.

60 **"I've stopped being in such an awful hurry"**: Ibid.

61 **"There has to be something close to your heart"**: Ibid., 146.

61 **"I have often wondered why"**: Arthur Kinnan to MKR, July 22, 1919.

62 **"I'm so low that I owe"**: Arthur Kinnan to MKR, August 4, 1919.

62 **piece about the local Y's health center**: MKR, "A Sanitorium Without Mud Baths or Mineral Water," Louisville *Courier-Journal*, October 24, 1920, p. 5. Reprinted in Tarr and Kinser, *Uncollected Writings*, 182–85.

63 **"About the time I was lisping"**: MKR, "The Only Woman State Bacteriologist in the United States," Louisville *Courier-Journal*, February 6, 1921, p. 6. Reprinted in Tarr and Kinser, *Uncollected Writings*, 186–89.

63 **"O for the virile pen"**: MKR, "A Member of the Louisville Board of Fire Underwriters," Louisville *Courier-Journal*, March 27, 1921, 4.

64 **"a wild outcropping of girls"**: Ishbel Ross, *Ladies of the Press: The Story of Women in Journalism by an Insider* (New York: Harper & Row, 1936), 7.

64 **"A girl might be asked"**: Ibid., 22.

64 **"invaded the front pages"**: Ibid., 23.

65 **"astonish, bemuse"**: Ibid., 262.

65 **"It was a rough school"**: MKR interview with Robert Van Gelder in his *Writers and Writing* (New York: Scribner, 1946), 242–43.

66 **Evidence lies in the first page**: MKR, "Jenny," unpublished manuscript, Marjorie Kinnan Rawlings Papers, University of Florida.

67 **"the sole secret reason"**: MKR, *Blood of My Blood*, 159–60.

67 **"It's on a knoll, and overlooks little hills"**: MKR to Charles Rawlings, January 1922.

68 **"Everything possible is done"**: MKR, *Blood of My Blood*, 163.

68 **"She had lived too long in other lives"**: Ibid.

68 **"I did not know that so little"**: Ibid., 168.

CHAPTER SIX: ROCHESTER

69 **One piece landed on the front page**: "Wife Tells of Forgotten Home." Sunday, October 15, 1922. A local woman suffers a head injury and amnesia.

69 **" 'Come Back,' Cries Bride"**: MKR, *Rochester Evening Journal*, October 8, 1922.

70 **"Lonely Spinster Had Premonition"**: MKR, *Rochester Evening Journal*, October 22, 1922.

70 **" 'Easiest Thing in World' "**: MKR, *Rochester Evening Journal*, November 16, 1922.

70 **"The Cookie Jar Keeps Husbands"**: MKR, *Rochester Evening Journal*, October 27, 1922.

70 **"Path to Slimness Is Mountainous"**: MKR, *Rochester Evening Journal*, October 19, 1922.

70 "Girl's Charm Goes Farthest": MKR, *Rochester Evening Journal*, October 16, 1922.

71 "Now about this Gray business": Charles Rawlings to MKR, November 23, 1922.

72 "with a warm and tender iron": MKR to Charles Rawlings, November 1922.

72 "You say you aren't trying to make me 'confess'": MKR to Charles Rawlings, November 1922.

73 "Someday, I shall write a great feminist novel": MKR to Charles Rawlings, November 1922.

74 "goes out into the woodshed": MKR, *Blood of My Blood*, 169.

75 "not only a third cousin": Editor's Note, *Five O'Clock*, April 22, 1924. Reprinted in Rodger L. Tarr and Brent Kinser, eds., *The Uncollected Writings of Marjorie Kinnan Rawlings* (Gainesville: University Press of Florida, 2007), 233.

75 "This is the last of a series": Editor's Note, *Five O'Clock*, May 20, 1924. Reprinted in Tarr and Kinser, *Uncollected Writings*, 241.

75 "the scantier the costume": MKR, "Tragic Drama at the Corinthian Stirs Rochester's Elite," *Five O'Clock*, April 22, 1924. Reprinted in Tarr and Kinser, *Uncollected Writings*, 233–35.

76 "She picked out her own assignments": Henry Clune, *Rochester Democrat and Chronicle*, January 16, 1943, p. 25.

76 "a very small affair": MKR to Ethel Fairmont Beebe, January 1925.

76 highly publicized Rochester love quartet: MKR, "The Price of Marguerite," *World*, September 5, 1926. Reprinted in Tarr and Kinser, *Uncollected Writings*, 244–50.

76 two completed fiction manuscripts: "Under the Lily Pond" and "The Heaven of Arlette," manuscripts, Marjorie Kinnan Rawlings Papers, University of Florida.

77 "This series is an entirely": Editor's note quoted in Rodger L. Tarr, ed., *Songs of a Housewife: Poems by Marjorie Kinnan Rawlings* (Gainesville: University Press of Florida, 1997), 4.

77 "I like the sound of silver": MKR, "The Symphony of Supper-time," *Rochester Democrat and Chronicle*, November 20, 1926. Reprinted in Tarr, *Songs*, 35.

79 "We both got in a panic": MKR to Ethel Fairmont Beebe, July 1928.

80 "Written 1928": *Blood of My Blood* manuscript, Marjorie Kinnan Rawlings Papers, University of Florida.

CHAPTER SEVEN: THE CREEK

81 "When I came to the Creek": MKR, *Cross Creek* (New York: Scribner, 1942), 9.

81 "You have in you that fatal drop of Pearce blood": Quoted in Elizabeth Silverthorne, *Marjorie Kinnan Rawlings: Sojourner at Cross Creek* (Woodstock, NY: Overlook, 1988), 56.

81 "It is more important to live the life": Ibid., 56–57.

84 "everything from barn and field rats": MKR to Ethel Fairmont Beebe, July 28, 1929.

84 "If you didn't like cats and dogs": Idella Parker, *Marjorie Rawlings' Perfect Maid* (Gainesville: University Press of Florida, 1992), xiii.

84 "The life here is one adventure after another": MKR to Ethel Fairmont Beebe, July 28, 1929.

85 "The Crackers, the natives here": Ibid.

85 "by displaying an air": J. T. Glisson, *The Creek* (Gainesville: University Press of Florida, 1993), 85.

86   "Mrs. Rawlings, a pretty woman": Ibid., 82.

87   "kicked like a Jersey mule": Dessie Smith Prescott, interview by Leland Hawes, March 30, 1990, Ocala, FL, Leland Hawes Collection, the University of Florida Digital Collections.

87   "and then I was turned loose": MKR to Ernest Hemingway, September 1936. Courtesy of the John F. Kennedy Presidential Library and Museum and the Norton S. Baskin Literary Trust.

87   "We usually just got the dogs off": Dessie Smith Prescott, interview by Leland Hawes, March 30, 1990, Ocala, FL, Leland Hawes Collection, the University of Florida Digital Collections.

88   "She was the logical census taker for our district": MKR, Cross Creek, 49.

88   "an 'old maid politician' ": Glisson, The Creek, 17.

89   "These places in Florida": Harriett Beecher Stowe, Palmetto Leaves (Boston: J. F. Osgood, 1873), 52.

90   "little thatched roof workshop": Marjory Stoneman Douglas to MKR, August 21, 1931.

90   "You ask how I happened to become interested": MKR to Alfred Dashiell, n.d.

91   "Sam Whitman, whose daddy's daddy killed a bear": MKR, "Georgia Money," from "Cracker Chidlings," Scribner's Magazine (February 1931): 127–34.

91   "painted her portrait of backwoods life": Ocala Evening Star, January 30, 1931.

91   "so true, that I have softened": MKR, letter to the editor, Ocala Evening Star, February 2, 1931.

93   "she couldn't hold the beam on the gator": Buren Clayton, "Gator Hunting with Marjorie Kinnan Rawlings," Florida Times-Union, November 13, 1966.

93   "the powers that be": High Springs Telegram, March 27, 1931.

93   "Kipling was right": Ocala Evening Star, April 11, 1931

94   "like a bird-dog": MKR, "Jacob's Ladder," Scribner's Magazine (April 1931): 351–66.

94   "He drew out the long, leathery neck": Ibid.

95   "A magnolia sixty feet tall": Ibid.

96   "If, after reading this letter": Maxwell Evarts Perkins to MKR, November 19, 1930.

96   "The ending I have worked out does": MKR to MEP, December 24, 1930.

96   "purports to be a 'human document' ": Gainesville News, April 3, 1931.

96   "Ocala, Marion county Fla. people": Norman Tuttle, editorial, Miami Herald, April 9, 1931.

CHAPTER EIGHT: *SOUTH MOON UNDER*

98   "Is there any chance": MEP to MKR, February 3, 1931.

98   "I am vibrating with material": MKR to MEP, March 31, 1931.

98   "You would be by far": MEP to MKR, April 13, 1931.

99   "I really ought not to trouble you": MEP to MKR, June 26, 1931.

99   "a boy as indigenous to the scrub": MKR to MEP, June 30, 1931.

99   "He was a man's man": MKR, letter to Ellery Sedgwick, Atlantic Monthly, August 14, 1931.

100 "Dear Mrs. Rawlings": Ellery Sedgwick to MKR, August 28, 1931.

100 "I have voluminous notes": MKR to MEP, November 4, 1931.

102 "I knew the manuscript": MKR to Ethel Fairmont Beebe, April 1932.

102   "Chuck sold a sponge story": MKR, Cracker notes, undated. Marjorie Kinnan
      Rawlings Papers, University of Florida.

102   "Chuck's disposition is still rotten": MKR to Ethel Fairmont Beebe, April 1932.

102   "Everything in the bean story is true": Ibid.

103   "nothing more than any woman acquaintance": Jack Carberry, "'It Is So Beau-
      tiful,' Says Girl Taken into Home of Admirer's Ex-Wife," International News Ser-
      vice, in the *Rochester Evening Journal,* December 5, 1922.

103   "bring it up to meet your high critical standards": MKR to MEP, August 1, 1932.

104   "My suggestions come only": MEP to MKR, August 23, 1932.

104   "Your diagnosis and prescription": MKR to MEP, August 31, 1932.

104   "One of those books": MKR to MEP, October 6, 1932.

105   "a vulgar woman with an obscene tongue": Ibid.

105   "If you like the book": MKR to MEP, November 2, 1932.

105   "By the way, this is my only copy": MKR to MEP, November 7, 1932.

105   "day by day": MKR to MEP, November 12, 1932.

105   "I am anxious to know": Ibid.

106   "The more I think about it": MKR to MEP, November 1932.

106   "soothed with copious draughts": MKR to MEP, November 18, 1932.

106   "It sounds like an affectation": Ibid.

106   "Don't let me emasculate": Ibid.

106   "in a crude state": Charles Rawlings to MEP, November 23, 1932.

107   "I don't want to tell Mrs. Rawlings": MEP to Charles Rawlings, December 3,
      1932.

107   "I think we shall end": MKR to MEP, December 3, 1932.

107   "Southern egg-nog all morning": MKR to Arthur Kinnan, January 3, 1933.

107   "Can it be that": Arthur Kinnan to MKR, February 6, 1933.

108   "LENGTH OF ALLIGATOR": MEP to MKR, January 26, 1933.

108   "THIRTY INTENTIONAL": MKR to MEP, January 28, 1933.

108   "more generous than I had expected": MKR to MEP, March 3, 1933.

108   "But if the road had been hard": MKR, *South Moon Under* (New York: Scribner,
      1933), 305.

108   "Perhaps all men": Ibid., 327.

108   "thoughts that are the author's": Herschel Brickell, *New York Herald Tribune,*
      March 5, 1933.

108   "a people and a setting new to literary fiction": Percy Hutchison, *New York
      Times,* March 5, 1933.

CHAPTER NINE: COMING APART

111   "What a man's man you have become": Bee McNeil to MKR, May 10, 1933.

111   "Mrs. Rawlings has reproduced": Carl Bohnenberger, *Florida Times-Union,* Feb-
      ruary 26, 1933.

112   "a Cracker couldn't do it": Edith Pope to MKR, January 25, 1933.

112   "Everyone tells me with great pride": MKR to MEP, late March 1933.

113   "a blue smear through the marsh": MKR, *Cross Creek,* 343, 347.

113   Dessie recalled: Dessie Smith Prescott, interview by Leland Hawes, March 30, 1990,
      Ocala, FL, Leland Hawes Collection, the University of Florida Digital Collections.

113   an article about Dutch oven cookery: MKR, *Sunrise,* February 1932.

114   According to Dessie: Dessie Smith Prescott, interview by Leland Hawes, March

30, 1990, Ocala, FL, Leland Hawes Collection, the University of Florida Digital Collections.

114 "Once I lost touch with the Creek": from "Hyacinth Drift," included in *Cross Creek*, 343–47.

114 "I can't say I'm sorry": MKR to MEP, April 13, 1933.

114 "I've been well marooned": MKR, *New York Herald Tribune*, June 8, 1933.

115 "My most fun has been coming home": Charles Rawlings to MKR, May 26, 1933.

115 "The first is a 'kindly' king": Arthur Kinnan to MKR, October 2, 1933.

116 "I'd never seen them walking together": J. T. Glisson, interview by the author, February 15, 2016, home of J.T. Glisson, Micanopy, FL.

116 "Marjorie and I are too high-strung": J. T. Glisson, *The Creek*, 85.

117 "All we knew": J. T. Glisson, interview by the author, February 15, 2016, home of J.T. Glisson, Micanopy, FL.

117 "Any good journalist": MKR to MEP, March 3, 1933.

117 "I am so weary of the Faulkner": MKR to MEP, March 18, 1933.

117 "It would be designed": MEP to MKR, June 10, 1933.

118 "If you sit quietly at table": MKR to Samuel Wright, September 20, 1933.

118 "My dear foolish Zelma": MKR to Zelma Cason, September 21, 1933.

118 After her trip to England, Marjorie celebrated another: MKR and Fred Tompkins, "Alligators," *Saturday Evening Post*, September 23, 1933, pp. 16–17, 36, 38.

119 In October, *Scribner's Magazine* published: MKR, "Benny and the Bird Dogs," *Scribner's Magazine* (October 1933): 193–200.

119 "My friends call me": MKR to MEP, November 14, 1939.

119 "I happen to be in a distressed": MKR to MEP, October 4, 1933.

119 a clean brew out of spring-fed water: description from Dessie Smith Prescott, interview by Leland Hawes, March 30, 1990, Ocala, FL, Leland Hawes Collection, the University of Florida Digital Collections.

119 "in the very core of the scrub": MKR to MEP, October 4, 1933.

120 "The truth is the best part of a man is a boy": MEP to MKR, October 27, 1933.

121 "like being handed a medal": MKR to MEP, November 11, 1933.

121 "I've wanted to meet you": Norton S. Baskin, interview by Danielle Flood, August 8, 1988, Marjorie Kinnan Rawlings Papers, University of Florida.

122 "Dear Chuck: The divorce was granted": MKR to Charles Rawlings, November 11, 1933.

122 "glad she and I can go our ways": Ibid.

122 "Came home to find": Ibid.

122 "My development, for some reason": Charles Rawlings to MKR, early 1934.

122 "We were never happy for very long": MKR to Bee Humiston McNeil, September 1, 1934.

123 "Mankind could go on a vast": MKR research notes, Marjorie Kinnan Rawlings Papers, University of Florida.

123 "We didn't hear a word from him": J. T. Glisson, interview by the author, February 15, 2016, home of J.T. Glisson, Micanopy, FL.

124 "His health was shot": Ibid.

124 "I think her ear was a great, great ear": Charles Rawlings, interview by Jean Wardlow.

CHAPTER TEN: *GOLDEN APPLES*

125 "It is going to be nip and tuck": MKR to Ida Tarrant, June 2, 1934.

126 "It would be impossible for me": MKR, "The Ancient Enmity," *Cross Creek*, 75.

127 "has something of your peculiarly": MKR to MEP, February 17, 1934.
127 "He writes fine novels, but": MEP to MKR, February 28, 1934.
127 "You do encourage me": MKR to MEP, February 11, 1934.
128 "I never did feel comfortable": MEP to Ernest Hemingway, November 28, 1934, in Matthew J. Bruccoli, ed., *The Only Thing That Counts: The Ernest Hemingway/Maxwell Perkins Correspondence, 1925–1947* (New York: Scribner, 1996), 217.
128 "I could have gone on reading": MEP to MKR, June 7, 1934.
128 "I hope you haven't thrown away": MKR to MEP, July 6, 1934.
128 "I despise working with an outline": MKR to MEP, July 31, 1934.
128 In its August 1934 issue: MKR, "The Pardon," *Scribner's Magazine* (August 1934): 95–98.
129 "it does not seem to be quite right": MEP to MKR, August 7, 1934.
129 "I will bring up a live rattlesnake": MKR to MEP, August 9, 1934.
129 "The truth is you are a writer": MEP to MKR, August 10, 1934.
129 "I ran out of anything to read": MKR to MEP, October 18, 1934.
129 "But even through my intense": MKR to MEP, November 9, 1934.
130 "My great fear is": MKR to MEP, November 17, 1934.
130 "Don't take Henry James too seriously": MEP to MKR, November 23, 1934.
130 was not "a success": MEP to MKR, December 13, 1934.
130 "I am staying home from a deer-hunt": MKR to MEP, December 1934.
132 "A car driving up to the gate": MKR, *Cross Creek*, 42.
132 "There was the little cottage": Neal Smith to his mother, June 1935, Marjorie Kinnan Rawlings Papers, University of Florida.
133 "My God": MKR to MEP, February 19, 1935.
134 "I wish the Cosmopolitan sale": Ibid.
134 "Thought it was only muscular injury": MKR to MEP, March 30, 1935.
134 "Dr. Tigert is a prig": MKR to MEP, February 11, 1935.
135 "The very worst has happened": MKR to MEP, April 26, 1935.
135 "I told them to do their own cutting": MKR to MEP, May 18, 1935.
135 "But you are not thinking of this book": MEP to MKR, May 28, 1935.
135 "relief and despair": MKR to MEP, May 31, 1935.
135 "There are lots of three-name writers": MKR to MEP, June 10, 1935.
135 "The question of treatment": MEP to MKR, June 18, 1935.
136 "How can I do such sheer *bad writing*": MKR to MEP, July 4, 1935.

CHAPTER ELEVEN: WHAT ABOUT A NOVEL ABOUT A BOY

137 "What in hell": Arthur Kinnan to MKR, February 7, 1935.
137 "Try as I would": Arthur Kinnan to MKR, January 12, 1931.
137 "Gross foolishness—admitted, Marj": Arthur Kinnan to MKR, January 23, 1931.
138 "colorless, and uninteresting": Arthur Kinnan to MKR, August 5, 1930.
138 "She is Kinnan through and through": Arthur Kinnan to MKR, January 23, 1931.
138 "started her career nicely": Raymond J. Krantz, "Olympia-Nanaimo Cruiser Race," *MotorBoating* (September 1933): 37.
138 "principally through the children": Arthur Kinnan to MKR, May 15, 1933.
138 "peculiarly sweet and child-like": MKR to MEP, August 2, 1935.
138 "I had the comfort of knowing": MKR to MEP, August, 1935.
139 "Your beloved Ocala": Otto Lange to MKR, September 20, 1935.
139 "The forward-looking American": Ibid.
139 "You proved yourself the best": Ibid.

140 "The near-Chaucerian dialect": Percy Hutchison, *New York Times*, October 6, 1935.

140 "There is a tenderness": Henry Seidel Canby, *Saturday Review of Literature*, October 5, 1935.

141 "Peace and ecstasy": MKR, *Golden Apples* (New York: Scribner, 1935), 222.

141 "A man, by himself": Ibid., 222–23.

141 "In his love he takes": Ibid., 223.

141 "But no one makes note": MKR to MEP, October 15, 1935.

141 "the hell of publishing": MKR to MEP, November 6, 1935.

142 "Tordell is excellent": James Branch Cabell to MKR, September 15, 1941.

142 "Often I cross out a phrase": MKR to James Branch Cabell, October 4, 1945, in Jacqueline J. Wilken, "Selected Letters of Marjorie Kinnan Rawlings to James Branch Cabell" (M.A. thesis, Virginia Commonwealth University, May 1993).

142 "It is ridiculous to put your book": MEP to MKR, December 20, 1935.

142 "You have not changed at all": Edwin Roedder to MKR, October 6, 1935.

142 "in the Florida vein": MKR to MEP, October 16, 1935.

143 "out of the world flavor": MKR to MEP, November 5, 1935.

143 "She seemed impossible": MKR, *Cross Creek*, 82.

143 One day, according to Dessie Smith: Dessie Smith Prescott, interview by Leland Hawes, March 30, 1990, Ocala, FL, Leland Hawes Collection, the University of Florida Digital Collections.

144 Drink was the only thing: MKR, *Cross Creek*, 92.

144 But a year later: Dessie Smith Prescott, interview by Leland Hawes, March 30, 1990, Ocala, FL, Leland Hawes Collection, the University of Florida Digital Collections.

144 "I know I got to go": MKR, *Cross Creek*, 95.

145 "grown up in dogwood and holly": MKR to MEP, December 18, 1935.

145 "What a joy and a relief": Otto Lange to MKR, March 2, 1936.

145 "Did you feel me thinking of you": Otto Lange to MKR, February 21, 1935.

145 "It is useless for me": MKR to MEP, March 9, 1936.

145 "convinced me that I must be": Otto Lange to MKR, March 25, 1936.

145 "one of your vitriolic": Otto Lange to MKR, April 24, 1936.

146 "keeping a necessary detachment": MKR to MEP, May 20, 1936.

146 "I am not a professional writer": Thomas Wolfe, *The Story of a Novel* (New York: Scribner, 1936), 1–2.

146 "It's unbearable—its honesty": MKR to MEP, June 1, 1936.

CHAPTER TWELVE: THE WIDENING CIRCLE

147 "We eat leisurely": MKR, *Cross Creek*, 4.

147 "disagreeable and obstreperous": Wallace Stevens to MKR, February 20, 1936. Her personal reflection of the evening is jotted on the back of the letter.

148 "Mrs. Frost laughed so hard": Clifford Lyons, note attached to MKR's letter to Lyons, February 19, 1941. In the note, Lyons recalls the first meeting of MKR and Frost.

148 "At fifty-five, Mrs. Grinnell": H. W. Major, "American Game Fish," *MotorBoating* (April 1934): 37.

148 Mrs. Grinnell had written: Mrs. Oliver C. Grinnell, *American Big Game Fishing* (New York: Derrydale Press, 1935).

148 "The man astonished me": MKR to MEP, June 18, 1936.

149 "It is an odd thing": MEP to MKR, July 8, 1936.

150   "I have a big, sloppy, easy-going place": MKR to Ernest Hemingway, August 1, 1936. Courtesy of the John F. Kennedy Presidential Library and Museum and the Norton S. Baskin Literary Trust.

151   "They are not much hunted": MKR to Ernest Hemingway, early September 1936. Courtesy of the John F. Kennedy Presidential Library and Museum and the Norton S. Baskin Literary Trust.

152   "make their own plot": MKR to MEP, July 14, 1936.

152   "If I try to express in a few sentences": MKR to MEP, July 31, 1936.

152   "None of the fear and torment": MKR to MEP, August 27, 1936.

152   "Now I think I have discovered": MKR to Ernest Meyer, January 30, 1937.

153   "overcome with the beauty of his style": MKR to Edith Pope, July 14, 1936.

153   "She's interested in the old days": MKR to MEP, August 27, 1936.

153   "She has accepted my withdrawal": MKR to Ida Tarrant, late summer 1936.

154   In an account more than fifty years later: Dessie Smith Prescott, interview by Leland Hawes, March 30, 1990, Ocala, FL, Leland Hawes Collection, the University of Florida Digital Collections.

154   "Brought my Proust and my pointer": MKR to MEP, September 22, 1936.

155   "I don't see how any journalist": MKR to MEP, September 30, 1936.

155   "but I thought that something": MEP to MKR, October 7, 1936.

155   "It simply took me off my feet": MKR to F. Scott Fitzgerald, October 24, 1936.

156   "only sherry and table wine": MKR to MEP, October 25, 1936.

156   "The book resolves itself": MKR to F. Scott Fitzgerald, October 25, 1936.

157   "The word means something very special": MKR, "A Mother in Mannville," reprinted in *Short Stories by Marjorie Kinnan Rawlings,* ed. Rodger L. Tarr (Gainesville: University Press of Florida, 1994), 245.

158   "droop-eared, sway-backed": MKR, "Varmints," reprinted in *Short Stories by Marjorie Kinnan Rawlings,* 237, 241–42. Also appeared in MKR's short story collection *When the Whippoorwill* (New York: Scribner, 1940).

158   "I am not coming to hunt": Arthur Kinnan to MKR, October 25, 1936.

159   "Spiders swung comfortably": MKR, *Cross Creek,* 183.

159   "the ease and smoothness": Arthur Kinnan to MKR, January 30, 1937.

159   "a woman of intelligence": MKR to MEP, February 25, 1937.

159   Florida "lacks the rough ruggedness": Arthur Kinnan to MKR, January 30, 1937.

CHAPTER THIRTEEN: *THE YEARLING*

160   "perfectly delirious": MKR to MEP, August 27, 1936.

160   "I do not know when I have ever": MKR to MEP, October 16, 1936.

160   "I assure you the fabric": MKR to MEP, November 1936.

160   "The Louisville flood meant nothing": MKR to MEP, January 1937.

161   "anything they do": Ibid.

161   "on the point of exploding": MKR to MEP, February 25, 1937.

161   "back on your hands": Arthur Kinnan to MKR, March 15, 1937.

161   "I lost my hard-won abstraction": MKR to MEP, April 22, 1937.

161   "I really think she": C. Blackburn Miller to MKR, December 6, 1937.

161   "I wished I had argued": MKR to MEP, June [13?], 1937.

162   "Why didn't you tell me": MKR to MEP, June 18, 1937.

162   "I've missed you woefully": Otto Lange to MKR, July 21, 1937.

162   "It is a good thing": Otto Lange to MKR, August 26, 1937.

162   "That last night at your house": Otto Lange to MKR, September 28, 1937.

162 **In a letter to Julia Scribner:** MKR to JSB, August 9, 1944.

162 **"He was the quiet one":** David Nolan, interview by the author, October 17, 2016, St. Augustine, Florida.

163 **"lots of blue pencil":** MKR to MEP, October 20, 1937.

163 **"The relation of fact to fiction":** "On the Relationship Between Fact and Fiction," notes, Marjorie Kinnan Rawlings Papers, University of Florida.

164 **"Hope you find the book":** MKR to MEP, December 2, 1937.

165 **"The truth is the book is":** MEP to MKR, December 13, 1937.

165 **"After completing such a book":** MEP to MKR, December 23, 1937.

165 **"with as cold an eye as possible":** MKR to MEP, January 23, 1938.

166 **"I always regretted":** MKR to MEP, March 2, 1938.

166 **"It looks even worse":** "Hitler and Shirt-Tails," *Palm Beach Post,* January 7, 1938.

166 **"I fired my young grove":** MKR to MEP, December 29, 1937.

167 **"food and coffee and liquor":** Ibid.

167 **"I have never read such art":** Hamilton Holt to MKR, May 14, 1938.

167 **"The fact is, you are":** Hamilton Holt to MKR, July 1, 1938.

167 **"the skillful counterpoint":** Charles Poore, *New York Times,* April 1, 1938.

168 **"lesser members of the fraternity":** William Soskin, *New York Herald Tribune,* April 3, 1938.

168 **"The thing about *The Yearling*":** Edith H. Walton, *New York Times Book Review,* April 3, 1938.

168 **"The hunger of one person":** Otto Lange to MKR, January 30, 1938.

168 **"We all want you":** Otto Lange to MKR, May 12, 1938.

169 **"It is so lovely":** Marjory Stoneman Douglas to MKR, August 28, 1938.

169 **"I feel that you must be a generous":** MKR to Frank Kelley, n.d.

CHAPTER FOURTEEN: PULITZER

170 **"Wire me at Ft. Knox":** Otto Lange to MKR, May 12, 1938.

170 **"Even if I had never seen you":** MEP to MKR, June 10, 1938.

171 **"If you'd gone through with it":** Quoted in MKR to Norman Berg, June 25, 1938.

171 **"Statistics don't mean anything":** Ibid.

171 **"fished hard in all kinds of weather":** MKR to MEP, July 11, 1938.

171 **"extremely nervous":** Margaret, "Author Tells of 'Hot' Trip From Bimini," *Miami Daily News,* July 10, 1938.

171 **"She wore a cotton print dress":** Margaret, "Author Tells of 'Hot' Trip From Bimini," *Miami Daily News,* July 10, 1938.

171 **"I cannot and will not":** MKR to MEP, July 11, 1938.

172 **"poached eggs so fresh":** MKR, "Now Nationally Known Author Recalls Visits on Farm in Holly Township," *Holly Herald,* June 30, 1938

172 **"We will switch back to Barklay's":** NSB to MKR, July 31, 1938. Barclay's (misspelled by Norton) is a brand of whiskey.

172 **"He was all alone":** MEP to MKR, July 26, 1938.

172 **"a burden that I never realized":** Ibid.

173 **"If I get on my feet":** Thomas Wolfe to MEP, in *Editor to Author: The Letters of Maxwell E. Perkins,* ed. John Hall Wheelock (New York: Scribner, 1950), 141–42.

173 **"I know you think I":** MKR to MEP, May 14, 1938.

173 **"said that the writer must wait between books":** MKR to MEP, August 30, 1938.

174 **"I'd get in the Ford and ride":** "Author of 'Lamb in His Bosom,' Here, Tells How She Gathered Material for Her Book," *Atlanta Constitution,* November 26, 1933, p. 7.

175 "It was a close squeak": MKR to Norman Berg, June 25, 1938.

175 "the last thing": MEP to MKR, September 19, 1938.

175 "His very touching letter": MKR to MEP, September 21, 1938.

176 "As you know, the United States": Margaret Mitchell to MKR, December 7, 1938.

176 "I reminded them": MKR to Margaret Mitchell, March 6, 1939.

176 "I had been told you had a grove": Margaret Mitchell to MKR, December 20, 1938.

177 "running the termites down": MKR to MEP, December 6, 1938.

177 "He looked just the same": MKR to Bee Humiston McNeil, January 9, 1939.

177 "would happen sooner or later": MKR to MEP, December 8, 1938.

177 "I should think Chuck": Bee Humiston McNeil to MKR, January 31, 1939.

177 her time was too valuable: MEP to MKR, December 6, 1938.

177 "very exhausting and unrewarding": MEP to MKR, December 12, 1938.

177 "$8000 for 8 weeks": MKR to MEP, December 8, 1938.

178 She was fighting for writing time: MKR wire to MEP, December 11, 1938.

178 "We can guarantee no parties": Edith Pope to MKR, May 11, 1938.

178 "pleading need of noninterruption": MKR to MEP, January 12, 1939.

178 "I refuse to let them lick me": Arthur Kinnan to MKR, May 10, 1937.

178 "I am of course much upset": MKR to MEP, January 2, 1939.

179 According to Marjorie: Marjorie's full account can be found in "Black Shadows," Cross Creek, 180–204.

179 "The old woman, who I had": MKR to MEP, January 16, 1939. This anecdote was later included in "Black Shadows."

180 "The Scotch in me rebelled": MKR to MEP, February 22, 1939.

180 "he didn't give a damn": Ibid.

180 "It is a pity": Ibid.

181 "Fell into bed more dead than alive": MKR to NSB, May 1939.

181 on page 17: "Pulitzer Awards Are Won by Four Newspapermen," Cincinnati Enquirer, May 2, 1939, p. 17.

181 "Saw the Pulitzer announcement": MKR to NSB, May, 1939.

181 "any of those things too much to heart": MKR to Norman Berg, June 14, 1939.

181 "Hell, no": Quoted in Elizabeth Silverthorne, Marjorie Kinnan Rawlings: Sojourner at Cross Creek (Woodstock, NY: Overlook, 1988), 182.

182 "Author Amazed, Reads She Won Pulitzer Prize": Jane Williams, Mansfield News-Journal, May 3, 1939, 2.

CHAPTER FIFTEEN: *WHEN THE WHIPPOORWILL*

183 "a lot of drunken fun": MKR to Norman Berg, June 14, 1939.

183 "A book of description": MEP to MKR, May 9, 1939.

183 "it would be absurd to begin": MKR to MEP, May 13, 1939.

183 "succession of sketches": Ibid.

184 "I think it all comes down, basically": MKR to Fritz Dashiell, June 29, 1939.

185 "I hate to have to run from my own home": MKR to MEP, August 14, 1939.

185 "I have been forced to wonder": Ibid.

185 Max reassured her: MEP to MKR, August 17, 1939.

185 "When a woman has wanted more of a man": MKR to NSB, August 10, 1939.

186 "in rags and tatters": MKR to MEP, August 29, 1939.

186 "Cocks Must Crow," and "The Enemy": Saturday Evening Post, November 25, 1939, and January 20, 1940.

186 **"The Pelican's Shadow":** *New Yorker,* January 6, 1940.

186 **"In the Heart":** *Collier's,* February 3, 1940.

187 **"As quietly as a hostess":** Molly Clowes, Louisville *Courier-Journal,* October 5, 1939, p. 10.

187 **"I always come back from Louisville":** MKR to MEP, October 18, 1939.

187 **"a wave of pity came over me":** MKR to Mark Ethridge, October 22, 1939.

188 **"Said not to ever let anyone":** MKR to NSB, October 5, 1939.

188 **"with a bird of Paradise":** Margaret Mitchell to MKR, December 7, 1938.

188 **"With [Mitchell's] passion for law-suits":** MKR to Bernice Baumgarten, late 1938 or 1939.

188 **"Yet the customs of travel":** MKR, "Regional Literature of the South," *English Journal,* (February 1940): 89–97.

189 **"for the first time since leaving":** Ibid., 388–89. These quotes were jotted down and appended to the manuscript by the editor.

189 **"Went to the Christmas punch tasting":** MKR to NSB, November 30, 1939.

190 **"The grove and the farmhouse":** MKR to MEP, December 14, 1939.

190 **"We expect to have a swell time":** MKR to Norman Berg, November, 1939.

190 **"the town is in a frenzy":** Margaret Mitchell to MKR, November 8, 1939.

191 **"almost straight journalism":** MKR to MEP, February 27, 1940.

191 **"I'll be damned":** MKR to MEP, January 2, 1940.

191 **"He was hard on people":** Karen Kushner, telephone interview by the author, September 2015.

191 **"Feisty and opinionated":** Tom Consolino, telephone interview by the author, August 23, 2017.

192 **"You are a little boy":** John Steinbeck, *Cup of Gold: A Life of Henry Morgan, Buccaneer, with Occasional Reference to History* (New York: Penguin Classics, 1995), 22–23.

192 **"There is no alternative":** MKR to Norman Berg, February 3, 1940.

193 **"I'm more than perfunctorily sorry":** MKR to Norman Berg, March 18, 1940.

193 **"I present you the gun":** MKR to Norman Berg, December 9, 1946.

194 **"your" shotgun:** Norman Berg to MKR, September 16, 1949. ("The dove season opens this afternoon. When I carry your shotgun into the field, I'll be thinking of you. I prize it very much.")

194 **"the key to his combative":** Pat Conroy, letter to Cliff Gaubert, January 15, 2007. Courtesy of the Pat Conroy Archive, Irvin Department of Rare Books and Special Collections, University of South Carolina Libraries.

194 **"a rejected suitor":** MKR to Julia Scribner Bigham, October 8, 1940.

194 **"The youngster who wins the part":** "MGM to Use Miami Boy For Lead In New Movie," *Miami News,* February 28, 1940, p. 23.

194 **"How smart of you":** Margaret Mitchell to MKR, March 5, 1940.

194 **"I would like to tell you":** JSB to MKR, March 15 or 14, 1940.

195 **"The story about Margaret Mitchell":** MKR to JSB, undated letter, 1940.

195 **"I have really missed you":** MKR to JSB, undated letter, 1940.

195 **"The 4th from now on":** JSB to MKR, April 1, 1940.

195 **"the long steady stream":** MKR to MEP, April 1, 1940.

195 **"entirely too handsome":** *Miami News,* March 20, 1940, p. 24.

196 **"The boy must be twelve years old":** "Hollywood Crew On Silver Springs Site To Plan Production of 'The Yearling,'" *Miami News,* April 10, 1940, p. 11.

196 **"I am furious at myself":** MKR to MEP, April 1, 1940.

196 **"Ate in the vast dining-room":** MKR to NSB, April 2, 1940.

196 **"much too nice for the way I live":** MKR to NSB, April 1940.

196 **"if I can beat it":** MKR to MEP, April 7, 1940.

197   **"being happy while he worked":** Ibid.

197   **"I have wondered and wondered":** Ibid.

CHAPTER SIXTEEN: TODAY'S WOMAN

198   **"excellently, even in these":** MEP to MKR, May 16, 1940.

198   **"not so much in deeper knowledge":** Edith H. Walton, "Tales of the Florida Crackers," *New York Times Book Review*, April 28, 1940.

198   **"as good reporting of life":** *Atlantic Monthly*, June 1940.

199   **"You are just a born story-teller":** Margaret Mitchell to MKR, March 5, 1940.

199   **"I do not kindle":** James Branch Cabell to MKR, June 11, 1940.

199   **"Dear Malveeeeeeena":** MKR to Malvina Hoffman, May 15, 1940. Courtesy of the Malvina Hoffman papers, Getty Research Institute, and the Norton S. Baskin Literary Trust.

199   **"They thought there was a trick":** *Miami News*, May 26, 1940, p. 11.

199   **"Don't be surprised":** Edward Lawrence to MKR, May 22, 1941.

200   **"My hair literally stood on end":** MKR to JSB, May 1940.

200   **"I couldn't tell whether he was pulling my leg":** MKR to MEP, May 14, 1940.

200   **"People have popped in unannounced":** MKR to JSB, May 1940.

200   **"A stop-by for lunch":** Norton Baskin, interview by Danielle Flood, August 8, 1988.

201   **"I prefer to review":** MKR to Stetson Kennedy, August 11, 1942.

201   **"for it does no good":** MEP to MKR, June 1940.

201   **"Mama, you reckon":** MKR to MEP, May 24, 1940.

201   **"The Ivory Tower long since":** MKR to MEP, June 6, 1940.

202   **"It's possible that I'm asking":** MKR to NSB, June [12?], 1940.

202   **"There are so many things":** MKR to MEP, July 22, 1940.

202   **"You cannot have it":** MEP to MKR, July 26, 1940.

203   **"stuck at the creek":** MKR to JSB, June 22, 1940.

203   **"When he went off on a fresh trail":** MKR to JSB, July 22, 1940.

203   **"Was quite disappointed":** MKR to NSB, July [31?], 1940.

203   **"I was very much distressed":** MKR to Norman Berg, August 26, 1940.

204   **"Marriage is a little like death":** MKR to JSB, August 7, 1940.

204   **"Understanding, deeply kind, shrewdly observant":** Sarah Shields Pfeiffer, "Today's Woman," *Christian Science Monitor*, September 4, 1940.

205   wrote a parody: MKR, "Yesterday's Woman: An Exclusive Interview with Lollie Pop Twitter," manuscript, Marjorie Kinnan Rawlings Papers, University of Florida.

206   **"There are so many pitfalls":** MKR to MEP, September 3, 1940.

207   **"the great flaw of most autobiographies":** MKR to MEP, January 13, 1944.

207   **"He is obviously in a much better":** MKR to MEP, September 19, 1940.

207   **"It could and even must be":** MEP to MKR, September 20, 1940.

207   **"As matters stand":** Ibid.

208   **"There are lots of people who think":** Ibid.

208   **"people reflect their background":** V. Jackson, "Campus Comment," *Oshkosh Northwestern*, Oshkosh, WI, October 14, 1940.

208   Another question: Ibid.

209   **"Now that we are in our declining years":** Ibid.

209   Other classmates offered memories: Remarks at the Marjorie Kinnan Rawlings Banquet, Memorial Union, October 8, 1940, manuscript, Marjorie Kinnan Rawlings Papers, University of Florida.

CHAPTER SEVENTEEN:
GOOD WOMEN, MARRIAGE, AND A MEMOIR

210 **"and I have only now gotten":** MKR to MEP, November 25, 1940.

210 **"Of course you need not":** MEP to MKR, November 28, 1940.

211 **A native of nearby Reddick:** The account of Idella's hiring comes predominantly from her memoir *Marjorie Rawlings' Perfect Maid* (Gainesville: University Press of Florida, 1992).

212 **"My new darky maid":** MKR to JSB, November 25, 1940.

212 **"They shouldn't call it that":** Ibid.

212 **"low metabolism":** MKR to JSB, January 1, 1941.

213 **"He suffered by having":** MEP to MKR, January 4, 1941.

213 **Scott's life was more tragic than his death:** MKR to MEP, January 1941.

213 **"the courtesy often extended":** MKR, "In the Heart," reprinted in *Short Stories by Marjorie Kinnan Rawlings,* ed. Rodger L. Tarr (Gainesville: University Press of Florida, 1994), 315–19.

214 **"a temporary paralysis":** MKR to MEP, March 3, 1941.

214 **"I suffer from it all the time":** MKR to JSB, January 4, 1941.

214 **"Why? Why?? Why???":** Grace Kinnan to MKR, December 28, 1944.

215 **"the Southern peasants":** Ellen Glasgow to Irita Van Doren, September 8, 1933, in *Perfect Companionship: Ellen Glasgow's Selected Correspondence with Women,* ed. Pamela R. Matthews (Charlottesville: University of Virginia Press, 2005), 139.

215 **"seems to me to be":** Ellen Glasgow to MKR, April 16, 1939.

215 **"a tremendous hit":** James Branch Cabell to MKR, April 9, 1941.

215 **"The reality of a dream":** MKR to Ellen Glasgow, July 19, 1941, in Matthews, *Perfect Companionship,* 210.

216 a **"thrilling sense of friendship and sympathy":** Ellen Glasgow to MKR, July 24, 1941.

216 **"I simply don't feel good enough":** MKR to NSB, April 1, 1941.

217 **"The White House and its friends":** Louisville *Courier-Journal*, April 2, 1941, p. 15.

217 **"did your trick":** MKR to NSB, April 2, 1941.

217 **"Surely a man in his loneliness":** MKR, "The Provider," reprinted in Tarr, *Short Stories,* 326–37.

217 **"You changed instantly":** MKR to NSB, September 1941.

218 **"They convinced me my moods":** MKR to JSB, September 24, 1941.

218 **"see the whole picture":** MKR to NSB, October 1, 1941.

218 **"I am to ease up":** MKR to MEP, October 12, 1941.

218 **"a well-trained and perceptive internist":** Dana Atchley, *Physician: Healer and Scientist* (New York: Macmillan, 1961), 68.

219 **"alert, open watchfulness":** Anne Morrow Lindbergh, *Against Wind and Tide: Letters and Journals, 1947–1986* (New York: Pantheon, 2012), 105.

219 **"the things that I could identify":** MKR to NSB, October 11, 1941.

219 **"the source of my peculiar":** MKR to NSB, October [13?], 1941.

219 **"I'm giving you a chance":** MKR to NSB, October 11, 1941.

219 **"As you know, I have been ready":** NSB to MKR, October 6, 1941.

219 **"It is just right that this marriage':** Ellen Glasgow to MKR, February 24, 1942.

220 **"I have used true names":** MKR to MEP, September 15, 1941.

220 **"What really binds the book together":** MEP to MKR, September 29, 1941.

220 **"No actual autobiography":** MKR to Norman Berg, December 9, 1946.

220 **"As to the question of libel":** MEP to MKR, September 29, 1941.

220 "It has been such a funny pain": MKR to NSB, November 1941.

221 "I think you are most blessed": MEP to MKR, December 5, 1941.

221 "a brilliant new chapter": "Castle Warden Opens Here With Norton Baskin, Host At Pretty Informal Cocktail Party," *St. Augustine Record,* December 1941

221 "this gregarious hotel man": Interview with Norton Baskin, St. Augustine *Compass,* May 19, 1988.

221 "She was a bad judge of people": NSB, interview by Danielle Flood, August 8, 1988.

222 "change some names": MEP to MKR, December 9, 1941.

222 "a great many minor changes": MKR to MEP, December 12, 1941.

222 Later, she pointed out: MKR to MEP, January 12, 1942.

222 "could have been written only": Katherine Woods, "In the Land of 'The Yearling,'" *New York Times Book Review,* March 15, 1942.

223 "They say that the staunchest": Lewis Gannett, *New York Herald Tribune,* March 16, 1942.

223 "Like all her books": "Books: Enchanted Land," *Time,* March 23, 1942.

223 Sometime in April: Patricia Nassif Acton, *Invasion of Privacy: The Cross Creek Trial of Marjorie Kinnan Rawlings* (Gainesville: University Press of Florida, 1988), 24.

223 "very heavy fan mail": MKR to MEP, June 19, 1942.

223 Some readers were either naïve: MKR to Lieutenant Commander E. Mixon, U.S. Navy, August 13, 1943.

224 "a very appealing little volume": MEP to MKR, April 21, 1942.

CHAPTER EIGHTEEN: WARTIME, ZORA

225 "I had thought": MKR to MEP, March 1942.

226 "A brown girl goes out": Yola Miller Sigerson, *The Art of Compassion: A Biography of Sigrid Undset* (Bloomington: Xlibris, 2006), 237.

226 "Please don't hurry her": Ibid., 237.

227 "speaking at 'Rallies'": Sigrid Undset to MKR, April 24, 1942.

227 "Every week almost I learn": Sigrid Undset to MKR, January 6, 1943.

227 "There is a woman": MKR to JSB, April 7, 1942.

228 "We have the dim-out": MKR to MEP, June 19, 1942.

228 "I simply associate": MKR to Edith Pope, July 16, 1942.

229 "She gives no great quantity of milk": MKR, *Cross Creek Cookery* (New York: Scribner, 1942), 199.

229 "which I discovered": Ibid., 111.

229 "met the most wonderful woman": NSB, interview by Danielle Flood, August 8, 1988.

230 Norton, however, assured Marjorie: Ibid.

230 "a lush, fine-looking": MKR to Edith Pope, July 7, 1942.

230 "staked out a conservative position": Carla Kaplan, *Zora Neale Hurston: A Life in Letters* (New York: Doubleday, 2002), 5.

231 "theatrical modesty and duplicity": Hilton Als, *White Girls* (San Francisco: McSweeney's, 2013), 97.

231 "the lie of their pretended humanism": James Baldwin, *No Name in the Street* (New York: Vintage, 2007), 85.

231 "Mrs. Rawlings, kind as she was": Idella Parker, *Marjorie Rawlings' Perfect Maid* (Gainesville: University Press of Florida, 1992), iii.

231 "in the absence of other and adequate": "University of Florida May Have First Negro Student This Summer," Associated Press, June 14, 1941; seen in the *Greenville News,* June 14, 1941.

232 "reasonably accurate": MKR, *Cross Creek,* 180.

232 "By all her principles": MKR to Edith Pope, July 7, 1942.

232 she found it "rather creepy": MKR to MEP, July 23, 1942.

233 "A war of ideas": Franklin D. Roosevelt, letter to W. W. Norton, chairman of the Council on Books in Wartime, December 1, 1942.

233 In some cities: Nick Wynne and Richard Moorhead, *Florida in World War II: Floating Fortress* (Charleston: History Press, 2010), 55.

234 "That meal was a symphony": MKR to MEP, August 21, 1942.

234 "May I commend you": Alexander P. Haley to MKR, April 29, 1944.

235 "I am afraid that it is utterly futile": MKR to John Temple Graves, manuscript, Marjorie Kinnan Rawlings Papers, University of Florida.

238 "The scarcity of natural resources": Earle H. Clapp, quoted in Gerald W. Williams, *The USDA Forest Service: The First Century,* rev. ed. (Washington, DC: USDA Forest Service Office of Communication, 2005), 87.

238 "It has destroyed his future": MKR, "Trees for Tomorrow," *Collier's,* May 8, 1943.

239 "As you grow older": MKR to JSB, November 11, 1942.

240 "interwoven with brilliant vignettes": Wilma Lord Perkins, *New York Post,* December 2, 1942.

240 "the Army seems to have been": Lewis Gannett, *New York Herald Tribune,* December 25, 1942.

240 "only a dinner with you": Mary Meade, "Cross Creek: Here Comes Mary Meade," *Chicago Tribune,* November 15, 1942.

240 "Only the expert dare attempt": MKR, *Cross Creek Cookery,* 32.

240 "Actually, I think he is pleased": MKR to Edith Pope, November 2, 1942.

CHAPTER NINETEEN: LAWSUIT

242 "Zelma is an ageless spinster": MKR, *Cross Creek,* 357–58.

243 "It is charged": seen in the *Philadelphia Inquirer,* " 'Character' in Book Sues Miss Rawlings," February 3, 1943.

243 "Let's turn to the book": E. D. Lambright, "Cross Creek in Court," *Tampa Tribune,* February 7, 1943.

243 "I think the Declaration": MKR to Phil May, February 5, 1943.

244 "If it were in New York": MEP to MKR, February 5, 1943.

245 "It's probably the most perfect": Quoted in Patricia Nassif Acton, *Invasion of Privacy: The Cross Creek Trial of Marjorie Kinnan Rawlings* (Gainesville: University Press of Florida, 1988), 23.

245 "Had my abdominal X-ray": MKR to NSB, February [26?], 1943.

246 "a huge jar of Martinis": MKR to NSB, February 26, 1943 (separate letter from that above).

246 "I know only that I love you": MKR to NSB, March 5, 1943.

246 "You know I will cooperate": NSB to MKR, March 8, 1943.

246 "certain medical practices": NSB to MKR, February 25, 1943.

246 "to prove she is *the* Zelma": NSB to MKR, February 26, 1943.

246 "The models are pretty enough": NSB to MKR, March 9, 1943.

246 Norton had held back: Ibid.

247 "It looks as though": MKR to NSB, March 22, 1943.

247 "together in a tangle": Ibid.

247 "the height of indiscretion": MKR to NSB, April [4?], 1943.

247 "you are an artist": MKR to JSB, March 26, 1943.

248 "Twenty-one guns!": Zora Neale Hurston to MKR, May 16, 1943.

249 "You did a thing I like": Ibid.

249 "As the years went by": Idella Parker, *Marjorie Rawlings' Perfect Maid* (Gainesville: University Press of Florida, 1992), 117.

249 "On the right-hand side": Ibid.

250 "all but held up": MKR to Edith Pope, July 14, 1943.

250 "I could hardly hope for you to understand": NSB to MKR, April [15?], 1943.

250 "work in the front lines": MKR to Norman Berg, July 6, 1943.

251 "I feel a little better": MKR to NSB, July 28, 1943.

251 "what people are saying": MKR to Edith Pope, July 14, 1943.

251 "not chilled, or, as it were": James Branch Cabell to MKR, June 26, 1943.

252 "a certain inevitability": MKR to MEP, June 17, 1943.

252 "the consciousness of the principal character": MKR to MEP, August 2, 1943.

252 "You asked me once": Ibid.

253 "How I wish that I were not doing": Zora Neale Hurston to MKR, August 21, 1943.

253 "The Negro writer": MKR to NSB, August 23, 1943.

254 "When she and I have finished": Ibid.

254 "The offer from Zora": NSB to MKR, September 19, 1943.

254 "is not nearly sufficient": Quoted in Acton, *Invasion of Privacy*, 56.

254 "It shouldn't worry us": NSB to MKR, September 1, 1943.

254 Marjorie replied with new information: MKR to NSB, September 4, 1943.

255 "I have always enjoyed her": MKR to NSB, November 18, 1943.

CHAPTER TWENTY: WHAT IS HOME?

256 "We all talk like Hemingway": NSB to MKR, July 20, 1943.

256 "I do two push-ups": NSB to MKR, August 31, 1943.

256 "The terrain was as different": NSB to MKR, September 4, 1943.

257 "as obscure as some of the more": NSB to MKR, October 20, 1943.

257 "would be replete with boredom": NSB to MKR, September 5, 1943.

257 "with lots of lattice work": NSB to MKR, September 15, 1943.

257 "leaves the impression that": NSB to MKR, December 6, 1943.

257 "Four of us roamed": NSB to MKR, October 31, 1943.

257 "Don't even think that anything": NSB to MKR, October 11, 1943.

257 "Don't ever put off writing me": NSB to MKR, September 16, 1943.

257 "You are given a truck": NSB to MKR, October 17, 1943.

258 "retire to the bathroom": NSB to MKR, November 6, 1943.

258 "I think that if I did not write you": NSB to MKR, November 14, 1943.

258 "For probably the first time in my life": NSB to MKR, November 23, 1943.

258 "If you have really never been in it": MKR to NSB, December 20, 1943.

259 "She is in a perilous": MKR to NSB, October 20, 1943.

259 "I have been unable quite": MKR to NSB, October 30, 1943.

260 "It is a magnificent thing": MKR to NSB, October 17, 1943.

260 "It went into the stream-of-consciousness": MKR to NSB, October 18, 1943.

260 "Where has Koestler been": MKR to Norman Berg, November 27, 1943.

260 "so he is evidently carrying": MKR to NSB, November 27, 1943.

260   **"I have forced myself"**: MKR to Norman Berg, November 27, 1943.

260   **"a tough bunch"**: MKR to NSB, August 16, 1943.

260   **"I am toying with the idea"**: MKR to NSB, August 11, 1943.

261   **"For a long time I have been awakening"**: MKR to NSB, August 19, 1943.

261   **"Something of my old desire"**: MKR to NSB, September 23, 1943.

261   **"There were so many unhappy details"**: MKR to NSB, October 29, 1943.

262   **"I thought I would get great satisfaction"**: NSB to MKR, December 1943

262   **"the waste and the horrors of war"**: NSB to MKR, December 25, 1943.

262   **"Well, I had the most mixed emotions"**: MKR to NSB, December 22, 1943.

264   **"Dearest I am whipped down"**: MKR to NSB, December 22, 1943 (second letter).

264   **"was that I had been"**: MKR to NSB, December 29, 1943.

265   **"The rioters were the lowest"**: MKR to NSB, February 5, 1944.

265   **"What I wanted to do"**: Trudi McCullough, "'Strange Fruit,' Southern Woman's Novel, Plea Against Segregation," Associated Press, seen in the *St. Louis Post-Dispatch,* April 9, 1944.

265   **"so devastating and accurate"**: MKR to NSB, February 10, 1944.

266   **"Southerners don't want to think"**: Edith Pope to MKR, March 2, 1944.

266   **"an old shack of a church"**: MKR to NSB, February 14, 1944.

266   **"You have never been hated"**: MKR to NSB, February 16, 1944.

266   **"You will gain nothing"**: NSB to MKR, March 15, 1944.

267   **"And you got up"**: MKR to NSB, February 27, 1944.

267   **"They don't shout like the sanctifiers"**: MKR to NSB, February 28, 1944.

267   **"but they really did their stuff"**: MKR to NSB, March 1, 1944.

268   **"You can't force men"**: MKR to NSB, April 14, 1944.

268   a court decision in Montgomery: Arthur A. Madison v. State of Alabama.

268   **"We haven't had that"**: MKR to NSB, May 29, 1944.

268   **"close to the heart"**: MKR to NSB, June 23, 1944.

269   **"I still have to fight"**: MKR to NSB, June 28, 1944.

269   **"I get over the necessary embrace"**: MKR to NSB, July 8, 1944.

269   inspired an anxious dream: NSB to MKR, August 4, 1944.

269   **"for a certain spurious sort"**: MKR to NSB, May 7, 1944.

269   **"I cut as far to the right"**: MKR to NSB, March 13, 1944.

270   **"I don't believe I have ever been"**: JSB to MKR, March 16, 1944.

270   **"With all due admission"**: MKR to JSB, May 19, 1944.

270   **"This is truly one of life's"**: NSB to MKR, May 11, 1944.

CHAPTER TWENTY-ONE: ON TRIAL

272   *New Yorker* in the coming months: "The Shell" appeared on December 9, 1944; "Miriam's Houses" on November 24, 1945; and "Black Secret" on September 8, 1945.

273   **"At the moment"**: "Florida: A Land of Contrasts," *Transatlantic,* October 1944. Reprinted in Rodger L. Tarr and Brent Kinser, eds., *The Uncollected Writings of Marjorie Kinnan Rawlings* (Gainesville: University Press of Florida, 2007), 302–08.

273   **"Take the lies of California"**: "Florida: An Affectionate Tribute," *Congressional Record,* March 2, 1945, H1692–93; reprinted in Tarr and Kinser, *Uncollected Writings,* 310–11.

274   **"for breach of which"**: Quoted in Patricia Nassif Acton, *Invasion of Privacy: The Cross Creek Trial of Marjorie Kinnan Rawlings* (Gainesville: University Press of Florida, 1988), 59.

274 **"portrays plaintiff"**: Ibid.

275 **"upon the same legal basis"**: Ibid., 68.

275 **"feels that autobiographies"**: Ibid., 69.

276 **"It was a fascinating experience"**: MKR to Edith Pope, March 7, 1945.

276 **"I am out of patience"**: MKR quoted in the *Tampa Times*, May 31, 1945.

276 **"clinging to the safety"**: MKR to JSB, May 19, 1944.

276 **"You make it sound"**: JSB to MKR, September 1944.

277 **"where the Germans destroyed"**: Sigrid Undset to MKR, November 24, 1945.

278 **"with the most idiotic"**: MEP to MKR, October 17, 1944.

278 **"And I hope the day is very near"**: G. S. Lobrano to MKR, January 2, 1948.

278 **"an advanced stage of melancholia"**: James Branch Cabell to MKR, November 3, 1945.

278 **"Go on with your book"**: Ellen Glasgow to MKR, November 17, 1945.

278 **"At the time of Ellen's death"**: MKR to James Branch Cabell, March 1946.

279 **"it was in response to that"**: MKR to MEP, December 7, 1945.

279 **"It does seem rather incongruous"**: MKR to Phil May, December 31, 1945.

280 **"Please come up and have a drink"**: MKR to Phil May, April 18, 1946.

280 **"In the long years of loneliness"**: MKR to Norman Berg, July 18, 1945.

281 **"The defense contends"**: "Trial Opens in Slander Suit Against Author," *Tampa Tribune*, May 21, 1946.

282 **"I've never used the Lord's name"**: "Made 'A Huzzy Out of a Lady,'" *Baltimore Sun*, May 22, 1946.

282 **"humiliated and mortified"**: J. A. Clendinen, "'Cross Creek' Spinster Tells Story in Court," *Tampa Tribune*, May 22, 1946.

282 **"now I know"**: Hampton Dunn, "Spinster Says Novel Made Friends Tease," *Tampa Times*, May 21, 1946.

282 **"I told her she took a lady"**: Ibid.

283 **"The lawyer was apparently"**: Hampton Dunn, "2nd Book Character Takes Stand at Trial," *Tampa Times*, May 22, 1946.

283 **"We can't try every character"**: Quoted in Acton, *Invasion of Privacy*, 90.

283 **"paid off" all the characters**: "Marjorie Rawlings On Stand in Defense Of Her Writing," *Fort Lauderdale News*, May 24, 1946.

283 **A local attorney said**: J. A. Clendinen, "15 Witnesses Testify for 'Cross Creek,'" *Tampa Tribune*, May 24, 1946.

284 **"dissected, analyzed"**: Ibid.

284 **"If all inelegant passages"**: Andy Anderson, "Rawlings Suit Nears Climax," *St. Petersburg Times*, May 24, 1946.

285 **"I was interpreting this lovely country"**: Quoted in Acton, *Invasion of Privacy*, 103.

285 **"She was a woman who didn't grow old"**: Quoted in Ibid., 104.

285 **"I was thinking of a man being more forceful"**: Hampton Dunn, "Hushed Courtroom Listens to Author," *Tampa Times*, May 24, 1946.

286 **asked Zelma's mother and brother**: J. A. Clendinen, "Mrs. Rawlings Defends Her 'Cross Creek,'" *Tampa Tribune*, May 25, 1946.

286 **"Phil May jumped up and said"**: MKR to MEP, June 5, 1946.

286 **"Well, she combined various"**: J. A. Clendinen, "Mrs. Rawlings Defends Her 'Cross Creek,'" *Tampa Tribune*, May 25, 1946.

286 **"Yes, I would call"**: Ibid.

287 **"love life is merciless"**: MKR, *Cross Creek*, 254.

287 **At one point, grasping at straws**: Andy Anderson, "Mrs. Rawlings Denies Cruelty," *Tampa Times*, May 27, 1946.

287 **"It is in my blood and bones"**: Quoted in Acton, *Invasion of Privacy*, 111.

CHAPTER TWENTY-TWO:
"I HAVE NEVER FELT MORE INADEQUATE"

289 "more in demand": Milton Plumb, "Author of 'Cross Creek' Says She's Worth $124,000," *Tampa Tribune,* May 28, 1946.

289 "it was something past Lewis Carroll's": James Branch Cabell, quoted in a letter by MKR to NSB, June 6, 1946.

289 "Zelma Cason, Florida social worker": *Time,* July 10, 1946.

290 "A person who redoubles": Paraphrased by MKR in a letter to MEP, June 18, 1946.

290 "It seems so crazy to me": Sigrid Undset to MKR, December 14, 1946.

290 "I can hear Zelma saying": MKR to NSB, September 25, 1946.

290 "The mountains give a great lift": MKR to Norman Berg, September 13, 1946.

291 "Most of them mulattoes": MKR to NSB, September 21, 1946.

291 "At first, the extremity": MKR to MEP, September 18, 1946.

291 "The story goes rapidly": MKR to NSB, September 2, 1946.

291 "could have died": MKR to MEP, April 30, 1947.

291 "I have paid with my life's blood": MKR to Walter O'Meara, n.d.

292 "The woman is a great American artist": MKR to NSB, December 1, 1946.

293 "In five minutes": UP story seen in the Canonsburg, PA, *Daily Notes,* December 24, 1946.

293 "Those movie people": *Central New Jersey Home News,* April 28, 1946.

293 "She wouldn't come to the place": *Chicago Tribune,* November 9, 1946.

293 "To be sure": Bosley Crowther, "*The Yearling,* Based on Novel by Marjorie Rawlings, Opens at Radio City, with Claude Jarman Jr. in Role of Jody," *New York Times,* January 24, 1947.

294 "and they and I cleaned up on it": Margaret Mitchell to MKR, February 4, 1947.

294 "I have never felt more inadequate": MKR to MEP, February 13, 1947.

294 "The Negro imagination": MKR, *Cross Creek,* 81.

294 "I have found that each of my books": MKR to MEP, February 13, 1947.

295 "Mrs. Rawlings had been working late": Edwin Way Teale, *North with the Spring* (New York: Dodd, Mead, 1951), 57.

295 However, in his private journal: Teale's journals courtesy of Archives and Special Collections, University of Connecticut Library, Archive Box 15, Volume 1 (142–47) and Volume 2 (1–37). With gratitude to Mary Z. Fuka.

297 "pretty much fairy-tale style": MKR to MEP, March 19, 1947.

297 "a little of the Negro quality": MEP to MKR, March 31, 1947.

297 In the *People's Voice:* "Anti-Negro Book Banned by School," *People's Voice,* September 14, 1946.

298 "I approve with all": "Author Explains Use of 'Nigger' in Book," *People's Voice,* November 9, 1946

298 she implied that southern Negroes: see Zora Neale Hurston's letter to the *Orlando Sentinel,* August 11, 1955, available at https://teachingamericanhistory.org/library/document/letter-to-the-orlando-sentinel/.

298 "How much satisfaction": Ibid.

299 "complete dignity to all Negroes": MKR to MEP, April 4, 1947.

299 "the world will be robbed": MEP to MKR, April 16, 1947.

299 That spring, Marjorie had another wreck: MKR to MEP, April 30, 1947.

299 Later, Idella told the story differently: Idella Parker, *Marjorie Rawlings' Perfect Maid* (Gainesville: University Press of Florida, 1992), 77–78.

300 "I had been obliged": MKR to Norman Berg, May 1, 1947.

300 "I don't know why I fool": MKR to Norman Berg, May 21, 1947.

300   **"settle the thing":** NSB to MKR, May 26, 1947.

300   **"I cannot allow a precedent":** MKR to Norman Berg, May 26, 1947.

301   **"I could have saved all kinds of trouble":** Quoted by MKR in a letter to Phil May, March 30, 1948.

CHAPTER TWENTY-THREE: A NEW OUTPOST

302   **"Several of us who had":** "Portrait of a Magnificent Editor as Seen Through His Letters," *Publishers' Weekly* (April 1950): 1573–74. Reprinted in Rodger L. Tarr and Brent Kinser, eds., *The Uncollected Writings of Marjorie Kinnan Rawlings* (Gainesville: University Press of Florida, 2007), 334–37.

303   **"and on which he could not save":** MKR to Norman Berg, June 22, 1947.

303   **"panic, the sense of falling":** Marcia Davenport, *Too Strong for Fantasy* (New York: Scribner, 1967), 405.

303   **"the best":** Quoted in A. Scott Berg, *Max Perkins: Editor of Genius* (New York: Dutton, 1978), 449.

303   **"I felt inclined":** MKR to Norman Berg, June 22, 1947.

303   **"The almost indefinable quality":** MKR to Charles Scribner, July 3, 1947.

303   **"I went into his office":** MKR to Bernice Gilkyson, July 9, 1947.

303   **"Mrs. Young is 'mothering' me":** MKR to Bee McNeil, August 27, 1947.

303   **"There isn't a drop of liquor":** MKR to NSB, June 25, 1947.

304   **"I have lost ten pounds":** MKR to Norman Berg, July 30, 1947.

304   **"You will love it as much":** MKR to NSB, July 14, 1947.

305   **"Your castles are a little far flung":** NSB to MKR, July 21, 1947.

305   **"having felt insecure all my life":** MKR to NSB, June 10, 1950.

305   **"Get your work done":** MKR to NSB, July 14, 1947.

305   **"Sometimes I sit":** MKR to NSB, July 17, 1947.

306   **"Should books be planned out":** "If You Want to be a Writer," *The Book of Knowledge Annual,* ed. E. V. McLoughlin (New York: Grolier Society, 1948), 247–49. Reprinted in Tarr and Kinser, *Uncollected Writings,* 325–29.

306   **"where I came from":** NSB to MKR, August 3, 1947.

306   **"One sonnet needs reworking":** MKR to Norman Berg, August 22, 1947.

306   **"make a lot of money from it":** NSB to MKR, August 15, 1947.

306   **"Every nail that has been driven":** NSB to MKR, October 1, 1947.

307   **"It must seem hard to write":** JSB to MKR, July 1, 1947.

307   **"I think it damned white":** NSB to MKR, September 24, 1947.

307   **"I enjoyed him very much":** NSB to MKR, Ibid.

308   **"shocked by the new size":** MKR to Norman Berg, November 4, 1947.

308   **"like a bird in passage":** Ibid.

308   **"She was more than happy about it":** Ibid.

308   **"in which you stand on your head":** MKR to NSB, November 14, 1947.

308   **"I just hope so earnestly":** Wilmer Kinnan to MKR, January 4, 1948.

308   **Hodding Carter, whose long piece:** Hodding Carter, "The Civil Rights Issue as Seen in the South: A Mississippi Editor Analyzes the Factors That Lie Beneath the Great Controversy," *New York Times,* March 21, 1948.

309   **"I shall have to make a different":** MKR to Norman Berg, March 30, 1948.

309   **"I cannot resist":** MKR to James Branch Cabell, May 16, 1948, in Jacqueline J. Wilken, "Selected Letters of Marjorie Kinnan Rawlings to James Branch Cabell" (M.A. thesis, Virginia Commonwealth University, May 1993).

309   **"I was no longer":** Ibid.

309 **She had first captured national attention:** Farah Jasmine Griffin, *Harlem Nocturne: Women Artists and Progressive Politics During World War II* (New York: BasicCivitas, 2013), 23.

309 **"to know my own people":** Quoted in "Pearl in Our Midst: In Memoriam—Pearl Primus (November 29, 1919–October 29, 1994)," *Dance Research Journal* 27, no. 1 (Spring 1995): 80–82.

310 **"and my book suddenly":** MKR to NSB, June 14, 1948.

310 **"intervention of a transcendent":** Pierre Lecomte du Noüy, *Human Destiny* (New York: Longmans, Green, 1947), 38.

310 **"Without much to hang onto":** MKR to NSB, September 28, 1948.

311 **"The expressions are for the most part":** Zora Neale Hurston to MKR, December 22, 1948.

CHAPTER TWENTY-FOUR: THE COSMIC NOVEL

312 **"I may be at a crossroads":** MKR to Norman Berg, January 9, 1949.

312 **"I have never read a book":** MKR to Norman Berg, January 26, 1949.

313 **"in recognition of":** "Berg Is Editor for Macmillan," *Atlanta Constitution,* October 25, 1943.

313 **"It will not be enough":** MKR to Norman Berg, February 4, 1949.

314 **"Do not ever question yourself":** Ibid.

314 **"I am very much worried about you":** Norman Berg to MKR, February 1949.

314 **"I cannot blame environment":** MKR to Norman Berg, February 19, 1949.

315 **"to transport you":** Norman Berg to MKR, March 2, 1949.

315 **"We are in the middle":** Sigrid Undset to MKR, February 4, 1949.

315 **"I don't know if it is the same":** Sigrid Undset to MKR, March 29, 1949.

316 **"Everything is too beautiful":** MKR to Norman Berg, May 11, 1949.

316 **"When you brace yourself":** JSB to MKR, November 15, 1949.

316 **"is almost inarticulate":** MKR to Norman Berg, July 27, 1949.

317 **"I am writing privately":** Ibid.

317 **"I love and need you":** Quoted by MKR in a letter to NSB, August 2, 1949.

317 **"Of course, Norman doesn't know":** MKR to NSB, August 2, 1949.

317 **"Norman's reaction to your letter":** NSB to MKR, August 1949.

317 **"You may do anything you wish":** MKR to Norman Berg, August 8, 1949.

318 **"bread and butter and Bourbon":** Ibid.

318 **"I cannot bring":** MKR to NSB, August 1, 1949.

318 **"hands on hips":** MKR to NSB, August 16, 1949.

318 **"I cannot help wondering":** MKR to NSB, March 22, 1950.

318 **"The South seems so shabby":** MKR to Norman Berg, November 10, 1949.

318 **"Mis' Piety put her thin":** MKR to Norman Berg, December 29, 1949.

319 **"Norton was simply furious":** MKR to Norman Berg, January or February 1950.

319 **"They appeared soon after":** Ibid.

319 **"with what art":** MKR to NSB, March 14, 1950.

320 **"Ain't got my mind composed":** MKR to NSB, March 1950 (second letter).

CHAPTER TWENTY-FIVE: FERMENT

321 **"I should be the last person":** MKR to Norman Berg, early April 1950.

321 **"There is so much to be done":** Norman Berg to MKR, April 11, 1950.

321   "It appears that you might": Ibid.

322   "When I want to make Idella feel good": MKR to NSB, April 11, 1950.

322   "tampering with the bar bottles": NSB to MKR, April 5, 1950.

322   "I understand her left-over": MKR to NSB, June 20, 1950.

323   "You see, Ase <u>thinks</u>": MKR to Norman Berg, June 30, 1950.

323   "I love him with the same tearing": MKR to NSB, June 10, 1950.

323   When Frost asked: MKR to Norman Berg, June 30, 1950.

324   "A mature human being": Norman Berg to MKR, June 27, 1950.

324   "Each of us who knows": MKR to Norman Berg, June 30, 1950.

324   "collapsed on them": MKR to Norman Berg, July 1950.

324   "It fed my soul": MKR to NSB, July 18, 1950.

324   "The fight has not yet begun": Pearl Primus to MKR, October 8, 1949.

324   "Some of the African tribes": MKR to NSB, August 6, 1950.

325   "Can't seem to find a doctor": MKR to NSB, [August?] 1950.

325   "You have told me": NSB to MKR, August 1950.

325   "was cold sober": MKR to NSB, August 23, 1950.

325   "Shit-fire, honey": Ibid.

325   "Martha is one of the most sex-conscious": MKR to JSB, January 21, 1948.

325   "Hemingway says always": MKR to Norman Berg, September 18, 1950.

325   "Blast those heart-breaking little": MKR to NSB, July 13, 1950.

325   "I am at once frightened": MKR to Norman Berg, September 18, 1950.

326   "The book is not <u>fluid</u> enough": MKR to NSB, October 19, 1950.

326   "I was driving very slowly": MKR to JSB, October 25, 1950.

326   "With my own doubts": MKR to NSB, November 3, 1950.

326   "Why was she all alone": MKR to NSB, Ibid.

327   "I have become so conscious of": NSB to MKR, November 10, 1950.

327   "Daddy called me up": JSB to MKR, February 12, 1951.

327   "I seem not to have written": MKR to JSB, February 19, 1951.

327   "There is absolutely no doubt in my mind": NSB to MKR, February 24, 1951.

328   "The valuable thing you have done for me": MKR to Norman Berg, February 28, 1950.

328   "I walked up to him": Norman Berg to MKR, March 4, 1951.

329   "She is magnificent": MKR to Norman Berg, May 28, 1951.

329   "God's in His heaven": MKR to Norman Berg, May 2, 1951.

329   "All my life I have hated": MKR to Norman Berg, May 31, 1951.

329   "Another girl, damn it": MKR to NSB, August 31, 1951.

330   "a stickler for manners": Sally Baskin Hooker, interview by the author, March 30, 2017, Daytona Beach, FL.

330   "You must not ever think of me": NSB to MKR, September 18, 1951.

CHAPTER TWENTY-SIX: LOSSES

331   "I am just about down": MKR to Bernice Gilkyson, January or February 1952.

331   "It seems so callous of me": MKR to NSB, January 18, 1952.

331   "Said when he read my recipe": MKR to NSB, January 3, 1952.

332   "Heaven knows to whom": MKR to Norman Berg, January 25, 1952.

332   "turned all spiritual": MKR to NSB, January 23, 1952.

332   "The loss, while severe": MKR to Norman Berg, February 13, 1952.

332   "remodeled the home": *Rochester Democrat and Chronicle,* February 1, 1952.

333   "I had planned a perfectly lovely": MKR to JSB, February 29, 1952.

333   "but for a year or two": MKR to Norman Berg, March 2, 1952.

333 **"by a Shelby Foote"**: MKR to Norman Berg, March 14, 1952.

333 **"I have survived in spite of you"**: MKR to Norman Berg, April 28, 1952.

333 **"We had two bad evenings"**: Norman Berg to MKR, May 12, 1952.

333 **"and hope and believe"**: MKR to Norman Berg, April 28, 1952.

334 **"I have never been so jittery"**: MKR to NSB, June 4, 1952.

334 **"I have read the ending"**: Norman Berg to MKR, June 13, 1952.

334 **"two unspeakable days"**: MKR to Norman and Julie Berg, June 29, 1952.

334 **"be prepared to hear"**: MKR, quoting Arthur, to NSB, December 1, 1949.

335 **"Do you know in general"**: Wilmer Kinnan to MKR, September 3, 1950.

335 **"great lovability will compensate"**: MKR to NSB, August 6, 1950.

335 **"this very hasty marriage"**: MKR to NSB, August 30, 1950.

335 **"She has had two previous husbands"**: MKR to NSB, September 8, 1950.

336 **"raising a whirlwind"**: Wilmer Kinnan to MKR, end of 1950 or early 1951.

336 **"What made me furious"**: MKR to NSB, June 11, 1951.

336 **"That would be worthwhile"**: MKR to NSB, June 20, 1951.

336 **"I don't believe this blind"**: MKR to NSB, June 25, 1951.

337 **"just what I idealize"**: Arthur Kinnan to MKR, June 29, 1951.

337 **"A lot of it has proved"**: MKR to NSB, June 25, 1951.

337 **"I feel more strongly"**: MKR to NSB, January 29, 1952.

337 **"There was six foot four"**: NSB to MKR, July 2, 1952.

338 **"Tell Arthur"**: MKR to NSB, July 21, 1952.

338 **"I kept myself from remarking"**: MKR to NSB, July 14, 1952.

338 **"I have never seen anything so pitiful"**: MKR to NSB, July 31, 1952.

339 **"and while I could get them on"**: MKR to NSB, July 21, 1952.

339 **"So I did, and the next morning"**: MKR to Norman Berg, August 10, 1952.

339 **"Nice as the man is"**: MKR to NSB, August 26, 1952.

340 **"I read night and morning"**: MKR to JSB, August 20, 1952.

CHAPTER TWENTY-SEVEN: "DOWN"

342 **"I shall not hurry the book"**: MKR to Norman Berg, August 30, 1952.

342 **"as though I intended"**: MKR to Norman Berg, September 19, 1952.

342 **"I am sure that my fatigue"**: MKR to Norman Berg, September 26, 1952.

342 **"I believe the state law requires"**: MKR quoted by the Associated Press; seen in the *Tampa Tribune,* September 10, 1952.

343 **In response:** Described in Elizabeth Silverthorne, *Marjorie Kinnan Rawlings: Sojourner at Cross Creek* (Woodstock, NY: Overlook, 1988), 323–24.

343 **"lit out way too fast"**: MKR to NSB, September 24, 1952.

343 **"My admiration for the Oldsmobile"**: MKR to Norman Berg, September 24, 1952.

343 **"I know what you write about"**: Norman Berg to MKR, September 29, 1952.

343 **"Marjorie Kinnan Rawlings has written"**: Coleman Rosenberger, "In This Luminous New Novel One Man's Story Is a Fable of Mankind," *New York Herald Tribune,* January 4, 1953.

344 **"Precious to her are"**: Paul Jordan Smith, "Father Stands Alone in Greedy Family," *Los Angeles Times,* January 4, 1953.

344 **"She has the gift of identifying"**: "Sad and Lonely, Sojourner Is Fine Job, but No Yearling," *Miami Herald,* January 4, 1953.

344 **"the lift of *The Yearling*"**: Louis Bromfield, "Case of the Wandering Wits," *Saturday Review,* January 3, 1953.

NOTES   391

344 "The book is really as much of a legend": Paul Engle, "Marjorie Rawlings' Legend-Like Story of a Man's Search," *Chicago Tribune*, January 11, 1953.

344 "Only a skillful and sensitive writer": *Atlantic Monthly*, February 1953.

344 "Since Ase is no conversationalist": *New York Herald Tribune*, January 10, 1953.

345 "Sometimes when Ase is meditating": Orville Prescott, "Books of the Times," *New York Times*, January 3, 1953.

345 "The Sojourner is a noble attempt": *New York World-Telegram*, January 7, 1953.

345 "Although you warned me": MKR to Norman Berg, January 2, 1953.

345 "I have never laid down a book": Geoffrey Marshall to MKR, April 15, 1953.

346 "man in relation to the cosmos": Norman Berg to MKR, January 5, 1953.

346 "I shall brazen it out": MKR to Norman Berg, January 2, 1953.

346 "in the Chinese coat": MKR to Norman Berg, early 1953.

347 "*The Sojourner* is already": MKR to Norman Berg, February 19, 1953.

347 "The cream of Richmond": MKR to JSB, March 18, 1953.

347 "Why, you must be Mrs. Rawlings": MKR to NSB, February 10, 1953.

347 "I am happy to report": NSB to MKR, February 11, 1953.

348 "Sorry that you lost a short": NSB to MKR, 1953.

348 "Darling, when you call me": NSB to MKR, February 21, 1953.

348 "the most amazing results": MKR to Norman Berg, May 9, 1953.

348 "None of my novels has satisfied me": MKR, "Mrs. Rawlings Adapts Characters to Meet Novel's Creative Need," *Los Angeles Times*, May 10, 1953.

348 "And that is about all I can say": MKR, *Los Angeles Times*, May 24, 1953.

349 "unaware of the local custom": MKR to the *St. Augustine Record*, April 14, 1953.

349 "It takes very little time": MKR to Norman Berg, May 18, 1953.

350 "knew or even knows": Norman Berg to MKR, May 14, 1953.

350 "The horrible thing that gets me": MKR to NSB, July 31, 1953.

350 "I have found some wonderful": NSB to MKR, late September 1953.

350 "where I could entertain": MKR to JSB, November 19, 1953.

351 "The child was produced": Associated Press, "Nephew of Novelist Located After 18 Months of Searching," *Fairbanks Daily News-Miner*, December 2, 1953.

351 "It is almost a year": Norman Berg to MKR, December 9, 1953.

352 "More than ever Ase felt": MKR, *The Sojourner* (New York: Scribner, 1953), 324.

352 "Today she will be buried": "Mrs. Rawlings, Pulitzer Prize Winner, Dies," *St. Petersburg Times*, p. 1.

352 "skill in reproducing the color": "Mrs. Rawlings, 57, Novelist, Is Dead," *New York Times*, December 16, 1953.

353 "Her novels have brought so many": Eleanor Roosevelt column, "My Day," seen in the *World*, Coos Bay, OR, December 28, 1953.

CHAPTER TWENTY-EIGHT: LEGACY

355 "As you read, bit by bit": Shirley Ann Grau, "Introduction," *Cross Creek*, Time Reading Program edition (New York: Time Incorporated, 1966), xv–xxi.

357 "One was as prim as a New England schoolteacher": Interview of NSB by Michael Gannon for WUFT-TV, 1983.

SELECTED BIBLIOGRAPHY

MANUSCRIPT COLLECTIONS

Ernest Hemingway Collection, Personal Papers, John F. Kennedy Presidential Library and Museum, Boston, MA

Malvina Hoffman Papers, Getty Research Institute, Research Library, Special Collections, Los Angeles, CA

Marcia Davenport Papers, Library of Congress, Washington, DC

Marjorie Kinnan Rawlings Papers, Special and Area Studies Collections, George A. Smathers Libraries, University of Florida, Gainesville, FL

Mary McLeod Bethune Papers: The Bethune Foundation Collection. Microfilm accessed at the University of Colorado

Norman S. Berg and Marjorie Kinnan Rawlings correspondence and manuscripts, Hargrett Rare Book and Manuscript Library, University of Georgia Special Collections, Athens, GA

Owen D. Young Collection, Special Collections, St. Lawrence University Libraries, Canton, NY

Pat Conroy Archive, Irvin Department of Rare Books and Special Collections, University of South Carolina Libraries, Columbia, SC

Pearl Primus Collection, American Dance Festival Archives, David M. Rubenstein Rare Book and Manuscript Library, Duke University, Durham, NC

ARTICLES

Acton, Patricia Nassif. "The Effect of the 'Cross Creek' Trial on the Writings of Marjorie Kinnan Rawlings." *Marjorie Kinnan Rawlings Journal of Florida Literature* 2 (1990): 57–71.

Bass, Ernest. "Marjorie Rawlings: The Second Generation." *Marjorie Kinnan Rawlings Journal of Florida Literature* 15 (2007): 1–14.

Bauer, Gerri. "Pollution in Paradise: Betrayal and the Nature of Salvation in Marjorie Kinnan Rawlings's 'A Crop of Beans' and *Golden Apples*." *Marjorie Kinnan Rawlings Journal of Florida Literature* 13 (2004): 34–57.

Bigelow, Gordon E. "Marjorie Kinnan Rawlings' Wilderness." *Sewanee Review* 73, no. 2 (1965): 299–310.

————, moderator. "Memories of Marjorie: A Conversation with Idella Parker and Dessie Prescott." *Marjorie Kinnan Rawlings Journal of Florida Literature* 2 (1990): 131–51.

Boggess, Carol. "Letters of Understanding: James Still's Correspondence with Marjorie Rawlings and Katherine Anne Porter, 1936–1945." *Appalachian Heritage* 8, no. 4 (2010): 53–62.

Booth, William. "Together but Not Equal: A 'Perfect' Maid's Bittersweet Story of Life with Marjorie Rawlings." *Washington Post*, January 5, 1993.

Bowman, Robert. "'Who Owns the Creek?' Rawlings and the Cracker Ethics of Nature." *Marjorie Kinnan Rawlings Journal of Florida Literature* 24 (2016): 79–104.

Cauthen, Sudye. "Sacred Place in the Work of Marjorie Kinnan Rawlings." *Marjorie Kinnan Rawlings Journal of Florida Literature* 11 (2002): 61–69.

Coyote, Peter. 1993. "Peter Coyote Interviews Norton Baskin for the Movie *Cross Creek*." *Marjorie Kinnan Rawlings Journal of Florida Literature* 5 (1993): 19–38.

Dukes, Thomas. "*Cross Creek* as the Autobiography of an Alienated Woman." *Marjorie Kinnan Rawlings Journal of Florida Literature* 2 (1990): 89–108.

Dunn, Lisa Kerr. "All My (Almost) Children: Rawlings's Ambivalence About Motherhood and Adoption." *Marjorie Kinnan Rawlings Journal of Florida Literature* 25 (2017): 1–12.

Edwards, Alexandra. "Entre Nous: Rawlings's Pre–World War II Fan Mail." *Marjorie Kinnan Rawlings Journal of Florida Literature* 25 (2017): 51–61.

Fleegler, Robert L. "Theodore G. Bilbo and the Decline of Public Racism, 1938–1947." *Journal of Mississippi History* 68 (Spring 2006): 1–27.

Friedman, Susan Stanford. "Women's Autobiographical Selves: Theory and Practice." In *The Private Self: Theory and Practice of Women's Autobiographical Writing*, edited by Shari Benstock, 34–62. Chapel Hill: University of North Carolina Press, 1988.

Gannon, Michael. "The Norton Baskin Interviews." *Marjorie Kinnan Rawlings Journal of Florida Literature* 26 (2018): 1–24.

Gilman, Owen W., Jr. "Idella: Marjorie Kinnan Rawlings' 'Perfect Maid.'" *Mississippi Quarterly*, 46, no. 4 (1993): 681–84.

Gottlieb, Robert. "Max and Marjorie: An Editorial Love Story." In *Lives and Letters*. New York: Farrar, Straus and Giroux, 2011.

Graham-Bertolini, Alison. "Marjorie Kinnan Rawlings and the Reckoning of Ideology." *Southern Quarterly* 43, no. 1 (October 2005): 49–62.

Hogue, Bev. "When Local Color Meets the Open Road: Rawlings and Hurston at the Crossroads." *Marjorie Kinnan Rawlings Journal of Florida Literature* 23 (2015): 3–28.

Hyman, Ann. "Supper With Dessie." *Marjorie Kinnan Rawlings Journal of Florida Literature* 5 (1993): 7–17.

Jones, Anne G., ed. "Knowing Marjorie: An Interview with Gordon Bigelow, Jake Glisson, and Idella Parker." *Rawlings Journal* 1 (1988): 50–66.

Jones, Carolyn M. "Race and the Rural in Marjorie Kinnan Rawlings's *Cross Creek*." *Mississippi Quarterly* 57, no. 2 (2004): 215–30.

King, Laura. "A 'Cosmic Maturity': Marjorie Kinnan Rawlings's Use of Rain in *The Yearling*." *Marjorie Kinnan Rawlings Journal of Florida Literature* 11 (2002): 45–59.

Lear, Ashley. "A Letter and a Dream: The Literary Friendship of Ellen Glasgow and Marjorie Kinnan Rawlings." *Marjorie Kinnan Rawlings Journal of Florida Literature* 20 (2012): 23–37.

Lende, Heather. "An Alaskan Writer Learns About the Writing Life from Marjorie Kinnan Rawlings." *Marjorie Kinnan Rawlings Journal of Florida Literature* 20 (2012): 75–92.

Lowe, John. "The Construction and Deconstruction of Masculinity in *The Yearling*." *Mississippi Quarterly* 57, no. 2 (2004): 231–46.

Makowsky, Veronica. "The Changing American Hero and the 'Eternal Bitch' in Marjorie Kinnan Rawlings's *The Sojourner*." *Mississippi Quarterly* 57, no. 2 (2004): 247–54.

Middendorf, Robert D., and Tarr, Rodger L. "The Will of Marjorie Kinnan Rawlings." *Marjorie Kinnan Rawlings Journal of Florida Literature* 15 (2007): 125–40.

Morris, Lloyd. "A New Classicist." *North American Review* 246, no. 1 (Autumn 1938): 179–84.

Nolan, David. "James Branch Cabell: FFV in Florida." *Marjorie Kinnan Rawlings Journal of Florida Literature* 5 (1993): 73–85.

Noles, Randy. "Pride and Privacy: *Cason vs. Baskin* and Cross Creek's Loss of Innocence." *Marjorie Kinnan Rawlings Journal of Florida Literature* 26 (2018): 81–91.

O'Sullivan, Maurice, and Lane, Jack C. "My Dear Mrs. Baskin: Marjorie Kinnan Rawlings and Hamilton Holt." *Marjorie Kinnan Rawlings Journal of Florida Literature* 17 (2009): 1–7.

Poole, Leslie Kemp. "Hunting for Bear: Tales of Teddy Roosevelt, William Faulkner, and Marjorie Kinnan Rawlings." *Marjorie Kinnan Rawlings Journal of Florida Literature* 20 (2012): 1–15.

———. " 'Marjorie's Wake': A Film Voyage into Florida's Nature Consciousness." *Florida Historical Quarterly* 90, no. 3 (Winter 2012): 331–53.

Poole, Leslie Kemp, and Hadley, Carol Courtney. "Marjorie and Zelma: Friendship Restored." *Marjorie Kinnan Rawlings Journal of Florida Literature*. 20 (2012): 39–50.

Prenshaw, Peggy Whitman. 1988. "Marjorie Kinnan Rawlings: Woman, Writer, and Resident of Cross Creek." *Marjorie Kinnan Rawlings Journal of Florida Literature* 1 (1988): 1–17.

Rankin, Cherie. "Blended Genres, Blended Lives: Marjorie Kinnan Rawlings's *Blood of My Blood*." *Marjorie Kinnan Rawlings Journal of Florida Literature* 12 (2003): 1–23.

Rawlings, Marjorie Kinnan. "Regional Literature of the South." *College English* 1, no. 5 (February 1940): 381–89.

Reich, Kathleen J. "Rollins College's Animated Magazine and the Hamilton Holt–Marjorie Kinnan Rawlings Correspondence." *Marjorie Kinnan Rawlings Journal of Florida Literature* 8 (1999): 51–62.

Rich, H. Alexandra. "Interpreters of Nature: Marjorie Kinnan Rawlings, Frank Lloyd Wright, and the 'Sense of Place.'" *Marjorie Kinnan Rawlings Journal of Florida Literature* 24 (2016): 33–48.

Richie, Rebecca. 1993. "The St. Johns River in the Work of Marjorie Kinnan Rawlings." *Marjorie Kinnan Rawlings Journal of Florida Literature* 5 (1993): 61–66.

Rieger, Christopher. "Don't Fence Me In: Nature and Gender in Marjorie Kinnan Rawlings's *South Moon Under*." *Mississippi Quarterly* 57, no. 2 (2004): 199–214.

Saffy, Edna. "Marjorie Kinnan Rawlings's Theory of Composition." *Marjorie Kinnan Rawlings Journal of Florida Literature* 2 (1990): 109–29.

Schmidt, Susan. "Finding a Home: Rawlings's Cross Creek." *Southern Literary Journal* 26, no. 2 (1994): 49–57.

Sharpless, Rebecca. "Neither Friends nor Peers: Idella Parker, Marjorie Kinnan Rawlings, and the Limits of Gender Solidarity at Cross Creek." *Journal of Southern History* 78, no. 2 (2012): 327–60.

———. "The Servants and Mrs. Rawlings: Martha Mickens and African American Life at Cross Creek." *Florida Historical Quarterly* 89, no. 4 (2011): 500–529.

Steiner, Michael C. "Regionalism in the Great Depression." *Geographical Review* 73, no. 4 (October 1983): 430–46.

Tarr, Anita. "In Mystic Company: The Master Storyteller in Marjorie Kinnan Rawlings's *The Yearling*." *Marjorie Kinnan Rawlings Journal of Florida Literature* 2 (1990): 23–34.

————. "Preserving Southern Culture: Marjorie Kinnan Rawlings's *The Yearling*." *Southern Quarterly* 54, nos. 3–4 (2017): 42–61.

Tarr, C. Anita. "The Evolution of a Southern 'Liberal': Marjorie Kinnan Rawlings and Race." *Marjorie Kinnan Rawlings Journal of Florida Literature* 15 (2007): 141–62.

Tarr, Rodger. "Hemingway's Lost Friend: Norton S. Baskin." *Hemingway Review* 25, no. 2 (2006): 136–39.

————. "The Premier of Premieres: Norton Baskin on *Gone with the Wind*." *Marjorie Kinnan Rawlings Journal of Florida Literature* 15 (2007): 15–30.

Turcotte, Florence M. "For This Is an Enchanted Land: Marjorie Kinnan Rawlings and the Florida Environment." *Florida Historical Quarterly* 90, no. 4 (2012): 488–504.

Watkins, James H. "Self-Location and the Racial Other: Reading *Cross Creek* as Southern Autobiography." *Marjorie Kinnan Rawlings Journal of Florida Literature* 11 (2002): 15–43.

Weiser, David K. "David and Esau in *The Yearling*." *Marjorie Kinnan Rawlings Journal of Florida Literature* 24 (2016): 67–77.

York, Lamar. "Edith Pope's *Colcorton*." *Marjorie Kinnan Rawlings Journal of Florida Literature* 19 (2011): 99–110.

————. "Marjorie Kinnan Rawlings's Rivers." *Southern Literary Journal* 9, no. 2 (Spring 1977): 91–107.

BOOKS

Acton, Patricia Nassif. *Invasion of Privacy: The Cross Creek Trial of Marjorie Kinnan Rawlings*. Gainesville: University Press of Florida, 1988.

Agee, James, and Walker Evans. *Let Us Now Praise Famous Men*. New York: Houghton Mifflin, 1941.

Belleville, Bill. *River of Lakes: A Journey on Florida's St. Johns River*. Athens: University of Georgia Press, 2000.

Bellman, Samuel. *Marjorie Kinnan Rawlings*. Boston: Twayne, 1974.

Benstock, Shari, ed. *The Private Self: Theory and Practice of Women's Autobiographical Writings*. Chapel Hill: University of North Carolina Press, 1988.

Berg, A. Scott. *Lindbergh*. New York: G. P. Putnam, 1998.

————. *Max Perkins: Editor of Genius*. New York: Dutton, 1978.

Bigelow, Gordon. *Frontier Eden: The Literary Career of Marjorie Kinnan Rawlings*. Gainesville: University of Florida Press, 1966.

Bigelow, Gordon, and Laura Monti. *Selected Letters of Marjorie Kinnan Rawlings*. Gainesville: University Press of Florida, 1983.

Bigham, Julia Scribner, ed. *The Marjorie Rawlings Reader*. New York: Scribner, 1956.

Bradley, Patricia. *Women and the Press: The Struggle for Equality*. Evanston: Northwestern University Press, 2005.

Bromfield, Louis. *The Farm*. New York: Harper & Row, 1933.

Bucke, Richard Maurice. *Cosmic Consciousness: A Study in the Evolution of the Human Mind*. Philadelphia: Innes & Sons, 1905. Reprint, Mansfield Centre, CT: Martino, 2010.

Burnett, Gene. M. *Florida's Past: People & Events That Shaped the State*. Vol. 1. Sarasota: Pineapple Press, 1991.

Cabell, James Branch, and A. J. Hanna. *The St. Johns: A Parade of Diversities*. New York: Farrar & Rinehart, 1943.

Caplan, Carla, ed. *Zora Neale Hurston: A Life in Letters*. New York: Doubleday, 2002.

Carter, W. Horace. *Return to Cross Creek*. Tabor City, NC: Atlantic, 1985.

Colum, Padraic, and Margaret Freeman Cabell, eds. *Between Friends: Letters of James Branch Cabell and Others.* New York: Harcourt, Brace & World, 1962.

Conroy, Pat. *My Reading Life.* New York: Doubleday, 2010.

Cowley, Malcolm. *Unshaken Friend: A Profile of Maxwell Perkins.* 1944. Reprint, Boulder: Roberts Rinehart, 1985.

Dardis, Tom. *The Thirsty Muse: Alcohol and the American Writer.* New York: Ticknor & Fields, 1989.

Davenport, Marcia. *Too Strong for Fantasy.* New York: Scribner, 1967.

Dearborn, Mary V. *Ernest Hemingway: A Biography.* New York: Knopf, 2017.

Edwards, Anne. *The Road to Tara: The Life of Margaret Mitchell.* Boston: Ticknor & Fields, 1983.

Egerton, John. *Speak Now Against the Day: The Generation Before the Civil Rights Movement in the South.* Chapel Hill: University of North Carolina Press, 1995.

Eksteins, Modris. *Rites of Spring: The Great War and the Birth of the Modern Age.* Boston: Houghton Mifflin, 1989.

Feeley, John J., Jr., and Rosie Dempsey. *Brookland.* Charleston, SC: Arcadia, 2011.

Froncek, Thomas, ed. *An Illustrated History of the City of Washington.* New York: Wings Books, 1992.

Fussell, Paul. *The Great War and Modern Memory.* New York: Oxford University Press, 1975.

Gannon, Michael, ed. *The New History of Florida.* Gainesville: University Press of Florida, 1996.

Gillette, Howard, Jr., ed. *Southern City, National Ambition: The Growth of Early Washington, D.C., 1800–1860.* Washington: George Washington University Center for Washington Area Studies, 1995.

Glasgow, Ellen. *A Certain Measure: An Interpretation of Prose Fiction.* New York: Harcourt, Brace, 1943.

———. *The Woman Within: An Autobiography.* New York: Harcourt Brace Jovanovich, 1954.

Glisson, J. T. *The Creek.* Gainesville: University Press of Florida, 1993.

Griffin, Farah Jasmine. *Harlem Nocturne: Women Artists and Progressive Politics During World War II.* New York: BasicCivitas, 2013.

Halsey, Margaret. *Color Blind: A White Woman Looks at the Negro.* New York: Simon & Schuster, 1946.

Hamsun, Knut. *Growth of the Soil.* Translated by Sverre Lyngstad. New York: Penguin Books, 2007.

Hobbs, Tameka Bradley. *Democracy Abroad, Lynching at Home: Racial Violence in Florida.* Gainesville: University Press of Florida, 2015.

Jacob, Kathryn Allamong. *Capital Elites: High Society in Washington, D.C., After the Civil War.* Washington: Smithsonian Institution Press, 1995.

James, Henry. *The Art of the Novel: Critical Prefaces.* New York: Scribner, 1934.

Jeans, James. *The Mysterious Universe.* New York: Macmillan, 1943.

Kazin, Alfred. *On Native Grounds.* New York: Harcourt, 1942.

Kennedy, Stetson. *Jim Crow Guide to the U.S.A.: The Laws, Customs and Etiquette Governing the Conduct of Nonwhites and Other Minorities as Second-Class Citizens.* London: Lawrence and Wishart, 1959.

Kirby, Jack Temple. *Mockingbird Song: Ecological Landscapes of the South.* Chapel Hill: University of North Carolina Press, 2006.

Kyvig, David E. *Daily Life in the United States, 1920–1940: How Americans Lived Through the "Roaring Twenties" and the Great Depression.* Chicago: Ivan R. Dee, 2004.

Laing, Olivia. *The Trip to Echo Spring: On Writers and Drinking.* New York: Picador, 2014.

Lear, Ashley Andrews. *The Remarkable Kinship of Marjorie Kinnan Rawlings and Ellen Glasgow.* Gainesville: University Press of Florida, 2018.

Lears, Jackson. *Rebirth of a Nation: The Making of Modern America, 1877–1920.* New York: HarperCollins, 2009.

Lecomte du Noüy, Pierre. *Human Destiny.* New York: Longmans, Green, 1947.

Lillios, Anna. *Crossing the Creek: The Literary Friendship of Zora Neale Hurston and Marjorie Kinnan Rawlings.* Gainesville: University Press of Florida, 2010.

Lindbergh, Anne Morrow. *Against Wind and Tide: Letters and Journals, 1947–1986.* New York: Pantheon, 2012.

Lowe, John. *Jump at the Sun: Zora Neale Hurston's Cosmic Comedy.* Urbana: University of Illinois Press, 1997.

Magee, Rosemary M., ed. *Friendship and Sympathy: Communities of Southern Women Writers.* Jackson: University Press of Mississippi, 1992.

Manning, Molly Guptill. *When Books Went to War: The Stories That Helped Us Win World War II.* New York: Houghton Mifflin Harcourt, 2014.

Mansfield, Katherine. *Stories.* Introduction by Marjorie Kinnan Rawlings. Cleveland: World Publishing, 1946.

Matthews, Pamela R., ed. *Perfect Companionship: Ellen Glasgow's Selected Correspondence with Women.* Charlottesville: University of Virginia Press, 2005.

McCarthy, Kevin M., ed. *The Book Lover's Guide to Florida.* Sarasota: Pineapple Press, 1992.

McDaniel, George W., and John N. Pearce, eds. *Images of Brookland: The History and Architecture of a Washington Suburb.* Revised and enlarged by Martin Aurand. Washington, DC: George Washington University, 1982.

McDonogh, Gary W. *The Florida Negro: A Federal Writers' Project Legacy.* Jackson: University Press of Mississippi, 1993.

McGuire, William Joseph. *A Study of Florida Cracker Dialect Based Chiefly on the Prose Works of Marjorie Kinnan Rawlings.* Gainesville: University of Florida Press, 1939.

Miller, Frederic M., and Howard Gillette Jr. *Washington Seen: A Photographic History, 1875–1965.* Baltimore: Johns Hopkins University Press, 1995.

Montague, Margaret Prescott. *Twenty Minutes of Reality: An Experience, with Some Illuminating Letters Concerning It.* New York: Dutton, 1917.

Mormino, Gary R. *Land of Sunshine, State of Dreams: A Social History of Modern Florida.* Gainesville: University Press of Florida, 2005.

Nevius, Blake. *Robert Herrick: The Development of a Novelist.* Berkeley and Los Angeles: University of California Press, 1962.

Nolan, David. *The Houses of St. Augustine.* Sarasota: Pineapple Press, 1995.

The 100 Best True Stories of World War II. New York: Wm. H. Wise, 1945.

Parini, Jay. *Robert Frost: A Life.* New York: Henry Holt, 1999.

Parker, Idella. *From Reddick to Cross Creek.* Gainesville: University Press of Florida, 1999.

———. *Marjorie Rawlings' Perfect Maid.* Gainesville: University Press of Florida, 1992.

Perry, Carolyn, and Mary Louise Weaks, eds. *The History of Southern Women's Literature.* Baton Rouge: Louisiana State University Press, 2002.

Pope, Edith. *Colcorton.* New York: Scribner, 1944.

Prenshaw, Peggy Whitman. *Composing Selves: Southern Women and Autobiography.* Baton Rouge: Louisiana State University Press, 2011.

Rawlings, Marjorie Kinnan. *Blood of My Blood.* Edited by Anne Blythe Meriwether. Gainesville: University Press of Florida, 2002.

———. *Cross Creek.* New York: Scribner, 1942.

———. *Cross Creek Cookery.* New York: Scribner, 1942.

———. *Golden Apples.* New York: Scribner, 1935.

———. *The Secret River.* New York: Scribner, 1955.

———. *Short Stories by Marjorie Kinnan Rawlings.* Edited by Rodger L. Tarr. Gainesville: University Press of Florida, 1994.

———. *The Sojourner.* New York: Scribner, 1953.

———. *South Moon Under.* New York: Scribner, 1933.

———. *When the Whippoorwill.* New York: Scribner, 1940.

———. *The Yearling.* New York: Scribner, 1938.

Reinitz, Neale. *William Ellery Leonard: The Professor and the Locomotive God.* Madison, NJ: Fairleigh Dickinson University Press, 2013.

Rieger, Christopher. *Clear-Cutting Eden: Ecology and the Pastoral in Southern Literature.* Tuscaloosa: University of Alabama Press, 2009.

Romans, Bernard. *A Concise Natural History of East and West Florida, 1775.* Facsimile reproduction. Gainesville: University of Florida Press, 1962.

Ross, Ishbel. *Ladies of the Press: The Story of Women in Journalism by an Insider.* New York: Harper & Row, 1936.

Rowe, Anne. *The Idea of Florida in the American Literary Imagination.* Gainesville: University Press of Florida, 1991.

Schwartz, Peggy, and Murray Schwartz. *The Dance Claimed Me: A Biography of Pearl Primus.* New Haven: Yale University Press, 2011.

Sharpless, Rebecca. *Cooking in Other Women's Kitchens: Domestic Workers in the South, 1865–1960.* Chapel Hill: University of North Carolina Press, 2010.

Sigerson, Yola Miller. *The Art of Compassion: A Biography of Sigrid Undset.* Bloomington: Xlibris, 2006.

Silverthorne, Elizabeth. *Marjorie Kinnan Rawlings: Sojourner at Cross Creek.* Woodstock, NY: Overlook, 1988.

Smith, Asa. *Smith's Illustrated Astronomy.* Boston: Nichols & Hall, 1868. Reprint, London: Forgotten Books.

Smith, Kathryn Schneider, ed. *Washington at Home: An Illustrated History of Neighborhoods in the Nation's Capital.* Baltimore: Johns Hopkins University Press, 2010.

Ste. Claire, Dana. *Cracker: The Cracker Culture in Florida History.* Gainesville: University Press of Florida, 2006.

Stephens, James M. *Cross Creek Reader's Guide.* James M. Stephens, 2003.

Stowe, Harriet Beecher. *Palmetto Leaves.* Boston: J. F. Osgood, 1873.

Tarr, Rodger L., ed. *As Ever Yours: The Letters of Max Perkins and Elizabeth Lemmon.* University Park: Pennsylvania State University Press, 2003.

———, ed. *Max and Marjorie: The Correspondence Between Maxwell E. Perkins and Marjorie Kinnan Rawlings.* Gainesville: University Press of Florida, 1999.

———. *Marjorie Kinnan Rawlings: A Descriptive Bibliography.* Pittsburgh: University of Pittsburgh Press, 1996.

———, ed. *The Private Marjorie: The Love Letters of Marjorie Kinnan Rawlings to Norton S. Baskin.* Gainesville: University Press of Florida, 2004.

———, ed. *Songs of a Housewife: Poems by Marjorie Kinnan Rawlings.* Gainesville: University Press of Florida, 1997.

Tarr, Rodger L., and Brent Kinser. *The Uncollected Writings of Marjorie Kinnan Rawlings.* Gainesville: University Press of Florida, 2007.

Teale, Edwin Way. *North with the Spring: A Naturalist's Record of a 17,000-Mile Journey with the North American Spring.* New York: Dodd, Mead, 1951.

Versluis, Arthur. *American Gurus: From Transcendentalism to New Age Religion.* New York: Oxford University Press, 2014.

Wheelock, John Hall, ed. *Editor to Author: The Letters of Maxwell E. Perkins*. New York: Scribner, 1950.

Wilkerson, Isabel. *The Warmth of Other Suns: The Epic Story of America's Great Migration*. New York: Random House, 2010.

Williamson, Scott Graham. *A Convoy Through the Dream*. New York: Macmillan, 1948.

Wolfe, Thomas. *The Story of a Novel*. New York: Scribner, 1936.

Weiner, Melissa F. *Power, Protest and the Public Schools: Jewish and African American Struggles in New York City*. New Brunswick: Rutgers University Press, 2010.

The WPA Guide to Florida: The Federal Writers' Project Guide to 1930s Florida. Written and compiled by the Federal Writers' Project of the Works Progress Administration for the State of Florida. Reprint, New York: Pantheon, 1984.

Wynne, Nick, and Richard Moorhead. *Florida in World War II: Floating Fortress*. Charleston: History Press, 2010.

ILLUSTRATION CREDITS

Marjorie interviewing Julian Bauknight: George Karger / The LIFE Images Collection via Getty Images.
Marjorie hunting: George Karger/The LIFE Images Collection via Getty Images.
Norman Berg: Hargrett Rare Book and Manuscript Library, University of Georgia.
Shotgun engraving: The Pat Conroy Archive, Irvin Department of Rare Books and Special Collections, University of South Carolina Libraries, Columbia, SC.
Zora Neale Hurston: Library of Congress, Prints & Photographs Division, Carl Van Vechten Collection; LC-DIG-van-5a52142.
Albert Stadler portrait: Artwork © 2020 Albert Stadler / Licensed by VAGA at Artists Rights Society (ARS), NY. Image: Sam and Robbie Vickers Florida Collection.
Marjorie, 1953: Library of Congress, Prints & Photographs Division, Carl Van Vechten Collection; LC-USZ62-106862.

All other images are courtesy of the Marjorie Kinnan Rawlings Collection, Department of Special and Area Studies Collections, University of Florida, Gainesville.

TEXT CREDITS

Excerpts from the following letters of Marjorie Kinnan Rawlings:

- to **Charles Rawlings,** September or October 1918; September 8, 1918; October 16?, 1918; October 10, 1918; October 1918; October 16, 1918; September 13, 1918; October 17, 1918; October 22, 1918; October 25, 1918; October 26, 1918; December 20, 1918; November 15, 1918; November 23, 1918; December 15, 1918; January 1922; November 1922; November 1922; November, 1922; November 11, 1933

- to **Julia Scribner (Bigham),** February 26, 1949; August 7, 1939 or 1940; May 1940; August 7, 1940; November 25, 1940; January 1, 1941; September 24, 1941; April 7, 1942; November 11, 1942; March 26, 1943; May 19, 1944; January 21, 1948; October 25, 1950; February 29, 1952; August 20, 1952; March 18, 1953; and several undated letters

- to **Ethel Freemont Beebe,** January 1925; July 28, 1929

- to **Arthur Kinnan,** January 3, 1933

- to **Samuel Wright,** September 20, 1933

- to **Bee McNeill,** September 1, 1934

- to **Ida Tarrant,** June 2, 1934

- to **Ernest Meyer,** January 30, 1937

- to **Edith Pope,** July 14, 1936; July 16, 1942; July 7, 1942; November 30, 1942; July 14, 1943; March 7, 1945

- to **C. Blackburn Miller,** December 13, 1936

- to **Bernice Baumgartner,** March 6, 1939; November or December, 1939 to **Norman Berg,** June 14, 1939; February 3, 1940; March 18, 1940; December 9, 1946; August 26, 1940; December 9, 1946; July 6, 1943; July 18, 1945; September 13, 1946; May 1, 1947; May 21, 1947; May 26, 1947; June 7, 1947; June 22, 1947; August 22, 1947; November 4, 1947; January 9, 1949; January 26, 1949; February 4, 1949; February 19, 1949; May 11, 1949; July 27, 1949; August 8, 1949; Nov. 10, 1949; November 29, 1949; ca. December 1949; January or February, 1950; April 1950; June 30, 1950; July 1950; September 18, 1950; February 28, 1951; May 28, 1951; May 2, 1951; May 31, 1951; January 25, 1952; February 13, 1952; March 2, 1952; March 14, 1952; ND, 1952; April 28, 1952; August 10, 1952; August 30, 1952; September 19, 1952; September 26; September 24, 1952; January 2, 1953; ND, early 1953; February 19, 1953

to **Norman and Julie Berg,** June 29, 1952

to **Dashiell,** June 29, 1939

to **Mark Ethridge,** October 22, 1939

to **Stetson Kennedy,** August 11, 1942

to **John Temple Graves,** undated

to **Philip May,** February 5, 1943; December 31, 1945; April 18, 1946

to **James Branch Cabell,** March 1946 and undated

to **Zelma Cason,** ND, 1933

to **Norton Baskin,** September 21, 1946; June 10, 1950

to **Walter O'Meara,** undated

to **Charles Scribner,** July 3, 1947

to **Bernice Gilkyson,** ND, 1947

to **Bee McNeill,** August 27, 1947

From Marjorie Kinnan Rawlings Papers, Department of Special and Area Studies Collections, George A. Smathers Libraries, University of Florida. Letters reprinted courtesy of John Sundeman, as Trustee for the Norton S. Baskin Literary Trust.

INDEX